White Rose MATHS

White Rose Maths Edition

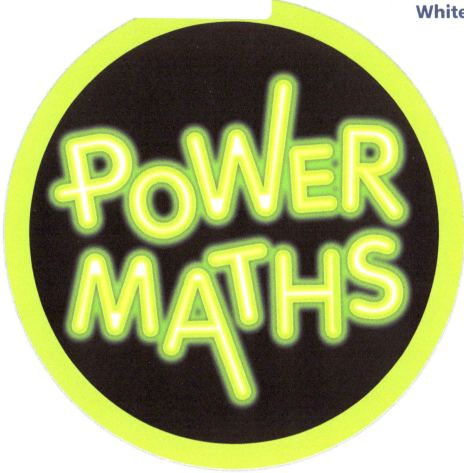

POWER MATHS

Year 6B
A Guide to Teaching for Mastery

Series Editor: Tony Staneff
Lead author: Josh Lury

Pearson

Contents

Introduction to the author team

Power Maths arises from the work of maths mastery experts who are committed to proving that, given the right mastery mindset and approach, **everyone can do maths**. Based on robust research and best practice from around the world, *Power Maths* was developed in partnership with a group of UK teachers to make sure that it not only meets our children's wide-ranging needs but also aligns with the National Curriculum in England.

Power Maths – White Rose Maths edition

This edition of *Power Maths* has been developed and updated by:

Tony Staneff, Series Editor and Author

Vice Principal at Trinity Academy, Halifax, Tony also leads a team of mastery experts who help schools across the UK to develop teaching for mastery via nationally recognised CPD courses, problem-solving and reasoning resources, schemes of work, assessment materials and other tools.

Josh Lury, Lead Author

Josh is a specialist maths teacher, author and maths consultant with a passion for innovative and effective maths education.

The first edition of *Power Maths* was developed by a team of experienced authors, including:

- **Tony Staneff and Josh Lury**
- **Trinity Academy Halifax** (Michael Gosling CEO, Emily Fox, Kate Henshall, Rebecca Holland, Stephanie Kirk, Stephen Monaghan and Rachel Webster)
- **David Board, Belle Cottingham, Jonathan East, Tim Handley, Derek Huby, Neil Jarrett, Stephen Monaghan, Beth Smith, Tim Weal, Paul Wrangles** – skilled maths teachers and mastery experts
- **Cherri Moseley** – a maths author, former teacher and professional development provider
- **Professors Liu Jian and Zhang Dan**, Series Consultants and authors, and their team of mastery expert authors: **Wei Huinv, Huang Lihua, Zhu Dejiang, Zhu Yuhong, Hou Huiying, Yin Lili, Zhang Jing, Zhou Da and Liu Qimeng**

  Used by over 20 million children, Professor Liu Jian's textbook programme is one of the most popular in China. He and his author team are highly experienced in intelligent practice and in embedding key maths concepts using a C-P-A approach.

- **A group of 15 teachers and maths co-ordinators**

  We consulted our teacher group throughout the development of *Power Maths* to ensure we are meeting their real needs in the classroom.

What is *Power Maths*?

Created especially for UK primary schools, and aligned with the new National Curriculum, *Power Maths* is a whole-class, textbook-based mastery resource that empowers every child to understand and succeed. *Power Maths* rejects the notion that some people simply 'can't do' maths. Instead, it develops growth mindsets and encourages hard work, practice and a willingness to see mistakes as learning tools.

Best practice consistently shows that mastery of small, cumulative steps builds a solid foundation of deep mathematical understanding. *Power Maths* combines interactive teaching tools, high-quality textbooks and continuing professional development (CPD) to help you equip children with a deep and long-lasting understanding. Based on extensive evidence, and developed in partnership with practising teachers, *Power Maths* ensures that it meets the needs of children in the UK.

Power Maths and Mastery

Power Maths makes mastery practical and achievable by providing the structures, pathways, content, tools and support you need to make it happen in your classroom.

To develop mastery in maths, children must be enabled to acquire a deep understanding of maths concepts, structures and procedures, step by step. Complex mathematical concepts are built on simpler conceptual components and when children understand every step in the learning sequence, maths becomes transparent and makes logical sense. Interactive lessons establish deep understanding in small steps, as well as effortless fluency in key facts such as tables and number bonds. The whole class works on the same content and no child is left behind.

Power Maths

- Builds every concept in small, progressive steps
- Is built with interactive, whole-class teaching in mind
- Provides the tools you need to develop growth mindsets
- Helps you check understanding and ensure that every child is keeping up
- Establishes core elements such as intelligent practice and reflection

The *Power Maths* approach

Everyone can!

Founded on the conviction that every child can achieve, *Power Maths* enables children to build number fluency, confidence and understanding, step by step.

Child-centred learning

Children master concepts one step at a time in lessons that embrace a concrete-pictorial-abstract (C-P-A) approach, avoid overload, build on prior learning and help them see patterns and connections. Same-day intervention ensures sustained progress.

Continuing professional development

Embedded teacher support and development offer every teacher the opportunity to continually improve their subject knowledge and manage whole-class teaching for mastery.

Whole-class teaching

An interactive, whole-class teaching model encourages thinking and precise mathematical language and allows children to deepen their understanding as far as they can.

What's different in the new edition?

If you have previously used the first editions of *Power Maths*, you might be interested to know how this edition is different. All of the improvements described below are based on feedback from *Power Maths* customers.

Changes to units and the progression

⚡ The order of units has been slightly adjusted, creating closer alignment between adjacent year groups, which will be useful for mixed age teaching.

⚡ The flow of lessons has been improved within units to optimise the pace of the progression and build in more recap where needed. For key topics, the sequence of lessons gives more opportunities to build up a solid base of understanding. Other units have fewer lessons than before, where appropriate, making it possible to fit in all the content.

⚡ Overall, the lessons put more focus on the most essential content for that year, with less time given to non-statutory content.

⚡ The progression of lessons matches the steps in the new White Rose Maths schemes of learning.

Lesson resources

⚡ There is a Quick recap for each lesson in the Teacher Guide, which offers an alternative lesson starter to the Power Up for cases where you feel it would be more beneficial to surface prerequisite learning than general number fluency.

⚡ In the **Discover** and **Share** sections there is now more of a progression from 1 a) to 1 b). Whereas before, 1 b) was mainly designed as a separate question, now 1 a) leads directly into 1 b). This means that there is an improved whole-class flow, and also an opportunity to focus on the logic and skills in more detail. As a teacher, you will be using 1 a) to lead the class into the thinking, then 1 b) to mould that thinking into the core new learning of the lesson.

⚡ In the **Share** section, for KS1 in particular, the number of different models and representations has been reduced, to support the clarity of thinking prompted by the flow from 1 a) into 1 b).

⚡ More fluency questions have been built into the guided and independent practice.

⚡ Pupil pages are as easy as possible for children to access independently. The pages are less full to provide greater focus on key ideas and instructions. Also, more freedom is offered around answer format, with fewer boxes scaffolding children's responses; squared paper backgrounds are used in the Practice Books where appropriate. Artwork has also been revisited to ensure the highest standards of accessibility.

New components

480 Individual Practice Games are available in *ActiveLearn* for practising key facts and skills in Years 1 to 6. These are designed in an arcade style, to feel like fun games that children would choose to play outside school. They can be accessed via the Pupil World for homework or additional practice in school – and children can earn rewards. There are Support, Core and Extend levels to allocate, with Activity Reporting available for the teacher. There is a Quick Guide on *ActiveLearn* and you can use the Help area for support in setting up child accounts.

There is also a new set of lesson video resources on the Professional Development tile, designed for in-school training in 10- to 20-minute bursts. For each part of the *Power Maths* lesson sequence, there is a slide deck with embedded video, which will facilitate discussions about how you can take your *Power Maths* teaching to the next level.

Your *Power Maths* resources

Pupil Textbooks

Discover, **Share** and **Think together** sections promote discussion and introduce mathematical ideas logically, so that children understand more easily.

Using a Concrete-Pictorial-Abstract approach, clear mathematical models help children to make connections and grasp concepts.

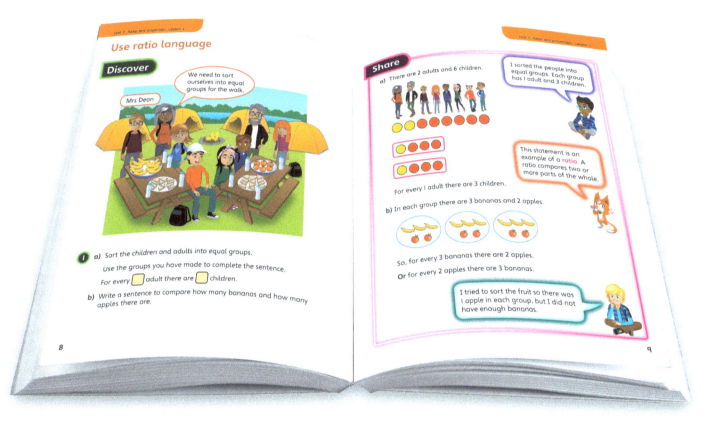

Appealing scenarios stimulate curiosity, helping children to identify the maths problem and discover patterns and relationships for themselves.

Friendly, supportive characters help children develop a growth mindset by prompting them to think, reason and reflect.

To help you teach for mastery, *Power Maths* comprises a variety of high-quality resources.

The coherent *Power Maths* lesson structure carries through into the vibrant, high-quality textbooks. Setting out the core learning objectives for each class, the lesson structure follows a carefully mapped journey through the curriculum and supports children on their journey to deeper understanding.

Pupil Practice Books

The Practice Books offer just the right amount of intelligent practice for children to complete independently in the final section of each lesson.

> Practice questions are finely tuned to move children forward in their thinking and to reveal misconceptions.

> The practice questions are for everyone – each question varies one small element to move children on in their thinking.

> Calculations are connected so that children think about the underlying concept.

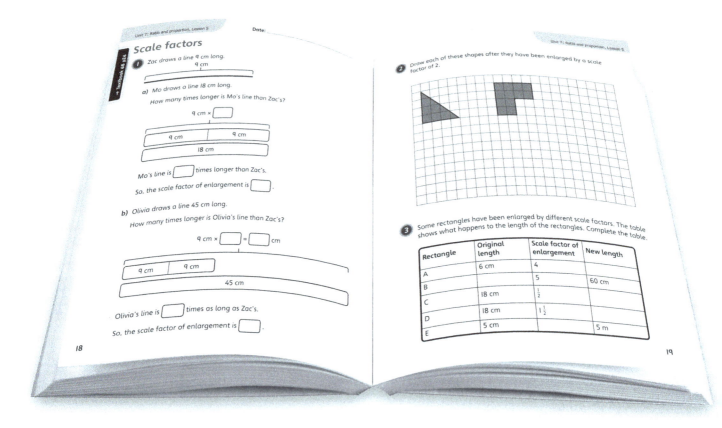

Challenge questions allow children to delve deeper into a concept.

Think differently questions encourage children to use reasoning as well as their mathematical knowledge to reach a solution.

> **Reflect** questions reveal the depth of each child's understanding before they move on.

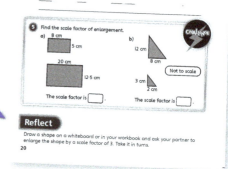

Online subscription

The online subscription will give you access to additional resources and answers from the Textbook and Practice Book.

eTextbooks

Digital versions of *Power Maths* Textbooks allow class groups to share and discuss questions, solutions and strategies. They allow you to project key structures and representations at the front of the class, to ensure all children are focusing on the same concept.

Teaching tools

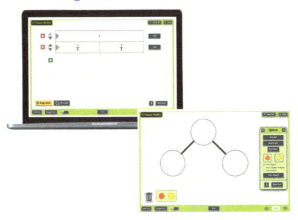

Here you will find interactive versions of key *Power Maths* structures and representations.

Power Ups

Use this series of daily activities to promote and check number fluency.

Online versions of Teacher Guide pages

PDF pages give support at both unit and lesson levels. You will also find help with key strategies and templates for tracking progress.

Unit videos

Watch the professional development videos at the start of each unit to help you teach with confidence. The videos explore common misconceptions in the unit, and include intervention suggestions as well as suggestions on what to look out for when assessing mastery in your students.

End of unit Strengthen and Deepen materials

The Strengthen activity at the end of every unit addresses a key misconception and can be used to support children who need it. The Deepen activities are designed to be low ceiling/high threshold and will challenge those children who can understand more deeply. These resources will help you ensure that every child understands and will help you keep the class moving forward together. These printable activities provide an optional resource bank for use after the assessment stage.

Individual Practice Games

These enjoyable games can be used at home or at school to embed key number skills (see page 6).

Professional Development videos and slides

These slides and videos of *Power Maths* lessons can be used for ongoing training in short bursts or to support new staff.

The *Power Maths* teaching model

At the heart of *Power Maths* is a clearly structured teaching and learning process that helps you make certain that every child masters each maths concept securely and deeply. For each year group, the curriculum is broken down into core concepts, taught in units. A unit divides into smaller learning steps – lessons. Step by step, strong foundations of cumulative knowledge and understanding are built.

Quick check on prerequisite skills and a warm-up for children.

Rich assessments show mastery of key skills combined with a pupil self-assessment and reflection opportunity.

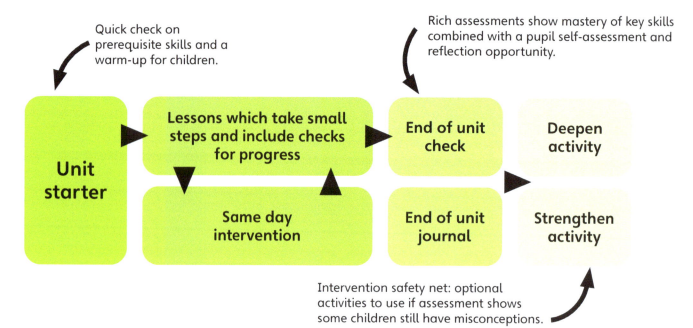

Intervention safety net: optional activities to use if assessment shows some children still have misconceptions.

Unit starter

Each unit begins with a unit starter, which introduces the learning context along with key mathematical vocabulary and structures and representations.

- The Textbooks include a check on readiness and a warm-up task for children to complete.

- Your Teacher Guide gives support right from the start on important structures and representations, mathematical language, common misconceptions and intervention strategies.

- Unit-specific videos develop your subject knowledge and insights so you feel confident and fully equipped to teach each new unit. These are available via the online subscription.

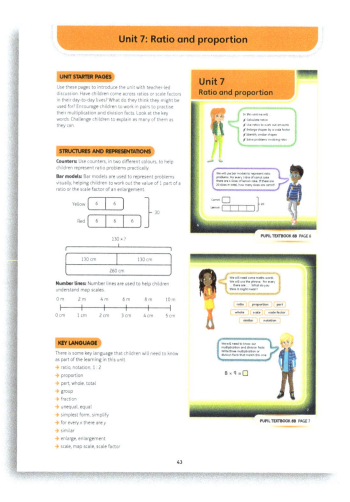

Lesson

Once a unit has been introduced, it is time to start teaching the series of lessons.

- Each lesson is scaffolded with Textbook and Practice Book activities and begins with a Power Up activity (available via online subscription) or the Quick recap activity in the Teacher Guide (see page 15).

- *Power Maths* identifies lesson by lesson what concepts are to be taught.

- Your Teacher Guide offers lots of support for you to get the most from every child in every lesson. As well as highlighting key points, tricky areas and how to handle them, you will also find question prompts to check on understanding and clarification on why particular activities and questions are used.

Same-day intervention

Same-day interventions are vital in order to keep the class progressing together. This can be during the lesson as well as afterwards (see page 28). Therefore, *Power Maths* provides plenty of support throughout the journey.

- Intervention is focused on keeping up now, not catching up later, so interventions should happen as soon as they are needed.

- Practice section questions are designed to bring misconceptions to the surface, allowing you to identify these easily as you circulate during independent practice time.

- Child-friendly assessment questions in the Teacher Guide help you identify easily which children need to strengthen their understanding.

End of unit check and journal

For each unit, the End of unit check in the Textbook lets you see which children have mastered the key concepts, which children have not and where their misconceptions lie. The Practice Books also include an End of unit journal in which children can reflect on what they have learned. Each unit also offers Strengthen and Deepen activities, available via the online subscription.

> The Teacher Guide offers different ways of managing the End of unit assessments as well as giving support with handling misconceptions.

> The End of unit check presents multiple-choice questions. Children think about their answer, decide on a solution and explain their choice.

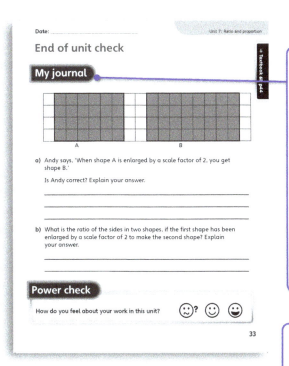

> The End of unit journal is an opportunity for children to test out their learning and reflect on how they feel about it. Tackling the 'journal' problem reveals whether a child understands the concept deeply enough to move on to the next unit.

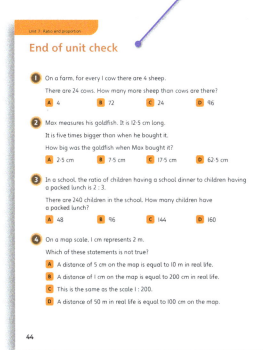

> In KS2, the End of unit assessment will also include at least one SATs-style question.

The *Power Maths* lesson sequence

At the heart of *Power Maths* is a unique lesson sequence designed to empower children to understand core concepts and grow in confidence. Embracing the National Centre for Excellence in the Teaching of Mathematics' (NCETM's) definition of mastery, the sequence guides and shapes every *Power Maths* lesson you teach.

Flexibility is built into the *Power Maths* programme so there is no one-to-one mapping of lessons and concepts and you can pace your teaching according to your class. While some children will need to spend longer on a particular concept (through interventions or additional lessons), others will reach deeper levels of understanding. However, it is important that the class moves forward together through the termly schedules.

Power Up 5 minutes

Each lesson begins with a Power Up activity (available via the online subscription) which supports fluency in key number facts.

The whole-class approach depends on fluency, so the Power Up is a powerful and essential activity.

The Quick recap is an alternative starter, for when you think some or all children would benefit more from revisiting pre-requisite work (see page 15).

TOP TIP

If the class is struggling with the task, revisit it later and check understanding.

Power Ups reinforce the two key things that are essential for success: times-tables and number bonds.

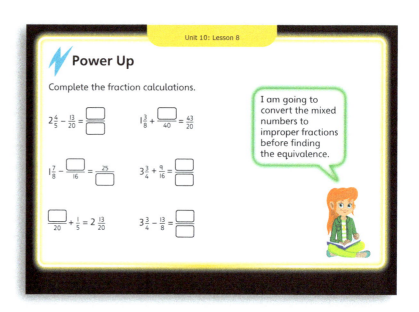

Unit 10: Lesson 8

Power Up

Complete the fraction calculations.

$2\frac{4}{5} - \frac{13}{20} = \frac{\square}{\square}$

$1\frac{3}{8} + \frac{\square}{40} = \frac{43}{20}$

$1\frac{7}{8} - \frac{\square}{16} = \frac{25}{\square}$

$3\frac{3}{4} + \frac{9}{16} = \frac{\square}{\square}$

$\frac{\square}{20} + \frac{1}{5} = 2\frac{13}{20}$

$3\frac{3}{4} - \frac{13}{8} = \frac{\square}{\square}$

I am going to convert the mixed numbers to improper fractions before finding the equivalence.

Discover 10 minutes

A practical, real-life problem arouses curiosity. Children find the maths through story telling.

A real-life scenario is provided for the **Discover** section but feel free to build upon these with your own examples that are more relevant to your class, or get creative with the context.

TOP TIP

Discover works best when run at tables, in pairs with concrete objects.

Question ❶ a) tackles the key concept and question ❶ b) digs a little deeper. Children have time to explore, play and discuss possible strategies.

Unit 7: Ratio and proportion, Lesson 8

Problem solving – ratio and proportion ❶

Discover

I need to make dinner for 6 people!

Toshi

Vegetable Curry
(serves 4)
Ingredients
300 g butternut squash, chopped
3 peppers, sliced
200 g coconut milk
48 g curry paste

❶ a) How many grams of curry paste does Toshi need for 6 people?

b) Toshi has 4 peppers.

Does he have enough peppers to make the curry for 6 people?

36

Share ⏱ 10 minutes

Teacher-led, this interactive section follows the **Discover** activity and highlights the variety of methods that can be used to solve a single problem.

TOP TIP

Pairs sharing a textbook is a great format for **Share**!

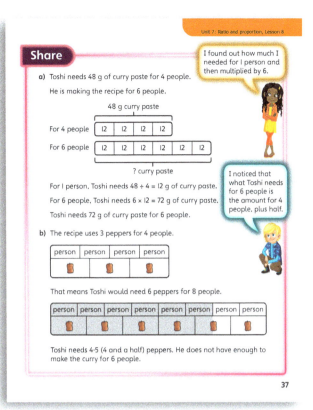

Your Teacher Guide gives target questions for children. The online toolkit provides interactive structures and representations to link concrete and pictorial to abstract concepts.

Bring children to the front to share and celebrate their solutions and strategies.

Think together

⏱ 10 minutes

Children work in groups on the carpet or at tables, using their textbooks or eBooks.

TOP TIP

Make sure children have mini whiteboards or pads to write on if they are not at their tables.

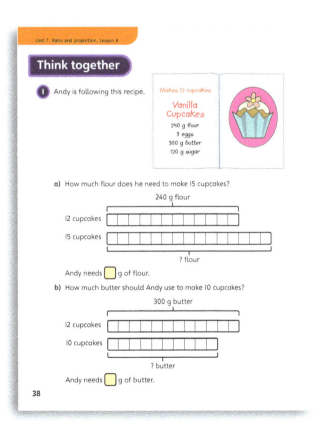

Using the Teacher Guide, model question ① for your class.

Question ② is less structured. Children will need to think together in their groups, then discuss their methods and solutions as a class.

In question ③ children try working out the answer independently. The openness of the **Challenge** question helps to check depth of understanding.

Unit 8: Algebra, Lesson 2

Date: _____

→ Textbook 6B p52

Find a rule – two steps

1 Complete the table.

IN
×2 +3
OUT

Input	1	2	3	4	5	n
Output	5					

2 a) Olivia has £25 in the bank. Each week she saves £3. Complete the table.

Week	1	2	3	4	5	10
Total savings	£28					

b) Complete the rule for how much Olivia has saved after y weeks.

After y weeks, Olivia has saved 25 + ☐ × ☐ pounds.

38

Unit 8: Algebra, Lesson 2

3 Here is a growing pattern of triangles made from sticks.

In a growing pattern, there is a rule for how it grows each time.

a) Complete the table.

Number of triangles	1	2	3	4	5	10	100
Number of sticks used							

b) Complete the rule.

To make n triangles, _____ sticks are used.

4 Ebo makes this pattern of houses. What is the rule for the number of sticks needed for a pattern with g houses?

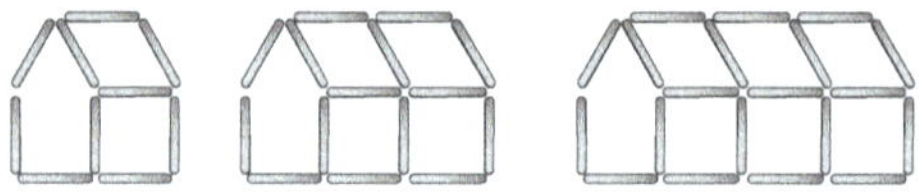

For g houses, you need _____ sticks.

39

Using the *Power Maths* Teacher Guide

Think of your Teacher Guides as *Power Maths* handbooks that will guide, support and inspire your day-to-day teaching. Clear and concise, and illustrated with helpful examples, your Teacher Guides will help you make the best possible use of every individual lesson. They also provide wrap-around professional development, enhancing your own subject knowledge and helping you to grow in confidence about moving your children forward together.

There is a Teacher Guide per year group for every term, with unit and lesson level guidance and support.

Never feel stuck! You will find ideas for introducing every unit and lesson and questions to encourage teacher reflection before and after each lesson.

Tips and advice on key elements such as C-P-A approaches, misconceptions, language, modelling growth mindsets and same day intervention.

Annotations for every Textbook and Practice Book page, providing prompts for key questions to ask to expose understanding and explanations as to why key questions have been chosen.

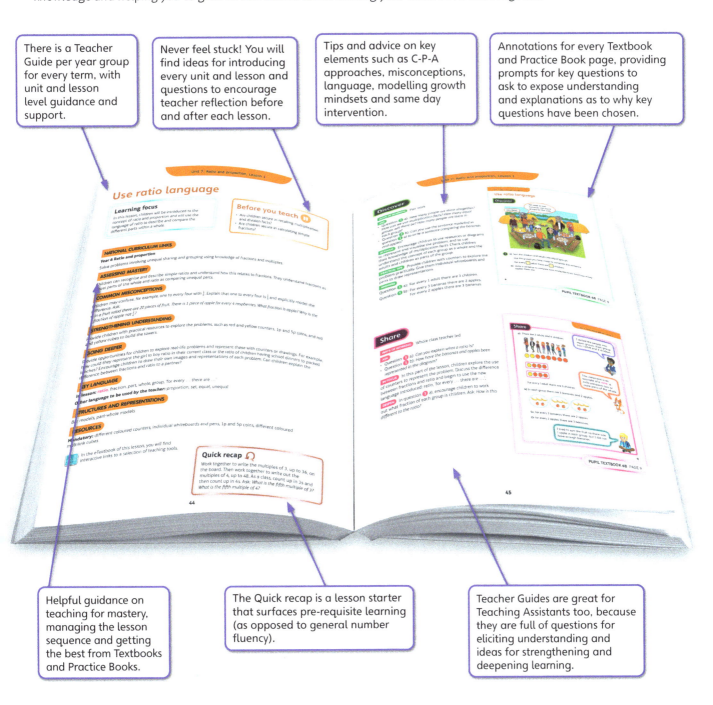

Helpful guidance on teaching for mastery, managing the lesson sequence and getting the best from Textbooks and Practice Books.

The Quick recap is a lesson starter that surfaces pre-requisite learning (as opposed to general number fluency).

Teacher Guides are great for Teaching Assistants too, because they are full of questions for eliciting understanding and ideas for strengthening and deepening learning.

At the end of each unit, your Teacher Guide helps you identify who has fully grasped the concept, who has not and how to move every child forward. This is covered later in the Assessment strategies section.

Power Maths Year 6, yearly overview

Textbook	Strand	Unit		Number of lessons
Textbook A / Practice Workbook A (Term 1)	Number – number and place value	1	Place value within 10,000,000	8
	Number – addition, subtraction, multiplication and division	2	Four operations (1)	8
	Number – addition, subtraction, multiplication and division	3	Four operations (2)	12
	Number - fractions	4	Fractions (1)	9
	Number - fractions	5	Fractions (2)	9
	Measurement	6	Measure – imperial and metric measures	5
Textbook B / Practice Workbook B (Term 2)	Ratio and proportion	7	Ratio and proportion	9
	Algebra	8	Algebra	11
	Number - fractions (including decimals and percentages)	9	Decimals	9
	Number - fractions (including decimals and percentages)	10	Percentages	8
	Measurement	11	Measure – perimeter, area and volume	11
Textbook C / Practice Workbook C (Term 3)	Statistics	12	Statistics	11
	Geometry – properties of shapes	13	Geometry – properties of shapes	12
	Geometry – position and direction	14	Geometry – position and direction	5
	Number – addition, subtraction, multiplication and division	15	Problem solving	14

Power Maths Year 6, Textbook 6B (Term 2) overview

Strand	Unit	Unit title	Lesson number	Lesson title	NC Objective 1	NC Objective 2
Ratio and proportion	7	Ratio and proportion	1	Use ratio language	Solve problems involving unequal sharing and grouping using knowledge of fractions and multiples	
Ratio and proportion	7	Ratio and proportion	2	Introduce the ratio symbol	Solve problems involving unequal sharing and grouping using knowledge of fractions and multiples	
Ratio and proportion	7	Ratio and proportion	3	Use ratio	Solve problems involving unequal sharing and grouping using knowledge of fractions and multiples	
Ratio and proportion	7	Ratio and proportion	4	Scale drawing	Solve problems involving similar shapes where the scale factor is known or can be found	
Ratio and proportion	7	Ratio and proportion	5	Scale factors	Solve problems involving similar shapes where the scale factor is known or can be found	
Ratio and proportion	7	Ratio and proportion	6	Similar shapes	Solve problems involving similar shapes where the scale factor is known or can be found	
Ratio and proportion	7	Ratio and proportion	7	Ratio problems	Solve problems involving unequal sharing and grouping using knowledge of fractions and multiples	
Ratio and proportion	7	Ratio and proportion	8	Problem solving – ratio and proportion (1)	Solve problems involving unequal sharing and grouping using knowledge of fractions and multiples	Solve problems involving the relative sizes of two quantities where missing values can be found by using integer multiplication and division facts
Ratio and proportion	7	Ratio and proportion	9	Problem solving – ratio and proportion (2)	Solve problems involving unequal sharing and grouping using knowledge of fractions and multiples	Solve problems involving the relative sizes of two quantities where missing values can be found by using integer multiplication and division facts
Algebra	8	Algebra	1	Find a rule – one step	Generate and describe linear number sequences	
Algebra	8	Algebra	2	Find a rule – two steps	Generate and describe linear number sequences	
Algebra	8	Algebra	3	Form expressions	Generate and describe linear number sequences	
Algebra	8	Algebra	4	Substitution (1)	Express missing number problems algebraically	Generate and describe linear number sequences
Algebra	8	Algebra	5	Substitution (2)	Express missing number problems algebraically	Generate and describe linear number sequences
Algebra	8	Algebra	6	Formulae	Use simple formulae	
Algebra	8	Algebra	7	Form and solve equations	Express missing number problems algebraically	
Algebra	8	Algebra	8	Solve one-step equations	Express missing number problems algebraically	
Algebra	8	Algebra	9	Solve two-step equations	Express missing number problems algebraically	
Algebra	8	Algebra	10	Find pairs of values	Find pairs of numbers that satisfy an equation with two unknowns	
Algebra	8	Algebra	11	Solve problems with two unknowns	Enumerate possibilities of combinations of two variables	Find pairs of numbers that satisfy an equation with two unknowns

Strand	Unit	Unit title	Lesson number	Lesson title	NC Objective 1	NC Objective 2
Number – fractions (including decimals and percentages)	9	Decimals	1	Place value to 3 decimal places	Identify the value of each digit in numbers given to three decimal places and multiply and divide numbers by 10, 100 and 1000 giving answers up to three decimal places	Solve problems which require answers to be rounded to specified degrees of accuracy
Number – fractions (including decimals and percentages)	9	Decimals	2	Round decimals	Identify the value of each digit in numbers given to three decimal places and multiply and divide numbers by 10, 100 and 1000 giving answers up to three decimal places	Solve problems which require answers to be rounded to specified degrees of accuracy
Number – fractions (including decimals and percentages)	9	Decimals	3	Add and subtract decimals	Solve problems which require answers to be rounded to specified degrees of accuracy	
Number – fractions (including decimals and percentages)	9	Decimals	4	Multiply by 10, 100 and 1,000	Identify the value of each digit in numbers given to three decimal places and multiply and divide numbers by 10, 100 and 1000 giving answers up to three decimal places	
Number – fractions (including decimals and percentages)	9	Decimals	5	Divide by 10, 100 and 1,000	Identify the value of each digit in numbers given to three decimal places and multiply and divide numbers by 10, 100 and 1000 giving answers up to three decimal places	
Number – fractions (including decimals and percentages)	9	Decimals	6	Multiply decimals by integers	Multiply one-digit numbers with up to two decimal places by whole numbers	
Number – fractions (including decimals and percentages)	9	Decimals	7	Divide decimals by integers	Use written division methods in cases where the answer has up to two decimal places	Solve problems which require answers to be rounded to specified degrees of accuracy
Number – fractions (including decimals and percentages)	9	Decimals	8	Fractions to decimals	Associate a fraction with division and calculate decimal fraction equivalents [for example, 0·375] for a simple fraction [for example, $\frac{3}{8}$]	Identify the value of each digit in numbers given to three decimal places and multiply and divide numbers by 10, 100 and 1000 giving answers up to three decimal places
Number – fractions (including decimals and percentages)	9	Decimals	9	Fractions as division	Associate a fraction with division and calculate decimal fraction equivalents [for example, 0·375] for a simple fraction [for example, $\frac{3}{8}$]	
Number – fractions (including decimals and percentages)	10	Percentages	1	Understand percentages	Recall and use equivalences between simple fractions, decimals and percentages, including in different contexts	
Number – fractions (including decimals and percentages)	10	Percentages	2	Fractions to percentages	Recall and use equivalences between simple fractions, decimals and percentages, including in different contexts	

Strand	Unit	Unit title	Lesson number	Lesson title	NC Objective 1	NC Objective 2
Number – fractions (including decimals and percentages)	10	Percentages	3	Equivalent fractions, decimals and percentages	Recall and use equivalences between simple fractions, decimals and percentages, including in different contexts	
Number – fractions (including decimals and percentages)	10	Percentages	4	Order fractions, decimals and percentages	Compare and order fractions, including fractions > 1	Recall and use equivalences between simple fractions, decimals and percentages, including in different contexts
Number – fractions (including decimals and percentages)	10	Percentages	5	Simple percentage of an amount	Solve problems involving the calculation of percentages [for example, of measures, and such as 15% of 360] and the use of percentages for comparison	Recall and use equivalences between simple fractions, decimals and percentages, including in different contexts
Number – fractions (including decimals and percentages)	10	Percentages	6	Percentage of an amount – 1%	Solve problems involving the calculation of percentages [for example, of measures, and such as 15% of 360] and the use of percentages for comparison	Recall and use equivalences between simple fractions, decimals and percentages, including in different contexts
Number – fractions (including decimals and percentages)	10	Percentages	7	Percentages of an amount	Solve problems involving the calculation of percentages [for example, of measures, and such as 15% of 360] and the use of percentages for comparison	Recall and use equivalences between simple fractions, decimals and percentages, including in different contexts
Number – fractions (including decimals and percentages)	10	Percentages	8	Percentages (missing values)	Recall and use equivalences between simple fractions, decimals and percentages, including in different contexts	Multiply one-digit numbers with up to two decimal places by whole numbers
Measurement	11	Measure – perimeter, area and volume	1	Shapes – same area	Recognise that shapes with the same areas can have different perimeters and vice versa	
Measurement	11	Measure – perimeter, area and volume	2	Area and perimeter	Recognise that shapes with the same areas can have different perimeters and vice versa	
Measurement	11	Measure – perimeter, area and volume	3	Area and perimeter – missing lengths	Recognise that shapes with the same areas can have different perimeters and vice versa	
Measurement	11	Measure – perimeter, area and volume	4	Area of a triangle – counting squares	Calculate the area of parallelograms and triangles	
Measurement	11	Measure – perimeter, area and volume	5	Area of a right-angled triangle	Calculate the area of parallelograms and triangles	
Measurement	11	Measure – perimeter, area and volume	6	Area of any triangle	Calculate the area of parallelograms and triangles	
Measurement	11	Measure – perimeter, area and volume	7	Area of a parallelogram	Recognise when it is possible to use formulae for area and volume of shapes	Calculate the area of parallelograms and triangles
Measurement	11	Measure – perimeter, area and volume	8	Problem solving – area	Calculate the area of parallelograms and triangles	
Measurement	11	Measure – perimeter, area and volume	9	Problem solving – perimeter	Recognise that shapes with the same areas can have different perimeters and vice versa	

Strand	Unit	Unit title	Lesson number	Lesson title	NC Objective 1	NC Objective 2
Measurement	11	Measure – perimeter, area and volume	10	Volume – count cubes	Calculate, estimate and compare volume of cubes and cuboids using standard units, including cubic centimetres (cm^3) and cubic metres (m^3), and extending to other units [for example, mm^3 and km^3]	Recognise when it is possible to use formulae for area and volume of shapes
Measurement	11	Measure – perimeter, area and volume	11	Volume of a cuboid	Calculate, estimate and compare volume of cubes and cuboids using standard units, including cubic centimetres (cm^3) and cubic metres (m^3), and extending to other units [for example, mm^3 and km^3]	Recognise when it is possible to use formulae for area and volume of shapes

Mindset: an introduction

Global research and best practice deliver the same message: learning is greatly affected by what learners perceive they can or cannot do. What is more, it is also shaped by what their parents, carers and teachers perceive they can do. Mindset – the thinking that determines our beliefs and behaviours – therefore has a fundamental impact on teaching and learning.

Everyone can!

Power Maths and mastery methods focus on the distinction between 'fixed' and 'growth' mindsets (Dweck, 2007).[1] Those with a fixed mindset believe that their basic qualities (for example, intelligence, talent and ability to learn) are pre-wired or fixed: 'If you have a talent for maths, you will succeed at it. If not, too bad!' By contrast, those with a growth mindset believe that hard work, effort and commitment drive success and that 'smart' is not something you are or are not, but something you become. In short, everyone can do maths!

Key mindset strategies

A growth mindset needs to be actively nurtured and developed. *Power Maths* offers some key strategies for fostering healthy growth mindsets in your classroom.

It is okay to get it wrong

Mistakes are valuable opportunities to re-think and understand more deeply. Learning is richer when children and teachers alike focus on spotting and sharing mistakes as well as solutions.

Praise hard work

Praise is a great motivator, and by focusing on praising effort and learning rather than success, children will be more willing to try harder, take risks and persist for longer.

Mind your language!

The language we use around learners has a profound effect on their mindsets. Make a habit of using growth phrases, such as, 'Everyone can!', 'Mistakes can help you learn' and 'Just try for a little longer'. The king of them all is one little word, 'yet'... I can't solve this...yet!' Encourage parents and carers to use the right language too.

Build in opportunities for success

The step-by-small-step approach enables children to enjoy the experience of success. In addition, avoid ability grouping and encourage every child to answer questions and explain or demonstrate their methods to others.

---

[1]Dweck, C (2007) *The New Psychology of Success*, Ballantine Books: New York

The *Power Maths* characters

The *Power Maths* characters model the traits of growth mindset learners and encourage resilience by prompting and questioning children as they work. Appearing frequently in the Textbooks and Practice Books, they are your allies in teaching and discussion, helping to model methods, alternatives and misconceptions, and to pose questions. They encourage and support your children, too: they are all hardworking, enthusiastic and unafraid of making and talking about mistakes.

Meet the team!

Creative Flo is open-minded and sometimes indecisive. She likes to think differently and come up with a variety of methods or ideas.

Determined Dexter is resolute, resilient and systematic. He concentrates hard, always tries his best and he'll never give up – even though he doesn't always choose the most efficient methods!

'Let's try again.'

'Mistakes are cool!'

'Have I found all of the solutions?'

'Let's try it this way...'

'Can we do it differently?'

'I've got another way of doing this!'

'I'm going to try this!'

'I know how to do that!'

'Want to share my ideas?'

Curious Ash is eager, interested and inquisitive, and he loves solving puzzles and problems. Ash asks lots of questions but sometimes gets distracted.

'What if we tried this...?'

'I wonder...'

'Is there a pattern here?'

Miaow!

Sparks the Cat

Brave Astrid is confident, willing to take risks and unafraid of failure. She's never scared to jump straight into a problem or question, and although she often makes simple mistakes she's happy to talk them through with others.

Mathematical language

Traditionally, we in the UK have tended to try simplifying mathematical language to make it easier for young children to understand. By contrast, evidence and experience show that by diluting the correct language, we actually mask concepts and meanings for children. We then wonder why they are confused by new and different terminology later down the line! *Power Maths* is not afraid of 'hard' words and avoids placing any barriers between children and their understanding of mathematical concepts. As a result, we need to be deliberate, precise and thorough in building every child's understanding of the language of maths. Throughout the Teacher Guides you will find support and guidance on how to deliver this, as well as individual explanations throughout the pupil Textbooks.

Use the following key strategies to build children's mathematical vocabulary, understanding and confidence.

Precise and consistent

Everyone in the classroom should use the correct mathematical terms in full, every time. For example, refer to 'equal parts', not 'parts'. Used consistently, precise maths language will be a familiar and non-threatening part of children's everyday experience.

Full sentences

Teachers and children alike need to use full sentences to explain or respond. When children use complete sentences, it both reveals their understanding and embeds their knowledge.

Stem sentences

These important sentences help children express mathematical concepts accurately, and are used throughout the *Power Maths* books. Encourage children to repeat them frequently, whether working independently or with others. Examples of stem sentences are:

'4 is a part, 5 is a part, 9 is the whole.'

'There are …. groups. There are …. in each group.'

Key vocabulary

The unit starters highlight essential vocabulary for every lesson. In the pupil books, characters flag new terminology and the Teacher Guide lists important mathematical language for every unit and lesson. New terms are never introduced without a clear explanation.

Mathematical signs

Mathematical signs are used early on so that children quickly become familiar with them and their meaning. Often, the *Power Maths* characters will highlight the connection between language and particular signs.

The role of talk and discussion

When children learn to talk purposefully together about maths, barriers of fear and anxiety are broken down and they grow in confidence, skills and understanding. Building a healthy culture of 'maths talk' empowers their learning from day one.

Explanation and discussion are integral to the *Power Maths* structure, so by simply following the books your lessons will stimulate structured talk. The following key 'maths talk' strategies will help you strengthen that culture and ensure that every child is included.

Sentences, not words

Encourage children to use full sentences when reasoning, explaining or discussing maths. This helps both speaker and listeners to clarify their own understanding. It also reveals whether or not the speaker truly understands, enabling you to address misconceptions as they arise.

Working together

Working with others in pairs, groups or as a whole class is a great way to support maths talk and discussion. Use different group structures to add variety and challenge. For example, children could take timed turns for talking, work independently alongside a 'discussion buddy', or perhaps play different *Power Maths* character roles within their group.

Think first – then talk

Provide clear opportunities within each lesson for children to think and reflect, so that their talk is purposeful, relevant and focused.

Give every child a voice

Where the 'hands up' model allows only the more confident child to shine, *Power Maths* involves everyone. Make sure that no child dominates and that even the shyest child is encouraged to contribute – and praised when they do.

Assessment strategies

Teaching for mastery demands that you are confident about what each child knows and where their misconceptions lie; therefore, practical and effective assessment is vitally important.

Formative assessment within lessons

The **Think together** section will often reveal any confusions or insecurities; try ironing these out by doing the first **Think together** question as a class. For children who continue to struggle, you or your Teaching Assistant should provide support and enable them to move on.

▶ Performance in practice can be very revealing: check Practice Books and listen out both during and after practice to identify misconceptions.

▶ The **Reflect** section is designed to check on the all-important depth of understanding. Be sure to review how the children performed in this final stage before you teach the next lesson.

End of unit check – Textbook

Each unit concludes with a summative check to help you assess quickly and clearly each child's understanding, fluency, reasoning and problem solving skills. Your Teacher Guide will suggest ideal ways of organising a given activity and offer advice and commentary on what children's responses mean. For example, 'What misconception does this reveal?'; 'How can you reinforce this particular concept?'

Assessment with young children should always be an enjoyable activity, so avoid one-to-one individual assessments, which they may find threatening or scary. If you prefer, the End of unit check can be carried out as a whole-class group using whiteboards and Practice Books.

End of unit check – Practice Book

The Practice Book contains further opportunities for assessment, and can be completed by children independently whilst you are carrying out diagnostic assessment with small groups. Your Teacher Guide will advise you on what to do if children struggle to articulate an explanation – or perhaps encourage you to write down something they have explained well. It will also offer insights into children's answers and their implications for next learning steps. It is split into three main sections, outlined below.

My journal is designed to allow children to show their depth of understanding of the unit. It can also serve as a way of checking that children have grasped key mathematical vocabulary. The question children should answer is first presented in the Textbook in the Think! section. This provides an opportunity for you to discuss the question first as a class to ensure children have understood their task. Children should have some time to think about how they want to answer the question, and you could ask them to talk to a partner about their ideas. Then children should write their answer in their Practice Book, using the word bank provided to help them with vocabulary.

The **Power check** allows pupils to self-assess their level of confidence on the topic by colouring in different smiley faces. You may want to introduce the faces as follows:

Each unit ends with either a Power play or a Power puzzle. This is an activity, puzzle or game that allows children to use their new knowledge in a fun, informal way.

Progress Tests

There are *Power Maths* Progress Tests for each half term and at the end of the year, including an Arithmetic test and Reasoning test in each case. You can enter results in the online markbook to track and analyse results and see the average for all schools' results. The tests use a 6-step scale to show results against age-related expectation.

How to ask diagnostic questions

The diagnostic questions provided in children's Practice Books are carefully structured to identify both understanding and misconceptions (if children answer in a particular way, you will know why). The simple procedure below may be helpful:

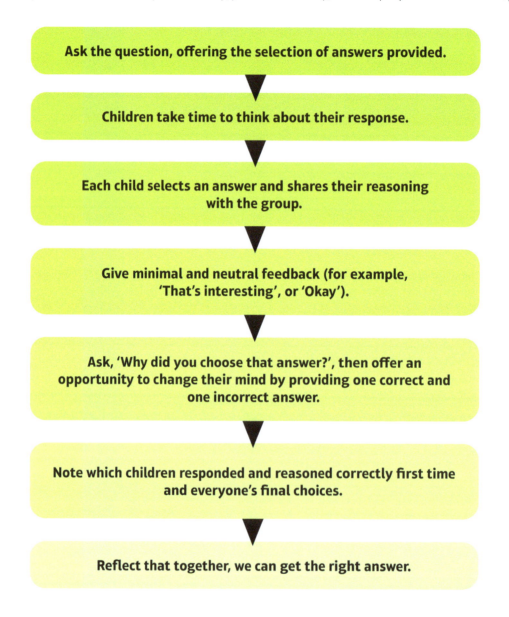

Ask the question, offering the selection of answers provided.

Children take time to think about their response.

Each child selects an answer and shares their reasoning with the group.

Give minimal and neutral feedback (for example, 'That's interesting', or 'Okay').

Ask, 'Why did you choose that answer?', then offer an opportunity to change their mind by providing one correct and one incorrect answer.

Note which children responded and reasoned correctly first time and everyone's final choices.

Reflect that together, we can get the right answer.

Keeping the class together

Traditionally, children who learn quickly have been accelerated through the curriculum. As a consequence, their learning may be superficial and will lack the many benefits of enabling children to learn with and from each other.

By contrast, *Power Maths'* mastery approach values real understanding and richer, deeper learning above speed. It sees all children learning the same concept in small, cumulative steps, each finding and mastering challenge at their own level. Remember that when you teach for mastery, EVERYONE can do maths! Those who grasp a concept easily have time to explore and understand that concept at a deeper level. The whole class therefore moves through the curriculum at broadly the same pace via individual learning journeys.

For some teachers, the idea that a whole class can move forward together is revolutionary and challenging. However, the evidence of global good practice clearly shows that this approach drives engagement, confidence, motivation and success for all learners, and not just the high flyers. The strategies below will help you keep your class together on their maths journey.

Mix it up

Do not stick to set groups at each table. Every child should be working on the same concept, and mixing up the groupings widens children's opportunities for exploring, discussing and sharing their understanding with others.

Recycling questions

Reuse the Textbook and Practice Book questions with concrete materials to allow children to explore concepts and relationships and deepen their understanding. This strategy is especially useful for reinforcing learning in same-day interventions.

Strengthen at every opportunity

The next lesson in a *Power Maths* sequence always revises and builds on the previous step to help embed learning. These activities provide golden opportunities for individual children to strengthen their learning with the support of Teaching Assistants.

Prepare to be surprised!

Children may grasp a concept quickly or more slowly. The 'fast graspers' won't always be the same individuals, nor does the speed at which a child understands a concept predict their success in maths. Are they struggling or just working more slowly?

Same-day intervention

Since maths competence depends on mastering concepts one by one in a logical progression, it is important that no gaps in understanding are ever left unfilled. Same-day interventions – either within or after a lesson – are a crucial safety net for any child who has not fully made the small step covered that day. In other words, intervention is always about keeping up, not catching up, so that every child has the skills and understanding they need to tackle the next lesson. That means presenting the same problems used in the lesson, with a variety of concrete materials to help children model their solutions.

We offer two intervention strategies below, but you should feel free to choose others if they work better for your class.

Within-lesson intervention

The **Think together** activity will reveal those who are struggling, so when it is time for practice, bring these children together to work with you on the first practice questions. Observe these children carefully, ask questions, encourage them to use concrete models and check that they reach and can demonstrate their understanding.

After-lesson intervention

You might like to use the **Think together** questions to recap the lesson with children who are working behind expectations during assembly time. Teaching Assistants could also work with these children at other convenient points in the school day. Some children may benefit from revisiting work from the same topic in the previous year group. Note also the suggestion for recycling questions from the Textbook and Practice Book with concrete materials on page 27.

The role of practice

Practice plays a pivotal role in the *Power Maths* approach. It takes place in class groups, smaller groups, pairs, and independently, so that children always have the opportunities for thinking as well as the models and support they need to practise meaningfully and with understanding.

Intelligent practice

In *Power Maths*, practice never equates to the simple repetition of a process. Instead we embrace the concept of intelligent practice, in which all children become fluent in maths through varied, frequent and thoughtful practice that deepens and embeds conceptual understanding in a logical, planned sequence. To see the difference, take a look at the following examples.

Traditional practice

- Repetition can be rote – no need for a child to think hard about what they are doing

- Praise may be misplaced

- Does this prove understanding?

Intelligent practice

- Varied methods – concrete, pictorial and abstract

- Equation expressed in different ways, requiring thought and understanding

- Constructive feedback

All practice questions are designed to move children on and reveal misconceptions.

Simple, logical steps build onto earlier learning.

C-P-A runs throughout – different ways of modelling and understanding the same concept.

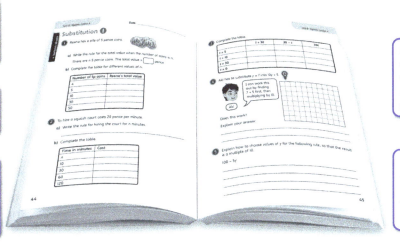

Conceptual variation – children work on different representations of the same maths concept.

Friendly characters offer support and encourage children to try different approaches.

A carefully designed progression

The Practice Books provide just the right amount of intelligent practice for children to complete independently in the final sections of each lesson. It is really important that all children are exposed to the practice questions, and that children are not directed to complete different sections. That is because each question is different and has been designed to challenge children to think about the maths they are doing. The questions become more challenging so children grasping concepts more quickly will start to slow down as they progress. Meanwhile, you have the chance to circulate and spot any misconceptions before they become barriers to further learning.

Homework and the role of parents and carers

While *Power Maths* does not prescribe any particular homework structure, we acknowledge the potential value of practice at home. For example, practising fluency in key facts, such as number bonds and times-tables, is an ideal homework task. You can share the Individual Practice Games for homework (see page 6), or parents and carers could work through uncompleted Practice Book questions with children at either primary stage.

However, it is important to recognise that many parents and carers may themselves lack confidence in maths, and few, if any, will be familiar with mastery methods. A Parents' and Carers' evening that helps them understand the basics of mindsets, mastery and mathematical language is a great way to ensure that children benefit from their homework. It could be a fun opportunity for children to teach their families that everyone can do maths!

Structures and representations

Unlike most other subjects, maths comprises a wide array of abstract concepts – and that is why children and adults so often find it difficult. By taking a concrete-pictorial-abstract (C-P-A) approach, *Power Maths* allows children to tackle concepts in a tangible and more comfortable way.

Non-linear stages

Concrete

Replacing the traditional approach of a teacher working through a problem in front of the class, the concrete stage introduces real objects that children can use to 'do' the maths – any familiar object that a child can manipulate and move to help bring the maths to life. It is important to appreciate, however, that children must always understand the link between models and the objects they represent. For example, children need to first understand that three cakes could be represented by three pretend cakes, and then by three counters or bricks. Frequent practice helps consolidate this essential insight. Although they can be used at any time, good **concrete models are an essential first step in understanding.**

Pictorial

This stage uses pictorial representations of objects to let children 'see' what particular maths problems look like. It helps them make connections between the concrete and pictorial representations and the abstract maths concept. Children can also create or view a pictorial representation together, enabling discussion and comparisons. The *Power Maths* teaching tools are fantastic for this learning stage, and bar modelling is invaluable for problem solving throughout the primary curriculum.

Abstract

Our ultimate goal is for children to understand abstract mathematical concepts, symbols and notation and of course, some children will reach this stage far more quickly than others. To work with abstract concepts, a child must be comfortable with the meaning of and relationships between concrete, pictorial and abstract models and representations. The C-P-A approach is not linear, and children may need different types of models at different times. However, when a child demonstrates with concrete models and pictorial representations that they have grasped a concept, we can be confident that they are ready to explore or model it with abstract symbols such as numbers and notation.

Use at any time and with any age to support understanding

Variation helps visualisation

Children find it much easier to visualise and grasp concepts if they see them presented in a number of ways, so be prepared to offer and encourage many different representations.

For example, the number six could be represented in various ways:

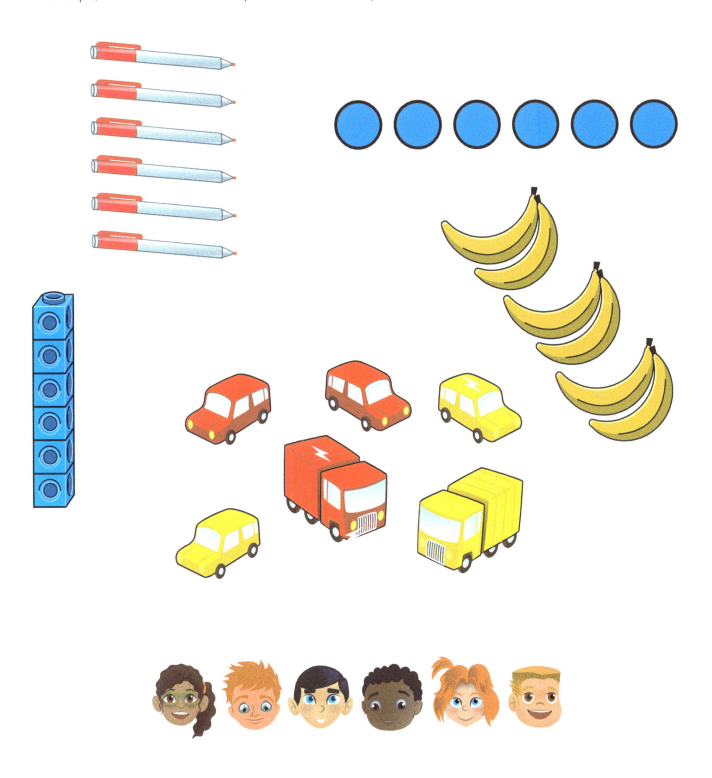

Practical aspects of *Power Maths*

One of the key underlying elements of *Power Maths* is its practical approach, allowing you to make maths real and relevant to your children, no matter their age.

Manipulatives are essential resources for both key stages and *Power Maths* encourages teachers to use these at every opportunity, and to continue the Concrete-Pictorial-Abstract approach right through to Year 6.

The Textbooks and Teacher Guides include lots of opportunities for teaching in a practical way to show children what maths means in real life.

Discover and Share

The **Discover** and **Share** sections of the Textbook give you scope to turn a real-life scenario into a practical and hands-on section of the lesson. Use these sections as inspiration to get active in the classroom. Where appropriate, use the **Discover** contexts as a springboard for your own examples that have particular resonance for your children – and allow them to get their hands dirty trying out the mathematics for themselves.

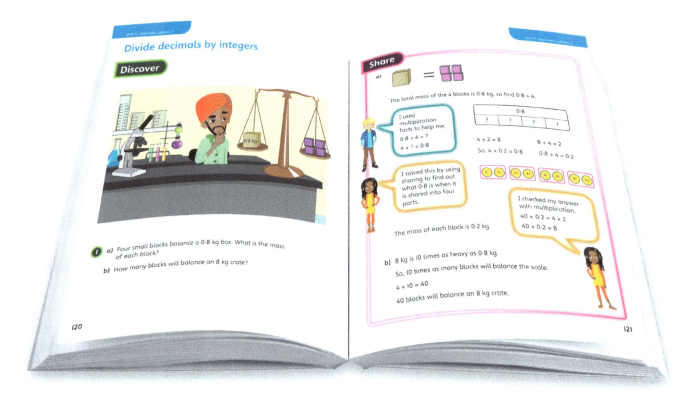

Unit videos

Every term has one unit video which incorporates real-life classroom sequences.

These videos show you how the reasoning behind mathematics can be carried out in a practical manner by showing real children using various concrete and pictorial methods to come to the solution. You can see how using these practical models, such as part-whole and bar models, helps them to find and articulate their answer.

Mastery tips

Mastery Experts give anecdotal advice on where they have used hands-on and real-life elements to inspire their children.

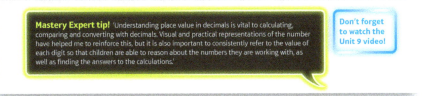

Mastery Expert tip! 'Understanding place value in decimals is vital to calculating, comparing and converting with decimals. Visual and practical representations of the number have helped me to reinforce this, but it is also important to consistently refer to the value of each digit so that children are able to reason about the numbers they are working with, as well as finding the answers to the calculations.'

Don't forget to watch the Unit 9 video!

Concrete-Pictorial-Abstract (C-P-A) approach

Each **Share** section uses various methods to explain an answer, helping children to access abstract concepts by using concrete tools, such as counters. Remember, this isn't a linear process, so even children who appear confident using the more abstract method can deepen their knowledge by exploring the concrete representations. Encourage children to use all three methods to really solidify their understanding of a concept.

Pictorial representation – drawing the problem in a logical way that helps children visualise the maths

Concrete representation – using manipulatives to represent the problem. Encourage children to physically use resources to explore the maths.

Abstract representation – using words and calculations to represent the problem.

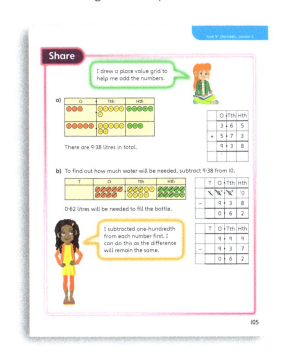

Practical tips

Every lesson suggests how to draw out the practical side of the **Discover** context.

You'll find these in the **Discover** section of the Teacher Guide for each lesson.

PRACTICAL TIPS Provide children with counters to explore the problem practically. Give them individual whiteboards and pens to draw representations.

Resources

Every lesson lists the practical resources you will need or might want to use. There is also a summary of all of the resources used throughout the term on page 39 to help you be prepared.

RESOURCES

Mandatory: place value grids, counters
Optional: number lines

Working with children below age-related expectation

This section offers advice on using *Power Maths* with children who are significantly behind age-related expectation. Teacher judgement will be crucial in terms of where and why children are struggling, and in choosing the right approach. The suggestions can of course be adapted for children with special educational needs, depending on the specific details of those needs.

General approaches to support children who are struggling

Keeping the pace manageable

Remember, you have more teaching days than *Power Maths* lessons so you can cover a lesson over more than one day, and revisit key learning, to ensure all children are ready to move on. You can use the + and − buttons to adjust the time for each unit in the online planning. The NCETM's Ready-to-Progress criteria can be used to help determine what should be highest priority.

Same-day intervention

You could go over the Textbook pages or revisit the previous year's work if necessary (see Addressing gaps). Remember that same-day intervention can be within the lesson, as well as afterwards (see page 28). As children start their independent practice, you can work with those who found the first part of the lesson difficult, checking understanding using manipulatives.

Fluency sessions

Fit in as much practice as you can for number bonds and times-tables, etc., at other times of the day. If you can, plan a short 'maths meeting' for this in the afternoon. You might choose to use a Power Up you haven't used already.

Addressing gaps

Use material from the same topic in the previous year to consolidate or address gaps in learning, e.g. Textbook pages and Strengthen activities. The End of unit check will help gauge children's understanding.

Pre-teaching

Find a 5- to 10-minute slot before the lesson to work with the children you feel would benefit. The afternoon before the lesson can work well, because it gives children time to think in between. Recap previous work on the topic (addressing any gaps you're aware of) and do some fluency practice, targeting number facts etc. that will help children access the learning.

Focusing on the key concepts

If children are a long way behind, it can be helpful to take a step back and think about the key concepts for children to engage with, not just the fine detail of the objective for that year group (e.g. addition with a specific number of columns). Bearing that in mind, how could children advance their understanding of the topic?

Providing extra support within the lesson

Support in the Teacher Guide

First of all, use the Strengthen support in the Teacher Guide for guided and independent work in each lesson, and share this with Teaching Assistants, where relevant. As you read through the lesson content and corresponding Teacher Guide pages before the lesson, ask yourself what key idea or nugget of understanding is at the heart of the lesson. If children are struggling, this should help you decide what's essential for all children before they move on.

Annotating pages

You can annotate questions to provide extra scaffolding or hints if you need to, but aim to build up children's ability to access questions independently wherever you can. Children tend to get used to the style of the *Power Maths* questions over time.

Quick recap as lesson starter

The Quick recap for each lesson in the Teacher Guide is an alternative starter activity to the Power Up. You might choose to use this with some or all children if you feel they will need support accessing the main lesson.

Consolidation questions

If you think some children would benefit from additional questions at the same level before moving on, write one or two similar questions on the board. (This shouldn't be at the expense of reasoning and problem-solving opportunities: take longer over the lesson if you need to.)

Hard copy Textbooks

The Textbooks help children focus in more easily on the mathematical representations, read the text more comfortably, and revisit work from a previous lesson that you are building on, as well as giving children ownership of their learning journey. In main lessons, it can work well to use the e-Textbook for **Discover** and give out the books when discussing the methods in the **Share** section.

Reading support

It's important that all children are exposed to problem solving and reasoning questions, which often involve reading. For whole-class work you can read questions together. For independent practice you could consider annotating pages to help children see what the question is asking, and stem sentences to help structure their answer. A general focus on specific mathematical language and vocabulary will help children access the questions. You could consider pairing weaker readers with stronger readers, or read questions as a group if those who need support are on the same table.

Providing extra depth and challenge with *Power Maths*

Just as prescribed in the National Curriculum, the goal of *Power Maths* is never to accelerate through a topic but rather to gain a clear, deep and broad understanding. Here are some suggestions to help ensure all children are appropriately challenged as you work with the resources.

Overall approaches

First of all, remember that the materials are designed to help you keep the class together, allowing all children to master a concept while those who grasp it quickly have time to explore it in more depth. Use the Deepen support in the Teacher Guide (see below) to challenge children who work through the questions quickly. Here are some questions and ideas to encourage breadth and depth during specific parts of the lesson, or at any time (where no part of the lesson sequence is specified):

- **Discover**: 'Can you demonstrate your solution another way?'

- **Share**: Make sure every child is encouraged to give answers and engage with the discussion, not just the most confident.

- **Think together**: 'Can you model your answers using concrete materials? Can you explain your solution to a partner?'

- Practice: Allow all children to work through the full set of questions, so that they benefit from the logical sequence.

- **Reflect**: 'Is there another way of working out the answer? And another way?'
  'Have you found all the solutions?'
  'Is that always true?'
  'What's different between this question and that question? And what's the same?'

Note that the **Challenge** questions are designed so that all children can access and attempt them, if they have worked through the steps leading up to them. There may be some children in a given lesson who don't manage to do the **Challenge**, but it is not supposed to be a distinct task for a subset of the class. When you look through the lesson materials before teaching, think about what each question is specifically asking, and compare this with the key learning point for the lesson. This will help you decide which questions you feel it's essential for all children to answer, before moving on. You can at least aim for all children to try the **Challenge**!

Deepen activities and support

The Teacher Guide provides valuable support for each stage of the lesson. This includes Deepen tips for the guided and independent practice sections, which will help you provide extra stretch and challenge within your lesson, without having to organise additional tasks. If you have a Teaching Assistant, they can also make use of this advice. There are also suggestions for the lesson as a whole in the 'Going Deeper' section on the first page of the Teacher Guide section for that lesson. Every class is different, so you can always go a bit further in the direction indicated, if appropriate, and build on the suggestions given.

There is a Deepen activity for each unit. These are designed to follow on from the End of unit check, stretching children who have a firm understanding of the key learning from the unit. Children can work on them independently, which makes it easier for the teacher to facilitate the Strengthen activity for children who need extra support. Deepen activities could also be introduced earlier in the unit if the necessary work has been covered. The Deepen activities are on *ActiveLearn* on the Planning page for each unit, and also on the Resources page).

 Deepen Activities

1 a) Draw a vertical line to use as a scale. Label the top of the line as 100 ml. Mark the line to show 10 ml divisions.

b) Draw a line and label the top to show 80 ml. Mark the line to show 10 ml divisions.

 I tried to show 2 ml divisions but there were too many!

c) Draw a line and label the top to show 500 ml. Mark the line to show 20 ml divisions.

d) Show 360 ml on a scale, deciding what divisions to use.

2 a) Draw a vertical scale. Mark the bottom as 0 litres and the top as 10 litres.

Take turns with a partner to roll a dice four times to make a 4-digit capacity in millilitres. Mark the capacity on your scale.

Repeat until you have both marked five different capacities.

b) What is the largest capacity you have marked on the scale?

c) What is the largest capacity you could mark using the numbers you rolled?

Using the questions flexibly to provide extra challenge

Sometimes you may want to write an extra question on the board or provide this on paper. You can usually do this by tweaking the lesson materials. The questions are designed to form a carefully structured sequence that builds understanding step by step, but, with careful thought about the purpose of each question, you can use the materials flexibly where you need to. Sometimes you might feel that children would benefit from another similar question for consolidation before moving on to the next one, or you might feel that they would benefit from a harder example in the same style. It should be quick and easy to generate 'more of the same' type questions where this is the case.

When you see a question like this one (from Unit 2, Lesson 1), it's easy to make extra examples to do afterwards if you need them, maximising the number of exchanges if you want to make it tricky. You can also blot out more digits and ask children if this makes it easier or harder.

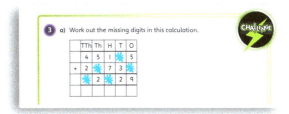

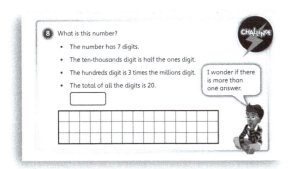

For this example (from Unit 1, Lesson 3), you could ask children to make up their own question(s) for a partner to solve, using 4 clues. (In fact, for any of these examples you could ask early finishers to create their own question for a partner.)

Here's an example (from Unit 4, Lesson 6) where the sum of two number cards is used in the question, but there are other combinations you could ask children to work out, for example, as an extra task at the end of the lesson.

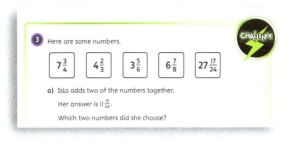

Besides creating additional questions, you should be able to find a question in the lesson that you can adapt into a game or open-ended investigation, if this helps to keep everyone engaged. It could simply be that, instead of answering 5 × 5 etc. on the page, they could build a robot with 5 lots of 5 cubes.

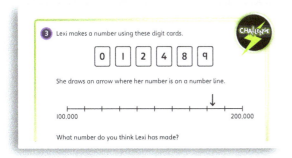

With a question like this (from Unit 1, Lesson 1), children could play a game where they have to guess their partner's mystery number, finding out each time if the guess is too high or too low.

See the bullets above for some general ideas that will help with 'opening out' questions in the books, e.g. 'Can you find all the solutions?' type questions.

Other suggestions

Another way of stretching children is through mixed ability pairs, or via other opportunities for children to explain their understanding in their own way. This is a good way of encouraging children to go deeper into the learning, rather than, for instance, tackling questions that are computationally more challenging but conceptually equivalent in level.

Using *Power Maths* with mixed age classes

Overall approaches

There are many variables between schools that would make it inadvisable to recommend a one-size-fits-all approach to mixed age teaching with *Power Maths*. These include how year groups are merged, availability of Teaching Assistants, experience and preference of teaching staff, range in pupil attainment across years, classroom space and layout, level of flexibility around timetables, and overall organisational structure (whether the school is part of a trust).

Some schools will find it best to timetable separate maths lessons for the different year groups. Others will aim to teach the class together as much as possible using the mixed age planning support on *ActiveLearn* (see the lesson exemplars for ways of organising lessons with strong/medium/weak correlation between year groups). There will also be ways of adapting these general approaches. For example, offset lessons where Year A start their lesson with the teacher, while Year B work independently on the practice from the previous lesson, and then start the next lesson with the teacher while Year A work independently; or teachers may choose to base their provision around the lesson from one year group and tweak the content up/down for the other group.

Key strategies for mixed age teaching

The mixed age teaching webinar on *ActiveLearn* provides advice on all aspects of mixed age teaching, including more detail on the ideas below.

Developing independence over time
Investing time in building up children's independence will pay off in the medium term.

Clear rationale
If someone asked, 'Why did you teach both Unit 3 and 4 in the same lesson/separate lessons?', what would your answer be?

Designing a lesson
1. Identify the core learning for each group
2. Identify any number skills necessary to access the core
3. Consider the flow of concepts and how one core leads to the other

Challenging all children
The questions are designed to build understanding step by step, but with careful thought about the purpose of each question you can tweak them to increase the challenge.

Multiple years combined
With more than two years together, teachers will inevitably need to use the resources flexibly if delivering a single lesson.

Enjoy the positives!

Comparison deepens understanding and there will be lots of opportunities for children, as well as misconceptions to explore. There is also in-built pre-teaching and the chance to build up a concept from its foundations. For teachers there is double the material to draw on! Mixed age teachers require a strong understanding of the progression of ideas across year groups, which is highly valuable for all teachers. Also, it is necessary to engage deeply with the lesson to see how to use the materials flexibly – this is recommended for all teachers and will help you bring your lesson to life!

List of practical resources

Year 6B Mandatory resources

Resource	Lesson
100 square	**Unit 10** Lesson 1
3D shapes (made of cubes)	**Unit 11** Lessons 10, 11
Bead strings	**Unit 10** Lesson 1
Coins (1p and 5p)	**Unit 7** Lesson 1
Counters	**Unit 7** Lessons 7, 9 **Unit 8** Lesson 10 **Unit 9** Lesson 1 **Unit 10** Lesson 5
Counters (different colours)	**Unit 7** Lesson 1
Counters (red and yellow)	**Unit 7** Lessons 2, 3
Cubes	**Unit 10** Lesson 5
Geoboards (and elastics)	**Unit 7** Lesson 6 **Unit 11** Lesson 2
Hundred grids	**Unit 10** Lesson 1
Isometric paper	**Unit 11** Lesson 10
Measuring tapes	**Unit 11** Lesson 1
Multilink cubes	**Unit 11** Lesson 11
Multilink cubes (different colours)	**Unit 7** Lesson 1
Pencils (coloured)	**Unit 11** Lesson 4
Place value counters	**Unit 9** Lessons 4, 5
Place value equipment	**Unit 9** Lesson 1
Place value grids	**Unit 9** Lessons 1, 4, 5, 6
Rulers	**Unit 7** Lesson 4 **Unit 11** Lessons 1, 3, 6, 7, 8, 9
Scissors	**Unit 11** Lesson 4
Squared paper	**Unit 7** Lesson 4 **Unit 11** Lessons 5, 6, 7, 8, 9
Whiteboard pens	**Unit 7** Lesson 1
Whiteboards (individual)	**Unit 7** Lessons 1, 9

Year 6B Optional resources

Resource	Lesson
10-sided dice	**Unit 10** Lesson 3
100 squares	**Unit 10** Lesson 2
2D shapes	**Unit 8** Lessons 2, 6
Balance scales	**Unit 8** Lesson 8
Base 10 equipment	**Unit 9** Lessons 4, 5, 7, 8 **Unit 10** Lessons 1, 4, 6
Bean bags	**Unit 10** Lesson 4
Blocks	**Unit 8** Lesson 9
Boxes or buckets	**Unit 10** Lesson 4
Bricks	**Unit 7** Lesson 9
Cardboard	**Unit 11** Lesson 7
Cardboard shapes	**Unit 11** Lesson 2
Chalk	**Unit 10** Lesson 3 **Unit 11** Lessons 6, 8
Coins	**Unit 7** Lesson 3 **Unit 8** Lessons 4, 11
Counters	**Unit 7** Lessons 4, 8 **Unit 8** Lessons 1, 3, 8, 9 **Unit 10** Lessons 1, 2, 6

Year 6B Optional resources – *continued*

Resource	Lesson
Cubes	**Unit 7** Lessons 3, 5, 7 **Unit 8** Lessons 1, 2, 8, 9
Digit cards	**Unit 8** Lesson 6
Fraction walls	**Unit 9** Lessons 8, 9
Graph paper	**Unit 9** Lesson 8
Hundred grids	**Unit 10** Lesson 2
Marbles	**Unit 7** Lesson 9
Measuring equipment	**Unit 9** Lesson 4
Measuring jugs	**Unit 9** Lesson 3
Measuring jugs (or cylinders)	**Unit 7** Lesson 8
Metre rulers	**Unit 9** Lesson 2 **Unit 11** Lesson 7
Multilink cubes	**Unit 11** Lesson 10
Multilink cubes (or printed versions)	**Unit 8** Lesson 7
Number lines	**Unit 9** Lessons 2, 6, 7
Paper (square sheets with area of 100 cm)	**Unit 11** Lesson 4
Paper squares	**Unit 11** Lesson 5
Pencils (coloured)	**Unit 11** Lesson 2
Pens (coloured)	**Unit 11** Lessons 6, 8, 9
Place value equipment	**Unit 9** Lesson 3
Place value grids	**Unit 9** Lessons 2, 7, 8, 9
Plastic money	**Unit 8** Lesson 2
Plates (10)	**Unit 9** Lesson 4
Printed tables	**Unit 8** Lesson 11
Rectangle (250 cm to 500 cm)	**Unit 9** Lesson 6
Rods	**Unit 11** Lesson 3
Rulers	**Unit 7** Lesson 5 **Unit 11** Lessons 2, 5, 6
Squared paper	**Unit 7** Lessons 5, 6 **Unit 11** Lesson 1
Sticks (small)	**Unit 8** Lessons 1, 2
Straws (or similar)	**Unit 11** Lessons 6, 9
Straws (or strips of paper)	**Unit 11** Lesson 3
String	**Unit 11** Lesson 3
String (or ribbon)	**Unit 7** Lesson 4
Strips of paper	**Unit 9** Lesson 9
Tape	**Unit 11** Lesson 3
Tape measures	**Unit 9** Lesson 2
Times-table lists	**Unit 9** Lesson 6
Toy trucks and cars	**Unit 7** Lesson 2
Transparent squared overlay	**Unit 11** Lesson 4
Triangular tiles made from cardboard	**Unit 11** Lesson 8
Water (coloured)	**Unit 7** Lesson 8
Weights	**Unit 8** Lesson 8
Whiteboards (individual)	**Unit 7** Lessons 2, 5, 8 **Unit 9** Lessons 4, 5

Getting started with *Power Maths*

As you prepare to put *Power Maths* into action, you might find the tips and advice below helpful.

STEP 1: Train up!

A practical, up-front full day professional development course will give you and your team a brilliant head-start as you begin your *Power Maths* journey. You will learn more about the ethos, how it works and why.

STEP 2: Check out the progression

Take a look at the yearly and termly overviews. Next take a look at the unit overview for the unit you are about to teach in your Teacher Guide, remembering that you can match your lessons and pacing to match your class.

STEP 3: Explore the context

Take a little time to look at the context for this unit: what are the implications for the unit ahead? (Think about key language, common misunderstandings and intervention strategies, for example.) If you have the online subscription, don't forget to watch the corresponding unit video.

STEP 4: Prepare for your first lesson

Familiarise yourself with the objectives, essential questions to ask and the resources you will need. The Teacher Guide offers tips, ideas and guidance on individual lessons to help you anticipate children's misconceptions and challenge those who are ready to think more deeply.

STEP 5: Teach and reflect

Deliver your lesson — and enjoy!

Afterwards, reflect on how it went… Did you cover all five stages? Does the lesson need more time? How could you improve it? What percentage of your class do you think mastered the concept? How can you help those that didn't?

Unit 7
Ratio and proportion

Mastery Expert tip! 'I found this unit to be a great opportunity to link with other curriculum areas and 'real' situations. The children calculated ratios during pond dipping and hunting for minibeasts in our forest school and were particularly engaged when challenged to draw a map for the school fair – to scale!'

Don't forget to watch the Unit 7 video!

WHY THIS UNIT IS IMPORTANT

This unit introduces children to the concept of ratio and proportion. Children will learn to recognise, describe and compare ratios and will represent them in different ways. They will learn how to use ratio notation to record and interpret ratios and will develop an understanding of how ratios relate to fractions. They will use a range of methods to calculate amounts from a given ratio, including totals and parts of groups, and will find the difference between unequal parts of a group. They will solve word problems and 2-step problems involving ratio and proportion.

This unit also introduces the concept of scale factors. Children will learn to interpret scales on plans and maps, using them to calculate actual size or distance. They will enlarge shapes by a given scale factor, will learn to identify whether two shapes are similar and will use calculations to deduce the scale factor.

WHERE THIS UNIT FITS

→ Unit 6: Measure – imperial and metric measures
→ **Unit 7: Ratio and proportion**
→ Unit 8: Algebra

In this unit, children use their knowledge of fractions, word problems and multiplication facts to calculate and use ratio and scale factors in a variety of contexts.

Before they start this unit, it is expected that children:
• understand fractions as $\frac{part}{whole}$ and are able to simplify fractions
• can recall multiplication and division facts
• can read word problems carefully, identify the information given and deduce what they need to find out.

ASSESSING MASTERY

Children who have mastered this unit will be able to demonstrate their understanding of ratio using the key language and ratio notation (1 : 2). They will be able to draw diagrams and models to represent problems involving ratio and use ratio to find totals of groups, parts of groups and the difference between unequal parts. They will be able to use scale factors confidently and compare two shapes or quantities of similar proportions.

COMMON MISCONCEPTIONS	STRENGTHENING UNDERSTANDING	GOING DEEPER
Children may confuse, for example, 1 : 4 with $\frac{1}{4}$.	Encourage children to draw diagrams and use practical resources to solve problems. Discuss the difference between fractions and ratio.	Provide opportunities for children to explore real-life problems. Encourage them to explain the difference between fractions and ratio.
Children may enlarge one edge of a shape by the scale factor, but not the others.	Encourage children to draw simple shapes and compare them. Demonstrate that when you enlarge a shape by a scale factor, the whole shape is enlarged.	Increase the complexity of the shape from lines and rectangles to triangles, irregular shapes and other polygons.
Children may add the scale factor rather than multiplying.	Ask children to cut string or ribbon to a given length and use it to measure out a second piece to a given scale factor.	Provide children with 2-step problems or problems with three parts to the ratio, for example 2 : 3 : 1.

Unit 7: Ratio and proportion

UNIT STARTER PAGES

Use these pages to introduce the unit with teacher-led discussion. Have children come across ratios or scale factors in their day-to-day lives? What do they think they might be used for? Encourage children to work in pairs to practise their multiplication and division facts. Look at the key words. Challenge children to explain as many of them as they can.

STRUCTURES AND REPRESENTATIONS

Counters: Use counters, in two different colours, to help children represent ratio problems practically.

Bar models: Bar models are used to represent problems visually, helping children to work out the value of 1 part of a ratio or the scale factor of an enlargement.

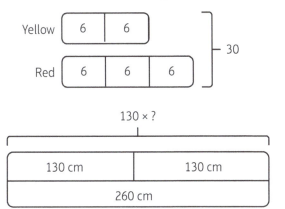

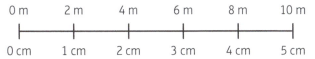

Number lines: Number lines are used to help children understand map scales.

0 m	2 m	4 m	6 m	8 m	10 m
0 cm	1 cm	2 cm	3 cm	4 cm	5 cm

KEY LANGUAGE

There is some key language that children will need to know as part of the learning in this unit.

→ ratio, notation, 1 : 2
→ proportion
→ part, whole, total
→ group
→ fraction
→ unequal, equal
→ simplest form, simplify
→ for every *x* there are *y*
→ similar
→ enlarge, enlargement
→ scale, map scale, scale factor

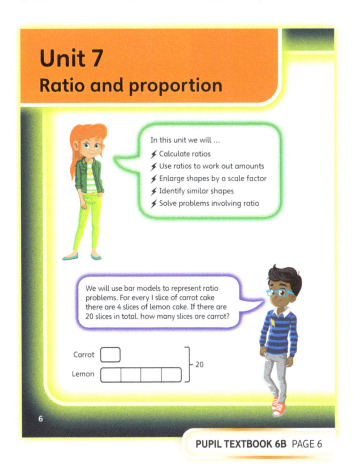

PUPIL TEXTBOOK 6B PAGE 6

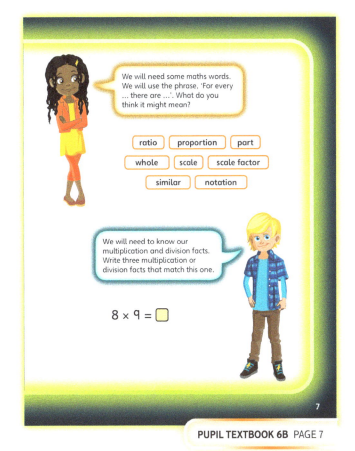

PUPIL TEXTBOOK 6B PAGE 7

Use ratio language

Learning focus

In this lesson, children will be introduced to the concept of ratio and proportion and will use the language of ratio to describe and compare the different parts within a whole.

Before you teach

- Are children secure in recalling multiplication and division facts?
- Are children secure in calculating simple fractions?

NATIONAL CURRICULUM LINKS

Year 6 Ratio and proportion

Solve problems involving unequal sharing and grouping using knowledge of fractions and multiples.

ASSESSING MASTERY

Children can recognise and describe simple ratios and understand how this relates to fractions. They understand fractions as equal parts of the whole and ratio as comparing unequal parts.

COMMON MISCONCEPTIONS

Children may confuse, for example, one to every four with $\frac{1}{4}$. Explain that one to every four is $\frac{1}{5}$ and explicitly model the difference. Ask:

- *In a fruit salad there are 20 pieces of fruit. There is 1 piece of apple for every 4 raspberries. What fraction is apple? Why is the fraction of apple not $\frac{1}{4}$?*

STRENGTHENING UNDERSTANDING

Provide children with practical resources to explore the problems, such as red and yellow counters, 1p and 5p coins, and red and yellow cubes to build the towers.

GOING DEEPER

Provide opportunities for children to explore real-life problems and represent these with counters or drawings. For example, how could they represent the girl to boy ratio in their current class or the ratio of children having school dinners to packed lunches? Encourage children to draw their own images and representations of each problem. Can children explain the difference between fractions and ratio to a partner?

KEY LANGUAGE

In lesson: ratio, fraction, part, whole, group, 'for every … there are …'

Other language to be used by the teacher: proportion, set, equal, unequal

STRUCTURES AND REPRESENTATIONS

Bar models, part-whole models

RESOURCES

Mandatory: different coloured counters, individual whiteboards and pens, 1p and 5p coins, different coloured multilink cubes

 In the eTextbook of this lesson, you will find interactive links to a selection of teaching tools.

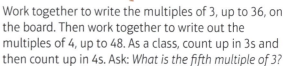

Quick recap

Work together to write the multiples of 3, up to 36, on the board. Then work together to write out the multiples of 4, up to 48. As a class, count up in 3s and then count up in 4s. Ask: *What is the fifth multiple of 3? What is the fifth multiple of 4?*

Discover

WAYS OF WORKING Pair work

ASK

- Question ① a): *How many people are there altogether? How can we use multiplication facts? How many equal groups will there be? How many people are there in each group?*
- Question ① b): *Can you use the sentence modelled in question ① a) to write a sentence comparing the bananas and apples?*

IN FOCUS Encourage children to use resources or diagrams to represent and visualise the problem, and to use their knowledge of multiplication facts. Check children understand the concept of each group as a whole and the adults and children as parts of the group.

PRACTICAL TIPS Provide children with counters to explore the problem practically. Give them individual whiteboards and pens to draw representations.

ANSWERS

Question ① a): For every 1 adult there are 3 children.

Question ① b): For every 3 bananas there are 2 apples.
For every 2 apples there are 3 bananas.

PUPIL TEXTBOOK 6B PAGE 8

Share

WAYS OF WORKING Whole class teacher led

ASK

- Question ① a): *Can you explain what a ratio is?*
- Question ① b): *How have the bananas and apples been represented in the diagram?*

IN FOCUS In this part of the lesson, children explore the use of counters to represent the problem. Discuss the difference between fractions and ratio and begin to use the new language introduced: ratio, 'for every … there are …'.

DEEPEN In question ① a), encourage children to work out what fraction of each group is children. Ask: *How is this different to the ratio?*

PUPIL TEXTBOOK 6B PAGE 9

Think together

WAYS OF WORKING Whole class teacher led (I do, We do, You do)

ASK

- Question **1**: *Can you represent this question using counters? How many groups can you make?*
- Question **1**: *What is the difference between the two statements? Do you need different diagrams for each one?*
- Question **2**: *Who thinks Danny is correct? Can you put the coins into equal groups?*

IN FOCUS Encourage children to use counters of two different colours to represent the problems visually. In question **3**, Astrid and Ash invite children to consider the relationship between fractions and ratio. Ensure children understand ratio as comparing unequal parts of the whole and fractions as equal parts of the whole. In question **3** b), children should identify that the size of the tower can change but the ratio and fractions remain the same.

STRENGTHEN Encourage children to use other visual representations, in addition to the counters, to help them visualise the problems. For example, in question **2**, provide children with eight 1p coins and six 5p coins to explore the problem practically. Similarly, in question **3**, provide red and yellow cubes to enable children to build the towers.

DEEPEN Deepen understanding by providing children with red and yellow cubes and challenging them to create towers, similar to those in question **3**, for a partner. Ask children to write a ratio sentence for each tower and answer questions such as: *What fraction of the tower is red? What fraction is yellow?*

ASSESSMENT CHECKPOINT Can children use counters and diagrams to group the items and find the ratios? Can children show clear understanding of the difference between ratio and fractions?

ANSWERS

Question **1**: For every 2 cheese sandwiches, there is 1 cucumber sandwich. For every 1 cucumber sandwich, there are 2 cheese sandwiches.

Question **2**: Danny is correct. 8 : 6 simplifies to 4 : 3.

Question **3** a): Both towers have 1 red cube with more than 1 yellow cubes. The shorter tower has 1 red cube and 2 yellow cubes. The taller tower has 1 red cube and 6 yellow cubes.

Question **3** b): $\frac{3}{5}$ of the tower is red. $\frac{2}{5}$ of the tower is yellow.

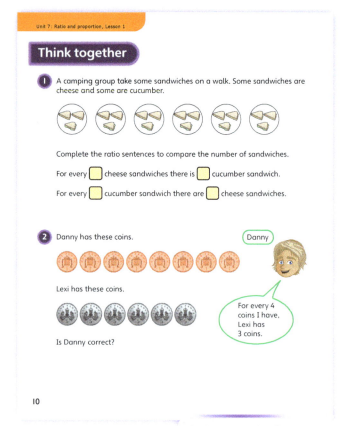

PUPIL TEXTBOOK 6B PAGE 10

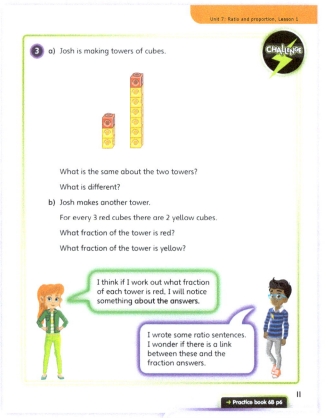

PUPIL TEXTBOOK 6B PAGE 11

Practice

WAYS OF WORKING Independent thinking

IN FOCUS Questions **1**, **2** and **3** require children to use the language of ratio to interpret and describe groups that represent parts of a whole. In question **4**, children are challenged to draw given ratios, the reverse of previous tasks. In question **5**, children match statements using the language of ratio to corresponding representations and then attempt to draw their own representation of a given ratio statement.

STRENGTHEN Reinforce the language of ratio and fractions by providing images representing ratios and fractions and asking children to describe them. Continue to encourage children to use counters, then drawings, to represent the problems visually.

DEEPEN Provide children with squared paper and ask them to colour in shapes to represent different ratios. In question **6**, challenge children to record their findings systematically in a table.

ASSESSMENT CHECKPOINT Are children differentiating between fractions and ratios? Do they recognise that the parts of the ratio (total amount of parts) add up to the denominator in the fraction? Can children draw a given ratio confidently?

ANSWERS Answers for the **Practice** part of the lesson can be found in the *Power Maths* online subscription.

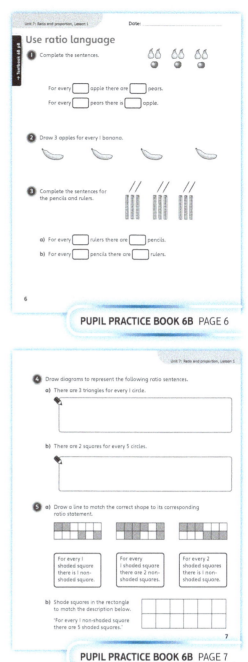

PUPIL PRACTICE BOOK 6B PAGE 6

PUPIL PRACTICE BOOK 6B PAGE 7

Reflect

WAYS OF WORKING Pair work

IN FOCUS This is an open-ended task, inviting children to demonstrate what they have learnt about ratio and fractions. Encourage children to compare and discuss the ratio and fractions. Challenge children to draw different amounts of fruit with the same ratio.

ASSESSMENT CHECKPOINT Check that children are using the language of ratio and fractions confidently when writing statements describing ratios. Are children able to identify fractions as part of the whole and ratios as part : part? Can children identify the common misconception? Can they identify the fractions of fruit?

ANSWERS Answers for the **Reflect** part of the lesson can be found in the *Power Maths* online subscription.

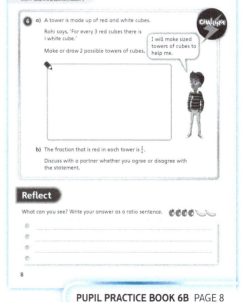

PUPIL PRACTICE BOOK 6B PAGE 8

After the lesson ⏸

- How confidently are children using the new vocabulary of ratio and proportion?
- Do children prefer concrete manipulatives (counters) or drawing diagrams to represent the problems?

Introduce the ratio symbol

Learning focus

In this lesson, children will compare ratios, explore different representations of ratio and identify ratios from given amounts or diagrams.

Before you teach

- How can you develop and refine children's own representations of each problem?
- Can you link this lesson to other curriculum work or a current topic?
- Are children secure in using measures (millilitres and litres)?

NATIONAL CURRICULUM LINKS

Year 6 Ratio and proportion

Solve problems involving unequal sharing and grouping using knowledge of fractions and multiples.

ASSESSING MASTERY

Children can use their understanding of ratio to compare ratios and explore different representations of the same ratio. They can identify ratios from given amounts and diagrams. Children can confidently use ratio notation and the ratio symbol ':' to record and interpret ratios.

COMMON MISCONCEPTIONS

Children may record ratios the wrong way around. For example, when looking at a picture of 3 yellow counters and 2 red counters, children may incorrectly write the ratio of yellow to red counters as 2 : 3 rather than 3 : 2. Ask:
- *How do you know which number comes first when writing a ratio? Can a ratio be written in more than one way?*

STRENGTHENING UNDERSTANDING

Provide children with individual whiteboards to draw representations of the problems using symbols. Use objects such as toy trucks and cars to create given scenarios.

GOING DEEPER

Provide children with 4 red counters and 5 yellow counters and ask them to record the ratio in as many ways as they can. Repeat for different amounts of counters.

KEY LANGUAGE

In lesson: ratio, 'for every … there are …', fraction, simplest form

Other language to be used by the teacher: proportion, set, multiplication, addition, subtraction, total, whole, part, group, ratio

RESOURCES

Mandatory: red and yellow counters

Optional: individual whiteboards, toy trucks and cars

 In the eTextbook of this lesson, you will find interactive links to a selection of teaching tools.

Quick recap

Draw six triangles and three stars on the board. Say:
The six triangles are a part and the three stars are a part. The collection of all the shapes is the whole.

Ask children to discuss how to describe the parts and the whole using the part-to-part relationship (for every … there are …) and the part-to-whole relationship (… out of …).

Discover

WAYS OF WORKING Pair work

ASK

- Question **1** b): *Can you draw a picture of Emma's next t-shirt? What ratio does Emma say she is going to use? Is there more than one answer? Can you work systematically to find different answers?*

IN FOCUS In question **1** a), children's initial response may be to count the stars and suns, concluding that for every 6 stars there are 9 suns. Ask children if they can simplify this. Encourage them to put the stars and suns into groups. Discuss the benefits of finding the simplest form, for example being able to calculate other quantities using the same ratio. In question **1** b), ensure children identify the ratio of stars to suns and encourage them to explore the question by drawing examples. Ask if there is more than one answer and encourage children to work systematically, for example by creating a table.

PRACTICAL TIPS Provide children with red and yellow counters. Individual whiteboards and pens could be used to draw sketches of the problem.

ANSWERS

Question **1** a): There are 6 stars and 9 suns. On the t-shirt, for every 2 stars there are 3 suns.

Question **1** b): On Emma's next t-shirt, for every 1 star there are 3 suns. The ratio of stars to suns is 1 : 3. There could be 1 star and 3 suns, 2 stars and 6 suns, 3 stars and 9 suns and so on.

Share

WAYS OF WORKING Whole class teacher led

ASK

- Question **1** a): *How does Sparks write the ratio? Why do we need to write the ratio in its simplest form?*
- Question **1** b): *Did you find more than one answer?*

IN FOCUS In question **1** a), Sparks introduces ratio notation and ':' as the ratio symbol. Provide children with several ratios and ask them to write each one using the notation. For example, 'For every 1 star there are 2 suns' should be written as 1 : 2.

DEEPEN Encourage children to extend the table in question **1** b). Ask children, for example, how many suns there would be if Emma printed 12 stars (12 × 3 = 36).

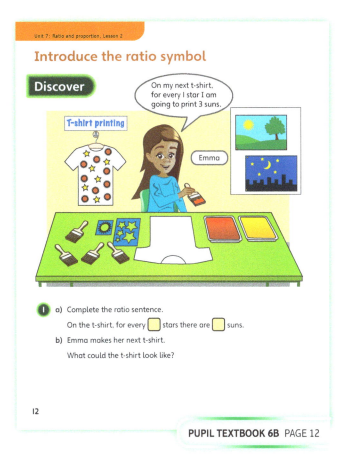

PUPIL TEXTBOOK 6B PAGE 12

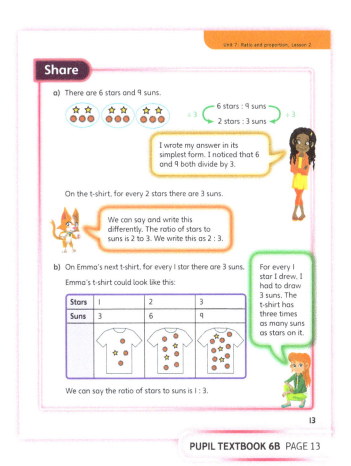

PUPIL TEXTBOOK 6B PAGE 13

Think together

Whole class teacher led (I do, We do, You do)

ASK

- Question **1**: *Have you found each answer in its simplest form? How did you work it out?*
- Question **2**: *What does 2 : 1 mean? Can this be written in a different way? How would you write the number of trucks as a fraction of all the vehicles?*
- Question **3**: *How did you compare the rectangles? Did you use fractions, ratio or both in your answer?*

IN FOCUS In question **2**, encourage children to explore the ratio of trucks to cars using yellow and red counters to represent them. Discuss what 2 : 1 means. Ask children if it can be written in a different way (for every 2 trucks there is 1 car). Suggest children draw and complete a table to work out different possibilities. Ask questions such as: *How many cars are there if there are 6 trucks? How many trucks are there if there are 6 cars?* You could use a table like the following one to give examples of numbers in a 2 : 1 ratio.

Trucks	2	4	6	8	10
Cars	1	2	3	4	5

Discuss Lexi's mistake (adding the 2 and the 1 to conclude that there are three times as many trucks as cars).

STRENGTHEN If children have trouble visualising the problem in question **2**, encourage them to model the scenario with toy cars and trucks. Suggest that they sort the toys into groups of 2 trucks and 1 car and use the groupings to help them draw their table.

DEEPEN In question **2**, ask children to work out how many cars there would be if there were 20 trucks. Ask them to explain the method they used to find their answer. Is there a quicker way of doing it?

ASSESSMENT CHECKPOINT Check that children are using the ratio notation confidently. Are they able to visualise a scenario from a given ratio? Ensure children are finding the answers in their simplest form.

ANSWERS

Question **1** a): For every 1 square there are 2 circles.
Or the ratio of squares to circles is 1 : 2.

Question **1** b): For every 2 squares there are 5 circles.
Or the ratio of squares to circles is 2 : 5.

Question **2**: Zac and Jamilla are correct, as the number of trucks is double the number of cars, so if there are 12 cars there will be 24 trucks. Lexi is incorrect. She has mistakenly added the two parts of the ratio together, confusing it with the fraction of the trucks ($\frac{2}{3}$) and of the cars ($\frac{1}{3}$).

Question **3**: Both rectangles have the same ratio. For every 1 white square there are 3 red squares. The ratio of white to red squares is 1 : 3. In both rectangles the fraction of white squares is $\frac{1}{4}$ ($\frac{4}{16}$ and $\frac{6}{4}$ both simplify to $\frac{1}{4}$). In both rectangles the fraction of red squares is $\frac{3}{4}$ ($\frac{12}{16}$ and $\frac{18}{24}$ both simplify to $\frac{3}{4}$). The rectangles are different sizes.

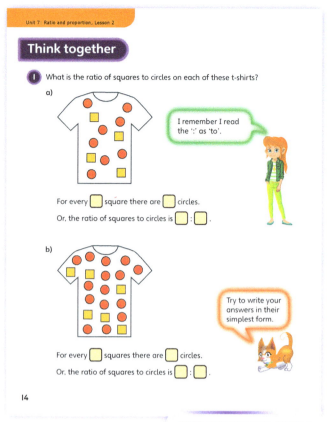

PUPIL TEXTBOOK 6B PAGE 14

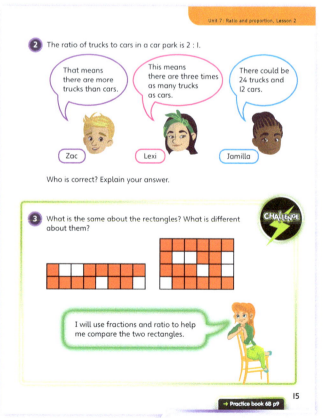

PUPIL TEXTBOOK 6B PAGE 15

50

Practice

WAYS OF WORKING Independent thinking

IN FOCUS In question ②, children should recognise that the first number in the ratio represents the first object in the statement. So, 1 : 2 represents jars to tins and 2 : 1 would represent tins to jars. Question ④ provides an opportunity for children to practise visualising and representing a scenario from a given ratio. Ensure children are able to increase the groups of circles and triangles to have more than six shapes in each box. To answer question ⑥, children need to be secure in using millilitres and litres. They should identify that 250 ml goes into $1\frac{1}{2}$ litres six times.

STRENGTHEN Provide children with individual whiteboards and encourage them to draw diagrams to help them visualise each problem. In question ⑥, for example, suggest children draw glasses to represent each 250 ml of orange juice and lemonade. How many glasses do they need to draw to make $1\frac{1}{2}$ litres? How many of their glasses should be orange juice? How many should be lemonade?

DEEPEN Provide children with several rectangles drawn on squared paper. Ask them to shade the squares to represent different ratios. Challenge children to write their own problems using the same format as question ⑥. Suggest they swap questions with a partner. Can they explain how they worked out the answer?

ASSESSMENT CHECKPOINT Check that children are using ratio notation confidently. Do they understand that the first number in the ratio represents the first object in the statement? For example, in question ④, have children drawn their answers the correct way round? (For example, if the ratio of triangles to circles is 3 : 1 there should be 6 triangles and 2 circles, rather than 6 circles and 2 triangles.)

ANSWERS Answers for the **Practice** part of the lesson can be found in the *Power Maths* online subscription.

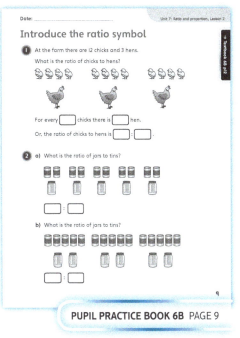

PUPIL PRACTICE BOOK 6B PAGE 9

PUPIL PRACTICE BOOK 6B PAGE 10

Reflect

WAYS OF WORKING Pair work

IN FOCUS This section gives children an opportunity to demonstrate their understanding of ratio notation, in particular that the first number in a ratio represents the first object in the statement. Encourage them to use images or counters to explore the ratios before constructing their answer.

ASSESSMENT CHECKPOINT Are children able to explain the difference between 2 : 1 and 1 : 2? Does their answer show clear understanding that the first number in the ratio represents the first object in the statement?

ANSWERS Answers for the **Reflect** part of the lesson can be found in the *Power Maths* online subscription.

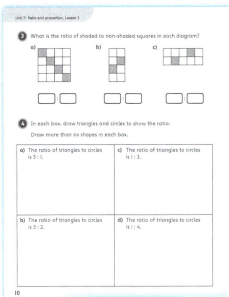

PUPIL PRACTICE BOOK 6B PAGE 11

After the lesson ⏸

• Are children able to use ratio notation correctly?
• Can they write the ratios in their simplest form?

Use ratio

Learning focus

In this lesson, children will use ratios to calculate totals and amounts and will consider the different methods that can be used.

Before you teach

- How will you support children with ratio notation?
- How will you encourage children to use the most efficient method to solve each problem, rather than the method they feel most comfortable with?

NATIONAL CURRICULUM LINKS

Year 6 Ratio and proportion

Solve problems involving unequal sharing and grouping using knowledge of fractions and multiples.

ASSESSING MASTERY

Children can use a range of methods to calculate amounts using a given ratio. They are able to find parts of a group or totals and compare parts of a group (by answering, 'How many more …' questions).

COMMON MISCONCEPTIONS

Children may confuse fractions and ratios. For example, children often think $\frac{3}{5}$ is 3 : 5 rather than 3 : 2. Emphasise that in a fraction the denominator gives the total number of parts, whereas in a ratio the total number of parts is found by adding: 3 parts + 2 parts = 5 parts in total. A fraction is $\frac{part}{whole}$ and a ratio is part : part. Ask:

- *What is the difference between a fraction and a ratio? What is the total number of parts in the fraction $\frac{3}{4}$? What about in the ratio 3 : 4?*

STRENGTHENING UNDERSTANDING

Use bar models to demonstrate visually the difference between fractions and ratios. Using counters to represent fractions and ratios will also help children to gain an understanding of the difference between the two.

GOING DEEPER

Challenge children to create their own bar models to represent each problem. Suggest that children who can confidently solve a 2-step problem work in pairs to create their own 2-step questions.

KEY LANGUAGE

In lesson: ratio, fraction, 'for every … there are …'

Other language to be used by the teacher: group, unequal, diagram, bar model, part

RESOURCES

Mandatory: red and yellow counters

Optional: cubes, coins

 In the eTextbook of this lesson, you will find interactive links to a selection of teaching tools.

Quick recap

Write the ratio 3 : 2 on the board. Ask children to use cubes, counters or other sorting objects to represent this ratio. Share the examples as a class.

Discover

WAYS OF WORKING Pair work

ASK

- Question **1** a): *What is the ratio of children that walk to school to children that catch the school bus? How can we write this ratio? Can we see all the children in the picture?*

IN FOCUS Encourage children to explore different ways to represent the problem. Could they draw a diagram, or use counters? Discuss what information they have been given, that is, the ratio and the number of children that walk to school (one part of the total). Ask what information is missing (the total and the number of children that catch the school bus) and what they need to find (the number of children that catch the school bus – the other part). Ask: *How can you use the ratio to find the number of children that catch the school bus?*

PRACTICAL TIPS Provide children with different coloured counters to represent children that walk to school and children that catch the school bus and encourage them to explore the problem practically.

ANSWERS

Question **1** a):

Question **1** b): Children could draw a table or divide 12 by 3 and multiply the answer by 2. 8 children catch the bus.

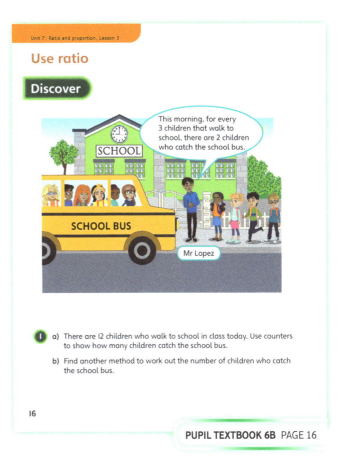

Use ratio

Discover

1 a) There are 12 children who walk to school in class today. Use counters to show how many children catch the school bus.

b) Find another method to work out the number of children who catch the school bus.

16

PUPIL TEXTBOOK 6B PAGE 16

Share

WAYS OF WORKING Whole class teacher led

ASK

- Question **1** a): *Which method do you prefer?*
- Question **1** b): *Which method do you think is most efficient?*

IN FOCUS Discuss the different methods used in question **1** b). Which method do children prefer and why? Do they find one of the methods quicker than the others? How do they know the total number of children? Consider the link between the fractions and ratio. Remind children that a fraction is $\frac{part}{whole}$ and a ratio is part : part.

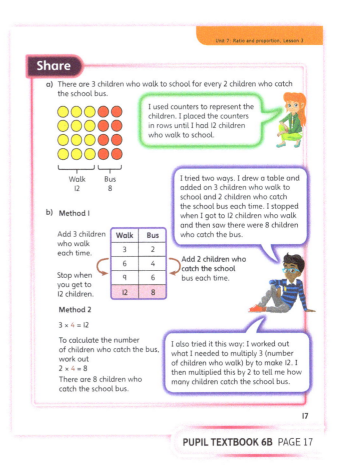

Share

a) There are 3 children who walk to school for every 2 children who catch the school bus.

Walk 12   Bus 8

I used counters to represent the children. I placed the counters in rows until I had 12 children who walk to school.

b) **Method 1**

Add 3 children who walk each time.

Walk	Bus
3	2
6	4
9	6
12	8

Stop when you get to 12 children.

Add 2 children who catch the school bus each time.

I tried two ways. I drew a table and added on 3 children who walk to school and 2 children who catch the school bus each time. I stopped when I got to 12 children who walk and then saw there were 8 children who catch the bus.

Method 2

3 × 4 = 12

To calculate the number of children who catch the bus, work out

2 × 4 = 8

There are 8 children who catch the school bus.

I also tried it this way: I worked out what I needed to multiply 3 (number of children who walk) by to make 12. I then multiplied this by 2 to tell me how many children catch the bus.

17

PUPIL TEXTBOOK 6B PAGE 17

Think together

WAYS OF WORKING Whole class teacher led (I do, We do, You do)

ASK

• Question **1**: *Explain the method you have chosen.*

IN FOCUS Encourage children to choose the method they feel most confident with when answering question **1**. Model the methods discussed in **Share** (using or drawing counters, creating a table and calculating the answer).

Using the table method for question **2** will enable children to answer both parts of the question at the same time. Encourage children to recognise this, asking whether they can see a benefit to using a table over the other methods.

STRENGTHEN If children need support working out the answer to question **3**, provide them with conkers and leaves (or other practical resources).

DEEPEN To extend children's learning in question **2**, ask them to work out how many shapes there would be altogether if there were 7 triangles. Challenge children to create a pattern using natural resources (such as sticks, stones, acorns and leaves) and work out the ratio. How many *x* will they need if they use a specified number of *y*?

ASSESSMENT CHECKPOINT Assess the confidence with which children are using their chosen method to answer the questions. Can they explain their method clearly? Have they chosen the most efficient method? Do children recognise that by using the table method in question **2**, they can answer parts a) and b) at the same time?

ANSWERS

Question **1**: There are 5 children not wearing a bib. The ratio of bib to no bib is 2 : 1. If the 2 parts = 10, then 1 part will equal 5. $10 \div 2 = 5$

Table

Bibs	Not bibs
2	1
4	2
6	3
8	4
10	5

Calculation
$2 \times 5 = 10$
$1 \times 5 = 5$

Question **2** a): There are 15 squares. 1 : 3 = 5 : 15. The number of triangles has increased 5 times, so the number of squares must also increase 5 times. $5 \times 3 = 15$

Question **2** b): There are 6 triangles. 1 : 3 = 6 : 18. The number of squares has increased 6 times ($18 \div 3 = 6$), so the number of triangles must also increase 6 times. $6 \times 1 = 6$

Question **3** a): They need 10 leaves. The ratio of conkers to leaves is 3 : 2.
15 conkers ÷ 3 = 5 groups of 3 conkers.
5 groups of 2 leaves = $5 \times 2 = 10$ leaves.

Question **3** b): 20 is not divisible by 3 so only 18 conkers can be used to make complete groups.
18 ÷ 3 = 6 groups of 3 conkers. 6 groups of 2 leaves = $6 \times 2 = 12$ leaves. They need 12 leaves with 18 conkers.

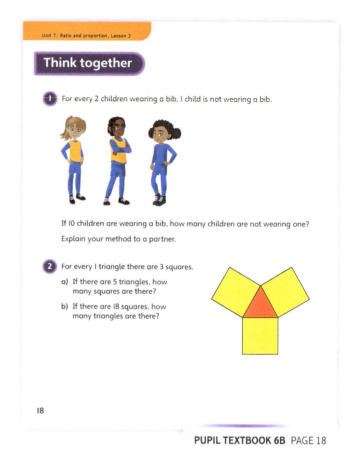

Think together

1 For every 2 children wearing a bib, 1 child is not wearing a bib.

If 10 children are wearing a bib, how many children are not wearing one?
Explain your method to a partner.

2 For every 1 triangle there are 3 squares.
a) If there are 5 triangles, how many squares are there?
b) If there are 18 squares, how many triangles are there?

18

PUPIL TEXTBOOK 6B PAGE 18

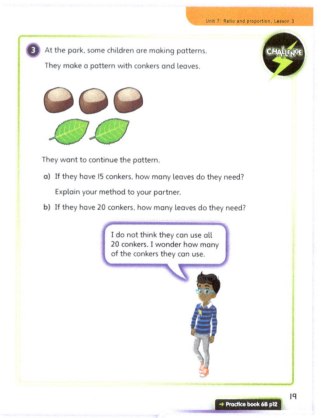

3 At the park, some children are making patterns.
They make a pattern with conkers and leaves.

They want to continue the pattern.
a) If they have 15 conkers, how many leaves do they need?
Explain your method to your partner.
b) If they have 20 conkers, how many leaves do they need?

I do not think they can use all 20 conkers. I wonder how many of the conkers they can use.

19

→ Practice book 6B p12

PUPIL TEXTBOOK 6B PAGE 19

Practice

WAYS OF WORKING Independent thinking

IN FOCUS Question **6** provides children with the opportunity to solve a 2-step question. The first step is to work out how many sheep there are, before subtracting the total number of sheep from the number of cows. Encourage children to recognise that drawing pictures or counting counters to solve the problem will take a long time; it will be more efficient to multiply or create a table. Question **7** provides the added challenge of using money notation. Children could use 5p and 10p coins to solve the problem practically.

STRENGTHEN If children need support using the table method, provide table headings and the first row or two. Demonstrate how the numbers change from row to row and encourage children to draw in arrows, showing what each row increases by, as a visual reminder.

DEEPEN Adapt some of the questions into 2-step problems. For example, for question **4**, ask: *For every 1 clown fish there are 4 box fish. If the fish tank contains 20 clown fish, how many more box fish than clown fish are there in the tank?* For question **5**, ask: *For every 2 squares there are 5 rectangles. If the pattern has 18 squares, how many more rectangles than squares are there?*

THINK DIFFERENTLY In question **5**, children explore how the ratio can inform the possible size of each of the parts. They should notice that if there is an odd number of squares, there cannot be a whole number of rectangles.

ASSESSMENT CHECKPOINT Can children use the language of ratio confidently? Are they able to choose the most efficient method to solve each problem? Are children able to solve 2-step problems involving ratio?

ANSWERS Answers for the **Practice** part of the lesson can be found in the *Power Maths* online subscription.

Reflect

WAYS OF WORKING Pair work

IN FOCUS By giving children the ratio (3 : 4) but not the total number of balloons, this question requires children to recognise that for every group of balloons there are 3 large and 4 small. From this they should conclude that there will always be more small balloons, regardless of how many balloons there are in total. Children can use a table or manipulatives to prove this.

Large balloons	Small balloons
3	4
6	8
9	12

ASSESSMENT CHECKPOINT Do children recognise that the ratio remains the same when the total changes? Are they able to explain why there are always more small balloons than large ones and prove their answer with a table, for example? Do they use the correct notation when answering the question?

ANSWERS Answers for the **Reflect** part of the lesson can be found in the *Power Maths* online subscription.

After the lesson ⏸

- Which methods do children find most useful? Can they explain why they prefer a particular method?
- Are children confident using ratio notation?

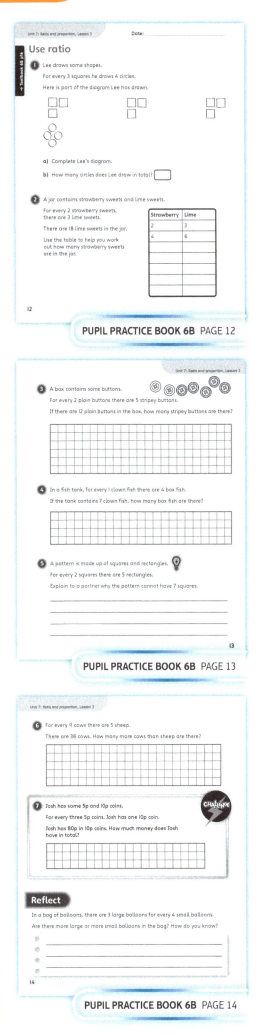

PUPIL PRACTICE BOOK 6B PAGE 12

PUPIL PRACTICE BOOK 6B PAGE 13

PUPIL PRACTICE BOOK 6B PAGE 14

Scale drawing

Learning focus

In this lesson, children will interpret scales on maps and plans. They will measure lines on the map or plan and calculate the length in real life.

Before you teach

- How and when will you introduce the new vocabulary?
- Do children need a reminder of ratio notation?
- Are children secure in finding the perimeter of a shape?

NATIONAL CURRICULUM LINKS

Year 6 Ratio and proportion

Solve problems involving similar shapes where the scale factor is known or can be found.

ASSESSING MASTERY

Children can interpret and understand scales used on maps and plans. They can measure a line or 2D shape and increase or decrease it by a given scale factor, to calculate the 'real-life' size.

COMMON MISCONCEPTIONS

Children may add the scale, rather than multiplying. For example, if a line measures 4 cm and is increased by a scale of 1 : 3, children may give the answer 4 + 3 = 7 cm rather than 4 × 3 = 12 cm. Ask:

- *What does a scale of 1 : 3 mean? What does the 1 stand for? What about the 3? How can you use the scale to work out the length of something in real life?*

STRENGTHENING UNDERSTANDING

Begin with increasing a line by a scale factor. Model the concept visually using counters. Ask children to cut string or ribbon to a given length, then use the string to measure out a second piece using a scale of 1 : *x*.

GOING DEEPER

Increase the complexity of the shape from basic lines and boxes, to triangles, irregular shapes and other polygons. Ask children to calculate the perimeters.

KEY LANGUAGE

In lesson: scale, ratio, **notation**, plan, map scale

Other language to be used by the teacher: proportion, measure, increase, decrease, scale factor, bar model, ratio, scale diagram

STRUCTURES AND REPRESENTATIONS

Number lines, bar models

RESOURCES

Mandatory: ruler, squared paper

Optional: counters, ribbon or string

 In the eTextbook of this lesson, you will find interactive links to a selection of teaching tools.

Quick recap ↻

Show an eraser, for example, and set the class a treasure hunt challenge. Ask: *Can you find something twice as long as this piece of stationery? What about three times as long? How about ten times as long?*

Discover

WAYS OF WORKING Pair work

ASK

- Question ①: *What scale is the plan drawn to? What does this mean?*
- Question ①: *What units are the distances in on the plan? (cm) What about in real life? (m)*
- Question ①: *How can you calculate the size of items on the plan in real life? What operation could you use?*

IN FOCUS The plan in question ① introduces the concept of scale. Encourage children to explore the plan and measure the different objects represented on it. Discuss the idea of scale and why it is useful. Do children understand why the units change?

PRACTICAL TIPS Provide children with a selection of resources with which to take measurements from the plan. This could include rulers and ribbon or string. Counters could also be used to help children to visualise the concept. For example, if the length of the fence is 6 counters on the plan, it will be 12 counters in real life. Lead children to recognise that the counters representing the line on the plan are worth 1 cm each, but those representing the fence in real life are worth 1 m each.

ANSWERS

Question ① a): The row of trees is 8 m long in real life.

Question ① b): The perimeter of the sandpit is 28 m in real life.

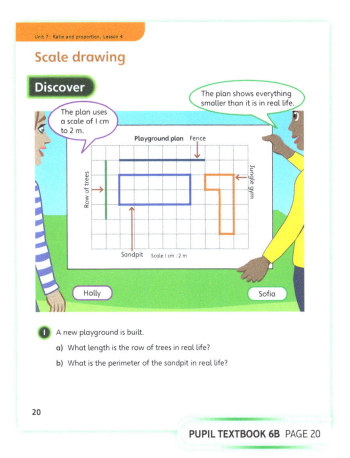

Scale drawing

Discover

The plan uses a scale of 1 cm to 2 m.

The plan shows everything smaller than it is in real life.

Playground plan   Fence

Row of trees

Jungle gym

Sandpit   Scale 1 cm : 2 m

Holly   Sofia

① A new playground is built.
a) What length is the row of trees in real life?
b) What is the perimeter of the sandpit in real life?

20

PUPIL TEXTBOOK 6B PAGE 20

Share

WAYS OF WORKING Whole class teacher led

ASK

- Question ① a): *Why is it important that a plan is drawn to scale? Who might use a plan and why?*
- Question ① a): *Did anyone use a map scale like Dexter?*
- Question ① b): *How does the bar model help you to answer the question?*

IN FOCUS This question will help children to see the connection between scale and ratio. Sparks prompts children to recognise that a scale of 1 cm : 2 m means that for every 1 cm on the plan there are 2 m in real life. Explain that both the map scale and the bar model used in this section show the relationship between 1 cm on the plan and 2 m in real life. Ask children to draw a bar model to represent question ① a) and a map scale to represent question ① b). Discuss which representation children prefer and why.

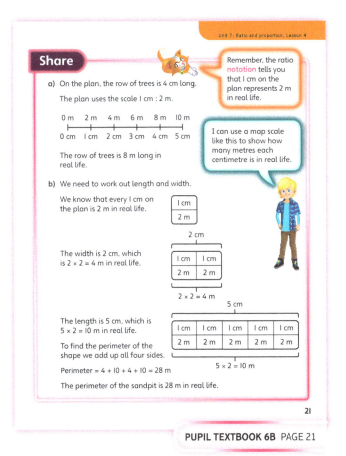

Share

Remember, the ratio notation tells you that 1 cm on the plan represents 2 m in real life.

a) On the plan, the row of trees is 4 cm long.

The plan uses the scale 1 cm : 2 m.

0 m   2 m   4 m   6 m   8 m   10 m

0 cm   1 cm   2 cm   3 cm   4 cm   5 cm

The row of trees is 8 m long in real life.

I can use a map scale like this to show how many metres each centimetre is in real life.

b) We need to work out length and width.

We know that every 1 cm on the plan is 2 m in real life.

| 1 cm |
| 2 m |

The width is 2 cm, which is 2 × 2 = 4 m in real life.

2 cm

| 1 cm | 1 cm |
| 2 m | 2 m |

2 × 2 = 4 m

The length is 5 cm, which is 5 × 2 = 10 m in real life.

5 cm

| 1 cm | 1 cm | 1 cm | 1 cm | 1 cm |
| 2 m | 2 m | 2 m | 2 m | 2 m |

5 × 2 = 10 m

To find the perimeter of the shape we add up all four sides.

Perimeter = 4 + 10 + 4 + 10 = 28 m

The perimeter of the sandpit is 28 m in real life.

21

PUPIL TEXTBOOK 6B PAGE 21

Think together

Unit 7: Ratio and proportion, Lesson 4

Think together

WAYS OF WORKING Whole class teacher led (I do, We do, You do)

ASK

- Question ❶: *What is a scale?*
- Question ❶: *How does a scale relate to a ratio?*
- Question ❷: *What diagrams could you draw to help you? Do you prefer a map scale or a bar model?*

IN FOCUS In question ❸, children will need to recognise that the second plan, with a scale of 1 : 200, does not have unit measurements on it. Discuss what this means and why it might not have units. Ask what the 200 could represent (for example, 200 mm, 200 cm, 200 m). Encourage children to conclude that 200 cm is the same as 2 m and therefore the scales are the same. Explain that if no measurement units are given on a scale, the measurement unit remains the same. For example, 1 cm : 200 cm is written as 1 : 200.

STRENGTHEN Give children different examples of scales and ask them to write or say a sentence for each. For example:

Scale	Sentence
1 cm : 3 m	For every 1 cm on the map there are 3 m in real life.
4 m : 2 km	For every ☐ m on the plan there are ☐ km in real life.

DEEPEN Challenge children to write some scales in a different way. Alternatively, give them a selection of scales (some of which are the same) and ask them to match them up. For example:

1 cm : 3 m	1 cm : 300 cm	0·01 m : 3 m
2 m : 5 m	200 cm : 500 cm	2,000 mm : 5,000 mm
1 km : 10 km	1,000 m : 10,000 m	2 m : 2 km
1 cm : 25,000 cm	1 cm : 250 m	200 cm : 2,000 m

ASSESSMENT CHECKPOINT Can children confidently use a scale to calculate real-life lengths from a plan? Assess whether children understand that, if no measurement units are given on a scale, the measurement unit is the same. For example, 1 cm : 200 cm is written as 1 : 200. Look for clear understanding in question ❸ of why Kate is correct.

ANSWERS

Question ❶ a): The length of the flower bed is 30 m in real life. The width of the flower bed is 15 m in real life.

Question ❶ b): The length of the path is 27·5 m in real life.

Question ❷: The distance is 90 m in real life.

Question ❸ a): Kate is correct. The second plan is 1 cm to 200 cm. 200 cm = 2 m, so 1 cm : 2 m is the same as 1 cm : 200 cm. When a scale does not state the units, they are the same units.

Question ❸ b): The height of the roof is 10 m in real life.

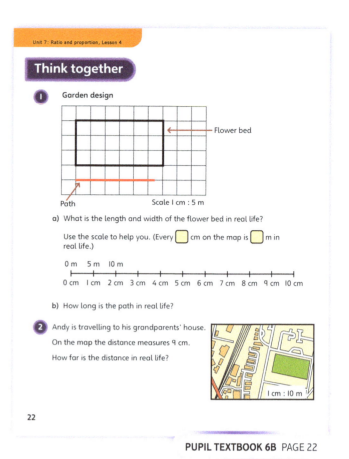

PUPIL TEXTBOOK 6B PAGE 22

PUPIL TEXTBOOK 6B PAGE 23

Practice

WAYS OF WORKING Independent thinking

IN FOCUS Questions ❸ and ❺ will require children to understand that when no units are given on a scale, the units for both the plan and real life are the same. For example, the scale 1 : 25,000 is 1 cm : 25,000 cm. Ask children if this can be written as metres or kilometres. For example, what is 12 cm on the map equal to in km or m? In question ❺, children will need to consider what information they have been given and what they need to find out. So, they should first calculate the perimeter of the irregular octagon in real life (400). This will give them the perimeter of the rectangle in real life, from which they can work out the missing scale (8 × ☐ = 400).

STRENGTHEN Encourage children to practise drawing scale diagrams. Provide them with a list of scales and ask them to sketch scale diagrams to match.

DEEPEN Provide children with squared paper and challenge them to create their own problems for a partner, based on question ❺.

ASSESSMENT CHECKPOINT Assess whether children are confident working with scales. In question ❶, are they confident when using a scale to add something to a plan? In question ❸, check children understand that when a scale does not have any units, the units for both sides are the same (for example, 1 : 25,000 is 1 cm : 25,000 cm).

ANSWERS Answers for the **Practice** part of the lesson can be found in the *Power Maths* online subscription.

Reflect

WAYS OF WORKING Independent thinking

IN FOCUS This question requires children to understand and explain that if no unit measurements are given, the two sides of the scale have the same units. Children will recognise that 200 cm is the same as 2 m. They may recognise that (without a map, plan or model to check) 1 : 200 could be 1 mm : 200 mm or 1 cm : 200 cm or 1 m : 200 m, whereas 1 cm : 2 m specifies the measurements.

ASSESSMENT CHECKPOINT Are children able to explain the similarities and differences between the two scales? Do their explanations show clear understanding of a scale without units? Can they write the same scale in different ways?

ANSWERS Answers for the **Reflect** part of the lesson can be found in the *Power Maths* online subscription.

After the lesson ⏸

- Can children make the link between visual representations and the calculations needed?
- Do children understand that if a scale does not have any units, the units are the same? Are they able to use this understanding to explain the differences between two scales?

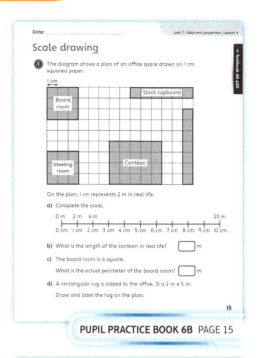

PUPIL PRACTICE BOOK 6B PAGE 15

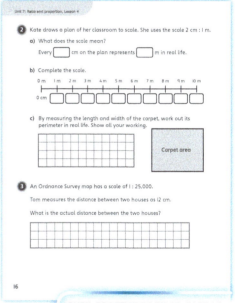

PUPIL PRACTICE BOOK 6B PAGE 16

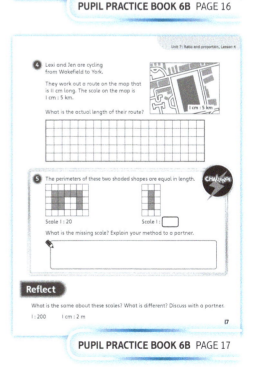

PUPIL PRACTICE BOOK 6B PAGE 17

Scale factors

Learning focus

In this lesson, children are provided with measurements and will find the scale factor. They will then apply the scale factor to calculate further measurements.

Before you teach

- Are children secure in multiplying whole numbers by decimals or by fractions?
- Are children familiar with the term 'scale factor'? If they have come across this before, discuss what context it was used in.

NATIONAL CURRICULUM LINKS

Year 6 Ratio and proportion

Solve problems involving similar shapes where the scale factor is known or can be found.

ASSESSING MASTERY

Children can use visual representations, models and calculations to deduce the scale factor of two similar shapes or measurements. They can apply their knowledge in different contexts. Children confidently use the scale factor to calculate measurements of enlargements.

COMMON MISCONCEPTIONS

Children may add the scale factor, rather than multiplying. They may also find the difference between two measurements, rather than how many times bigger one is than the other. Ask:

- If a line of 6 cm is increased by a scale factor 1 : 4, how long is the new line? How did you use the scale factor to work out the answer? Why is the answer not 10 cm? Two lines are 5 cm and 15 cm long. What is the scale factor? How did you work it out?

STRENGTHENING UNDERSTANDING

To ensure children are secure in their use of scale factors, focus on visual representations. Provide children with individual whiteboards and encourage them to draw bar models to help them answer the questions. Provide cubes and squared paper to enable children to explore questions practically.

GOING DEEPER

Once children are confidently using and calculating scale factors, challenge them to compare and enlarge more complex polygons. For example, provide them with irregular polygons drawn on squared paper and encourage them to enlarge them by different scale factors. Include scale factors less than 1, such as $\frac{1}{2}$ or $\frac{1}{4}$.

KEY LANGUAGE

In lesson: scale factor, bar model, enlarge, enlargement, multiply

Other language to be used by the teacher: ratio, proportion, increase, decrease, division, inverse

STRUCTURES AND REPRESENTATIONS

Bar models

RESOURCES

Optional: individual whiteboards, squared paper, cubes, rulers

 In the eTextbook of this lesson, you will find interactive links to a selection of teaching tools.

Quick recap

Give each child two objects of different sizes, such as a pencil and a ruler. Ask: *How many times longer is the ruler than the pencil? How many pencils could you line up along the ruler?*

Discover

WAYS OF WORKING Pair work

ASK

- Question **1** a): *What is a scale factor? What do you know about scale factors?*
- Question **1** a): *What visual representations could you use?*
- Question **1** b): *What information do you have? What calculations do you need to do?*

IN FOCUS In question **1** a), children are given two measurements to compare to find the scale factor. In question **1** b), children need to use the scale factor calculated in **1** a) to find the size of the tree from the given shadow length.

PRACTICAL TIPS Ask children to think about the bar models needed and to describe them in detail. Encourage children to draw their own bar models on individual whiteboards.

ANSWERS

Question **1** a): The scale factor is 2.

Question **1** b): The tree is 4 m tall.

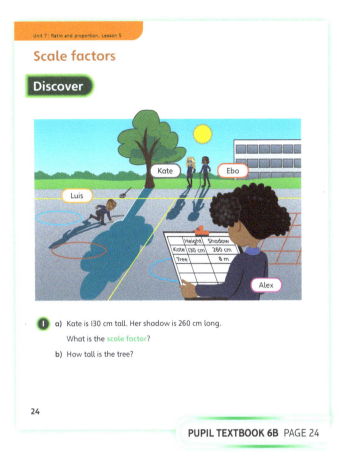

Scale factors

Discover

1 a) Kate is 130 cm tall. Her shadow is 260 cm long.

What is the scale factor?

b) How tall is the tree?

24

PUPIL TEXTBOOK 6B PAGE 24

Share

WAYS OF WORKING Whole class teacher led

ASK

- Question **1** a): *What is 130 cm long? What is 260 cm long? How many times bigger is Kate's shadow than her height?*
- Question **1** b): *What does the bar model show you? How can you use it to find the height of the tree?*

IN FOCUS In question **1** a), Dexter helps children to understand the relationship between how many *times* bigger Kate's shadow is than her. It is important to use the visual representation of the bar model to develop understanding. Encourage children to explain the bar model in their own words.

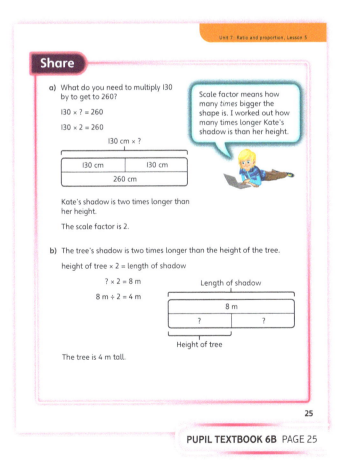

Share

a) What do you need to multiply 130 by to get to 260?

$130 \times ? = 260$

$130 \times 2 = 260$

Scale factor means how many *times* bigger the shape is. I worked out how many times longer Kate's shadow is than her height.

130 cm × ?

130 cm	130 cm
260 cm	

Kate's shadow is two times longer than her height.

The scale factor is 2.

b) The tree's shadow is two times longer than the height of the tree.

height of tree × 2 = length of shadow

$? \times 2 = 8 m$

$8 m \div 2 = 4 m$

Length of shadow

8 m	
?	?

Height of tree

The tree is 4 m tall.

25

PUPIL TEXTBOOK 6B PAGE 25

Think together

WAYS OF WORKING Whole class teacher led (I do, We do, You do)

ASK

• Question ❷: *What calculations do you need to do? Can you use the inverse to find or check answers?*

• Question ❷: *What happens if the scale factor is not a whole number?*

IN FOCUS In question ❶ c), the bar model is not given. This provides an opportunity to observe if children can draw their own bar model or work out the answer using calculations. In question ❷, children need to use a scale factor of $1\frac{1}{2}$. Discuss what happens when the scale factor is not a whole number.

STRENGTHEN To ensure children are confident using scale factors, focus on the bar models and describe them in detail. Ask children to draw their own bar models on individual whiteboards. Encourage children to use cubes to explore question ❷ practically, or to draw towers on squared paper. For question ❸, provide squared paper and encourage children to explore enlarging shapes by the given scale factors.

DEEPEN In question ❷, ask children to describe what happens when the scale factor is not a whole number. Encourage them to build towers with different scale factors and extend the table. For example, ask children how big the tower would be if it was enlarged by a scale factor of 0·25. Challenge children to investigate towers of different sizes. For example, what if the original tower is 10 cubes tall? Extend question ❸ by asking children to explore what happens to each side and to the perimeter of the shape.

ASSESSMENT CHECKPOINT Check children are multiplying, rather than adding or finding the difference. Are children able to draw accurate bar models and explain what they show? Are children confidently using scale factors of less than 1, or scale factors that are not whole numbers?

ANSWERS

Question ❶ a): The scale factor is 2.

Question ❶ b): The scale factor is 3.

Question ❶ c): The scale factor is 7.

Question ❷ a):

Scale factor	2	3	4	5	1
Number of cubes tall	16	24	32	40	12

Question ❷ b): The scale factor is 6.

Question ❷ c): The scale factor is $7\frac{1}{2}$.

Question ❸ a): To enlarge a shape by a scale factor of 2 means all the dimensions have been doubled (× 2).

Question ❸ b): To enlarge a shape by a scale factor of 3 means all the dimensions are trebled (× 3).

Question ❸ c): To enlarge a shape by a scale factor of $\frac{1}{2}$ means all the dimensions are halved (÷ 2).

Question ❸: Children should draw various pairs of shapes to show scale factors of 2, 3 and $\frac{1}{2}$.

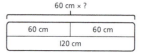

Unit 7: Ratio and proportion, Lesson 5

Think together

❶ Class 5 measure the length of the shadow of a pole at different times of the day.

The pole is 60 cm tall.

a) What is the scale factor when the shadow measures 120 cm?

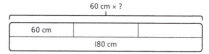

60 cm × ?

60 cm	60 cm

120 cm

b) What is the scale factor when the shadow measures 180 cm?

60 cm × ?

60 cm		

180 cm

c) What is the scale factor when the shadow measures 420 cm?

I will draw a bar model to help me work out the answer.

26

PUPIL TEXTBOOK 6B PAGE 26

---

❷ A tower is 8 cubes tall.

a) Complete the table to show the height of the tower after these scale factor enlargements.

Scale factor	2	3	4	5	$1\frac{1}{2}$
Number of cubes tall	16				

b) What is the scale factor when the tower is 48 cubes tall?

c) What is the scale factor when the tower is 60 cubes tall?

❸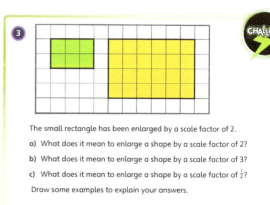

The small rectangle has been enlarged by a scale factor of 2.

a) What does it mean to enlarge a shape by a scale factor of 2?

b) What does it mean to enlarge a shape by a scale factor of 3?

c) What does it mean to enlarge a shape by a scale factor of $\frac{1}{2}$?

Draw some examples to explain your answers.

27

→ Practice book 6B p18

PUPIL TEXTBOOK 6B PAGE 27

Practice

WAYS OF WORKING Independent thinking

IN FOCUS Question ❶ provides an opportunity for children to practise working out scale factors using bar models. Encourage them to describe the bar models. What do they show? Can they draw their own bar model? In question ❷, a common misconception would be to only enlarge part of the shape, or one side. Ensure children enlarge all sides of the shape when drawing the enlargements.

STRENGTHEN In question ❶, discuss the bar models with children in detail. Encourage children to draw their own bar models on individual whiteboards. To cement understanding, provide children with rulers and encourage them to draw the lines. In question ❺, provide children with squared paper to draw the shapes. Encourage them to draw bar models to find the scale factor. Ensure children recognise that the scale factor is not a whole number.

DEEPEN Ask children to work in pairs and provide them with squared paper. Ask one child to draw a shape and challenge their partner to enlarge it. The original child must then calculate the scale factor their partner chose. Encourage them to use scale factors that are less than 1, or are not whole numbers.

ASSESSMENT CHECKPOINT Check that children can draw bar models to represent the problems. Can they explain what the bar models show? Are they able to enlarge a shape by a given scale factor? Can children explain what a scale factor is?

ANSWERS Answers for the **Practice** part of the lesson can be found in the *Power Maths* online subscription.

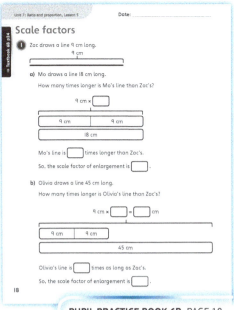

PUPIL PRACTICE BOOK 6B PAGE 18

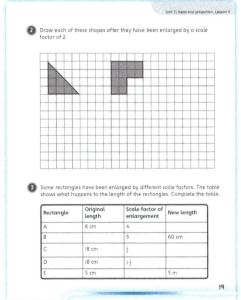

PUPIL PRACTICE BOOK 6B PAGE 19

Reflect

WAYS OF WORKING Pair work

IN FOCUS This question enables children to demonstrate their understanding of the term 'scale factor' and their knowledge of how to enlarge a shape (for example, that all sides need to be enlarged).

ASSESSMENT CHECKPOINT Can children explain that they need to multiply each side of the original shape by the scale factor to get the enlarged shape?

ANSWERS Answers for the **Reflect** part of the lesson can be found in the *Power Maths* online subscription.

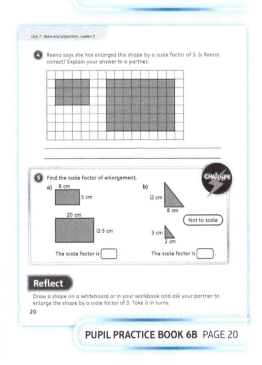

PUPIL PRACTICE BOOK 6B PAGE 20

After the lesson ⏸

- Can children describe the bar models in depth and explain how they relate to the calculations needed?
- Can children explain how to enlarge a shape by a scale factor?

Similar shapes

Learning focus

In this lesson, children will learn that for two shapes to be similar they must have the same proportions. They will identify if shapes are similar, deduce scale factors and draw similar shapes.

Before you teach

- Are children confident when enlarging shapes and calculating scale factors?
- Are children familiar with the term 'scale factor'?

NATIONAL CURRICULUM LINKS

Year 6 Ratio and proportion

Solve problems involving similar shapes where the scale factor is known or can be found.

ASSESSING MASTERY

Children can explain that similar shapes have the same proportions. They can compare two shapes, identify whether they are similar and use visual representations, models and calculations to deduce the scale factor. Children can draw similar shapes.

COMMON MISCONCEPTIONS

Children may think two shapes are similar because they are the same type of shape (both rectangles, for example) or have the same number of sides. Ensure children understand that for two shapes to be similar, the side lengths in both shapes must have the same proportions. Ask:

- *How can you tell if two shapes are similar? Will two rectangles always be similar? Why can an equilateral triangle not be similar to an isosceles triangle?*

STRENGTHENING UNDERSTANDING

Provide children with geoboards and elastic bands to make and compare shapes. Suggest they start with simple shapes but encourage them to make some more complex shapes. Challenge them to work with a partner to work out which of their shapes are similar and which are not.

GOING DEEPER

Provide children with more complex polygons drawn on squared paper, some of which are similar. Challenge them to compare the shapes and work out which ones are similar. Can they make changes to the other shapes to make them similar?

KEY LANGUAGE

In lesson: similar, corresponding, scale factor, enlargement, ratio

Other language to be used by the teacher: proportion, measure, increase, decrease, multiplication, division

STRUCTURES AND REPRESENTATIONS

2D shapes

RESOURCES

Mandatory: geoboards and bands

Optional: squared paper

 In the eTextbook of this lesson, you will find interactive links to a selection of teaching tools.

Quick recap

Ask children to draw three different examples of isosceles triangles, three different examples of scalene triangles and three different examples of equilateral triangles.

Discover

WAYS OF WORKING Pair work

ASK

- Question **1** a): *What is the same for each pair of shapes? What is different?*
- Question **1** a): *What do you think the term 'similar' means?*
- Question **1** a): *Is one shape an enlargement of the other? What is the scale factor? Are the shapes in proportion to each other?*

IN FOCUS Encourage children to discuss the pairs of shapes in the **Discover** picture. Ensure they can see that the large rectangle is an enlargement of the smaller rectangle, but the large triangle is not an enlargement of the smaller triangle. Although each of the sides in the big triangle is 3 squares longer than each of the sides in the small triangle, for the triangles to be similar each of the sides must be a multiple of the side length in the small triangle. Use this to lead into a discussion of what makes two shapes similar. In question **1** b), suggest children use their geoboards to try to make the triangles similar.

PRACTICAL TIPS Provide children with squared paper, geoboards and elastic bands to enable them to create the shapes themselves.

ANSWERS

Question **1** a): If two shapes are similar, then matching sides are all in the same ratio. Each side of Zac's larger rectangle is double the size of his smaller rectangle (the ratio is 1 : 2), so the rectangles are similar. One side of Lexi's larger triangle is double the size of the smaller one, but the other (vertical) side is not doubled (2 × 4 = 8 not 7), so her triangles are not in the same ratio and are not similar.

Question **1** b): Making the vertical side of the larger triangle 8 units would make the triangles similar.

Share

WAYS OF WORKING Whole class teacher led

ASK

- Question **1** a): *Why do you think the triangles are not similar, even though they both have a right angle?*

IN FOCUS In question **1** a), Dexter highlights a common misconception that two shapes are similar if they both have right angles, or have the same number of sides or the same number of angles. Encourage children to recognise that shapes must have the same proportions to be similar; that one shape is an enlargement of the other.
In question **1** b), suggest children use geoboards or squared paper to work this out practically. Encourage them to see that they could also change the height of the smaller triangle (to 3·5 units high).

Similar shapes

Discover

I want you to draw or make two shapes that are similar.

Zac

Lexi

Mr Jones

1 a) The two rectangles are similar, but the triangles are not.
What do you think it means for two shapes to be similar?

b) How can you make the two triangles similar?

28

PUPIL TEXTBOOK 6B PAGE 28

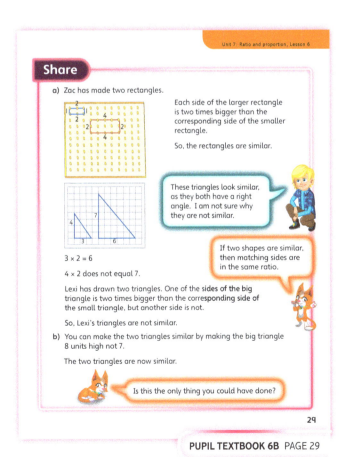

Share

a) Zac has made two rectangles.

Each side of the larger rectangle is two times bigger than the corresponding side of the smaller rectangle.

So, the rectangles are similar.

These triangles look similar, as they both have a right angle. I am not sure why they are not similar.

If two shapes are similar, then matching sides are in the same ratio.

3 × 2 = 6

4 × 2 does not equal 7.

Lexi has drawn two triangles. One of the **sides of the big** triangle is two times bigger than the **corresponding side of** the small triangle, but another side is not.

So, Lexi's triangles are not similar.

b) You can make the two triangles similar by making the big triangle 8 units high not 7.

The two triangles are now similar.

Is this the only thing you could have done?

29

PUPIL TEXTBOOK 6B PAGE 29

Think together

WAYS OF WORKING Whole class teacher led (I do, We do, You do)

ASK

- Question **1** a): *How can you find the scale factor of an enlargement?*
- Question **3**: *How is ratio linked to scale factor? How can you find the ratio of two side lengths?*
- Question **3**: *What does it mean for a shape to be similar to another shape?*

IN FOCUS Questions **1** and **2** give children an opportunity to practise calculating the scale factors of similar shapes. Remind children that the shapes are in proportion and all sides must be enlarged by the same scale factor. Question **3** requires children to link their previous knowledge of calculating ratio to scale factors and similar shapes.

STRENGTHEN Provide children with pairs of shapes drawn on squared paper to enable them to practise identifying which shapes are similar. Ask children to work in pairs to practise enlarging shapes by a given ratio or scale factor on geoboards.

DEEPEN Ask children to enlarge the first triangle in question **3** by different scale factors (for example 3, 5 or 10) and draw their answers on large sheets of squared paper.

ASSESSMENT CHECKPOINT Do children understand the term 'similar'? Can they find the scale factor of an enlargement? Can children find the ratio of similar shapes? Check that children can accurately draw similar shapes from a given ratio. Do they understand that the ratio 2 : 1 will produce a shape smaller than the original?

ANSWERS

Question **1** a): The scale factor is 2.

Question **1** b): The length is 20.

Question **1** c): The dimensions increase 3 times (× 3). The length will be 30 and the width 24.

Question **2**: The scale factor is 10. 1·5 × 10 = 15 or 15 ÷ 1·5 = 10.

Question **3** a): a : b = 1 : 2

Question **3** b): b : c = 1 : 1·5 = 2 : 3

Question **3** c): Children should draw two shapes where the dimensions of the second shape are 5 times the dimensions of the first shape. Children should draw two shapes where the dimensions of the second shape are half the dimensions of the first shape.

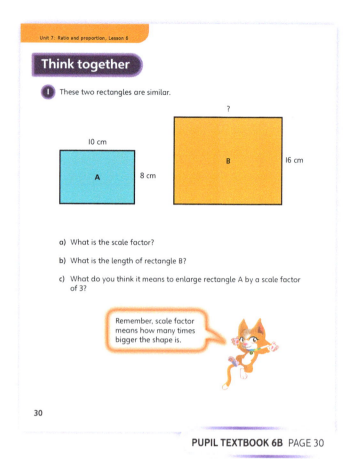

PUPIL TEXTBOOK 6B PAGE 30

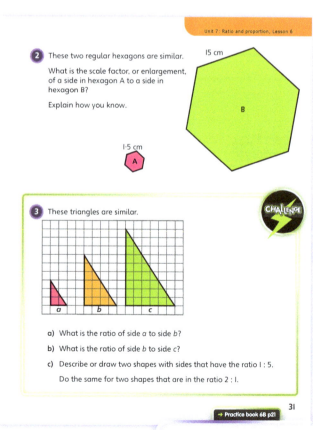

PUPIL TEXTBOOK 6B PAGE 31

Practice

WAYS OF WORKING Independent thinking

IN FOCUS Question ❶ b) highlights a common misconception. The two shapes are not similar as the vertical sides have not been enlarged by the same scale factor (they are not in proportion). Question ❷ provides an opportunity for children to practise drawing similar shapes. Question ❺ requires children to combine their understanding of scale factors, ratio and drawing similar (enlarged) shapes.

STRENGTHEN Provide children with squared paper and ask them to draw some simple shapes (a square, rectangle, triangle or parallelogram) to enlarge by different scale factors (2, 3, 5 or 10, for example). Help them to calculate the measurements (in squares) and use appropriate vocabulary (similar, ratio, scale factor) to discuss the shapes and enlargements.

DEEPEN Provide children with squared paper and challenge them to draw problems involving similar shapes with missing measurements, for a partner to solve.

ASSESSMENT CHECKPOINT Are children able to work out scale factors of enlargement with confidence? Check that when children draw similar shapes they enlarge all the sides in proportion. Can children use the key vocabulary correctly?

ANSWERS Answers for the **Practice** part of the lesson can be found in the *Power Maths* online subscription.

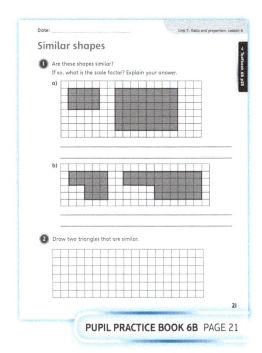

PUPIL PRACTICE BOOK 6B PAGE 21

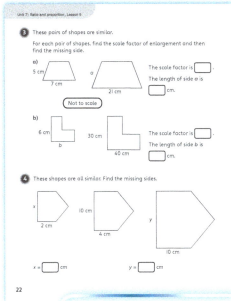

PUPIL PRACTICE BOOK 6B PAGE 22

Reflect

WAYS OF WORKING Pair work

IN FOCUS This section encourages children to consider what a ratio can tell them about two unknown, similar shapes. For example, it tells them that the shapes are in proportion as they are similar, that one shape is an enlargement of the other and that one shape is four times bigger than the other.

ASSESSMENT CHECKPOINT Can children use the mathematical terms similar, ratio, scale factor and enlargement? Do children understand that 1 : 4 means the enlargement is four times bigger than the original?

ANSWERS Answers for the **Reflect** part of the lesson can be found in the *Power Maths* online subscription.

After the lesson ❚❚

- Can children identify if shapes are similar?
- Can children use the key vocabulary confidently (similar, ratio, scale factor, enlargement)?
- Do children understand the connection between ratio and scale factor?

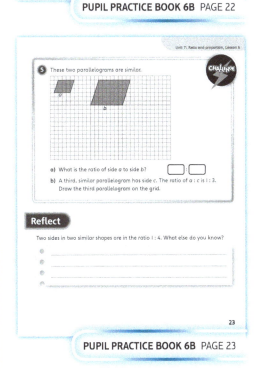

PUPIL PRACTICE BOOK 6B PAGE 23

Ratio problems

Learning focus

In this lesson, children will use ratios to deduce quantities.

Before you teach

- Based on previous lessons taught in this unit, are there any additional misconceptions you need to consider?
- Are children comfortable with bar models?

NATIONAL CURRICULUM LINKS

Year 6 Ratio and proportion

Solve problems involving unequal sharing and grouping using knowledge of fractions and multiples.

ASSESSING MASTERY

Children can interpret ratios recorded in different ways (1 : 2, 1 to 2, for every 1 x there are 2 y) and use this to deduce totals and parts of groups and to compare parts. They can use a variety of methods and visual representations, including counters, diagrams, tables and bar models, and can confidently explain what the representations mean. Children can use different contexts including money and measures.

COMMON MISCONCEPTIONS

Children may misuse addition in proportional problems. For example, if for every 1 white chocolate there are 2 milk chocolates, children may assume that for every 21 white chocolates there are 22 milk chocolates. Use visual representation to highlight this misconception. Ask:

- *For every 1 lemon sweet I have, I have 2 cola sweets. If I have 11 lemon sweets, how many cola sweets do I have? Why is the answer not 12?*
- Use different coloured counters or building blocks to represent the lemon and cola sweets.

STRENGTHENING UNDERSTANDING

Use a range of manipulatives, such as counters and cubes. Demonstrate different methods including tables, bar models and calculations.

GOING DEEPER

Extend to different contexts and introduce measures by asking questions such as: *Aki mixes 1·5 litres of orange squash. The ratio of orange squash to water is 1 : 5. How much water does he need?*

KEY LANGUAGE

In lesson: ratio, group, 'for every … there are …', parts, bar model, comparison, total

Other language to be used by the teacher: sets, unequal, diagram, ratio notation

STRUCTURES AND REPRESENTATIONS

Bar models

RESOURCES

Mandatory: counters

Optional: cubes

 In the eTextbook of this lesson, you will find interactive links to a selection of teaching tools.

Quick recap

Challenge the class to make or draw a representation to show the following ratios: 2 : 3, 1 : 3, 2 : 2, 4 : 2.

Discover

WAYS OF WORKING Pair work

ASK

- Question **1** a): *What information do you have? What do you need to find out?*
- Question **1** a): *Can you record the ratio in different ways?*
- Question **1** b): *What different methods could you use?*

IN FOCUS In question **1** a), children are asked to interpret the ratio statement and record the ratio. Can they record the ratio in different ways? (For example, 2 : 3, 2 to 3, for every 2 long balloons there are 3 round balloons, for every 3 round balloons there are 2 long balloons.) Question **1** b) gives children an opportunity to deduce the number of long and round balloons from the ratio. They could use a range of methods to find the answer, such as using counters, drawing a table or using multiplication calculations.

PRACTICAL TIPS Provide children with red and yellow counters to represent the balloons. Encourage them to sort the counters into groups of 2 yellow and 3 red. How many groups do they have? Help them to relate the groups of counters to each of the methods demonstrated in **Share**.

ANSWERS

Question **1** a): The ratio of long to round balloons is 2 : 3.

Question **1** b): There are 12 long and 18 round balloons.

Ratio problems

Discover

There are 30 balloons in the net.

For every 2 long balloons I inflated …

… I inflated 3 round ones.

Reena

Mr Jones   Ebo   Olivia

1 a) What is the ratio of round to long balloons in the net?

b) How many of the balloons are long?
   How many are round?

32

PUPIL TEXTBOOK 6B PAGE 32

Share

WAYS OF WORKING Whole class teacher led

ASK

- Question **1** a): *How is the ratio written? What symbol is used?*
- Question **1** b): *Is Dexter's method most like Method 1 or 2? Is Flo's method most like Method 1 or 2?*

IN FOCUS In question **1** b), Flo's method is most like Method 1. In calculating 30 ÷ 5 = 6, you work out that there are 6 groups of 5 balloons in 30. Help children understand that this is only the first step. To work out how many long balloons there are in total, you need to multiply the number of groups (6) by the number of long balloons in each group (2). Similarly for round balloons.

Dexter's method is most like Method 2. The table is an efficient way of counting balloons in the correct ratio of 2 : 3 until you reach 30 balloons in total. Since each column shows the running total of that type of balloon, the last row will tell you the total number of long balloons and the total number of round balloons.

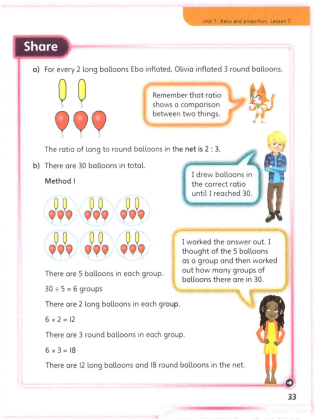

Share

a) For every 2 long balloons Ebo inflated, Olivia inflated 3 round balloons.

Remember that ratio shows a comparison between two things.

The ratio of long to round balloons in the net is 2 : 3.

b) There are 30 balloons in total.

Method 1

I drew balloons in the correct ratio until I reached 30.

I worked the answer out. I thought of the 5 balloons as a group and then worked out how many groups of balloons there are in 30.

There are 5 balloons in each group.

30 ÷ 5 = 6 groups

There are 2 long balloons in each group.

6 × 2 = 12

There are 3 round balloons in each group.

6 × 3 = 18

There are 12 long balloons and 18 round balloons in the net.

33

PUPIL TEXTBOOK 6B PAGE 33

Think together

WAYS OF WORKING   Whole class teacher led (I do, We do, You do)

ASK

• Question **2**: *Which method will you use and why?*
• Question **2**: *What information do you have? What do you need to find out?*

IN FOCUS   In question **1**, children can choose a method or experiment with different methods (counters, grouping or a table). Question **2** encourages children to choose the most efficient method of solving the problem. The scaffolding should lead them to recognise that drawing 154 coins, counting out 154 counters or drawing a table will take a long time and therefore be inefficient. Can children apply the grouping method instead?

£2 + £5 = £7 in each group
154 ÷ 7 = 22 groups of £7
6A raises £2 in each group: £2 × 22 = £44
6B raises £5 in each group: £5 × 22 = £110

Question **3** introduces children to the concept of using a bar model to find totals and amounts from a ratio. Ask children what each bar might represent. What information does this show us?

STRENGTHEN   Ask children to use all the methods (shown in **Share**) to answer the questions. This will allow them to practise and deepen their understanding of ratio, as well as how the different methods work.

DEEPEN   Ask children to work in pairs and provide them with red and yellow counters. Ask one child from each pair to create sets of unequal groups using the counters and the other to create a bar model to represent the ratio. They can then swap over.

ASSESSMENT CHECKPOINT   Can children select an efficient method? Are children secure in using bar models?

ANSWERS

Question **1** a): 7 children do karate. 21 ÷ 3 = 7

Question **1** b): 14 children do tennis. 21 ÷ 3 = 7
    7 × 2 = 14

Question **2**: 154 ÷ (2 + 5) = 154 ÷ 7 = 22
    22 × 2 = 44, 6A raises £44.
    22 × 5 = 110, 6B raises £110.

Question **3** a): Explanations may vary but answers should focus on sharing balloons between parts.

Question **3** b): For **Think together** question **1**: Children need to show the ratio karate : tennis is 1 : 2. The bar model needs to show a total of 21 with parts of 7 for karate and 14 for tennis. They should be able to show how they reach the correct answers for this question.

For **Think together** question **2**: Children need to show the ratio 6A : 6B is 2 : 5. The bar models need to show parts to make £44 for 6A and parts to show £110 for 6B. They should be able to show how they reach the correct answers for this question.

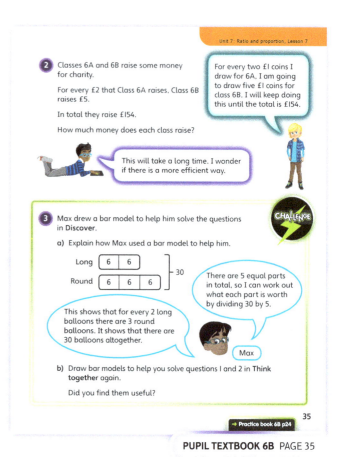

PUPIL TEXTBOOK 6B PAGE 34

PUPIL TEXTBOOK 6B PAGE 35

Practice

WAYS OF WORKING Independent thinking

IN FOCUS Question ❶ provides an opportunity for children to solve a ratio problem using a bar model. The bar model is partially drawn to provide scaffolding. Question ❷ requires children to draw their own bar model to answer the question. Question ❻ will require children to assess the information they have been given and identify what it means and what they need to work out. Children may find it helpful to draw a bar model to help them visualise the problem. Alternatively, they may feel confident enough to use multiplication calculations:

3 + 7 = 10 parts
7 − 3 = 4, so 4 parts = 560
1 part = 560 ÷ 4 = 140
140 × 3 = 420, 140 × 7 = 980, 420 + 980 = 1,400

STRENGTHEN If children need support drawing their own bar model in question ❷, discuss how to construct one using a simple ratio. For example, for 15 cars in the ratio of 1 red car for every 2 blue cars, demonstrate that the three parts of the ratio are represented by the three 'parts' of the bar model. Explain that the value of each 'part' is the same and can be found by dividing the total number of cars by the number of parts – in this example, 15 ÷ 3 = 5. Discuss how this value is recorded on the bar model and used to work out the number of cars of each colour.

DEEPEN Challenge children to work in pairs to draw and interpret their own bar models.

THINK DIFFERENTLY In question ❺, ensure children understand that they are looking for how much *more* money Zac receives. Encourage children to draw a bar model to represent the problem. This should help them see that they do not need to calculate how much Zac and Jamie receive, they can simply multiply 2 × £6 = £12.

ASSESSMENT CHECKPOINT Can children interpret bar models? Are they able to draw bar models to help them visualise ratio problems?

ANSWERS Answers for the **Practice** part of the lesson can be found in the *Power Maths* online subscription.

Reflect

WAYS OF WORKING Pair work

IN FOCUS This question gives children the total and the ratio and requires them to calculate the parts, explaining their method. They will need to interpret the ratio notation and choose an effective method for working out the answer.

ASSESSMENT CHECKPOINT Can children interpret the ratio notation 2 : 3? Look for depth of understanding of the method children use to work out their answer. Does their explanation demonstrate an understanding that they must first work out what each part of the ratio is worth, before multiplying the value of each part by the number of parts to find the correct answer?

ANSWERS Answers for the **Reflect** part of the lesson can be found in the *Power Maths* online subscription.

After the lesson ⏸

- Do children effectively apply their prior knowledge of ratio?
- Do children find the bar model useful?
- Are children confident using ratio notation?

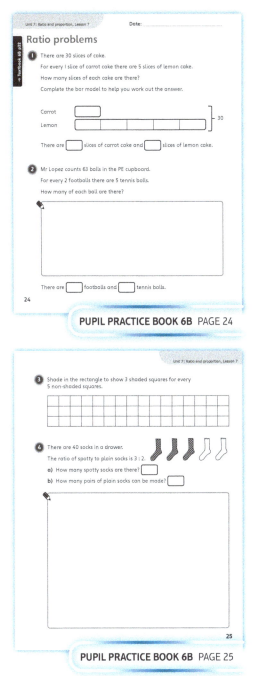

PUPIL PRACTICE BOOK 6B PAGE 24

PUPIL PRACTICE BOOK 6B PAGE 25

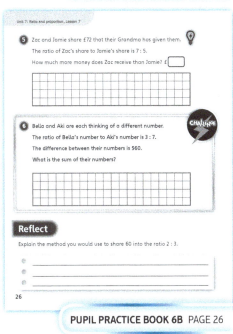

PUPIL PRACTICE BOOK 6B PAGE 26

Problem solving – ratio and proportion

Learning focus

In this lesson, children will solve problems involving proportion where the scale is not a whole number. They will use their knowledge of fractions and multiples and will compare and discuss different methods to solve the same question.

Before you teach ⏸

- Are children secure when using measurements such as grams and kilograms within word problems?

NATIONAL CURRICULUM LINKS

Year 6 Ratio and proportion

Solve problems involving unequal sharing and grouping using knowledge of fractions and multiples.

Solve problems involving the relative sizes of two quantities where missing values can be found by using integer multiplication and division facts.

ASSESSING MASTERY

Children can compare different proportions where the scale is not a whole number. They can choose an effective method to solve a problem and can work through the steps systematically. Children can use their knowledge of multiples and number facts to work out the answer.

COMMON MISCONCEPTIONS

Children may only complete one step of a 2-step problem, ending up with the wrong answer. They may also use the wrong calculations, for example adding rather than multiplying, when working through a problem. Ask:

- *Amelia has a recipe for ice cream sundaes. It makes 5 sundaes. The recipe asks for 30 g of chocolate sauce. Amelia decides to make 3 sundaes instead. How much chocolate sauce does she need? What calculations do you need to use? Why is the answer not 6 g?*

STRENGTHENING UNDERSTANDING

Encourage children to represent each problem using a variety of images and models, for example bar models, number lines, counters and diagrams. Discuss how each method is helpful and which one works best for them, and for each individual problem.

GOING DEEPER

Challenge children to write 2-step ratio problems for their partner and to use the different methods to solve them. Encourage them to discuss which method is most effective for each problem and why.

KEY LANGUAGE

In lesson: multiply

Other language to be used by the teacher: ratio, proportion, scale, amount, divide, fractions

STRUCTURES AND REPRESENTATIONS

Bar models, number lines

RESOURCES

Optional: counters, individual whiteboards

 In the eTextbook of this lesson, you will find interactive links to a selection of teaching tools.

Quick recap ↻

Revise measure scales by drawing a number line as a scale from 0 to 1 kg. Ask children to point to 100 g, 500 g, 250 g, 750 g, 200 g and 800 g on the number line.

Discover

WAYS OF WORKING Pair work

ASK

- Question ❶ a): *How many people is the recipe for? How much curry paste is used for each person?*
- Question ❶ a): *What models can you use to represent the problem? Is there more than one way to solve the problem?*
- Question ❶ b): *What steps could you take to work out how many peppers Toshi needs?*

IN FOCUS Questions ❶ a) and ❶ b) require children to recognise that more than one step is needed to work out the answer. Encourage children to discuss the method they used, drawing diagrams if this is helpful. There is more than one possible method (for example, adding half of the quantity again, or working out the quantity needed for 1 person and multiplying it by 6).

PRACTICAL TIPS Provide children with individual whiteboards so they can sketch models and ideas, helping them to visualise the problem.

ANSWERS

Question ❶ a): $48 \div 4 \times 6 = 72$. Toshi needs 72 g of curry paste for 6 people.

Question ❶ b): $3 \div 4 \times 6 = 4\frac{1}{2}$. Toshi needs $4\frac{1}{2}$ peppers for 6 people, so he does not have enough.

PUPIL TEXTBOOK 6B PAGE 36

Share

WAYS OF WORKING Whole class teacher led

ASK

- Question ❶ a): *Whose method is more effective, Flo's or Dexter's?*
- Question ❶ a): *What method did you use? How does your method compare to Dexter's and Flo's?*
- Question ❶ b): *How many peppers would be needed for 10 people?*

IN FOCUS Two possible methods are suggested for question ❶ a). Encourage children to discuss which method is more effective and why. Lead children to realise that Flo's method will work for any number of people. For example, Flo could use her method to calculate how many peppers would be needed to serve 10 people. Discuss the models demonstrated in this section and what they show. Challenge children to draw their own bar model to find out how much coconut milk is needed for 6 people.

DEEPEN Ask children to rewrite the recipe to serve 10 people.

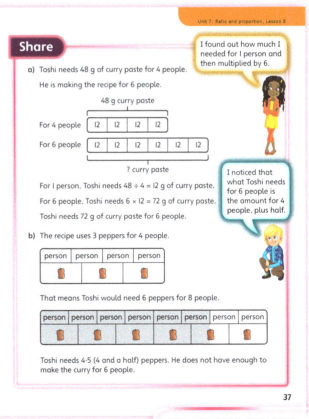

PUPIL TEXTBOOK 6B PAGE 37

Think together

Whole class teacher led (I do, We do, You do)

ASK

- Question **1**: *Can you draw a diagram to represent the problem? Which method will you use?*
- Question **2**: *Which method, or methods, would work best to complete the table?*

IN FOCUS Encourage children to consider different methods to solve the problems. In question **2**, lead children to recognise that they can complete the table both by calculating the cost for 1 person and multiplying, and by doubling the costs they already have (if 3 people cost £7·50, 6 people will cost £7·50 × 2 = £15). Question **3** highlights a misconception. Astrid halves the time each pair gets on the tennis court because the number of pairs is halved, when she should instead double the time each pair gets. Use a diagram to demonstrate this to children and explain that if there are fewer players, they each get more time (120 ÷ 3 = 40 mins).

1 pair	1 pair	1 pair	1 pair	1 pair	1 pair	6 pairs
20 minutes	20 minutes	20 minutes	20 minutes	20 minutes	20 minutes	120 minutes

1 pair	1 pair	1 pair	3 pairs
120 minutes			

STRENGTHEN Encourage children to draw diagrams or bar models to help them understand the questions. Provide children with some simple recipes and ask them to work in pairs to calculate how much of each ingredient they would need to serve different numbers of people.

DEEPEN Challenge children to use the recipe in question **1** to create a table showing how much flour is needed for different numbers of cupcakes. Encourage them to discuss the method they used with a partner.

ASSESSMENT CHECKPOINT Check children can explain their calculations in question **1** using the bar models. Look for understanding in question **3** that, although the number of pairs of tennis players has halved, the time they get on the court has doubled.

ANSWERS

Question **1** a): 240 ÷ 12 × 15 = 300. Andy needs 300 g of flour.

Question **1** b): 300 ÷ 12 × 10 = 250. Andy needs 250 g of butter.

Question **1** c): 120 ÷ 12 = 10. 200 ÷ 10 = 20. Andy could make 20 cupcakes.

Question **2**:

Number of people	3	6	15	30	40
Total cost	£7·50	£15	£37·50	£75	£100

Question **3** a): 6 × 20 minutes = 120 minutes.
120 minutes ÷ 3 pairs = 40 minutes.
Each pair would get 40 minutes.

Question **3** b): 120 minutes ÷ 8 pairs = 15.
Each pair would get 15 minutes.

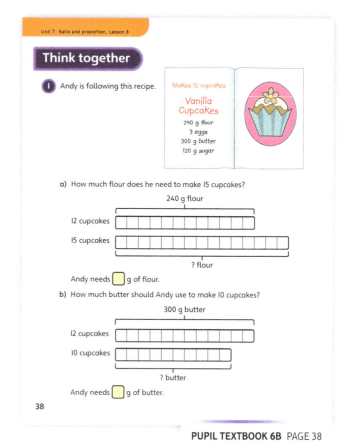

PUPIL TEXTBOOK 6B PAGE 38

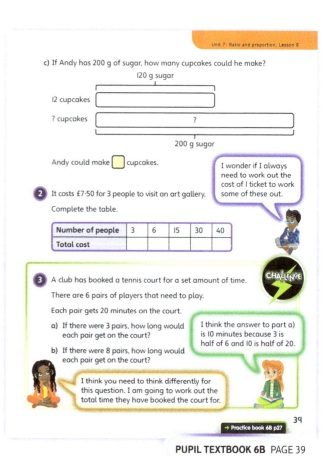

PUPIL TEXTBOOK 6B PAGE 39

74

Practice

WAYS OF WORKING Independent thinking

IN FOCUS Question ① provides an opportunity for children to practise a 2-step problem with the scaffolding of a partially drawn bar model. Encourage children to draw their own models and diagrams to represent the remaining problems. Ensure children complete all the steps of each problem. In question ⑤, children will have to take several steps to work out the answer. They should notice that both sets of scales have the same number of cubes. Lead them to recognise that subtracting the left scales from the right scales will give them the weight of 4 spheres (360 g). They can then use this to work out the weight of 1 sphere (90 g). The next step is to work out the weight of 2 cubes (220 g), then 1 cube (110 g) and use this to work out the weight of 5 cubes (550 g).

STRENGTHEN Encourage children to use different models and visual representations to represent the problems, for example bar models, number lines or their own diagrams/sketches. Challenge children to adapt a recipe they are making in another area of the curriculum, or one they like to make at home. Encourage them to weigh out and select ingredients in the correct quantities.

DEEPEN Provide children with a basic menu with some prices missing. Ask them to work in pairs to write and solve questions based on the menu. For example, *Lexi bought 3 coffees and 2 pieces of cake. It cost £13·60 in total. How much did each piece of cake cost if 1 coffee costs £2·20?*

THINK DIFFERENTLY Ensure children read question ④ carefully. The price of the chips is given first, followed by the price of the fish. However, the question asks children to find the cost of the fish, then the chips. Do children realise that to find the cost of 6 bags of chips, they can simply double the cost of 3 bags of chips?

ASSESSMENT CHECKPOINT Can children explain how the models and diagrams represent the problems? Can they apply knowledge of multiples and number facts? Check that children are able to work through the steps of question ⑤ systematically and accurately to get the correct answer.

ANSWERS Answers for the **Practice** part of the lesson can be found in the *Power Maths* online subscription.

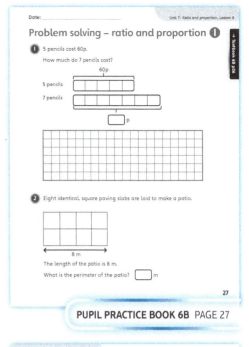

PUPIL PRACTICE BOOK 6B PAGE 27

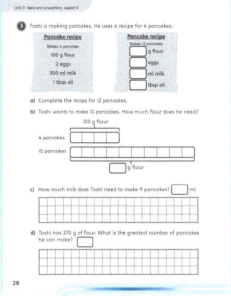

PUPIL PRACTICE BOOK 6B PAGE 28

Reflect

WAYS OF WORKING Independent thinking

IN FOCUS This section invites children to explain two different methods of solving the same problem. (Add half again; or divide by 6 to find the weight of 1 chocolate, then multiply by 9 to get the answer.)

ASSESSMENT CHECKPOINT Have children shown their workings clearly? Can they explain the two different methods clearly?

ANSWERS Answers for the **Reflect** part of the lesson can be found in the *Power Maths* online subscription.

After the lesson ⏸

- How confident are children when interpreting word problems involving more than one step?

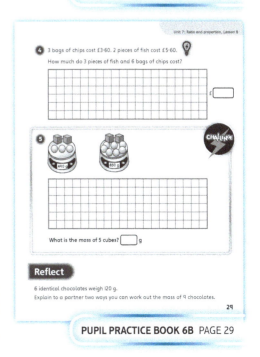

PUPIL PRACTICE BOOK 6B PAGE 29

Problem solving – ratio and proportion ②

Learning focus

In this lesson, children will solve a range of problems involving ratio, including 2-step problems.

Before you teach

- Are children confident calculating ratios?
- Are children confident solving 2-step problems?

NATIONAL CURRICULUM LINKS

Year 6 Ratio and proportion

Solve problems involving unequal sharing and grouping using knowledge of fractions and multiples.

Solve problems involving the relative sizes of two quantities where missing values can be found by using integer multiplication and division facts.

ASSESSING MASTERY

Children can demonstrate their understanding of ratio using the correct vocabulary and ratio notation (1 : 2) and can draw diagrams and models to represent problems involving ratio. They can calculate ratios and can use ratio to find totals of groups, parts of groups and the difference between unequal parts.

COMMON MISCONCEPTIONS

Children may misuse addition in proportional problems. For example, they may assume that if for every 1 red marble there are 2 blue marbles, then for every 21 red marbles there are 22 blue marbles. Use visual representations to highlight this misconception. Ask:

- *For every 3 red marbles Mo has, he has 4 blue ones. Mo has 12 red marbles. Zac thinks he must have 13 blue ones. Is he correct? Why not? How many blue marbles does Mo have?*

STRENGTHENING UNDERSTANDING

Encourage children to use manipulatives, such as counters, or diagrams to represent problems visually. Discuss in detail how to use a bar model to solve each problem. If children find it difficult to draw their own, provide a partially completed bar model.

GOING DEEPER

Challenge children who can confidently solve 2-step problems to solve problems where the ratio has three parts, for example 2 : 3 : 1. Ask: *In a bag of marbles, for every 2 red marbles there are 3 green marbles and 1 purple marble. There are 9 green marbles. How many marbles are in the bag in total?*

KEY LANGUAGE

In lesson: ratio, simplified, equal, part, whole, total

Other language to be used by the teacher: proportion, difference between, unequal

STRUCTURES AND REPRESENTATIONS

Bar models

RESOURCES

Mandatory: counters, individual whiteboards

Optional: measuring cylinders or jugs, coloured water, bricks, marbles

 In the eTextbook of this lesson, you will find interactive links to a selection of teaching tools.

Quick recap ↻

Revise measure scales by drawing a vertical number line as a scale from 0 to 1 l. Ask children to point to 100 ml, 500 ml, 250 ml, 750 ml, 200 ml and 800 ml on the number line.

Discover

Problem solving – ratio and proportion ②

Discover

① a) How much water does Sofia need to add to 350 ml of tomato feed?

b) Sofia gives the large tomato plant twice as much feed as the small plant.

If she gives the two plants 1,200 ml of feed in total, how much feed does each plant get?

40

PUPIL TEXTBOOK 6B PAGE 40

WAYS OF WORKING Pair work

ASK

- Question ① a): *What is the ratio of water to tomato feed?*
- Question ① a): *What models or diagrams could you use to represent the problem?*
- Question ① b): *How much more feed does the larger plant get compared with the smaller plant? Is there more than one way to solve the problem?*

IN FOCUS Question ① a) provides an opportunity for children to practise a 2-step problem. They will need to work out the ratio before using it to calculate the amount of water needed. Encourage children to explore different methods using models or diagrams.

PRACTICAL TIPS Provide children with measuring cylinders or jugs, water and coloured water to explore the problem practically.

ANSWERS

Question ① a): 200 ml feed = 800 ml water.
50 ml feed = 800 ÷ 4 = 200 ml of water.
350 ml feed = 7 × 200 = 1,400 ml of water.
Sofia needs to add 1,400 ml of water to 350 ml of tomato feed.

Question ① b): 1,200 ÷ 3 = 400 ml. The small plant gets 400 ml of feed.
400 × 2 = 800 ml. The big plant gets 800 ml of feed.

Share

Share

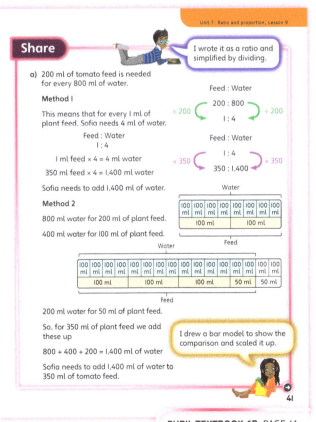

a) 200 ml of tomato feed is needed for every 800 ml of water.

Method 1

This means that for every 1 ml of plant feed, Sofia needs 4 ml of water.

Feed : Water
1 : 4

1 ml feed × 4 = 4 ml water

350 ml feed × 4 = 1,400 ml water

Sofia needs to add 1,400 ml of water.

Feed : Water
200 : 800
÷ 200   ÷ 200
1 : 4

Feed : Water
1 : 4
× 350   × 350
350 : 1,400

I wrote it as a ratio and simplified by dividing.

Method 2

800 ml water for 200 ml of plant feed.

400 ml water for 100 ml of plant feed.

Water							
100 ml	100 ml	100 ml	100 ml	100 ml	100 ml	100 ml	100 ml
100 ml				100 ml			

Feed

Water															
100 ml	100 ml	100 ml	100 ml	100 ml	100 ml	100 ml	100 ml	100 ml	100 ml	100 ml	100 ml	100 ml	100 ml	100 ml	100 ml
100 ml				100 ml				100 ml				50 ml		50 ml	

Feed

200 ml water for 50 ml of plant feed.

So, for 350 ml of plant feed we add these up

800 + 400 + 200 = 1,400 ml of water

Sofia needs to add 1,400 ml of water to 350 ml of tomato feed.

I drew a bar model to show the comparison and scaled it up.

41

PUPIL TEXTBOOK 6B PAGE 41

WAYS OF WORKING Whole class teacher led

ASK

- Question ① a): *Can you explain the bar models used in Method 2?*
- Question ① a): *There are two methods demonstrated for part a). Which method did you use?*
- Question ① b): *How many equal parts do you need to divide 1,200 into? Can you divide 12 into these equal parts and use your knowledge of multiplying by 100?*

IN FOCUS Question ① a) demonstrates two different methods. Discuss both methods and ask children which they prefer and why. Which method do they think is quickest and more efficient? Will both methods work in different situations?

In question ① b), the key thing children must realise is that they need to divide 1,200 by 3. Because the big plant requires twice as much as the little plant, 1,200 needs to be divided into 3 equal parts.

Think together

WAYS OF WORKING Whole class teacher led (I do, We do, You do)

ASK

- Question **1**: *Can you explain your chosen method?*
- Question **3**: *What is different about the ratio in this problem? Can you draw a bar model to help you solve the problem?*

IN FOCUS Question **1** provides scaffolding for both methods demonstrated in the **Share** section. Children are encouraged to consider the different methods and choose their favourite, or try both. Can they explain why they prefer their chosen method? Question **3** challenges children to solve a problem involving a ratio with three parts. They are encouraged to draw a bar model to help them solve the problem.

STRENGTHEN Encourage children to use counters to represent each problem. If children need support drawing their own bar model for question **3**, provide a partially completed bar model. Discuss how to work out how many parts the bar model should have and demonstrate how it can be used to solve the problem.

DEEPEN Create some thee-part ratio problems for children to solve. Ask them to explain to a partner how they worked them out. Challenge children to create their own three-part ratio problems and swap with a partner.

ASSESSMENT CHECKPOINT Assess whether children can use a given ratio to find an unequal part, the difference between parts and the total. Look for understanding of how a bar model can be used to solve a ratio problem. Check whether children can solve 2-step problems involving ratio.

ANSWERS

Question **1**: 27 ÷ 3 = 9
9 × 2 = 18
There are 18 children with winter birthdays at the club.

Question **2**: 3 × 110 = 330 g
110 + 330 = 440 g
The total mass of the parcels is 440 g.

Question **3**: 1 + 2 + 4 = 7
784 ÷ 7 = 112 km
First day = 1 × 112 = 112 km
Second day = 2 × 112 = 224 km
Third day = 4 × 112 = 448 km
She travels 224 km on the second day.

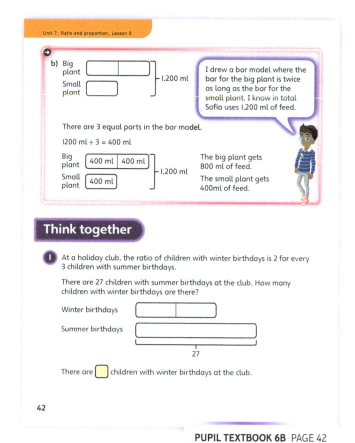

PUPIL TEXTBOOK 6B PAGE 42

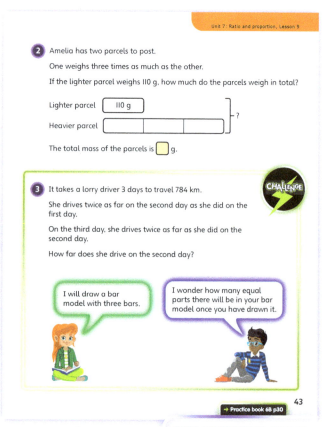

PUPIL TEXTBOOK 6B PAGE 43

Practice

WAYS OF WORKING Independent thinking

IN FOCUS In question **1**, children are encouraged to choose the method they prefer. To solve questions **3** and **4**, children will need to identify what information they have and what they need to work out. The questions provide scaffolding, encouraging children to use a bar model to solve the problems. In question **7**, encourage children to draw a bar model to represent the initial statement, that Lexi catches three times as many fish as Luis. Demonstrate how they can add to their bar model to represent the additional information and solve the problem.

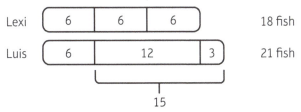

STRENGTHEN Encourage children to use a range of manipulatives to solve the problems practically, for example counters, bricks, marbles or natural objects.

DEEPEN Challenge children to solve three-part ratio problems. For example: *A florist is making a large bouquet of flowers. For every 4 roses in the bouquet, there are 3 lilies and 2 daffodils. There are 16 roses in the bouquet. How many flowers are there altogether?*

ASSESSMENT CHECKPOINT Assess whether children are answering the questions correctly and using an efficient method. Can children explain how to use a bar model to solve a ratio problem? Can they draw their own bar model to solve a problem? Check that children are using key vocabulary and ratio notation correctly.

ANSWERS Answers for the **Practice** part of the lesson can be found in the *Power Maths* online subscription.

Reflect

WAYS OF WORKING Independent thinking

IN FOCUS This section gives children an opportunity to consider whether they found a bar model helpful when solving the ratio problems. Encourage children to explain why a bar model is helpful. For example, it represents the problem visually.

ASSESSMENT CHECKPOINT Do children understand how a bar model works? Are they using the key vocabulary correctly?

ANSWERS Answers for the **Reflect** part of the lesson can be found in the *Power Maths* online subscription.

After the lesson ⏸

- How well do the prompts and questions from the characters promote learning of ratio?
- How carefully do children read the questions? Are they able to elicit the correct information?
- How confident are children in tackling problem solving?

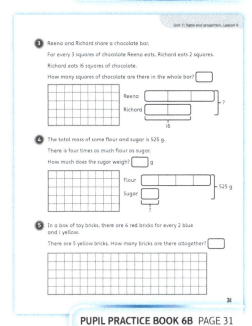

PUPIL PRACTICE BOOK 6B PAGE 30

PUPIL PRACTICE BOOK 6B PAGE 31

PUPIL PRACTICE BOOK 6B PAGE 32

End of unit check

Don't forget the unit assessment grid in your *Power Maths* online subscription.

WAYS OF WORKING Group work adult led

IN FOCUS These questions are designed to draw out misconceptions. Question **1** assesses children's ability to use a ratio to answer 'How many more?' questions. Question **4** assesses children's understanding of map scales. Question **5** requires children to work out a scale factor from a diagram and use it to calculate a missing measurement. Question **7** assesses children's ability to use ratios with three parts to calculate totals.

ANSWERS AND COMMENTARY

Children who have mastered the concepts in this unit will be able to use the key language of ratio and ratio notation. They will be able to draw diagrams and models to solve ratio problems, including finding totals of groups, parts of groups and the difference between unequal parts. They will understand how to use scale factors and be able to compare two shapes or quantities of similar proportions.

PUPIL TEXTBOOK 6B PAGE 44

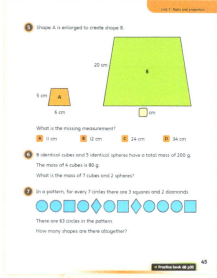

PUPIL TEXTBOOK 6B PAGE 45

Q	A	WRONG ANSWERS AND MISCONCEPTIONS	STRENGTHENING UNDERSTANDING
1	B	A suggests children have added 4 rather than multiplied by 4. D suggests children have not completed the second step of subtracting the number of cows from the number of sheep.	Give children an opportunity to use practical resources, such as counters, to represent the problems. Encourage them to draw bar models and diagrams to show what calculations are needed. Ensure children read and re-read the questions carefully. Ask: • *What is the key information you need to take from the question?* • *What do you need to work out?*
2	A	B, C and D indicate children have subtracted, added or multiplied by 5 instead of dividing by 5.	
3	C	A suggests children have calculated the value of 1 part. B suggests children have calculated the number of school dinners. D suggests children have confused ratio with fractions.	
4	D	100 cm on the map would be 200 m in real life.	
5	C	B suggests children have doubled the side of the shape. D suggests they have used the wrong ratio.	
6	156 g	An incorrect answer suggests children have not identified the key information or not completed all the steps required.	
7	108 shapes	An incorrect answer suggests children need help using ratios with 3 parts.	

My journal

WAYS OF WORKING Independent thinking

ANSWERS AND COMMENTARY

a) Andy is incorrect.
The length of rectangle B is 2 cm longer than rectangle A (6 + 2 = 8), but B has not been enlarged by a scale factor of 2.

b) The ratio of the sides is 1 : 2.
Ensure children give a general answer here (it does not need to be related to the rectangles in part a). Their answer should relate scale factor to ratio. The ratio is 1 : 2 because the enlarged shape is twice as big as the original shape.

If children need support explaining their answers, encourage them to draw a diagram to help. Ask:
• *What happens when you enlarge a shape by a scale factor?*
• *What does the 2 in the ratio tell us?*

Power check

WAYS OF WORKING Independent thinking

ASK

• *Do you think you could explain ratio to someone else?*
• *How confident are you at identifying similar shapes?*
• *Could you explain to someone how to enlarge a shape by a scale factor?*

Power play

WAYS OF WORKING Pair work

IN FOCUS Use this **Power play** as a fun way to check whether children can work in pairs to interpret and use scale factors on maps and plans. Challenge them to add other facilities to the plan, such as a hospital or restaurant, and to work out how far they are from Holly's house.

ANSWERS AND COMMENTARY

a) 1 cm represents 5,000 cm in real life. When no units are given on a scale, the units are the same.

b) The bus stop is 150 m from Holly's house.
On the plan, the bus stop is 3 cm from Holly's house. Each cm on the plan represents 5,000 cm in real life. This can be converted to metres by dividing by 100, so 1 cm on the plan represents 50 m in real life (1 cm : 50 m). This means 3 cm on the plan is 150 m in real life.

c) Check that children have marked two locations on the plan that are 7 cm from Holly's house. If they need help, ask:
• *How can you work out how many cm on the plan are equivalent to 350 m in real life?*
• *Can Holly walk in any direction or do you need to measure the distance along the grid lines?*

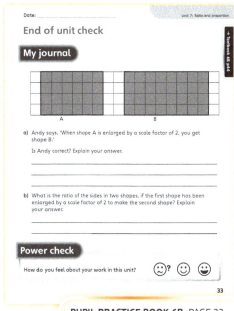

PUPIL PRACTICE BOOK 6B PAGE 33

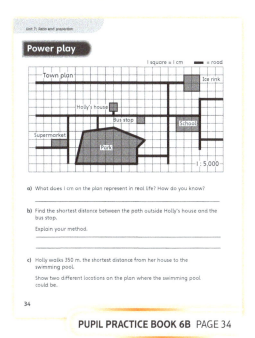

PUPIL PRACTICE BOOK 6B PAGE 34

After the unit ⏸

• What key indicators can you use to check that children are secure in their understanding of ratio and proportion?
• What strategies worked well to help children relate ratio and proportion to real-life situations?

Strengthen and **Deepen** activities for this unit can be found in the *Power Maths* online subscription.

Unit 8
Algebra

Don't forget to watch the Unit 8 video!

Mastery Expert tip! 'When teaching this unit, I enjoyed helping children view finding lots of answers for one equation as an exciting puzzle. It really helped those children who were worried about finding the 'right answer' to see that lots of answers could be fun and exciting!'

WHY THIS UNIT IS IMPORTANT

In this unit, children will generalise mathematical concepts and problems, representing them algebraically as expressions, formulae and equations. Children begin by finding rules that govern number patterns. They will represent the rules they find using pictures and abstract written recording, using letters to represent variables within a sequence. Once children are able to find a rule, they will follow a number pattern, find outputs from a given input number and use a rule to find a specific value and answer. Following this, children will investigate and record formulae for finding values linked to mathematical concepts such as the perimeter and area of 2D shapes. Finally, children will solve equations using algebraic notation. They will begin with 1-step equations, move on to 2-step equations where there is one solution, and then solve equations with multiple solutions.

WHERE THIS UNIT FITS

→ Unit 7: Ratio and proportion
→ **Unit 8: Algebra**
→ Unit 9: Decimals

This unit follows work on ratio, including scale factors and problem solving in the context of ratio and proportion. Here, children will solve real-life problems to find answers, use formulae and express missing numbers algebraically. Children will go on to use percentages, convert between fractions, decimals and percentages and find percentages of an amount.

Before they start this unit, it is expected that children:
- are confident in all four operations and can use them in the correct mathematical order
- can read and understand word problems
- have used bar models and are able to read and understand them.

ASSESSING MASTERY

Children will demonstrate mastery in this unit by fluently and reliably finding rules that govern number sequences, representing them pictorially and through algebraic notation. They will recognise the mathematical calculation needed to find values for a concept such as perimeter or area and will express these as algebraic formulae. Finally, children will be able to read, understand, write and solve 1- and 2-step algebraic equations, reliably finding an unknown number. They will recognise when an equation has more than one solution and will find multiple solutions to such an equation.

COMMON MISCONCEPTIONS	STRENGTHENING UNDERSTANDING	GOING DEEPER
Children may think an expression such as 2y means 2 + y.	Ask: *When you read it, does the expression 2y sound like '2 add y' or '2 ys'?* *Can you show 2y using a bar model? How does it differ to the bar model for 2 + y?*	Challenge children to write word problems that represent different types of equation such as: • those with only one solution • those with many solutions. Challenge children to share their word problems for a partner to solve.
When solving equations such as 36 − z = 23, children may solve the incorrect inverse calculation, calculating 23 + 36 instead of 36 − 23.	Ask: *Can you show the original equation as a bar model?* *Can you use the bar model to explain what calculation you could use to find the missing number more efficiently?*	

UNIT STARTER PAGES

Use these pages to introduce the focus to children. You can use the characters to explore different ways of working, too.

STRUCTURES AND REPRESENTATIONS

Bar model: The bar model is used in this unit to represent the different algebraic expressions, formulae and equations that children will meet and solve.

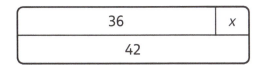

$$x + 36 = 42$$

Balance model: The balance model is used in this unit to help children visualise the concept of keeping an equation balanced, while trying to find an unknown number.

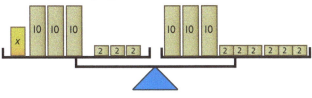

$$x + 36 = 42$$

2D shapes: 2D shapes are used in this unit to provide a context for the formulae children will create.

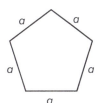 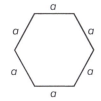

Tables: Tables are used in this unit to help children formulate and organise the different solutions to an equation they are working on.

KEY LANGUAGE

There is some key language that children will need to know as part of the learning in this unit.

→ pattern, growing pattern
→ sequence
→ rule
→ term
→ algebra, algebraic
→ expression
→ formula, formulae
→ substitute
→ generalise
→ operation
→ calculation, calculate
→ equation
→ inverse
→ solution
→ represent
→ value

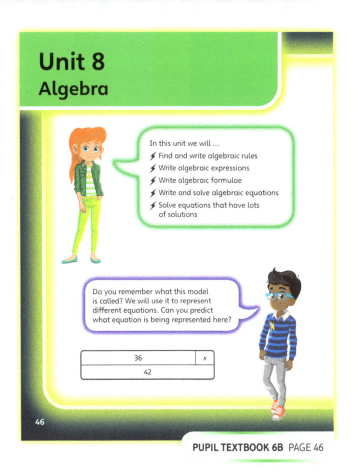

PUPIL TEXTBOOK 6B PAGE 46

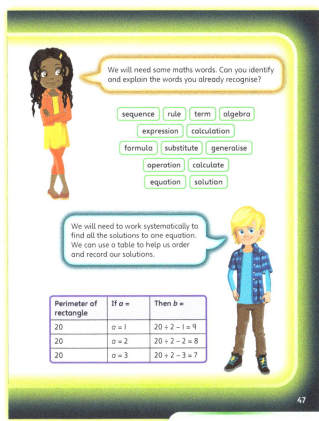

PUPIL TEXTBOOK 6B PAGE 47

Find a rule – one step

Learning focus

In this lesson, children will investigate number sequences and identify the algebraic rule that governs them. They will learn how to write these rules in a form that allows them to be applied generally.

Before you teach

- Are children confident recognising number patterns?
- What real-life contexts would this lesson fit into?

NATIONAL CURRICULUM LINKS

Year 6 Algebra

Generate and describe linear number sequences.

ASSESSING MASTERY

Children can explain what is similar and what is different about a sequence of numbers and, through this explanation, find the rule that governs the pattern. They can represent number patterns in different ways and use these representations to justify their ideas about the rule for a sequence.

COMMON MISCONCEPTIONS

Children may read and misunderstand a multiplicative number sequence as an additive one that adds a different number each time. For example, the sequence below:

Term	1	2	3	4	5
Number	4	8	12	16	20

Children may state that the rule for calculating the number from the term in this sequence is + 3, + 6, + 9, + 12, etc. Ask:
- *Is your rule the same each time? What same thing can you do to every number that results in the number pattern shown?*

STRENGTHENING UNDERSTANDING

For children who find recognising and explaining the rule governing a number pattern challenging, offer them the rule × 2. Ask: *If I gave you the number 1 and you applied that rule, what number would you have? How about 2, 3, 4? Can you make the pattern using counters?* Record these using a similar chart to those used in the lesson. Ask: *What clues are there in the chart that the numbers are multiplied by 2 each time?* Show children another chart with a different number pattern, for example, × 3. Do not show the rule. Ask: *How is this pattern similar to the previous pattern? How is it different? How could you work out from the clues what has happened to each number?*

GOING DEEPER

Challenge children to create a number sequence where two operations are carried out on a term before the number is found, for example, $n × 2 + 1$.

KEY LANGUAGE

In lesson: pattern, sequence, **rule**, represent

Other language to be used by the teacher: value

STRUCTURES AND REPRESENTATIONS

Charts

RESOURCES

Optional: cubes, counters, small sticks

In the eTextbook of this lesson, you will find interactive links to a selection of teaching tools.

Quick recap

Revise the 4 times-table. Practise counting up and back in 4s, from 0 to 100, and then from 100 to 0.

Discover

ASK

- Question **1** a): *What is the same and what is different about each new number in the sequence? What happens every time?*
- Question **1** a): *How many legs will 257 frogs have? What is the most efficient way of finding out?*
- Question **1** b): *What will you need to know to make a rule about the eyes on a frog?*

IN FOCUS Question **1** a) offers children the opportunity to begin following a rule for a number sequence. Encourage them to find and use the rule to find any term by asking for a number in the pattern that is too high to count. Question **1** b) develops children's understanding of rules by giving them the opportunity to create their own number sequence. Challenge children to prove their rule through building or drawing the pattern alongside the written numerals.

PRACTICAL TIPS Using cubes or counters, children could build and organise the pattern described in the **Discover** scenario to clearly show how the numbers are changing with each term. It may help children to use a consistent set of colours to make the pattern even clearer.

ANSWERS

Question **1** a): The number of legs is four times the number of frogs:
$4 \times a$ (where a is the number of frogs).

Question **1** b): Where a is the number of frogs, the number of eyes is $2 \times a$ and the number of mouths is $1 \times a$.

Share

ASK

- Question **1** a): *What is the most efficient way of finding how many legs there are on any number of frogs?*
- Question **1** b): *Can you write a calculation that represents the pattern for the number of ears on cats? Can you generalise your calculation so that it works with any number of cats?*

IN FOCUS At this point in the lesson, children should use specific examples to justify their generalisations. Encourage them to use examples from the chart showing the number of frogs and number of legs, draw out the general rule and find other examples that support their generalisations. Encourage children to draw up a similar bank of evidence for question **1** b). For both questions, ensure children understand how unknown or variable numbers in a calculation can be shown algebraically using letters.

PUPIL TEXTBOOK 6B PAGE 48

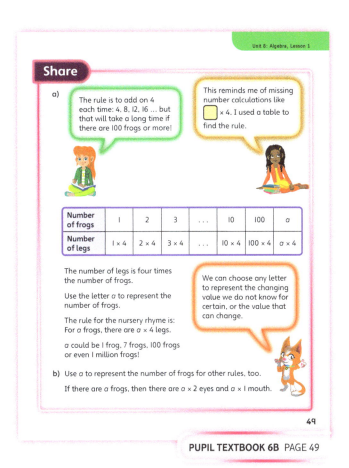

PUPIL TEXTBOOK 6B PAGE 49

Think together

Unit 8: Algebra, Lesson 1

Think together

WAYS OF WORKING Whole class teacher led (I do, We do, You do)

ASK

- Question ① a): *What number do you multiply the input by each time?*
- Question ②: *What calculation will find the number of shells for each number of bracelets?*
- Question ③ a): *How old would Lee have been when Jen was 26? 27? 28? How can you use this to help you?*
- Question ③ b): *What number will you begin investigating?*
- Question ③ c): *What is the same and what is different about how the numbers change each time?*

IN FOCUS Question ① uses a function machine context to represent the use of a known rule to find an unknown number. Question ② scaffolds the gathering and recording of the evidence children will need to find and prove an algebraic rule. Encourage children to demonstrate their reasoning by using resources and pictures alongside the abstract evidence shown in the table.

STRENGTHEN To help children understand how to write a function machine from the scenario given in question ②, you could model the situation using counters to represent the shells. You could make 1, 2 or 3 bracelets and help children make a connection between the number of bracelets and the number of counters (shells).

DEEPEN Question ③ deepens children's ability to find rules for number sequences by offering clues that will help them to find the rule in different ways. Ask: *How are the sequence and rule in question ③ b) similar to those in question ③ a)? How can recognising this help you find other algebraic rules in the future?*

ASSESSMENT CHECKPOINT Question ② assesses children's ability to use specific examples to find a general rule that governs a sequence. Question ③ assesses children's ability to look at number sequences that have been represented in different ways and investigate them to find the rule that governs them.

ANSWERS

Question ① a): Outputs: 3, 6, 9, 12, 15, 36, $3 \times n$ ($3n$)

Question ① b): Outputs: 11, 12, 13, 14, 26, 119, $n + 10$

Question ②: Number of shells: 6, 12, 18, 24, $m \times 6$ ($6m$)

Question ③ a): Jen's age: 34, 35, 36, 51, $n + 26$

Question ③ b): Ebo's age: 0, 10, 21, 33, $y - 47$

Question ③ c): If p is Amal's age, $p + 10 =$ Mrs Dean's age. When Amal is 75, Mrs Dean will be $75 + 10 = 85$. $p =$ Mrs Dean's age $- 10$ When Mrs Dean is 100, Amal will be $100 - 10 = 90$.

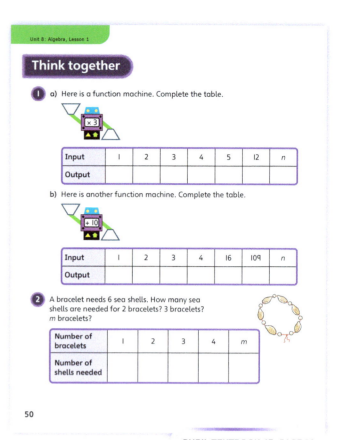

Think together

① a) Here is a function machine. Complete the table.

Input	1	2	3	4	5	12	n
Output							

b) Here is another function machine. Complete the table.

Input	1	2	3	4	16	109	n
Output							

② A bracelet needs 6 sea shells. How many sea shells are needed for 2 bracelets? 3 bracelets? m bracelets?

Number of bracelets	1	2	3	4	m
Number of shells needed					

50

PUPIL TEXTBOOK 6B PAGE 50

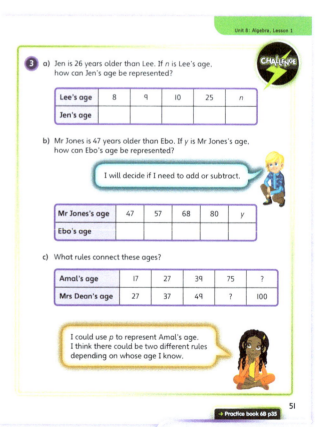

③ a) Jen is 26 years older than Lee. If n is Lee's age, how can Jen's age be represented?

CHALLENGE

Lee's age	8	9	10	25	n
Jen's age					

b) Mr Jones is 47 years older than Ebo. If y is Mr Jones's age, how can Ebo's age be represented?

I will decide if I need to add or subtract.

Mr Jones's age	47	57	68	80	y
Ebo's age					

c) What rules connect these ages?

Amal's age	17	27	39	75	?
Mrs Dean's age	27	37	49	?	100

I could use p to represent Amal's age. I think there could be two different rules depending on whose age I know.

51

→ Practice book 6B p35

PUPIL TEXTBOOK 6B PAGE 51

Practice

WAYS OF WORKING Independent thinking

IN FOCUS Question **1** uses a function machine to represent the rule for a number sequence. Question **2** scaffolds children's independent ability to investigate a number sequence and write the governing rule. In question **3**, encourage children to make or draw the patterns shown and transfer their understanding into a table to help them match the patterns to the rules accurately. For question **5**, children need to find and recognise number patterns and their rules using real-life contexts. Ask children to share their evidence for each solution, explaining how they came to their answer.

STRENGTHEN To strengthen children's ability to complete the table and find the matching rules in question **4**, ask: *Can you show the relationship between the times in a different way? If Zac has been painting for 30 minutes, how long will Kate have been painting for? If you have found one rule, what will its relationship with the other rule be? Can you show the relationship between the two rules using resources or a picture?*

DEEPEN If children are able to find the rules confidently in question **5**, ask: *Can you create your own table that shows a number pattern? Can a partner work out the rule for your pattern?*

ASSESSMENT CHECKPOINT Questions **2** and **6** assess children's ability to record number sequences and find the general rule that governs them. Look for children identifying the calculation that governs the *n*th term. The first table in question **6** shows an addition (*n* + 4), whereas the second shows a multiplication (2.5*y*). Help children to see that when a rule involves a multiplication, the numbers in the second row generally 'get bigger' much quicker than they do with an addition. Questions **3** and **5** assess children's ability to recognise number patterns and algebraic rules in different representations and contexts. Look for children explaining what they read in the clues, or saw in a picture, that allowed them to find the rule that governed the pattern. Question **4** assesses children's recognition that an algebraic rule can potentially be shown in more than one way, depending on which number is the variable. Look for children recognising how they could use their understanding of inverse operations.

ANSWERS Answers for the **Practice** part of the lesson can be found in the *Power Maths* online subscription.

Reflect

WAYS OF WORKING Independent thinking

IN FOCUS This question assesses children's understanding of algebraic notation and their understanding of how the different operations will affect an unknown variable differently. Encourage children to draw a picture to help support their thinking and apply their reasoning to a number of specific examples.

ASSESSMENT CHECKPOINT Look for children recognising *a* as an unknown variable. Children should be able to explain, using specific examples, how *a* × 5 is different to 5 + *a*. Children can support their thinking with pictures and possibly concrete resources.

ANSWERS Answers for the **Reflect** part of the lesson can be found in the *Power Maths* online subscription.

After the lesson

- Are children confident recognising and understanding how letters can be used to represent numbers in algebraic expressions?
- Can children find an algebraic rule in a number sequence?

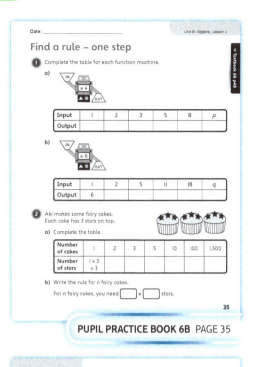

PUPIL PRACTICE BOOK 6B PAGE 35

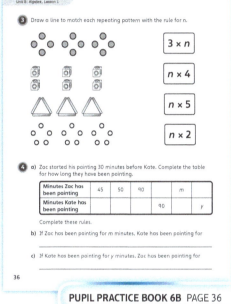

PUPIL PRACTICE BOOK 6B PAGE 36

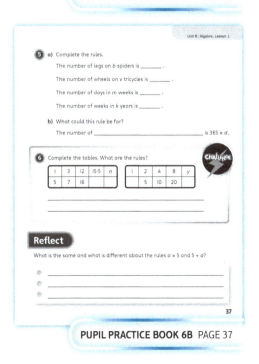

PUPIL PRACTICE BOOK 6B PAGE 37

Find a rule – two steps

Learning focus

In this lesson, children will find a rule for a number sequence that has more than one step. They will represent these sequences in a concrete, pictorial and abstract manner, focusing particularly on the algebraic expressions.

Before you teach

- Were there any unexpected misconceptions in the previous lesson about finding rules?
- How confident are children at using letters to represent unknown numbers?

NATIONAL CURRICULUM LINKS

Year 6 Algebra

Generate and describe linear number sequences.

ASSESSING MASTERY

Children can recognise and represent a rule in a number sequence that has more than one step, explain what is similar and what is different about a sequence of numbers and, through this, find the rule that governs the pattern. They can represent number patterns in different ways and use these representations to justify their ideas about the rule for a sequence.

COMMON MISCONCEPTIONS

Children may mistakenly assume that all number patterns start at 0 and, therefore, be unable to find the consistent rule governing a pattern that starts at any other number. Ask:
- *What is the first number in this sequence? What is the second number? Would the number be the same if the first number was 0?*

STRENGTHENING UNDERSTANDING

Offer children opportunities to build or model number sequences in different ways. Children could act out the money contexts and, as they talk through the context, write down the calculations they are carrying out. Ask: *How does the calculation that you have written change if you change the cost of each item? How does the calculation change if you change the starting amount?*

GOING DEEPER

Children could make up their own number sequence and write the rule that governs it. They could then hide some of the numbers in the pattern and challenge a partner to find the rule that governs their number sequence.

KEY LANGUAGE

In lesson: rule, pattern, growing pattern, **algebra**

Other language to be used by the teacher: sequence, term

STRUCTURES AND REPRESENTATIONS

Number line

RESOURCES

Optional: cubes, small sticks, 2D shapes, plastic money

 In the eTextbook of this lesson, you will find interactive links to a selection of teaching tools.

Quick recap

Ask children to work out the following 2-step calculations:

$4 + 3 \times 2$

$4 \times 3 + 2$

$4 - 3 \times 2$

$4 \times (3 - 2)$

Discuss the different steps that were needed for each one.

Discover

ASK

- Question **1** a): *Can you explain why the rule is not + 2?*
- Question **1** a): *How would this sequence change if 3 geese landed each time?*
- Question **1** b): *Why will 100 not be in the sequence? Can you prove it?*
- Question **1** b): *How many geese would need to land each time for there to be exactly 100 geese on the lake? Can you find more than one solution?*

IN FOCUS Some children may think the rule for question **1** a) is $n + 2$ or $n \times 2$ since 2 geese land each time. Ask them to prove whether this works for the first set of geese that land. Question **1** b) requires children to follow a number sequence using their understanding of number to support their reasoning. Encourage them to prove through pictures and concrete resources that, if the sequence begins on an odd number and 2 is added each time, it will never include an even number.

PRACTICAL TIPS Give children the opportunity to investigate this scenario with concrete resources. Encourage them to investigate how changing the numbers in the sequence changes it in different ways. For example, how does the sequence change if 8 geese are on the lake to begin with?

ANSWERS

Question **1** a): There will be $7 + n \times 2$ geese in total (where n is the number of additional pairs of geese that land).

Question **1** b): No, Richard is not correct because there will never be exactly 100 geese. The rule adds on a multiple of 2 to 7, so the answer will always be an odd number.

Share

ASK

- Question **1** a): *How do the cubes show what is the same and what is different about each iteration in the sequence?*
- Question **1** a): *How is this sequence different from those you looked at in the last lesson?*
- Question **1** a): *Why is 7 added to every step in the sequence?*
- Question **1** b): *How did you prove that exactly 100 geese will never be on the lake? Did you find a number of geese that could fly in so that exactly 100 geese will be on the lake at once?*

IN FOCUS It is important to ensure children understand the distinction between algebraic notation and the multiplication sign (i.e. using letters other than x to avoid confusion with the multiplication sign). Ask children to demonstrate their fluency and understanding by giving them the opportunity to practise through changing the parameters of the pattern slightly. Ask: *What would the algebraic expression look like if 3 geese or 4 geese flew in each time?*

PUPIL TEXTBOOK 6B PAGE 52

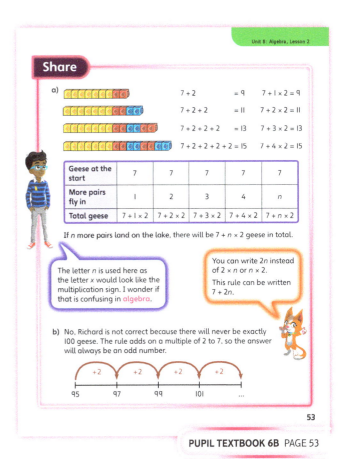

PUPIL TEXTBOOK 6B PAGE 53

Think together

WAYS OF WORKING Whole class teacher led (I do, We do, You do)

ASK

- Question **1**: *What number will you need to start with for each calculation?*
- Question **2**: *What calculation will you need to use to find the cost of any number of cups?*
- Question **3**: *Can you make the 5th term of this pattern? Does your calculation work for this term?*

IN FOCUS Question **1** uses a two-part function machine to represent a rule with two steps. This time, children are also asked to express the two functions as an algebraic rule. Question **2** helps to scaffold children's understanding of writing a two-step rule from a story problem. You might need to guide children to see that this rule will involve a subtraction as the amount of money Lexi has left will decrease as she buys more cups of lemonade.

STRENGTHEN To strengthen children's ability to find the rule in question **2**, it may help to give them the resources that will enable them to model or role play the scenario. Ask: *How does your model demonstrate the calculations needed to find how much money is left? Can you explain the calculations in the context of the story? Can you write them as abstract calculations? How would the calculations change if the number of cups changed?*

DEEPEN If children have solved question **3**, deepen their thinking and reasoning about the pattern shown by asking: *Are there any other ways of approaching the same sequence? What about if it had started with two sticks in place? How would this change the algebraic expression?*

ASSESSMENT CHECKPOINT Question **2** assesses children's ability to recognise the rules governing a number sequence and express them algebraically.

ANSWERS

Question **1** a): Outputs: 8, 11, 14, 20, 26, 35

Question **1** b): $n \times 3 + 5$ (or $3n + 5$)

Question **2**: Money left: 13, 11, 9, $15 - 2 \times a$ (or $15 - 2a$)

Question **3**: To make 3 squares, $4 + 3 \times 2$ sticks are used.
To make 4 squares, $4 + 3 \times 3$ sticks are used.
To make n squares, $4 + 3 \times (n - 1)$ sticks are used.

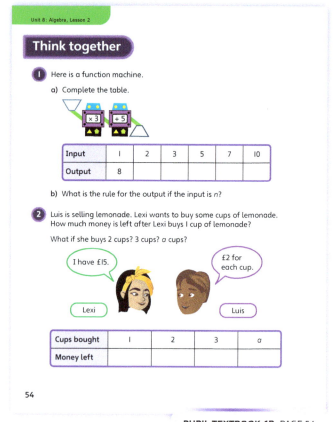

PUPIL TEXTBOOK 6B PAGE 54

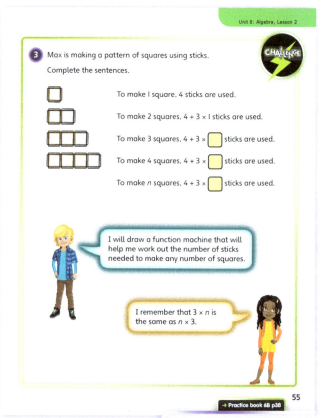

PUPIL TEXTBOOK 6B PAGE 55

Practice

WAYS OF WORKING Independent thinking

IN FOCUS Questions **1**, **2** and **3** present children with number sequences in different representations. Their thinking and evidence collection is scaffolded in these questions as they are provided with tables to organise their results. Question **4** presents children with a number sequence in which they need to find the rule, but also challenges them to collect and organise their own evidence. Encourage children to identify and explain how the methods shown in the previous questions can be applied here.

STRENGTHEN For questions **3** and **4**, offer children sticks to create the patterns shown. Ask: *What changes each time you find a new term in the sequence? Does the pattern increase or decrease? By how many? Where did the pattern start? Why is it important to know this?*

DEEPEN Question **5** deepens children's understanding of and reasoning with algebraic rules by challenging them to create their own number sequence that follows a consistent rule. Ask: *What operations will you need to use to create a growing pattern? How many different rules could you create that give the same number pattern?*

ASSESSMENT CHECKPOINT All questions in this lesson assess children's ability to recognise and understand number sequences and use their understanding to find a general rule that governs the sequence. Look for children collecting and organising the proof that their rule works in every instance of the number sequence, particularly in questions **4** and **5**, where a method of organisation is not provided. Question **5** assesses children's ability to create a number sequence and a rule that governs it.

ANSWERS Answers for the **Practice** part of the lesson can be found in the *Power Maths* online subscription.

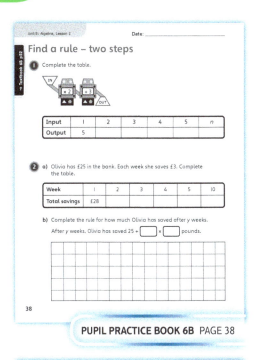

PUPIL PRACTICE BOOK 6B PAGE 38

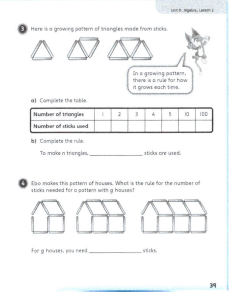

PUPIL PRACTICE BOOK 6B PAGE 39

Reflect

WAYS OF WORKING Independent thinking

IN FOCUS This question gives an opportunity to assess children's ability to put an algebraic expression into a context, rather than drawing one out from a given context as they have done elsewhere. Discuss the contexts they have met in the lesson so far. Could any similar contexts apply here?

ASSESSMENT CHECKPOINT Look for children applying a reasonable and appropriate context to the algebraic expression shown. For example, 'Isla has £100 and buys bags of marbles that cost £3 each. How much change does she get if she buys 1 bag? 2 bags? 3 bags? *y* bags?'

ANSWERS Answers for the **Reflect** part of the lesson can be found in the *Power Maths* online subscription.

After the lesson ⏸

- Are children able to recognise and find the rules for increasing sequences or decreasing sequences?
- How could you have included more concrete learning opportunities in this lesson?

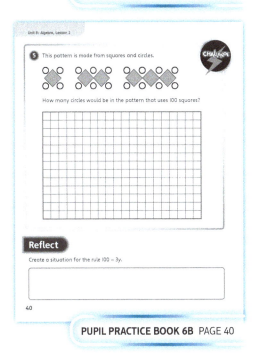

PUPIL PRACTICE BOOK 6B PAGE 40

Form expressions

Learning focus

In this lesson, children will apply their understanding of algebraic rules and investigate how they can be used to solve and generalise a contextual problem.

Before you teach

- Can children find number sequence rules that use all of the four operations?
- Are children confident finding the rule using one operation or more than one operation?

NATIONAL CURRICULUM LINKS

Year 6 Algebra

Generate and describe linear number sequences.

ASSESSING MASTERY

Children can represent a contextual problem as an algebraic expression and can use this to generalise the method of finding the solution. They can also use this expression to find a specific solution.

COMMON MISCONCEPTIONS

Children may neglect to use brackets in their algebraic expressions, leading to rules which do not represent the contextual problems correctly. Ask:

- *Does your rule represent the problem accurately? How can you prove it? How can you make sure the addition is carried out before the multiplication?*

In this lesson, children will need to get to grips with using the letter x in an algebraic expression as it is a letter that is commonly used. Ensure you discuss this with children and consider ways in which they could avoid confusing x with the multiplication sign. Ask:

- *What does each part of the expression mean? What does x mean?*

STRENGTHENING UNDERSTANDING

Before beginning the lesson, give children opportunities to find rules in number sequences. Begin with 1-step rules and move on to 2-step rules. Use multiple representations, such as counters showing number patterns, number patterns in the sides of shapes and number patterns shown using abstract numerals. For each, ask children what the rule is and how they could represent it as an algebraic expression.

GOING DEEPER

Children could be encouraged to write real-life problems similar to those seen in the lesson. Ask: *Can you write a problem that includes four variable numbers? How and why does the difficulty increase as you add more variables? Can you challenge a partner to find your algebraic rule and solve your problem?*

KEY LANGUAGE

In lesson: algebra, rule, input, output, function, operations

Other language to be used by the teacher: calculation

STRUCTURES AND REPRESENTATIONS

Bar model

RESOURCES

Optional: counters

 In the eTextbook of this lesson, you will find interactive links to a selection of teaching tools.

Quick recap

Challenge children to draw bar models that show:

15 + 10

5 + 5 + 5

3 × 4

3 × 4 + 5

Share and discuss their different interpretations.

Discover

WAYS OF WORKING Pair work

ASK

- Question ① a): *How can you organise and record the possible quantities of badges?*
- Question ① a): *Whose badges will you need to find the number of first? Second? Third?*
- Question ① a): *Can you write a rule that will find the number of everyone's badges, no matter how many Danny has?*
- Question ① b): *How many badges does Mo have if Danny has 4? How many does Jamilla have? How can you prove your solution?*

IN FOCUS Question ① a) offers children the opportunity to begin investigating and finding algebraic rules within a contextual problem. Encourage children to act out the scenario to help them identify the calculations behind the story. Question ① b) links this lesson with the previous one by looking for a specific term in the number sequence and using the rule to find it.

PRACTICAL TIPS Children could replicate this scenario with counters in the classroom. Once they have found the rules that express Mo and Jamilla's counters, ask children to investigate how the rules change as the context of the problem changes. For example, what would the rule be if Jamilla had 6 times as many badges as Mo? How many badges do Mo and Jamilla have if Danny has none? Children could also investigate how the operations could change, for example if Jamilla has half as many badges as Mo. For each scenario, children should write the new algebraic expression and compare the expressions to investigate what stays the same and what is different.

ANSWERS

Question ① a): The number of Mo's badges is $d + 6$.
The number of Jamilla's badges is $(d + 6) \times 2$.

Question ① b): $4 + 6 = 10$
Mo has 10 badges.
$(4 + 6) \times 2 = 20$ badges
Jamilla has 20 badges.

Share

WAYS OF WORKING Whole class teacher led

ASK

- Question ① a): *Did you record the rule for Mo's badges as $d + 6$? How does the bar model represent this rule?*
- Question ① a): *What mistake has Dexter made? Can you explain how he made it? How is the bar model for Jamilla's badges similar and different to the bar model for Mo's badges?*
- Question ① b): *Can you draw bar models to represent Danny having 10 badges?*

IN FOCUS Encourage children to find ways of using bar models to represent the algebraic rules they have created, including those which include division and subtraction. Doing this will support their understanding later in the lesson.

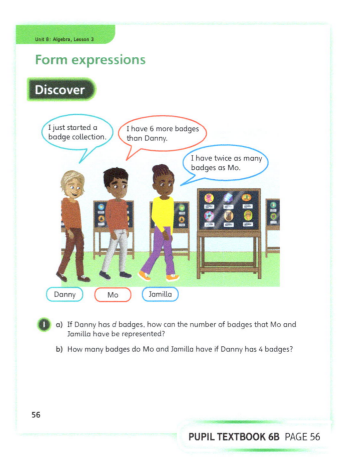

PUPIL TEXTBOOK 6B PAGE 56

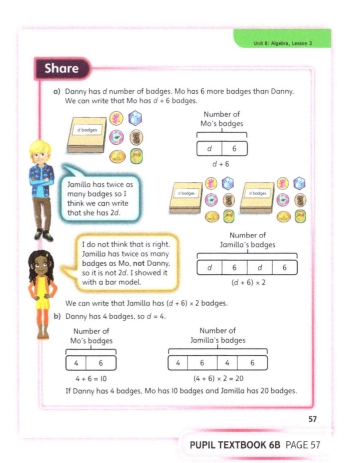

PUPIL TEXTBOOK 6B PAGE 57

Think together

WAYS OF WORKING Whole class teacher led (I do, We do, You do)

ASK

- Question **1** a): *How many multiples of snow globes does Bella have compared to Amelia?*
- Question **1** b): *What does the number 2 represent?*
- Question **1** c): *Can you draw a bar model to show your answer?*
- Question **2**: *Why do you need to do this in two steps? How are the operations different?*
- Question **3**: *What rules can you find that would work for the first term? How many solutions do you think there are?*

IN FOCUS Question **1** is important as it links a contextualised question, where it is necessary to find an algebraic rule, with the representation of the bar model. Use this bar model to support children when solving question **2** by discussing how a similar representation may help them.

STRENGTHEN To strengthen children's ability to identify a rule for question **3**, ask: *What 2-step calculation could you do which would begin with 1 and end with 4? Can you write some examples? Can you solve your calculations using the other starting numbers shown?*

DEEPEN Extend question **2** by asking children to use their understanding of bar models to help represent the problem. Ask: *How can you represent this question using a bar model? Explain how your bar model matches the function machine output. Why is it important to use brackets in this algebraic expression? How does the bar model help you to explain your thinking?*

ASSESSMENT CHECKPOINT Question **1** assesses children's understanding of the bar model and how it can represent an algebraic expression. Question **2** assesses children's ability to create an algebraic rule for a given set of operations. Look for children who recognise where the use of brackets is important. Question **3** assesses children's fluency with algebraic rules. Look for children who recognise that the same result can be found using multiple algebraic rules and can apply these rules fluently to other starting numbers.

ANSWERS

Question **1** a): Bella has 17 snow globes.

Question **1** b): The top bar shows the number of Amelia's snow globes as the letter *s*.
The bottom bar shows the number of Bella's snow globes.

Question **1** c): $3 \times s + 2$ (or $3s + 2$)

Question **2**: 7, 10, 25, 25·5, $(n + 10) \div 2$

Question **3**: There are many possible solutions, if the first function is a multiplication and the second is either an addition or subtraction.
There is only one solution where an addition is followed by a multiplication: $+ 1 \times 2$.
There are several solutions with an addition followed by a division. For example, $+ 7 \div 2$; $+ 11 \div 3$.
There are many possible solutions using a combination of 2 additions or an addition and a subtraction. For example, $+ 4 - 1$; $+ 1 + 2$.

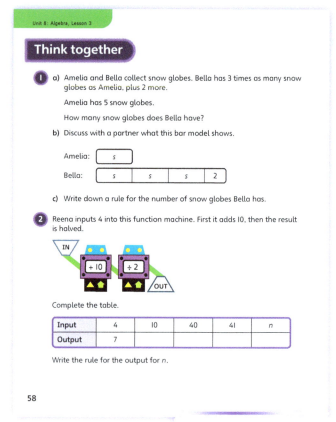

Think together

1 a) Amelia and Bella collect snow globes. Bella has 3 times as many snow globes as Amelia, plus 2 more.

Amelia has 5 snow globes.

How many snow globes does Bella have?

b) Discuss with a partner what this bar model shows.

Amelia: | *s* |

Bella: | *s* | *s* | *s* | 2 |

c) Write down a rule for the number of snow globes Bella has.

2 Reena inputs 4 into this function machine. First it adds 10, then the result is halved.

IN   + 10   ÷ 2   OUT

Complete the table.

Input	4	10	40	41	*n*
Output	7				

Write the rule for the output for *n*.

58

PUPIL TEXTBOOK 6B PAGE 58

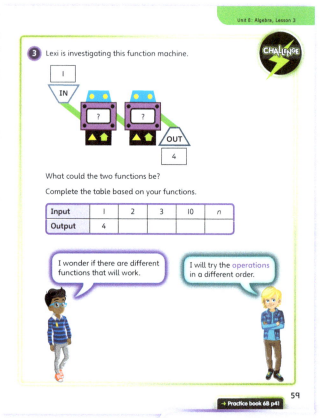

3 Lexi is investigating this function machine.

1

IN   ?   ?   OUT

4

What could the two functions be?

Complete the table based on your functions.

Input	1	2	3	10	*n*
Output	4				

I wonder if there are different functions that will work.

I will try the operations in a different order.

CHALLENGE

→ Practice book 6B p41

59

PUPIL TEXTBOOK 6B PAGE 59

Practice

WAYS OF WORKING Independent thinking

IN FOCUS Question ① scaffolds children's understanding of finding, representing and using a rule in a contextual story problem. When children are working on question ① c), encourage them to use the bar model they drew for question ① b) to help them find the number of guinea pigs Ambika has. This representation could also be used to explain their reasoning in question ① d).

STRENGTHEN To strengthen children's ability to find the rule for each of the function machines in question ②, ask: *Can you represent each function machine as a bar model? How can this help you find the rule? Will you need brackets for this rule?*

DEEPEN While solving question ④, deepen children's fluency and reasoning by asking: *Are there only two possible sets of functions for this question? Can you prove this? Would the functions you have chosen work if they were carried out in reverse order?*

THINK DIFFERENTLY Question ③ encourages children to recognise and explain the link between inverse operations. Children should recognise that the + 5 negates 5 of the – 15, effectively making one function of – 10. Encourage children to explain why this happens and to demonstrate their understanding using a bar model.

ASSESSMENT CHECKPOINT Question ② assesses children's ability to use algebraic rules to manipulate numbers. It also assesses their ability to record these rules using algebraic expressions. Question ③ assesses children's ability to recognise how numbers can be manipulated, using multiple algebraic rules, to achieve the same number pattern. Look for children finding multiple algebraic rules that result in the same numbers.

ANSWERS Answers for the **Practice** part of the lesson can be found in the *Power Maths* online subscription.

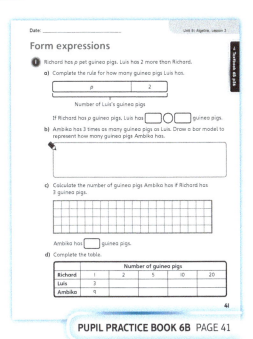

PUPIL PRACTICE BOOK 6B PAGE 41

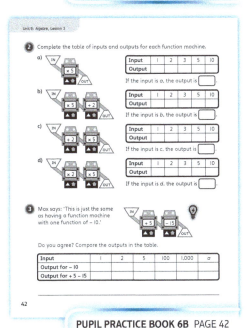

PUPIL PRACTICE BOOK 6B PAGE 42

Reflect

WAYS OF WORKING Independent thinking

IN FOCUS This question will allow you to assess children's ability to link their knowledge and understanding of number with their understanding of algebraic rules. Children may use a bar model to help them investigate the statement in this question.

ASSESSMENT CHECKPOINT Look for children who recognise that this method will not work, because of the + 2 element. Finding the answer when $m = 10$ and then multiplying by 10 will also multiply the 2 by 10, giving an incorrect answer.

ANSWERS Answers for the **Reflect** part of the lesson can be found in the *Power Maths* online subscription.

After the lesson ⏸

- Were children confident using the algebraic rules in this lesson?
- How fluently were children able to explain the link between the bar model and the algebraic rules in this lesson?

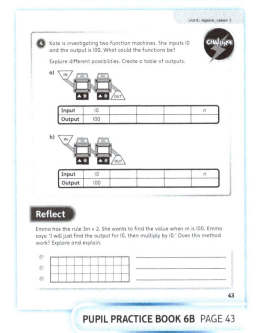

PUPIL PRACTICE BOOK 6B PAGE 43

Substitution

Learning focus

In this lesson, children will use their understanding of using algebraic rules to find the *n*th term in an algebraic sequence.

Before you teach

- How confident were children at using algebraic rules in the previous lesson?
- How will you provide extra support to those children still lacking confidence?

NATIONAL CURRICULUM LINKS

Year 6 Algebra

Express missing number problems algebraically.

Generate and describe linear number sequences.

ASSESSING MASTERY

Children can recognise and explain how they can use an algebraic expression to find any given term in an algebraic sequence. Children can represent algebraic expressions in different pictorial and abstract ways and can use these representations to support their findings.

COMMON MISCONCEPTIONS

Children may assume that an expression such as $4n + 7$ can be completed in any order, and so add the 7 before multiplying. Ask:

- *Can you represent this expression with a picture? How many + 7s are there in your picture? Have you multiplied them by 4? Can you remember the order of operations? Does it apply here?*

STRENGTHENING UNDERSTANDING

As in the previous lesson, provide opportunities for children to find rules in number sequences. Recap 1-step rules if necessary before moving on to 2-step rules.

GOING DEEPER

Encourage children to create their own algebraic rules with two or more steps. Ask: *What story context would work well with your algebraic expression? Can you make it so you have the same operation both times?*

KEY LANGUAGE

In lesson: substitute, rule, expression

Other language to be used by the teacher: term, sequence, algebra, algebraic, *n*th

STRUCTURES AND REPRESENTATIONS

Number line

RESOURCES

Optional: coins

 In the eTextbook of this lesson, you will find interactive links to a selection of teaching tools.

Quick recap

Ask children to draw bar models to represent the following expressions:

$12 + a$

$3 \times b$

$c + d + 5$

$2 \times e + 3$

Discover

WAYS OF WORKING Pair work

ASK

• Question **1** a): *What is the algebraic rule that governs this number sequence?*
• Question **1** a): *Could you find any number in the sequence?*
• Question **1** b): *Can you prove your thinking with a bar model? Are there any other models you could use?*

IN FOCUS Question **1** a) links this lesson with children's previous learning about finding algebraic rules. By following the rule and finding the first four terms, children should be able to recognise how to find the 13th term and identify patterns in the algebraic sequence. Question **1** b) challenges children to link their understanding of number with their understanding of algebraic expressions. Once children have answered the question, encourage them to investigate what happens to the score if the value of *n* increases by 100 or 1,000.

PRACTICAL TIPS Children could suggest other items that could be collected in the game and the points attributed to their new items. Children should investigate how this changes the result of the algebraic sequence.

ANSWERS

Question **1** a): 5, 10, 15, 20, *n* × 5 (or 5*n*)
The rule is 5*n* which means *n* × 5.
If *n* = 13, 5*n* = 5 × 13 = 65 points
If the value of *n* is 13, you will have 65 points.

Question **1** b): If *n* = 23, you will have 115 points.
Method 1: 5 × 23 = 115
Method 2: 5 × 13 + 5 × 10 = 65 + 50 = 115

Share

WAYS OF WORKING Whole class teacher led

ASK

• Question **1** a): *Why is the multiplication sign removed from the algebraic expression?*
• Question **1** a): *Is there a maximum number that n could stand for?*
• Question **1** b): *Can you draw a bar model to represent the same calculation as the number line?*
• Question **1** b): *Did you choose to use a number line? Explain how yours is the same as and different to the one on the page.*

IN FOCUS Give children the opportunity to experience finding the *n*th term using different operations. Encourage them to consider how the algebraic expression would change if there was a collectible in the game that subtracted 5 from the score or halved the score.

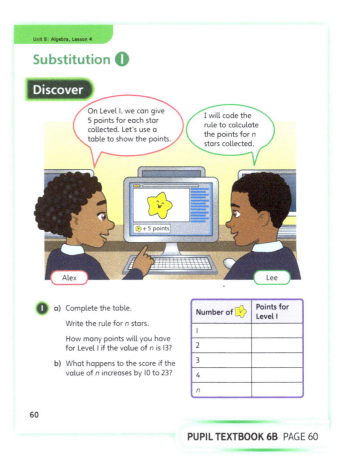

PUPIL TEXTBOOK 6B PAGE 60

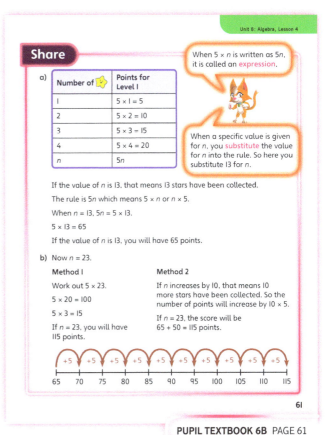

PUPIL TEXTBOOK 6B PAGE 61

Think together

Whole class teacher led (I do, We do, You do)

ASK

- Question **1**: *What changes each time another lightning bolt is collected? Can you write an algebraic expression that can find the points for any number of lightning bolts?*
- Question **2**: *How is this algebraic sequence different to the one in question* **1***?*
- Question **3**: *What is the same and what is different about the numbers the two expressions make?*

IN FOCUS In questions **1** and **2**, children investigate algebraic sequences and find the *n*th term of each one. When solving question **2**, ensure children recognise how this rule requires them to use a different operation as well as multiplication.

STRENGTHEN Support children in identifying the rule for a question. Ask: *Can you represent the problem in a concrete way? Can you use your concrete representation to draw a bar model or number line to represent the problem? What calculation is used? Which number can change? How will you use this to create the algebraic expression?*

DEEPEN Question **3** b) deepens children's reasoning and fluency with algebraic expressions and their knowledge of number. Ask: *Would the patterns you have noticed still be present if you added a different number from the one you subtracted?*

ASSESSMENT CHECKPOINT Questions **1** and **2** assess children's ability to recognise and record an algebraic rule for a number sequence and any term in the number sequence.

ANSWERS

Question **1** a): $15 \times m = 15m$

Question **1** b): When $m = 9$, points = 135; when $m = 10$, points = 150; when $m = 11$, points = 165.

Question **2** a): $100 - 3 \times k$

Question **2** b): When $k = 10$, $100 - 3 \times 10 = 100 - 30 = 70$
When $k = 20$: $100 - 3 \times 20 = 100 - 60 = 40$
When $k = 30$: $100 - 3 \times 30 = 100 - 90 = 10$

Question **2** c): When $k = 33$: $100 - 3 \times 33 = 100 - 99 = 1$
When $k = 34$: $100 - 3 \times 34 = 100 - 102 = {}^-2$
$k = 34$ means you lose all your 100 points.

Question **3** a):

	2p + 1	2p − 1
Substitute p = 1	2 × 1 + 1 = 3	2 × 1 − 1 = 1
Substitute p = 15	2 × 15 + 1 = 31	2 × 15 − 1 = 29
Substitute p = 101	2 × 101 + 1 = 203	2 × 101 − 1 = 201
Substitute p = 1,213	2 × 1,213 + 1 = 2,423	2 × 1,213 − 1 = 2,425

Children should notice that the answer is always odd because $2p$ always gives an even number.

Question **3** b): Various answers are possible. Children should notice that the answer is always odd, because $10p$ gives an even number.

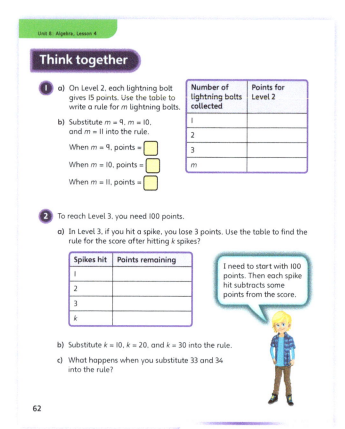

PUPIL TEXTBOOK 6B PAGE 62

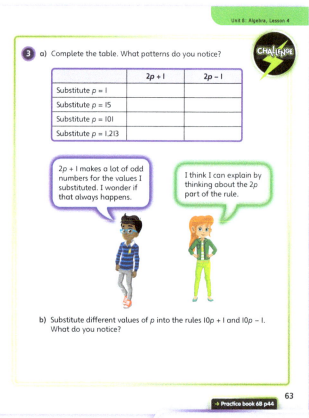

PUPIL TEXTBOOK 6B PAGE 63

Practice

WAYS OF WORKING Independent thinking

IN FOCUS In question **1**, encourage children to use coins to create the given problem to check their understanding, before representing it as an abstract calculation. In question **3**, children investigate the effect of different operations on numbers within an algebraic expression. Encourage them to explain what they have noticed about how the numbers differ and to back this up with pictorial evidence, possibly using a bar model.

STRENGTHEN If children find it challenging to explain how to find multiples of 10 in question **5**, ask: *Can you find and record the first 10 terms in the sequence? What do you notice about the expressions that result in a multiple of 10? What other numbers do you predict will have a similar result? How are they similar and different to those you have investigated?*

DEEPEN Question **6** challenges children to reason about algebraic expressions using the multiple representations they have used in previous lessons. Ask: *Is there a more efficient way to record this algebraic rule? How many ys would you need to subtract for every result to be a multiple of 7?*

THINK DIFFERENTLY Question **4** reinforces the idea that it is important to be careful when solving algebraic expressions and use the correct order of operations. Children should recognise that adding before multiplying will result in the added 7 being multiplied, as well as the variable number.

ASSESSMENT CHECKPOINT Questions **1** and **2** assess children's ability to find an algebraic rule and use it to find different terms in a number sequence. Look for children recognising the vocabulary in the problem that gives them information about which operations to use. Questions **5** and **6** assess children's awareness of how different numbers can influence an algebraic expression and number sequence.

ANSWERS Answers for the **Practice** part of the lesson can be found in the *Power Maths* online subscription.

Reflect

WAYS OF WORKING Independent thinking

IN FOCUS Once children have shared their reasoning about the given expression, they can be encouraged to show their fluency further by creating a different expression that will always result in an even number. Children can also be challenged to create an expression that always results in an odd number.

ASSESSMENT CHECKPOINT Look for children recognising that the result will always be an even number. This is due to the variable being doubled, which will result in an even number, before 4 (another even number) is added to it. As both numbers are even, every result will be even.

ANSWERS Answers for the **Reflect** part of the lesson can be found in the *Power Maths* online subscription.

After the lesson

- Did you help children identify where these skills would be useful in a real-world context?
- How confident were children with the use of the new vocabulary in this lesson?

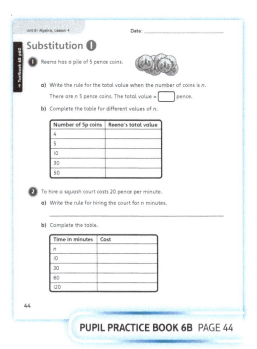

PUPIL PRACTICE BOOK 6B PAGE 44

PUPIL PRACTICE BOOK 6B PAGE 45

PUPIL PRACTICE BOOK 6B PAGE 46

Substitution

Learning focus

In this lesson, children will create algebraic expressions that generalise the rule in a number sequence. They will use these expressions to find the *n*th term in a sequence.

Before you teach ⏸

- Were there any misconceptions about using rules from the previous lesson that you will need to plan for in this lesson?

NATIONAL CURRICULUM LINKS

Year 6 Algebra

Express missing number problems algebraically.

Generate and describe linear number sequences.

ASSESSING MASTERY

Children can reliably find and record an algebraic expression using any of the four operations and brackets if necessary. Children can fluently use these expressions to find the *n*th term in a number sequence and can use their understanding to solve contextual problems.

COMMON MISCONCEPTIONS

Children may think an expression such as 2*y* means 2 + *y*. Ask:
- *Does the expression 2y sound like '2 add y' or '2 ys'? Can you show 2 ys using a bar model? How does it differ to the bar model for 2 + y?*

STRENGTHENING UNDERSTANDING

To strengthen children's ability to link bar models to algebraic expressions, it may help to show them bar models that represent different 1-step calculations using the four different operations. Ask: *How does each bar model differ? How are they similar? How can you recognise any given operation in another bar model?* Show children one of the bar models given in this lesson. Ask: *Can you spot any parts of this bar model that are similar to those you just looked at? Which operation do they match?*

GOING DEEPER

Challenge children to write their own contextual word problem that requires an algebraic expression with three or more steps. Once they have done so, ask them to represent their problem using a bar model.

KEY LANGUAGE

In lesson: expression

Other language to be used by the teacher: term, sequence, algebra, algebraic, *n*th

STRUCTURES AND REPRESENTATIONS

Bar model

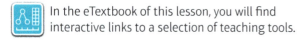 In the eTextbook of this lesson, you will find interactive links to a selection of teaching tools.

Quick recap

Challenge children to substitute the value *p* = 5 into each of these expressions, and to solve the resulting calculation:

10 + *p*

10 − *p*

3*p*

Discover

WAYS OF WORKING Pair work

ASK

- Question **1** a): *What algebraic rule governs this sequence? How will you use the rule to find out how much water is lost in a day? Can you represent the rule using a picture?*
- Question **1** b): *How will you include the 50 ml of water in the algebraic rule? Are you adding or multiplying the 50 ml?*

IN FOCUS Question **1** a) gives children an opportunity to find an algebraic expression and apply it to a specific term in a sequence. When children are solving this, encourage them to apply their understanding and fluency with number by investigating how much water will be lost in two days, a week, a month, a year, and so on. Question **1** b) develops the algebraic expression they created in question **1** a), by challenging children to find an expression that adds 50 ml to the multiples of 20 ml they find.

PRACTICAL TIPS When investigating the context shown in the picture, children could investigate how much water is lost per hour if the total amount of water lost over *t* hours is 20 ml. For example, if *t* = 4, then the tap will have leaked 5 ml of water per hour. For each example, children could investigate how much water would be lost in total over the course of a day and whether there are patterns or relationships evident in their findings.

ANSWERS

Question **1** a): If *t* is the number of hours, the rule is 20 × *t* (or 20*t*).

Question **1** b): If *n* is the number of hours, the rule is 50 + 20 × *n* (or 50 + 20*n*).

Share

WAYS OF WORKING Whole class teacher led

ASK

- Question **1** a): *How is an algebraic expression like the rules you have used?*
- Question **1** a): *Does your rule match the expression shown?*
- Question **1** a): *How can you use the expression to find how much water would be lost in a week or a month?*
- Question **1** b): *How does the bar model show whether you need to add or multiply the 50?*
- Question **1** b): *Is Astrid correct? If not, can you explain her mistake?*

IN FOCUS Encourage children to describe the rules they create as expressions from this point on. Children could create their own algebraic expressions, using all four operations, and link them to contexts similar to the one in the book.

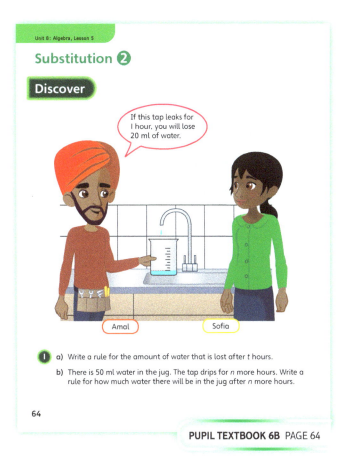

Substitution ②

Discover

If this tap leaks for 1 hour, you will lose 20 ml of water.

Amal

Sofia

1 a) Write a rule for the amount of water that is lost after *t* hours.

b) There is 50 ml water in the jug. The tap drips for *n* more hours. Write a rule for how much water there will be in the jug after *n* more hours.

64

PUPIL TEXTBOOK 6B PAGE 64

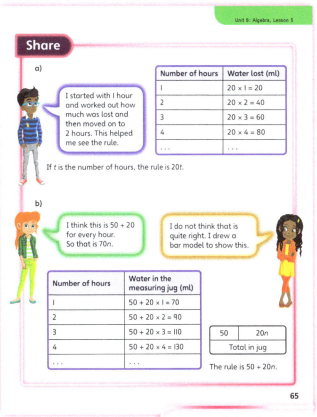

Share

a)

I started with 1 hour and worked out how much was lost and then moved on to 2 hours. This helped me see the rule.

Number of hours	Water lost (ml)
1	20 × 1 = 20
2	20 × 2 = 40
3	20 × 3 = 60
4	20 × 4 = 80
. . .	. . .

If *t* is the number of hours, the rule is 20*t*.

b)

I think this is 50 + 20 for every hour. So that is 70*n*.

I do not think that is quite right. I drew a bar model to show this.

Number of hours	Water in the measuring jug (ml)
1	50 + 20 × 1 = 70
2	50 + 20 × 2 = 90
3	50 + 20 × 3 = 110
4	50 + 20 × 4 = 130
. . .	. . .

50	20*n*
Total in jug	

The rule is 50 + 20*n*.

65

PUPIL TEXTBOOK 6B PAGE 65

Think together

WAYS OF WORKING Whole class teacher led (I do, We do, You do)

ASK

- Question ①: *What happens to the 150 l on the first day?*
- Question ②: *How does the bar model represent the problem? Can you write the algebraic expression that represents this problem? How does it link to the bar model?*
- Question ③ a): *Which operation is shown in each bar model? How can you prove it?*

IN FOCUS Question ① supports children in finding the general algebraic expression by giving them a suggested table that they can use to begin investigating the results when the number of days is changed. For question ②, encourage children to use the bar model to explain how they found the expression that governs the number sequence.

STRENGTHEN For each bar model in question ③ a), ask children to substitute a small value for *m* such as 1 or 2. This should help them to see what happens to *m* in each expression and support them in identifying which operation is shown.

DEEPEN When solving question ③ b), children could deepen their understanding, reasoning and fluency with the concept by following the suggested line of thinking further. Ask: *Do the things you have noticed continue if you substitute m with 12? What about if you work the other way and try 96? Are the patterns still evident?*

ASSESSMENT CHECKPOINT Questions ① and ② assess children's ability to draw out an algebraic expression from a contextualised problem. In question ③ b), children should use their understanding of additive and multiplicative reasoning to explain the different ways the numbers change.

ANSWERS

Question ①: After a week, 136 litres are left in the barrel. The expression is $150 - 2w$.

Question ② a): $720 - 20y$

Question ② b):

Time taken	Your calculation	Sand left in the hourglass (grams)
10 minutes	$720 - 20 \times 10$	520 g
20 minutes	$720 - 20 \times 20$	320 g
30 minutes	$720 - 20 \times 30$	120 g

Question ③ a): $m + 10$
$m - 30$
$\frac{1}{3}m, \frac{1}{3}m, \frac{1}{3}m$
$2m + 12$

Question ③ b): When $m = 48$:
$m + 10 = 48 + 10 = 58$
$m - 30 + 30 = 48 - 30 + 30 = 48$
$m - 30 = 48 - 30 = 18$
$\frac{1}{3}m + \frac{1}{3}m + \frac{1}{3}m = 16 + 16 + 16 = 48$
$2m + 12 = 2 \times 48 + 12 = 96 + 12 = 108$
When $m = 24$:
$m + 10 = 24 + 10 = 34$
$m - 30 + 30 = 24$
$\frac{1}{3}m + \frac{1}{3}m + \frac{1}{3}m = 8 + 8 + 8 = 24$
$2m + 12 = 2 \times 24 + 12 = 60$

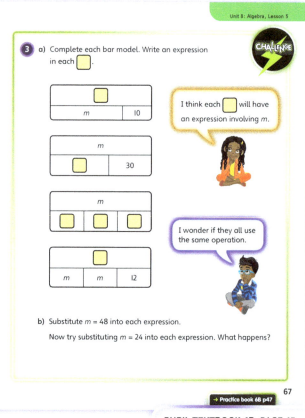

PUPIL TEXTBOOK 6B PAGE 66

PUPIL TEXTBOOK 6B PAGE 67

Practice

WAYS OF WORKING Independent thinking

IN FOCUS Question ❶ a) links children's understanding of the bar model to their understanding of finding an algebraic expression. Encourage children to record the beginning of the number sequence using a table to help them spot the patterns and find the expression that governs the sequence.

STRENGTHEN Questions ❸ and ❹ develop children's independent understanding of the four operations in algebraic expressions, represented using bar models. It may be beneficial to encourage children to substitute *a* or *y* for a number of their choosing, to help them begin to visualise the calculations necessary to formulate the algebraic expression. Ask: *Can you choose a number for a or y to represent? How will doing this help you to visualise and find a solution?*

DEEPEN Question ❺ deepens children's understanding, fluency and reasoning with the bar model representation of algebraic expressions by challenging children to interpret more complicated representations. Once children have successfully interpreted the bar models shown in the question, challenge them to create their own similar representations. Ask: *Can you use what you have learnt today to create a bar model that represents a similar algebraic expression?*

ASSESSMENT CHECKPOINT Questions ❶, ❸ and ❺ assess children's understanding of how bar models can represent algebraic expressions. Look for children explaining how the different operations are represented in bar models. Question ❷ assesses children's ability to find an algebraic expression that can be used to solve a contextual word problem.

ANSWERS Answers for the **Practice** part of the lesson can be found in the *Power Maths* online subscription.

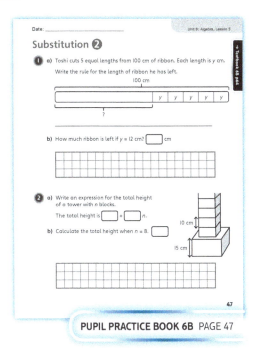

PUPIL PRACTICE BOOK 6B PAGE 47

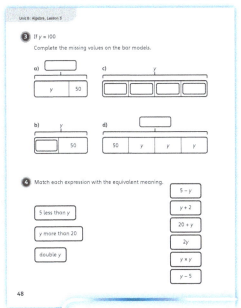

PUPIL PRACTICE BOOK 6B PAGE 48

Reflect

WAYS OF WORKING Independent thinking

IN FOCUS This question will offer the opportunity to assess whether children can fluently use algebraic expressions to find a given term and whether they can represent this term using a bar model. Encourage children to describe and show what the bar model will look like if the number that *y* is multiplied by changes.

ASSESSMENT CHECKPOINT Look for children accurately drawing a bar model and using it to work out the calculation they need to make to find the value of *y*.

ANSWERS Answers for the **Reflect** part of the lesson can be found in the *Power Maths* online subscription.

After the lesson ⏸

- Were children able to recognise how the bar model can represent all four operations in an algebraic expression?
- Can children use bar models to interpret more complicated algebraic representations?

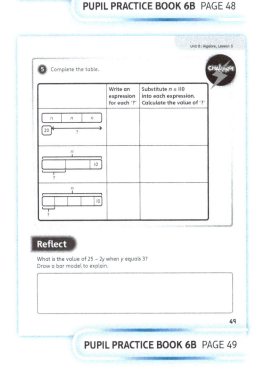

PUPIL PRACTICE BOOK 6B PAGE 49

Formulae

Learning focus

In this lesson, children will find and record algebraic formulae. They will link these formulae to different real-life contexts and use them to spot patterns.

Before you teach ⏸

- What real-life contexts could you include in this lesson where creating a formula could be useful?
- How will you ensure children know the difference between a formula and an expression?

NATIONAL CURRICULUM LINKS

Year 6 Algebra

Use simple formulae.

ASSESSING MASTERY

Children can write algebraic formulae, fluently demonstrating their understanding of the relationship between two different quantities. They can substitute numbers from a specific example of a number relationship with letters to find a general formula.

COMMON MISCONCEPTIONS

Children may assume that a formula such as $4b + 5$ will equal $9b$. Ask:
- *What would the full calculation be if you substituted b with 2? What number are you multiplying by 2? What will you add 5 to?*

STRENGTHENING UNDERSTANDING

Create a calculation with digit cards such as $5 + 6 \div 2$. Ask: *What number could you substitute with a letter? What would happen if the letter represented 1? How would that change the calculation? Can you find a pattern by trying different numbers?*

GOING DEEPER

Challenge children to write the formulae for the area or perimeter of different shapes. Once they have done this, they can challenge a partner to guess which shape the formula is for, based on the calculation the formula represents. Ask: *Which shape does this formula represent? Explain how you know.*

KEY LANGUAGE

In lesson: formula, formulae, algebra, substitute, pattern

Other language to be used by the teacher: expression, generalise

STRUCTURES AND REPRESENTATIONS

2D shapes

RESOURCES

Optional: 2D shapes, digit cards

 In the eTextbook of this lesson, you will find interactive links to a selection of teaching tools.

Quick recap ↻

Challenge children to substitute the value $q = 10$ into each of these expressions, and to evaluate each one:

$10q - 1$

$150 - 3q$

$4q - 28$

$100 - 10q$

Discover

WAYS OF WORKING Pair work

ASK

- Question **1** a): *When finding the perimeter of different hexagons, what numbers change and what numbers stay the same? What is the same and what is different about regular hexagons and regular pentagons? How will this be reflected in the two rules?*
- Question **1** b): *How are the perimeters different between the pentagons and the hexagons? How are the two hexagon perimeters different to each other?*

IN FOCUS Question **1** a) lays the foundations for introducing the concept of a formula. Question **1** b) shows children how a formula can be used to find the relationship between two quantities, in this instance a single side length and the total perimeter. (Note that the term formula is defined in **Share**.) Encourage children to try different types of numbers to see if they can be substituted into the rule (formula), for example, decimal numbers.

PRACTICAL TIPS Encourage children to find the rule for the sides of several regular 2D polygons using 2D shape manipulatives. What do they notice is the same and different about the rules they create? Children could then be encouraged to discuss other concepts they could find rules for, such as the area of 2D shapes.

ANSWERS

Question **1** a): Perimeter of a regular pentagon:
$a + a + a + a + a = a \times 5 = 5a$
Perimeter of a regular hexagon:
$a + a + a + a + a + a = a \times 6 = 6a$

Question **1** b): When $a = 6$:
$5a = 5 \times 6 = 30$ cm
$6a = 6 \times 6 = 36$ cm
When $a = 12$:
$5a = 5 \times 12 = 60$ cm
$6a = 6 \times 12 = 72$ cm
Children should notice that when the value of a is doubled, the perimeter of each shape is also doubled.

Share

WAYS OF WORKING Whole class teacher led

ASK

- Question **1** a): *What do you think 'formula' means? What does 'a' represent in the formula? Could you represent the formula as a bar model? Did you create the same formulae? Explain how yours are similar or different.*
- Question **1** b): *What links did you find between the perimeters of the shapes? What can you explain about the pattern?*

IN FOCUS At this point in the lesson, it will be important to ensure children understand how a formula shows the relationship between two quantities. Encourage children to explain how a formula is different to the algebraic expressions they have been studying up until now.

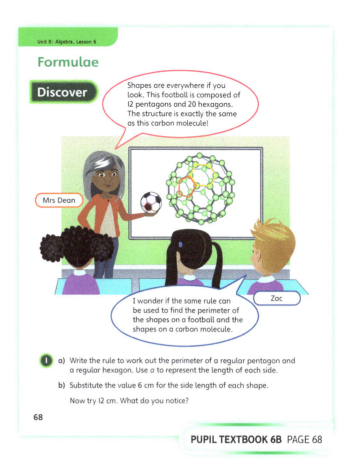

PUPIL TEXTBOOK 6B PAGE 68

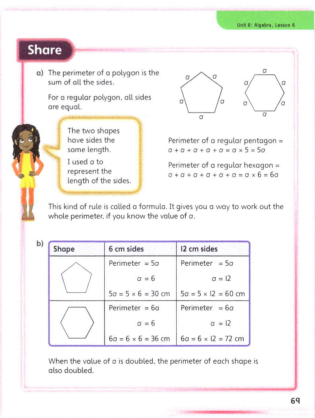

PUPIL TEXTBOOK 6B PAGE 69

Think together

Unit 8: Algebra, Lesson 6

Think together

WAYS OF WORKING Whole class teacher led (I do, We do, You do)

ASK

- Question **1** a): *Can you multiply the same number by 4 as there are four sides?*
- Question **1** b): *How will the calculation you create be similar and different to the formula?*
- Question **2**: *Do you need the picture of the rectangle to find the area if you have the formula?*
- Question **3** a): *Can you support your formulae with a pictorial representation?*

IN FOCUS Questions **1** and **2** secure children's understanding of how formulae can be used to generalise and find the properties of 2D shapes. Encourage children to recognise how a picture offers a specialised example of a concept, whereas a formula offers a generalised representation that covers all examples of the concept.

STRENGTHEN To help children convert the calculations into a general formula in question **3** a), ask: *What could you replace each number with to show it could represent any number? What letter will replace the 1? What letter will replace the other 1? Can your formula apply to the other calculations?*

DEEPEN When children are investigating formulae that can be reversed, as in questions **1**, **2** and **3** a), ask: *Why can these formulae be written either way round? Can you write a formula that can only be written in one way?*

ASSESSMENT CHECKPOINT Questions **1** and **2** assess children's ability to convert a mathematical calculation into a general formula, allowing them to apply it to other examples of the same concept. Look for children substituting numbers in a specific example with letters.

ANSWERS

Question **1** a): Perimeter = $a + b + a + b = 2a + 2b$
Children might also find the answer as $(a + b) \times 2$.

Question **1** b): Perimeter = $2 \times 10 + 2 \times 8 = 20 + 16 = 36$ m

Question **2** a): Area = $a \times b$

Question **2** b): Area of the shape = $7 \times 5 = 35$ cm^2

Question **3** a): Children should use a pair of letters, such as a and b, to write the equation $a + b = b + a$.

Question **3** b): Children use a pair of letters to write the equations:
$(a + b) \times c = a \times c + a \times b$
$a \times (b + c) = a \times b + a \times c$

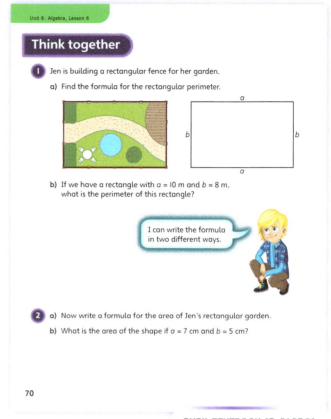

PUPIL TEXTBOOK 6B PAGE 70

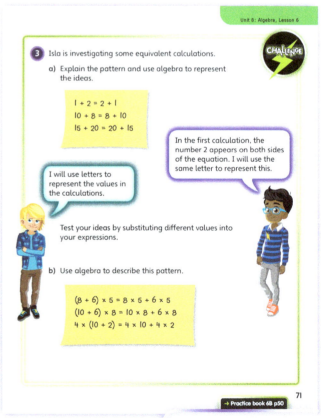

PUPIL TEXTBOOK 6B PAGE 71

Practice

WAYS OF WORKING Independent thinking

IN FOCUS Question ➊ links children's understanding of the properties of 2D shapes (in particular, perimeter) with their new understanding of creating formulae to represent number relationships. Question ➋ presents the formula for converting feet into inches and provides practice for using this.

STRENGTHEN To strengthen children's ability to find all the necessary information to solve question ➌, ask: *Does the question give you all the information you need to answer it? What is the problem with the units of measure used in the question? How many hours are in two days?*

DEEPEN When solving question ➎, challenge children to create their own similar patterns within a formula. Ask: *Can you generalise your pattern to the point where it is represented only by letters? Can you make similar patterns using division?*

THINK DIFFERENTLY Question ➍ challenges children's assumptions regarding how a formula might change in the context of two shapes being used to create a compound shape. While children solve this, ask: *How many 'a' sides are there if the two squares are joined? How will you label the new longer side on the rectangle? What is its relationship to side 'a' on the square? How many 'a' lengths are there on the new rectangle?*

ASSESSMENT CHECKPOINT Questions ➊ and ➋ assess children's ability to create simple formulae based on the perimeters of 2D shapes and measurement conversions. Look for children using their understanding of the algebraic notation for multiplication when writing their expressions. Question ➌ assesses children's ability to use algebraic formulae to prove their thinking. Review their explanations of how the formulae they have used demonstrate their ideas.

ANSWERS Answers for the **Practice** part of the lesson can be found in the *Power Maths* online subscription.

Reflect

WAYS OF WORKING Independent thinking

IN FOCUS This question offers a final opportunity to assess children's ability to create formulae that represent a mathematical concept. Children could also be challenged to draw their own 2D shape and create the formula that represents the perimeter of it.

ASSESSMENT CHECKPOINT Look for children creating the formula:
perimeter = 2x + y.

ANSWERS Answers for the **Reflect** part of the lesson can be found in the *Power Maths* online subscription.

After the lesson ⏸

- Are children confident creating simple formulae?
- Can children describe the difference between a formula and an expression?

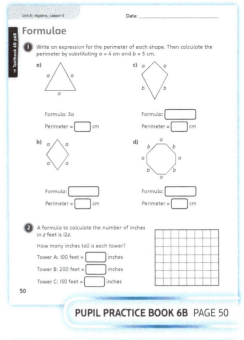

PUPIL PRACTICE BOOK 6B PAGE 50

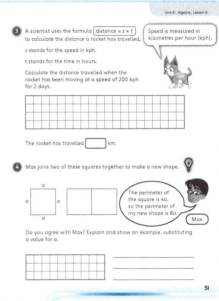

PUPIL PRACTICE BOOK 6B PAGE 51

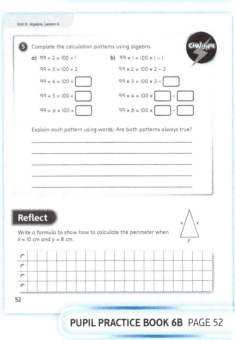

PUPIL PRACTICE BOOK 6B PAGE 52

Form and solve equations

Learning focus

In this lesson, children will read, understand and solve algebraic equations. They will represent equations in different ways and use these representations to support their reasoning.

Before you teach

- Are children confident about the difference between an expression and an equation?
- Do children realise that the key difference is that equations contain an equals sign, whilst expressions do not?

NATIONAL CURRICULUM LINKS

Year 6 Algebra

Express missing number problems algebraically.

ASSESSING MASTERY

Children can read and understand an algebraic equation. They can explain what the equation represents and show this in different ways. Children will be able to solve algebraic equations, fluently substituting letters for the correct numbers.

COMMON MISCONCEPTIONS

When solving equations such as $36 - v = 23$, children may solve the incorrect inverse calculation, calculating $23 + 36$ instead of $36 - 23$. Ask:

- *Can you show the original equation as a bar model? Can you use the bar model to explain what calculation you could use to find the missing number more efficiently?*

STRENGTHENING UNDERSTANDING

Children may benefit from being able to build bar models using manipulatives such as different numbers of multilink cubes, or printed paper versions of these. For an equation such as $160 = y + 75$, ask: *Can you draw the bar model? Which bar represents the 75? How could you turn the calculation around to find the missing number?*

GOING DEEPER

Children could draw bar models for equations that have more than one step. Ask: *What would the bar model be for $200 = 2y + 46$? Explain how you drew it.*

KEY LANGUAGE

In lesson: equation, unknown number

Other language to be used by the teacher: algebra, algebraic, calculate, calculation, operation, represent

STRUCTURES AND REPRESENTATIONS

Bar model, function machine

RESOURCES

Optional: multilink cubes (or printed versions)

 In the eTextbook of this lesson, you will find interactive links to a selection of teaching tools.

Quick recap

Ask children to work in pairs to solve these missing number calculations:

$2 + t = 11$

$100 - y = 45$

$p - 30 = 10$

$s \times 5 = 35$

Discover

WAYS OF WORKING Pair work

ASK

- Question **1** a): *Can you link the c in the equation to something in the picture?*
- Question **1** a): *What if there was a second item you did not know the price of? How would that change the equation?*
- Question **1** b): *What representation best suits this equation?*

IN FOCUS Question **1** a) leads children through their understanding of what the equation represents. While solving this question, encourage children to recognise the patterns in how each number affects the others in the equation, by investigating what happens if 80 is changed to another number, or if 230 is changed to another number. Question **1** b) offers children the opportunity to apply their previous learning to the current question.

PRACTICAL TIPS This concept could be linked to children's prior experience with missing number problems (such as 60 + ☐ = 100). Discuss how these two types of mathematical problem are similar and different. Encourage them to investigate whether it is possible to definitively solve an equation such as 80 + c + d = 230.

ANSWERS

Question **1** a): The *c* represents the cost of the kayak.
80 + *c* represents the total cost of the surfboard and the kayak.
80 + *c* = 230 means that the total cost of the surfboard and kayak is equal to £230.

Question **1** b): Several answers are possible. For example:
230 – 80 = 150.
The cost of the kayak is £150.

Share

WAYS OF WORKING Whole class teacher led

ASK

- Question **1** a): *Why does 80 + c represent the total cost of the two items? How is the equation different to a formula or expression?*
- Question **1** b): *How did you decide to record your representation of the equation? How is your method similar or different to those shown?*

IN FOCUS At this point in the lesson, children could develop their fluency with algebraic equations by writing their own using different operations. It will also be essential to discuss how using the inverse calculations can find the missing number more efficiently than trial and error.

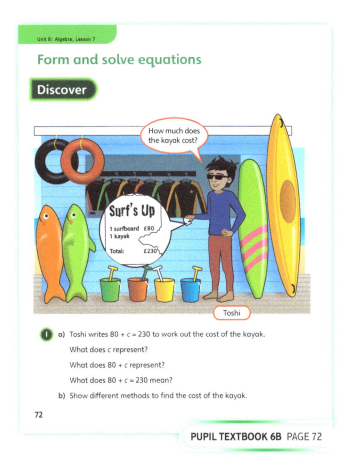

PUPIL TEXTBOOK 6B PAGE 72

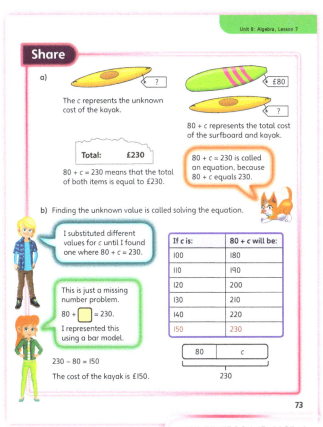

PUPIL TEXTBOOK 6B PAGE 73

Think together

Whole class teacher led (I do, We do, You do)

ASK

- Question **2**: *How does the bar model help to represent this equation? Why do you need to subtract in the equation? Use the question's story to prove your ideas.*
- Question **3**: *How could you represent each equation in a different way to help link it to a person more easily? Could any of the equations be linked to more than one person?*

IN FOCUS Questions **2** and **3** present children with equations that use operations not approached in the **Discover** section of the lesson. Discuss how the representations are similar and different to the addition seen in **Discover**.

STRENGTHEN To help children find the mystery numbers in question **3**, ask: *Which of the representations used so far could you use to help you find the mystery numbers? Is Ash's idea about drawing bar models a good one?*

DEEPEN Question **3** deepens children's understanding and reasoning around equations by giving them very similar looking equations that include different operations. Encourage children to show all the equations using the same type of pictorial representation and discuss what is the same and what is different about them to improve their fluency and understanding. Ask: *How has changing the operation changed your representation? Are the mystery numbers going to be the same?*

ASSESSMENT CHECKPOINT Question **2** assesses children's ability to solve an algebraic equation that includes subtraction. Look for children representing their thinking using bar models or a table of results and linking these to the context of the question and the equation itself. Question **3** assesses children's ability to solve algebraic equations which include any of the four operations. Look for children recognising how changing the operation used can change the solution of the equation and proving this using pictorial representations.

ANSWERS

Question **1**:

x	x + 25
1	26
2	27
5	30
6	31
7	32

Children should continue trying numbers to get to the correct result.

Question **2** a): $y - 35 = 85$
$y = 85 + 35 = £120$
The usual cost of the dinghy is £120.

Question **2** b): i) $s = 360 \div 3$
ii) $360 \div 3 = 120$
There are 120 wetsuits in 1 crate.

Question **3**: Kate: $\quad 9 + i = 45$
Alex: $\quad j - 9 = 45$
Richard: $\quad 45 = 9h$
Aki: $\quad 45 = k \div 9$

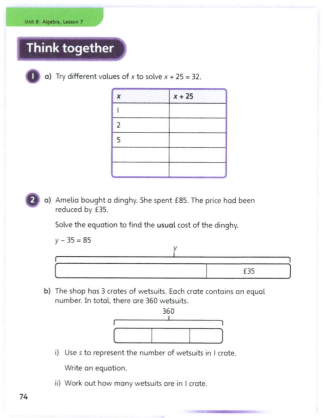

PUPIL TEXTBOOK 6B PAGE 74

PUPIL TEXTBOOK 6B PAGE 75

Practice

WAYS OF WORKING Independent thinking

IN FOCUS Question ② challenges children to solve a series of equations where the right-hand side is always the same but the unknown number (*a*) and the operation used are different each time. Ensure children understand that, even though the same letter is used in every equation and the right-hand side is always 15, the value of *a* is different each time.

STRENGTHEN To strengthen children's ability to solve the equations in question ③, ask: *Can you represent each equation using a picture? How does your picture help you find the inverse calculation to find the missing number?*

DEEPEN If children solve all four parts to question ⑤, they could deepen their understanding of each equation given by writing a real-life word problem. Ask: *Can you think of a real-life problem that would fit this equation?*

THINK DIFFERENTLY Question ④ focuses on the potential misconception of using the incorrect inverse operation to find an unknown number. Ask: *Can you represent the first equation using a bar model? Can you represent the inverse calculation Luis has created? What is the same and what is different about your models? Do they find the same number?*

ASSESSMENT CHECKPOINT Question ① assesses children's ability to substitute a given value into an algebraic expression, and then evaluate the expression. Look for children 'plugging' the given value of the variable into the expression confidently.

In question ②, look for children recognising that these are similar to missing number problems and solving them fluently as such.

Question ⑤ assesses children's ability to use their knowledge of inverse operations to create and solve an equation. Look for children recognising how to invert each operation to accurately find the missing number. They may use bar models to support their thinking.

ANSWERS Answers for the **Practice** part of the lesson can be found in the *Power Maths* online subscription.

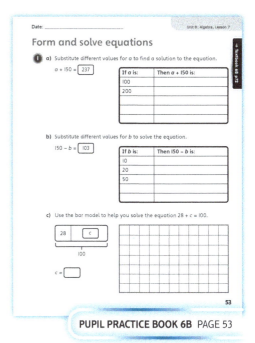

PUPIL PRACTICE BOOK 6B PAGE 53

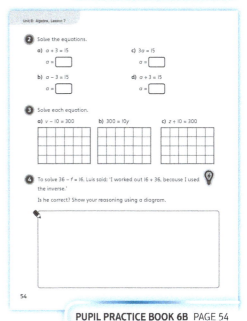

PUPIL PRACTICE BOOK 6B PAGE 54

Reflect

WAYS OF WORKING Independent thinking

IN FOCUS This question will offer an opportunity to make a final assessment of children's fluency and understanding of solving equations. Children may want to draw a bar model to represent the equation or create a table showing their possible solutions.

ASSESSMENT CHECKPOINT Look for children using one of the methods shown in the lesson. Children should be able to explain which of the methods they have chosen is more efficient at finding the missing number.

ANSWERS Answers for the **Reflect** part of the lesson can be found in the *Power Maths* online subscription.

After the lesson ⏸

- Can children accurately create an inverse calculation to find the missing number in an equation?

PUPIL PRACTICE BOOK 6B PAGE 55

Solve one-step equations

Learning focus

In this lesson, children will continue to develop their ability to solve equations, extending their understanding of using the inverse calculation to find the missing number in an equation.

Before you teach

- Do children already have some confidence in solving simple 1-step equations?

NATIONAL CURRICULUM LINKS

Year 6 Algebra

Express missing number problems algebraically.

ASSESSING MASTERY

Children can recognise and explain how to use the inverse calculation to that shown in an equation, to find an unknown number. Children can represent their thinking fluently using pictures and can use these pictures to support their reasoning.

COMMON MISCONCEPTIONS

When solving equations, such as $36 - z = 23$, children may solve the incorrect inverse calculation, finding $23 + 36$ instead of $36 - 23$. Ask:

- *Can you show the original equation as a bar model? Can you use the bar model to explain what calculation you could use to find the missing number more efficiently?*

STRENGTHENING UNDERSTANDING

Encourage children to investigate addition and subtraction using concrete manipulatives such as cubes and counters. For example, ask: *If I have 16 cubes and get 27 more, how many will I have? What if I start with 43 and take away 16? What if I subtract 27?* For each example, discuss how the calculations are linked and represent them using a bar model to link to this lesson.

GOING DEEPER

Challenge children to create equations for each other to solve. To develop their reasoning, ask: *What kinds of operation and what types of equation are more difficult to solve? What is the same and what is different about the most and least difficult equation you created?*

KEY LANGUAGE

In lesson: equation, missing number

Other language to be used by the teacher: inverse, algebra, algebraic

STRUCTURES AND REPRESENTATIONS

Bar model, balance model

RESOURCES

Optional: balance scales, weights, cubes, counters

 In the eTextbook of this lesson, you will find interactive links to a selection of teaching tools.

Quick recap

Ask children to draw diagrams to represent each of these equations:

$3a = 24$ $5 + b = 25$

Discover

WAYS OF WORKING Pair work

ASK

- Question **1** a): *What weights can you subtract from each side of the scale and still keep it balanced?*
- Question **1** a): *How does the balance scale help to show what calculation can be used to solve the equation?*
- Question **1** b): *What calculation can be used to solve the equation? How can you represent it?*

IN FOCUS Question **1** a) gives children a concrete opportunity to begin investigating how to use an inverse calculation to find a missing number in an algebraic equation. Once children have investigated the given scenario, they should be able to solve the equation in question **1** b). Encourage them to share their ideas and reasoning.

PRACTICAL TIPS Make this activity practical by using real weights and balance scales. Balance the scales using weights of your own. Turn one particular weight (which is different to all the others) away from children so they cannot see the mass written on the side. Children could investigate how to find the mystery weight. They might write an equation, or they might subtract other equal weights from both sides until the unknown weight is alone on one side of the equation. Children could then create and investigate their own similar equations, using weights on balance scales, and represent them as bar models and written equations.

ANSWERS

Question **1** a): The mystery weight is 6 kg.
Finding the mystery weight means you can replace the h in $h + 36 = 42$ with 6 to solve the equation.

Question **1** b): $h + 36 = 42$
$h = 42 - 36$
$h = 6$

Share

WAYS OF WORKING Whole class teacher led

ASK

- Question **1** a): *What weights did you subtract first? How heavy did you think the h weight was?*
- Question **1** b): *How is this equation similar and different to the one used in question **1** a)? Can you explain why the two questions have the same answer? How did you choose to represent the equation? How is your representation similar and different to the bar model shown?*

IN FOCUS It is important to give children the opportunity to develop their fluency and flexibility with using inverse operations to find missing numbers. Give them different equations and encourage them to investigate how they can be manipulated by swapping the numbers, as shown in questions **1** a) and **1** b). Children could investigate whether this has a similar result if carried out with equations that use the other three operations.

Unit 9: Algebra, Lesson 8

Solve one-step equations

Discover

You must both remove a weight from each side, but it must stay balanced.
Keep going until only the mystery weight remains on the left side.

Mr Jones

1 a) What is the mystery weight?
Explain how knowing this helps you solve the equation $h + 36 = 42$.

b) Solve the equation $36 + h = 42$.

76

PUPIL TEXTBOOK 6B PAGE 76

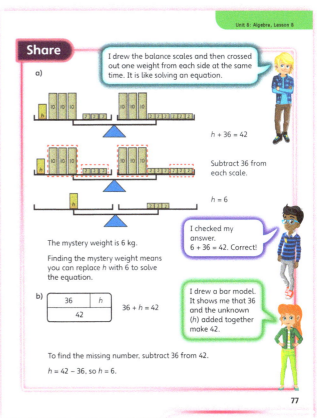

Unit 8: Algebra, Lesson 8

Share

a)

I drew the balance scales and then crossed out one weight from each side at the same time. It is like solving an equation.

$h + 36 = 42$

Subtract 36 from each scale.

$h = 6$

The mystery weight is 6 kg.

Finding the mystery weight means you can replace h with 6 to solve the equation.

I checked my answer.
6 + 36 = 42. Correct!

b)

36	h
42	

$36 + h = 42$

I drew a bar model. It shows me that 36 and the unknown (h) added together make 42.

To find the missing number, subtract 36 from 42.

$h = 42 - 36$, so $h = 6$.

77

PUPIL TEXTBOOK 6B PAGE 77

Think together

WAYS OF WORKING Whole class teacher led (I do, We do, You do)

ASK

• Question ❶: *Which weights are the same and which are different on the balance model? What will you do with the weights that are the same on the balance model?*
• Question ❷: *Can you explain how the bar models make the equations clear?*
• Question ❸ a): *Can you write an equation to represent each bar model?*
• Question ❸ b): *Can you draw a bar model for each of the equations?*

IN FOCUS Question ❶ gives children another opportunity to investigate solving equations through the context of balance scales. Question ❶ b) is particularly useful as it helps children recognise how other operations, in this case multiplication, can be represented through this context. While solving these questions, remind children how they could represent each equation with a bar model.

STRENGTHEN To help children solve the equations in question ❷, ask: *What is the inverse operation of that shown in the equation? How can this help you solve the equation? Can you link the inverse operation to the bar model shown?*

DEEPEN Question ❸ deepens children's reasoning about bar models by offering two similar models as possible representations of an equation. Ask: *Can you write a real-life problem that would represent the equation shown by each bar model? How are the two problems similar and different?*

ASSESSMENT CHECKPOINT Question ❶ assesses children's ability to solve equations that include addition and multiplication. Look for children recognising that, since there are three *a* weights, each of these must be the same as they are represented by the same letter; therefore one side of the equation is 3*a*. Question ❸ b) assesses children's fluency when solving equations.

ANSWERS

Question ❶ a): $y = 240 - 48 = 192$

Question ❶ b): $600 = 3a$

Question ❷ a): $t + 6 = 24$
$t = 24 - 6$
$t = 18$

Question ❷ b): $24 = 6m$
$m = 24 \div 6$
$m = 4$

Question ❸ a): The second bar model helps to solve the equation $n - 10 = 36$.
The first bar model shows $n + 10 = 36$.
$n - 10 = 36$
$n = 36 + 10$
$n = 46$

Question ❸ b): $y + 10 = 25$ $k - 10 = 25$
$y = 15$ $k = 35$
$10 + g = 25$ $25 - h = 10$
$g = 15$ $h = 15$
$5a = 30$ $4b = 600$
$a = 6$ $b = 150$

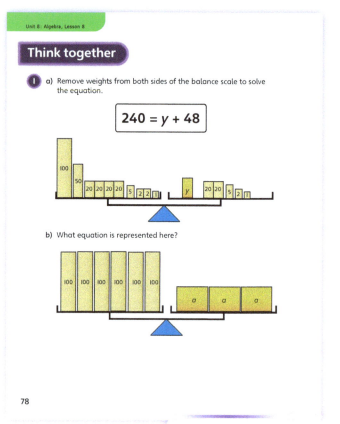

PUPIL TEXTBOOK 6B PAGE 78

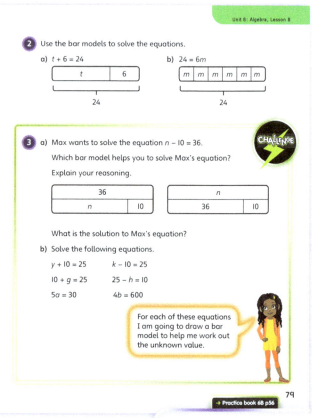

PUPIL TEXTBOOK 6B PAGE 79

Practice

WAYS OF WORKING Independent thinking

IN FOCUS Question ❶ is important as it presents children with an opportunity to develop their independent understanding of the pictorial representations of algebraic equations. In questions ❶ a) and b), encourage children to cross out the weights on either side until only the difference remains. In question ❸, discuss whether each equation could be represented with a balance model, a bar model, or both.

STRENGTHEN To strengthen children's ability to link the representations and equations in question ❷, ask: *What inverse operations would you use to help you find the missing number in each of these equations? What pictures can you see that represent these operations?*

DEEPEN Question ❹ deepens children's fluency and problem solving around equations. Ask: *Is it possible to create six different equations using the same three numbers? What is the highest number of equations you can create using the same three numbers? How does this number change if you always use the same two operations?*

ASSESSMENT CHECKPOINT Questions ❶ and ❷ assess children's ability to link pictorial representations with algebraic equations. Look for children reasoning confidently, using the pictorial representations to support their solutions to the equations. Question ❸ assesses children's ability to solve abstract equations. They may choose to use pictorial representations to support their solutions.

ANSWERS Answers for the **Practice** part of the lesson can be found in the *Power Maths* online subscription.

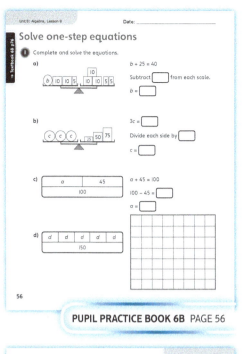

PUPIL PRACTICE BOOK 6B PAGE 56

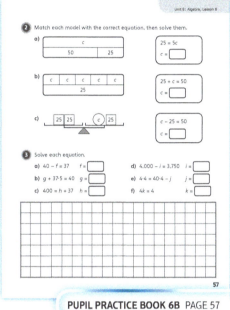

PUPIL PRACTICE BOOK 6B PAGE 57

Reflect

WAYS OF WORKING Pair work

IN FOCUS When solving this question, encourage children to compare their diagram with a partner's. Discuss how the diagrams are the same and how they are different.

ASSESSMENT CHECKPOINT Look for children representing the equation shown using either a bar model or a balance model. Children should also be able to give the linked inverse equation that will find the missing number.

ANSWERS Answers for the **Reflect** part of the lesson can be found in the *Power Maths* online subscription.

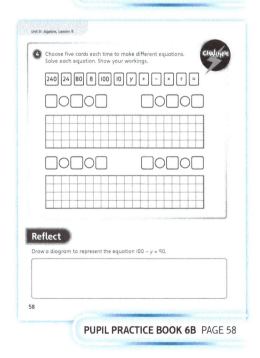

PUPIL PRACTICE BOOK 6B PAGE 58

After the lesson

- How confident are children at recognising how a balance model can be used to find an unknown number in an equation?
- Are children confident solving abstract equations?

Solve two-step equations

Learning focus

In this lesson, children will develop their ability to create algebraic equations based on contextual word problems. They will use this to find missing numbers in 2-step equations.

Before you teach

- Are children confident solving 1-step equations using balance models and bar models?
- What concrete resources could you use in this lesson to help them solve 2-step equations?

NATIONAL CURRICULUM LINKS

Year 6 Algebra

Express missing number problems algebraically.

ASSESSING MASTERY

Children can fluently read and understand a contextual word problem and, from it, can create a 2-step equation to solve it. They can then use this equation to find the solution to the problem.

COMMON MISCONCEPTIONS

Children may assume that, having written the equation that represents a word problem, they have found the calculation they can use to calculate the missing number, forgetting they need to solve the inverse of the equation. Ask:

- *Is it possible to solve the calculations shown in the equation? Explain how you will manipulate this equation so that you can find the missing number.*

STRENGTHENING UNDERSTANDING

Children may benefit from being given extra opportunities to explore finding inverse operations to solve algebraic equations in different contexts. For example, children could investigate arrays for multiplication and division.

GOING DEEPER

Challenge children to create real-life word problems for each other to solve. To develop their reasoning, ask: *What equation represents your word problem? Can you write a word problem that requires three calculations?*

KEY LANGUAGE

In lesson: equation

Other language to be used by the teacher: algebra, algebraic, calculation, calculate, unknown number

STRUCTURES AND REPRESENTATIONS

Bar model

RESOURCES

Optional: cubes, blocks, counters

 In the eTextbook of this lesson, you will find interactive links to a selection of teaching tools.

Quick recap

Ask children to solve these equations:

$3a = 24$

$5 + b = 25$

$20 - c = 10$

Discover

WAYS OF WORKING Pair work

ASK

- Question ① a): *What operations will be included in the equation? How could you represent this using a model? Is there more than one type of model you could use?*
- Question ① b): *How will you use your equation from question ① a) to work this out? What will you do first?*
- Question ① b): *What would the outcome have been if Lee's starting number was 8? What would Lee's starting number have been if the outcome was 23?*

IN FOCUS Question ① a) encourages children to begin considering how the problem can be represented as an algebraic equation. Children should develop this idea using pictorial representations such as the bar model and balance model, which they used in the previous lesson. When solving question ① b), encourage children to investigate what happens to the final number when the starting number is increased or decreased by 1. They could also investigate whether there is the same effect on the starting number when the output number is increased or decreased by 1.

PRACTICAL TIPS Once children have discussed how Kate managed to discover Lee's original number, encourage them to have a go at this for themselves. Ask children to list two calculations they will ask a partner to carry out on a number. Before carrying out the task, encourage children to write down the inverse calculations they will use to find the original number.

ANSWERS

Question ① a): $2a + 5 = 19$

Question ① b): Lee's number was 7.

Share

WAYS OF WORKING Whole class teacher led

ASK

- Question ① a): *Did you create the same equation? How was yours similar and different to the one shown?*
- Question ① a): *How did you use your equation to solve the problem? Is there only one solution to this problem?*
- Question ① b): *Did you use the balance model to represent the problem? Can you explain how the bar model shows this problem?*

IN FOCUS It is important to make sure children can recognise that, while finding the algebraic equation helps them to visualise and represent what is happening in the contextual problem, it does not solve it. Encourage children to notice how the equation needs inverting to enable them to find the missing number. Give them the opportunity to investigate how to invert different equations using all four operations.

PUPIL TEXTBOOK 6B PAGE 80

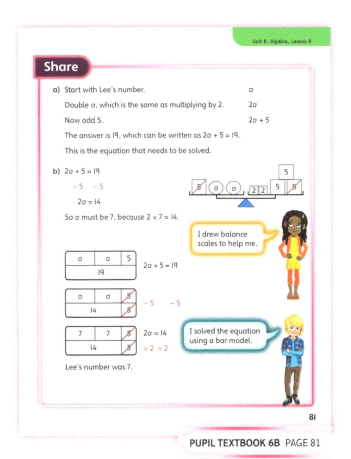

PUPIL TEXTBOOK 6B PAGE 81

Think together

WAYS OF WORKING Whole class teacher led (I do, We do, You do)

ASK

• Question ❶: *How can you tell which number needs to be subtracted? How will the bar model change once you have subtracted 4?*
• Question ❷: *How else can you represent these equations pictorially? Which pictorial representation works best and why?*
• Question ❸: *Is p more or less than 11? How do you know? What is the same and what is different about the two bar models?*

IN FOCUS Question ❶ shows a bar model as a representation of an equation. It would be beneficial to encourage children to also draw the balance model while solving this question. Children should use these visual representations when solving question ❷.

STRENGTHEN To help children solve the equations in question ❷, ask: *Can you draw this equation as a balance model? What can you do to both sides to remove one of the calculations, while keeping both sides balanced?*

DEEPEN Question ❸ a) challenges children to describe how a bar model represents a given 1-step equation. In question ❸ c), a second step with a different operation is added to the equation. Deepen children's thinking around this by asking them to write their own linked 1- and 2-step equations, and to represent them with bar models and balance models. Ask: *How does your representation change? How does the value of the missing number change?*

ASSESSMENT CHECKPOINT Question ❶ assesses children's awareness of how to keep an equation balanced as they work to find the missing number. Look for children making sure they carry out the same calculation on each side of the equation. Question ❷ assesses children's ability to solve an equation. Look for children independently identifying calculations they can use to negate parts of the equation, leaving only the number the letter represents.

ANSWERS

Question ❶: Lexi's number is 5.

Question ❷ a): $m = 11$

Question ❷ b): $q = 6$

Question ❸ a): The bar model shows that $p = 11 + 3$.
This can be rearranged as $p - 3 = 11$ because they are part of the same fact family.

Question ❸ b): $p - 3 = 11$
$p = 14$

Question ❸ c): This bar model shows that $2p = 11 + 3$.
This can be rearranged as $2p - 3 = 11$ because they are part of the same fact family.

Question ❸ d): $2p - 3 = 11$
$2p = 14$
$p = 7$

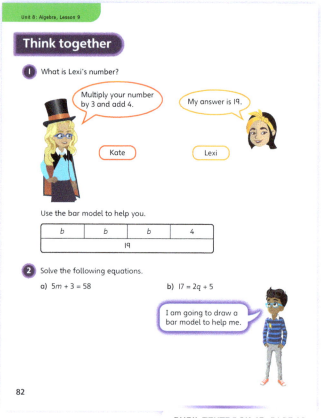

PUPIL TEXTBOOK 6B PAGE 82

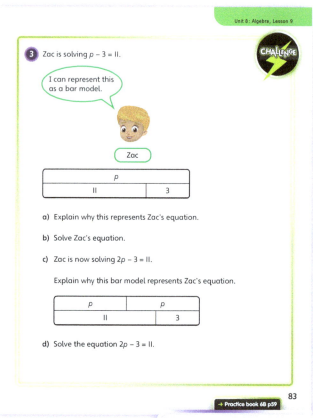

PUPIL TEXTBOOK 6B PAGE 83

Practice

Independent thinking

IN FOCUS Questions ❶, ❷ and ❸ give children the opportunity to work independently with the different models used to represent algebraic equations. In question ❷, encourage children to draw each equation using a different model.

STRENGTHEN To strengthen children's ability to create an equation to represent question ❹, ask: *Can you act out and talk through the story in the problem? Can you use your retelling to draw a bar model? How would you represent the bar model with an equation?*

DEEPEN While solving question ❺, deepen children's understanding and reasoning by asking: *In how many different ways can you represent each equation? Can you write a real-life word problem that fits each equation?*

THINK DIFFERENTLY Question ❸ explores the common error of solving only one part of a two-part equation. Children should observe that Olivia has correctly found the total on each side of the balance scale but has forgotten to divide 75 by 3 to find y.

ASSESSMENT CHECKPOINT Questions ❹, ❺ and ❻ assess children's ability to solve equations both abstractly and in contextual word problems. Look for children's organisation of their calculations and their independent choices regarding any pictorial representations they wish to use.

ANSWERS Answers for the **Practice** part of the lesson can be found in the *Power Maths* online subscription.

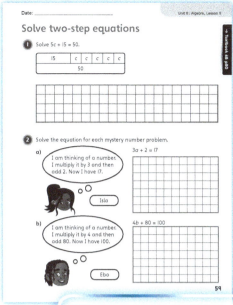

PUPIL PRACTICE BOOK 6B PAGE 59

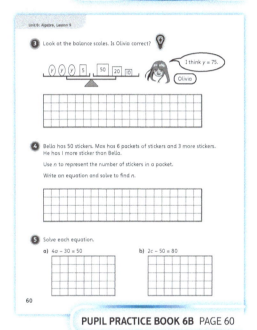

PUPIL PRACTICE BOOK 6B PAGE 60

Reflect

Independent thinking

IN FOCUS This question will offer a final opportunity to assess whether children can link algebraic equations with the bar model. It will also assess whether children are confident with the difference between the two 5s in the equation.

ASSESSMENT CHECKPOINT Look for children's confident use of the bar model to represent the equation.

ANSWERS Answers for the **Reflect** part of the lesson can be found in the *Power Maths* online subscription.

After the lesson ⏸

- Are children equally confident with abstract equations and equations in real-life contexts?
- How can you implement this learning in other areas of the curriculum?

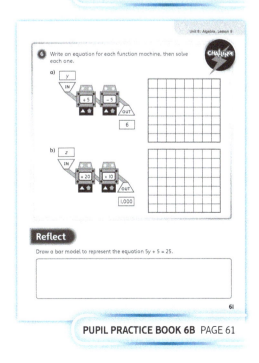

PUPIL PRACTICE BOOK 6B PAGE 61

Find pairs of values

Learning focus

In this lesson, children will use their understanding of creating algebraic equations to create equations they can use to find all solutions to a given problem with two missing values.

Before you teach

- Are children confident in recognising that some algebraic equations can have more than one solution?
- How will you support children who are more concerned about finding one 'right answer'?

NATIONAL CURRICULUM LINKS

Year 6 Algebra

Find pairs of numbers that satisfy an equation with two unknowns.

ASSESSING MASTERY

Children can read and understand a problem with two missing values and create an algebraic equation to represent it. They can recognise when a problem may have more than one solution and can use an algebraic equation to find all the possible solutions.

COMMON MISCONCEPTIONS

Children may think they do not have enough information to solve an equation where two values are missing, such $c + d = 10$. Although children cannot find one answer in these cases, encourage them that they need to look for pairs of numbers which satisfy the equation. Ask:

- *What if c represented 1? What would d mean in that case? What other numbers could c represent? How would that affect the value of d?*

STRENGTHENING UNDERSTANDING

If children find it challenging to accept that a mathematical problem may have more than one solution, give them opportunities to work with problems where there are multiple solutions, without needing to find equations to solve them.

GOING DEEPER

Encourage children to write their own word problems that have more than one solution for a pair of values. Ask: *What equation will solve your problem?*

KEY LANGUAGE

In lesson: solution, equation, formula

Other language to be used by the teacher: algebra, algebraic

STRUCTURES AND REPRESENTATIONS

Bar model, 2D rectilinear shapes, balance model

RESOURCES

Mandatory: counters

 In the eTextbook of this lesson, you will find interactive links to a selection of teaching tools.

Quick recap

Challenge children to find more than three different ways to complete this missing number problem:

$a + 99 = b$

Discover

Find pairs of values

Discover

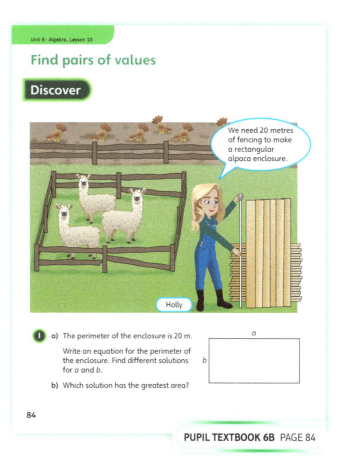

We need 20 metres of fencing to make a rectangular alpaca enclosure.

Holly

1 a) The perimeter of the enclosure is 20 m.

Write an equation for the perimeter of the enclosure. Find different solutions for a and b.

b) Which solution has the greatest area?

84

WAYS OF WORKING Pair work

ASK

• Question **1** a): *What is the same and what is different about each side of a rectangle? How could you represent these similarities and differences algebraically?*
• Question **1** b): *What algebraic formula will find the area of a rectilinear shape? Can you find the area of each possible rectangle?*

IN FOCUS Question **1** a) offers children the opportunity to begin investigating the sequence of numbers that can be created within the given parameters of the question. In questions **1** a) and **1** b), encourage children to record their findings in different ways. For example, using pictures to show the different-shaped enclosures and a table to write the abstract calculations and solutions.

PRACTICAL TIPS Encourage children to apply their understanding of 2D shapes and investigate how the equation would change if the shape of the enclosure was a pentagon. Following this line of enquiry, encourage children to create their own question with a different shape of enclosure and an appropriate number for the perimeter.

ANSWERS

Question **1** a): The perimeter is $2a + 2b$ or $(a + b) \times 2$.

Perimeter of rectangle	$a = ?$	$b = ?$
20	1	9
20	2	8
20	3	7
20	4	6
20	5	5
20	6	4

Question **1** b): Area is $a \times b$

The greatest area for the enclosure is $5 \text{ m} \times 5 \text{ m} = 25 \text{ m}^2$.

Share

Share

a)

I know the formula for the perimeter is $2a + 2b$ or $(a + b) \times 2$.

So $a + b$ must be equal to 10.

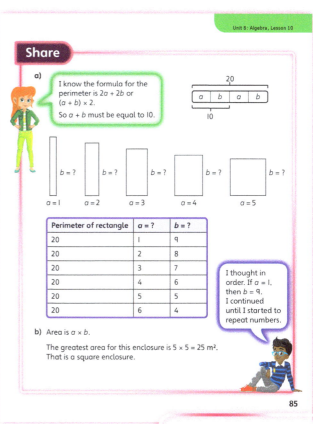

$b = ?$ $a = 1$

$b = ?$ $a = 2$

$b = ?$ $a = 3$

$b = ?$ $a = 4$

$b = ?$ $a = 5$

Perimeter of rectangle	$a = ?$	$b = ?$
20	1	9
20	2	8
20	3	7
20	4	6
20	5	5
20	6	4

I thought in order. If $a = 1$, then $b = 9$. I continued until I started to repeat numbers.

b) Area is $a \times b$.

The greatest area for this enclosure is $5 \times 5 = 25 \text{ m}^2$. That is a square enclosure.

85

WAYS OF WORKING Whole class teacher led

ASK

• Question **1** a): *Does your equation match the one given here? How is it the same? How is it different?*
• Question **1** b): *How did you find the area of each rectangle? Is a square always the shape with the largest area for a certain perimeter? How did you make sure you had found all the possible solutions?*

IN FOCUS Discuss Ash's comment and encourage children to notice that, in the context of the question, the results are not repeating. While the numbers inside the abstract calculations are repeating, the rectangles the numbers produce will be different. Discuss whether this is important or not and whether a 6 × 4 rectangle is different to a 4 × 6 rectangle.

Think together

WAYS OF WORKING Whole class teacher led (I do, We do, You do)

ASK

- Question **1** and **2**: *How many solutions do you predict this equation could have?*
- Question **3** b): *Can you explain why the pattern you have found in the coordinates is made?*

IN FOCUS For question **1**, encourage children to organise their findings logically to ensure they have found all the possible solutions. For question **2**, encourage children to consider why this equation has fewer possible solutions than the equation with addition as its operation. Children could investigate how the number of solutions would be different if it was $y + z = 36$. For question **3** a), encourage children to show their solutions on the grid using counters.

STRENGTHEN If children are struggling to find all the coordinates in question **3**, ask: *How could you use a table to organise your results? How can you use the table to make sure you have found all the possible solutions?*

DEEPEN When children have solved question **3**, encourage them to investigate whether there are other patterns they can create on a grid using an equation they have written to find the x and y coordinates. Ask: *Can you create an equation that will find coordinates that create a zig-zag line on the grid?*

ASSESSMENT CHECKPOINT Questions **1** and **2** assess children's ability to create equations that find multiple solutions for a single problem with two missing values. Look for children's fluent explanation of how their equation is able to find all possible results. Question **3** assesses children's ability to create equations that present solutions in ways that are very different to those they have experienced before. Look for children's ability to reason by applying their prior understanding to the new context.

ANSWERS

Question **1**:
Other values for m may be used, up to $m = 15$, $n = 0$.

$m = ?$	$n = ?$
0	15 – 0 = 15
1	15 – 1 = 14
2	15 – 2 = 13
3	15 – 3 = 12
4	15 – 4 = 11
5	15 – 5 = 10

Question **2**:
$y \times z = 36$

$y = ?$	$z = ?$
1	36
2	18
3	12
4	9
6	6

Question **3** a): There are multiple possible answers (see supplementary answer sheet). Children should notice that if they plot the values on the grid, they form a straight line.

Question **3** b): There are multiple possible answers (see supplementary answer sheet). Children should notice that if they plot the values on the grid, they form a straight line.

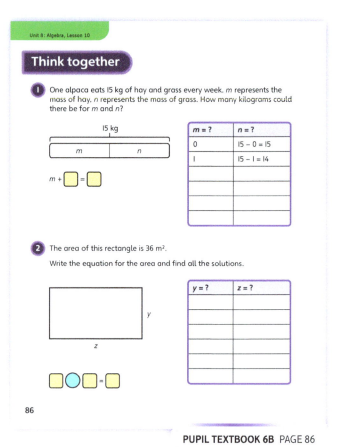

PUPIL TEXTBOOK 6B PAGE 86

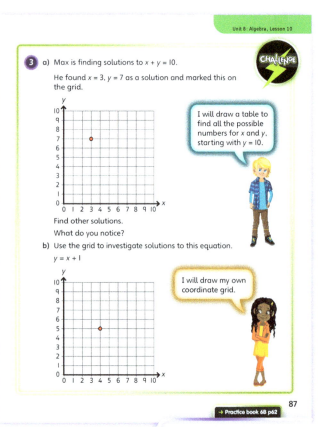

PUPIL TEXTBOOK 6B PAGE 87

Practice

WAYS OF WORKING Independent thinking

IN FOCUS Questions **1** and **2** help develop children's independent understanding of finding multiple solutions, using representations that children have used in their prior learning. Encourage children to use the structures and representations shown in these questions to support their reasoning in question **3**.

STRENGTHEN To strengthen children's ability to plot the points on the grid in question **4**, ask: *How can you use a table to make sure you have found all possible solutions? What is the same and what is different about the points the different equations find on the grid?*

DEEPEN Once children have found the solutions to question **5**, encourage them to create a similar question for a partner. Ask: *Is it more challenging to use odd or even numbers?*

ASSESSMENT CHECKPOINT Questions **1** and **2** assess children's independent ability to solve an equation and record and organise their results. Look for children organising their results logically to ensure they have found all potential solutions. Question **4** assesses children's ability to recognise patterns in the solutions of equations. Look for children accurately placing the points on the grid and discussing the similarities and differences between them.

ANSWERS Answers for the **Practice** part of the lesson can be found in the *Power Maths* online subscription.

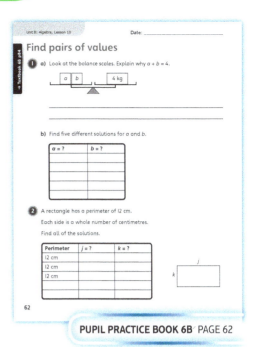

PUPIL PRACTICE BOOK 6B PAGE 62

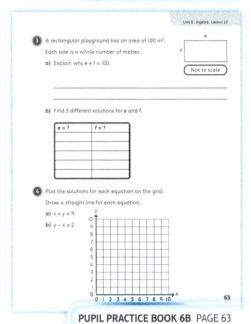

PUPIL PRACTICE BOOK 6B PAGE 63

Reflect

WAYS OF WORKING Independent thinking

IN FOCUS This question will offer the opportunity to assess children's fluency and reasoning around finding all solutions to an equation. Once children have written their explanations, encourage them to share their ideas with a partner and discuss how they are the same and different to each other.

ASSESSMENT CHECKPOINT Look for children explaining how to identify the equation needed to solve a problem and how to then find, record and organise the solutions. Children should be able to explain what method they have used to ensure they have found every possible solution.

ANSWERS Answers for the **Reflect** part of the lesson can be found in the *Power Maths* online subscription.

After the lesson ⏸

- Are children able to fluently and reliably find all the solutions to an equation with two missing values?
- Can children explain how they knew they had found every solution?

PUPIL PRACTICE BOOK 6B PAGE 64

Solve problems with two unknowns

Learning focus

In this lesson, children will continue to develop their ability to find all possible solutions to a given problem, this time including more than one variable, representing their solutions with algebraic equations.

Before you teach

- Are there any children who will find the idea of 'more than one solution' for equations with 2 unknowns difficult to accept?

NATIONAL CURRICULUM LINKS

Year 6 Algebra

Enumerate possibilities of combinations of two variables.

Find pairs of numbers that satisfy an equation with two unknowns.

ASSESSING MASTERY

Children can read and understand a problem with more than one variable and create an algebraic equation to represent it. They can recognise when a problem may have more than one solution and can use an algebraic equation to find all the possible solutions.

COMMON MISCONCEPTIONS

Children may, when finding multiple solutions to a problem, find solutions that do not work within the context of the question posed; they may insist these are working solutions because they fit the equation. Ask:
- *What would your solution look like if you applied it to the story question? Could your solution really work in the story?*

STRENGTHENING UNDERSTANDING

Some children may find it challenging to record their thinking in a structured way and efficiently enough, so that they still have time to find all the solutions to an equation. It may help to provide printed tables for these children to fill in, without needing to draw them. For example:

If ___ =	Then ___ =

GOING DEEPER

Children could write their own word problems that can be turned into an equation with multiple solutions. Ask: *Can you create a story problem that has more than one solution? How can you make your story problem more challenging or simpler? What can you change?*

KEY LANGUAGE

In lesson: solution, equation, value

Other language to be used by the teacher: algebra, algebraic

STRUCTURES AND REPRESENTATIONS

Bar model

RESOURCES

Optional: printed tables, coins

 In the eTextbook of this lesson, you will find interactive links to a selection of teaching tools.

Quick recap

Challenge children to find all the possible solutions for this equation, where *a* and *b* are both whole numbers:

$2a + b = 10$

Discover

Pair work

ASK

- Question **1** a): *How many solutions do you predict there are to this problem? How will you make sure you have found all the solutions? What equation can be used to solve this problem?*
- Question **1** b): *What will be similar about every number of chickens' legs?*
- Question **1** b): *Is there any number of chickens that would mean a number of rabbits could not work?*

IN FOCUS Question **1** a) is important as it links the problem shown with children's learning from the previous lesson. Encourage children to write their findings in a structured and organised way, considering how they will know when they have found all possible solutions. Question **1** b) encourages children to see how their understanding of number can be used to help them check their solutions for examples that will not fit the parameters of the problem. In this instance, the remaining number of rabbits' legs needs to be a multiple of 4.

PRACTICAL TIPS Encourage children to change the question using different animals to influence the numbers that are used in the problem. For example, children could investigate how the equation would change if they were using spiders and ants instead of rabbits and chickens.

ANSWERS

Question **1** a): $2a + 4y = 10$. The possible solutions are:
1 chicken, 2 rabbits; 3 chickens, 1 rabbit.

Question **1** b): There cannot be 2 or 4 chickens in the shelter, because this would mean there would have to be half a rabbit.
2 chickens = 4 legs, leaving 6 rabbit legs, and 4 chickens = 8 legs, leaving 2 rabbit legs.

Share

Whole class teacher led

ASK

- Question **1** a): *How many solutions did you find?*
- Question **1** a): *What equation found the possible solutions? Was there only one possible equation?*
- Question **1** b): *Is there a pattern to the solutions that are not possible? Could you use this pattern to predict all impossible combinations?*

IN FOCUS If children have not already investigated how different numbers of legs will change and influence the solutions, it will be important to do this now to help develop their fluency. Encourage children to recognise the patterns in the solutions, which ones are and are not possible, and whether this pattern is still evident when the numbers being used change.

PUPIL TEXTBOOK 6B PAGE 88

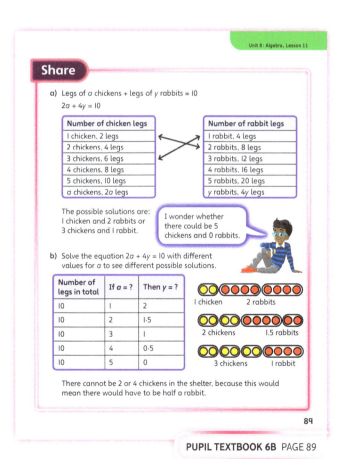

PUPIL TEXTBOOK 6B PAGE 89

Think together

WAYS OF WORKING Whole class teacher led (I do, We do, You do)

ASK

- Question **1**: *In terms of* m, *what is the total number of people sitting at tables of 6? Why? In terms of* n, *what is the total number of people sitting at tables of 4?*
- Question **2**: *Can you write an equation that represents this problem?*
- Question **3**: *How can you record and organise your solutions to be sure you have found them all?*

IN FOCUS In question **1**, help children to understand that the unknowns *m* and *n* represent the number of *tables*, not the number of *people* at a table. They already know that there are *m* tables of 6 people, so the total number of people sitting at tables of 6 is 6*m*. Likewise, the total number of people sitting at tables of 4 is 4*n*. The sum of these must be equal to 30, as the class needs 30 seats.

STRENGTHEN Question **2** challenges children with an equation that has many possible solutions. To help children find the correct one efficiently, ask: *Have you spotted a pattern in the results to the equation? Can you use this pattern to predict which equations you do not need to work out?*

DEEPEN Once children have solved question **3**, challenge them to give each equation a contextual word problem. Ask: *Can you write two linked story problems for the linked equations in question* **3** *a)?*

ASSESSMENT CHECKPOINT Question **1** assesses children's ability to represent the solutions to an equation both pictorially and abstractly. Look for children recognising where a solution does not fit the context of the problem (i.e. you cannot have half a table) and assess their fluency when explaining why. Question **2** assesses children's ability to work through a more abstract word problem with no pictorial support available. Look for children finding ways to solve the problem efficiently, by recognising the number patterns that begin to emerge as they find the first few solutions.

ANSWERS

Question **1**: 6*m* + 4*n* = 30. Possible solutions in the table:
 m = 1, *n* = 6; *m* = 3, *n* = 3; *m* = 5, *n* = 0.
 m = 2 leaves 18 which is not divisible by 4.
 m = 4 leaves 6 which is not divisible by 4.
 30 is not divisible by 4, so there cannot be only tables of 4.

Question **2**: There are 23 chickens and 12 rabbits in total.

Question **3** a): There are multiple possible answers.

Question **3** b): *d* + 30 = *y* − 70
 y is always 100 more than *d*.
 20*s* = 100 − 2*t*
 As the value of *s* increases by 1, the value of *t* decreases by 10.

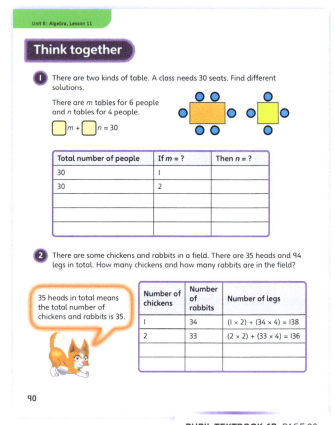

PUPIL TEXTBOOK 6B PAGE 90

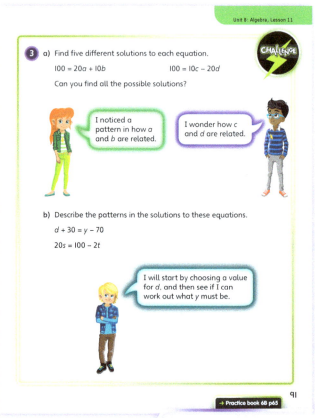

PUPIL TEXTBOOK 6B PAGE 91

Practice

WAYS OF WORKING Independent thinking

IN FOCUS Questions ❶ and ❷ challenge children to find solutions for problems that are based in contexts they will recognise from their own real-life experiences. Encourage children to write down the equation that will help them find the solutions to each of the problems given. Question ❹ is important as it challenges children to distinguish between solutions that work from those that do not work, within the given parameters of the question. Encourage children to share their reasoning as to why they have not included every iteration in the pattern of results and to justify their explanation with proof.

STRENGTHEN To strengthen children's ability to find the solutions in questions ❶, ❷ and ❸, ask: *Can you draw the problem? Can you use your drawing to create a bar model that represents the problem? Can you use your bar model to create an equation?*

DEEPEN Question ❺ uses more challenging number facts that rely on children's prior learning to enable them to find a working equation and its solutions. Ask: *Would the solutions be the same if Bella and Danny had added three of each kind of number together? How would the solutions be similar and different to those found with two numbers?*

ASSESSMENT CHECKPOINT Questions ❶, ❷ and ❸ assess children's ability to apply their understanding of equations and multiple solutions to different contexts. Look for children representing their working out using the models they have studied, for example, a bar model or a table listing the potential solutions. Children should also be able to explain fluently when they have found all the solutions and how they know.

ANSWERS Answers for the **Practice** part of the lesson can be found in the *Power Maths* online subscription.

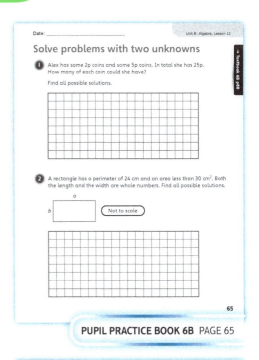

PUPIL PRACTICE BOOK 6B PAGE 65

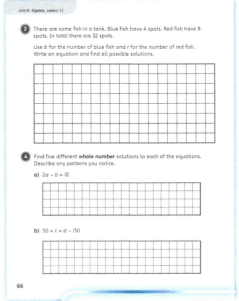

PUPIL PRACTICE BOOK 6B PAGE 66

Reflect

WAYS OF WORKING Independent thinking and pair work

IN FOCUS This question offers a good opportunity to assess children's understanding of the concept of equations with multiple solutions. This could also be used as an opportunity to assess their problem-solving and reasoning by asking children to swap their equations with a partner. Ask: *Does the equation work? If not, can you give advice on how to edit and improve it? Can you find at least four solutions to your partner's equation?*

ASSESSMENT CHECKPOINT Look for children reliably and fluently creating a working equation that has the potential for more than three solutions. Children may want to represent their thinking with a bar model first. If so, encourage them to explain how their bar model and equation are linked.

ANSWERS Answers for the **Reflect** part of the lesson can be found in the *Power Maths* online subscription.

After the lesson ⏸

- What was the most successful representation you used in this lesson? Why did it work so well?
- Have children mastered the concept of finding an equation that has multiple solutions?

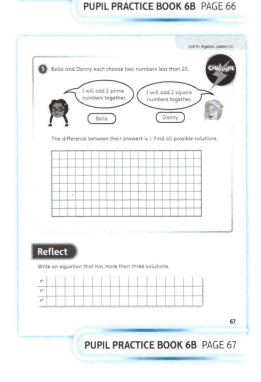

PUPIL PRACTICE BOOK 6B PAGE 67

End of unit check

> **Don't forget the unit assessment grid in your *Power Maths* online subscription.**

WAYS OF WORKING Group work adult led

IN FOCUS

- Question **1** assesses children's understanding of algebraic notation and their ability to read and understand an algebraic expression.
- Question **2** assesses children's ability to convert the representation of a function machine into an algebraic expression.
- Question **3** assesses children's ability to substitute a letter in an algebraic expression for a given number and use this to find the number the expression represents.
- Question **4** assesses children's ability to recognise an algebraic equation when represented as a bar model.
- Question **5** assesses children's ability to solve an algebraic equation.
- Question **6** is a SATs-style question, which assesses children's ability to find an unknown number in a 2-step equation that is represented as a bar model.
- Question **7** assesses children's ability to find different possible solutions to an equation with two variables.

ANSWERS AND COMMENTARY

Children will demonstrate mastery in this unit by recognising the mathematical calculation needed to find values for a concept, in the case of question **1** the number of wheels on a tricycle, and will be able to express these reliably as algebraic formulae. Children will be able to read, understand, write and solve one- and two-step algebraic equations, reliably finding an unknown number, and will be able to represent these through algebraic notation.

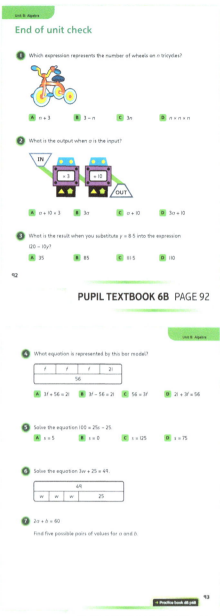

PUPIL TEXTBOOK 6B PAGE 92

PUPIL TEXTBOOK 6B PAGE 93

Q	A	WRONG ANSWERS AND MISCONCEPTIONS	STRENGTHENING UNDERSTANDING
1	C	A suggests that children have mistakenly interpreted the expression as saying each bike has 'plus 3' wheels.	**Balancing equations to find an unknown number:** Present the problem using the balance model. Ask: • *What can you take from both sides of the balance model and still keep the equation balanced?*
2	D	A suggests children have inverted the order of operations shown on the function machines.	
3	A	C indicates children have not multiplied 8·5 by 10.	**Creating algebraic expressions:** Help children to convert function machines into algebraic expressions. Ask:
4	D	A, B or C indicate children are unsure how to read, understand and use the bar model.	• *What does the first function machine do to the unknown number? How will the second function machine affect your expression?*
5	A	C indicates children haven't found the factor pair for 25 that would create 125, only substituted 25s with 125.	• Look for children using a table to find all possible values of *a* and *b*. They should be able to explain why *a* cannot be more than 30 and why *b* cannot be more than 60.
6	*w* = 8	Look for children relating the information in the bar model to the steps in the equation.	
7	A	Various answers are possible. *a* should be a number between 0 and 30.	

My journal

WAYS OF WORKING   Independent thinking

ANSWERS AND COMMENTARY

Children should be able to recognise the bar models as showing the equations:

- $3a + 5 = 20$
- $5b = 17 + 8$

Children should be able to confidently write a story problem that creates and represents a situation for each equation. To help children convert the bar models to equations, ask:

- *If you have three of the same letter, what expression can you use to represent this?*
- *How can you tell how much 5b is equal to? Explain how the bar model shows this.*

For children struggling to convert the equations into story problems, ask:

- *What if the numbers represented amounts of money?*
- *Could you create a 'Guess your number' magician story with these equations?*

Power check

WAYS OF WORKING   Independent thinking

ASK

- *How confident are you at representing a problem algebraically?*
- *Can you describe how to generalise a problem to help find many solutions?*
- *Can you explain how to keep an equation balanced?*

Power puzzle

WAYS OF WORKING   Pair work

IN FOCUS   Use this **Power puzzle** to challenge children's reasoning and problem-solving strategies. Children should be able to suggest a systematic method for finding and recording the rectangles within the grid. If they are struggling to begin, ask:

- *Has Flo identified all the types of rectangle that are shown in the grid?*
- *What other rectangles can you find?*
- *How will you make sure you have found all the examples of each type of rectangle?*

ANSWERS AND COMMENTARY   Children should find that there are 100 rectangles, including the squares, and 70 rectangles not including the squares. If children find any other number it is likely that they have miscounted, perhaps by losing track of which rectangles they have already counted. If this is the case, offer support on how to work systematically through problems such as this.

After the unit ⏸

- How has this unit developed children's ability to generalise mathematical concepts?
- What other mathematical concepts, beyond those met in the unit, could you apply these skills of generalisation to?

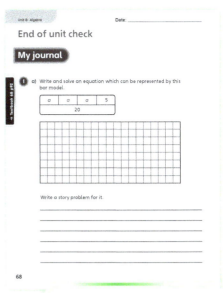

PUPIL PRACTICE BOOK 6B PAGE 68

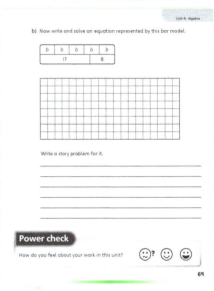

PUPIL PRACTICE BOOK 6B PAGE 69

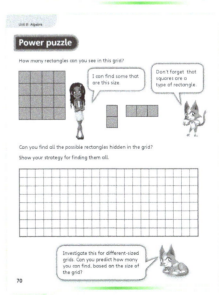

PUPIL PRACTICE BOOK 6B PAGE 70

Strengthen and **Deepen** activities for this unit can be found in the *Power Maths* online subscription.

Unit 9
Decimals

Don't forget to watch the Unit 9 video!

Mastery Expert tip! 'Understanding place value in decimals is vital to calculating, comparing and converting with decimals. Visual and practical representations of the number have helped me to reinforce this, but it is also important to consistently refer to the value of each digit so that children are able to reason about the numbers they are working with, as well as finding the answers to the calculations.'

WHY THIS UNIT IS IMPORTANT

In this unit, children will draw on their understanding of number and place value in order to calculate with decimals. They will learn to round, add and subtract numbers with up to 3 decimal places; multiply and divide decimals by multiples of 10, 100 and 1,000; multiply and divide decimals by whole numbers; and convert between fractions and decimals. The learning from this unit will support children's understanding of how decimals and fractions are related.

WHERE THIS UNIT FITS

→ Unit 8: Algebra

→ **Unit 9: Decimals**

→ Unit 10: Percentages

This unit builds on children's understanding of decimals and fractions as part of a whole and applies learning about multiplication and division methods to working with decimals.

Before they start this unit, it is expected that children:
- know how to multiply and divide whole numbers by powers of 10
- understand place value of decimals up to 2 decimal places
- know that decimals and fractions are ways of expressing a part of a whole.

ASSESSING MASTERY

Children will work confidently with decimals and explain the value of each digit. They will apply their knowledge of multiplication and division, including formal methods, in the context of decimals. Children will understand that decimals are a way of representing a part of a whole and will relate this to fractions. They will be able to convert fractions to decimals using division and recognise an increasing number of fraction or decimal equivalents.

COMMON MISCONCEPTIONS	STRENGTHENING UNDERSTANDING	GOING DEEPER
When multiplying and dividing decimals, children may fail to add necessary '0' placeholders, or fail to omit 0s at the end that are not needed.	Support children in exchanging with base 10 equipment. Use 1,000s block to represent 1, 100s blocks to represent tenths, 10s blocks to represent hundredths and 1s blocks to represent thousandths.	Explore area with decimals. Pose problems such as *find the area of a rectangle with sides 2.3 cm by 3 cm*. How could children work that out? Could they work out the answer in cm²? Can they work it out in mm²? Can they see a pattern to convert cm² to mm²?
Children may incorrectly compare numbers with different decimal places, for example, 0·5 < 0·48, by applying the idea that the more digits there are in a number, the larger it is.	The use of place value grids will help children to identify the value of each digit in a decimal number.	Ask children to make two numbers less than 1, a smaller number with 3 decimal places and a bigger number with 1 decimal place. Who can make the greatest difference between their numbers?

Unit 9: Decimals

UNIT STARTER PAGES

Use the unit starter pages of the **Textbook** to introduce the focus of the lessons. Use the characters to explore the vocabulary from the unit and to discuss the models being used.

STRUCTURES AND REPRESENTATIONS

Place value grid: This model can be used with counters or digits to demonstrate the value of each digit and to show exchanges taking place between columns.

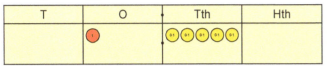

T	O		Tth	Hth
	●		ⓞ ⓞ ⓞ ⓞ ⓞ	

T	O		Tth	Hth
	1		5	

Bar model: This model can be used to visually represent division calculations. It can also be used with a number line to represent equivalence.

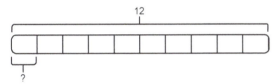

Number line: This model can be used to represent multiplication as repeated addition. It can also be used with a bar model to represent equivalence.

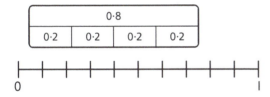

Short division: This model can be used to represent a fraction as division and to express a remainder as a decimal.

$$0 \cdot 3\ 7\ 5$$
$$8\overline{\smash{\big)}\,3 \cdot {}^3 0\ {}^6 0\ {}^4 0}$$

KEY LANGUAGE

There is some key language that children will need to know as part of the learning in this unit.

➜ multiply (×), divide (÷)

➜ decimal, recurring decimal, decimal place (dp), round

➜ placeholder

➜ place value, tenths, hundredths, thousandths

➜ factor, multiple, product

➜ group, share

➜ numerator, denominator

➜ convert, simplify, equivalent

➜ divisor, dividend, quotient, remainder

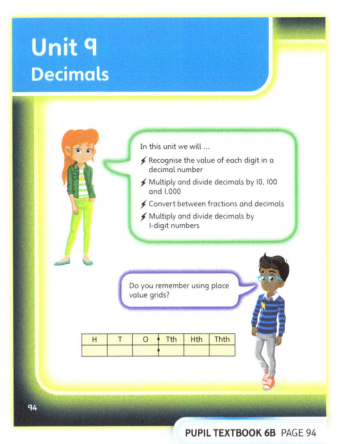

PUPIL TEXTBOOK 6B PAGE 94

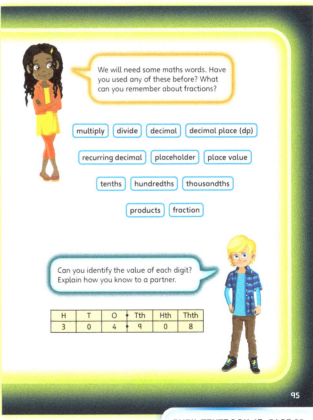

PUPIL TEXTBOOK 6B PAGE 95

131

Place value to 3 decimal places

Learning focus

In this lesson, children rehearse the place value of numbers, including decimals with tenths, hundredths and thousandths.

Before you teach

- Can children read and write decimal numbers accurately?
- Can children describe the link between simple decimals (such as 0·1 or 0·01) and fractions?

NATIONAL CURRICULUM LINKS

Year 6 Number – fractions (including decimals and percentages)

Identify the value of each digit in numbers given to three decimal places and multiply and divide numbers by 10, 100 and 1,000 giving answers up to three decimal places.

Solve problems which require answers to be rounded to specified degrees of accuracy.

ASSESSING MASTERY

Children can partition a given number into its component place value parts, and can recombine to find the whole.

COMMON MISCONCEPTIONS

Children may misunderstand the place value in numbers that have a placeholder 0, for example thinking that 7·06 partitions into 7 and 0·6. Ask:
- *What is the value of each digit in this number? What is the place value of the 0 in 7·06?*

STRENGTHENING UNDERSTANDING

Children can work with place value equipment to support their thinking and justify their decisions about the value of the digits in each number they encounter.

GOING DEEPER

Children can explore the place value of the digits in numbers that have more than one 0 as placeholders, for example, 20·002.

KEY LANGUAGE

In lesson: place value, decimal place, digit, tenth, hundredth, thousandth, part, whole, partition

Other language to be used by the teacher: column, value

STRUCTURES AND REPRESENTATIONS

Place value grid, part-whole model

RESOURCES

Mandatory: place value grids, counters, place value equipment

 In the eTextbook of this lesson, you will find interactive links to a selection of teaching tools.

Quick recap

Ask children to write the following decimals as fractions:

0·1	0·01	0·001
0·2	0·02	0·002

Discover

Pair work

ASK

- Question **1** a): *What do you notice about the two place value grids?*
- Question **1** a): *If you copy these numbers using your own place value grids, how many counters will you need?*
- Question **1** b): *Is the value of the digit '7' always just 7?*
- Question **1** b): *Can you write another number where the digit '7' has a value of 0·07?*

IN FOCUS Children use counters on place value grids to explore and compare the value of digits in two given numbers. One of the numbers has 1 decimal place and the other has 2 decimal places. However, the number with 1 decimal place also has counters in the tens and the ones columns and the number with 2 decimal places has a placeholder 0 in the ones column.

PRACTICAL TIPS Children should use counters on place value grids or other place value equipment to recreate each of the numbers in the question and to support their thinking when identifying the value of each digit. Draw their attention to the heading of each place value column.

ANSWERS

Question **1** a): Reena has made the number 0·37.
Andy has made the number 61·7.

Question **1** b): The value of the digit '7' is 7 hundredths in Reena's number.
The value of the digit '7' is 7 tenths in Andy's number.

Share

Whole class teacher led

ASK

- Question **1** a): *Why does Reena's number have '0' before the decimal place?*
- Question **1** a): *How do you say each of these numbers?*
- Question **1** b): *Why is the value of the digit '7' different in each of these numbers?*
- Question **1** b): *Can you write another decimal number that has a digit '7' in it?*

IN FOCUS Both of the numbers on the grids in this scenario have a digit '7', but crucially each 7 has a different place value. Discuss how children can identify the place value of each 7. Look at the position of the seven counters in each grid, focussing in particular on the column headings of each place value grid.

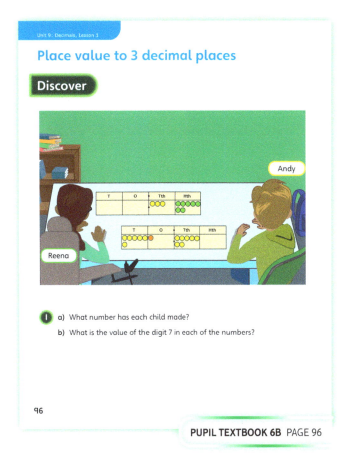

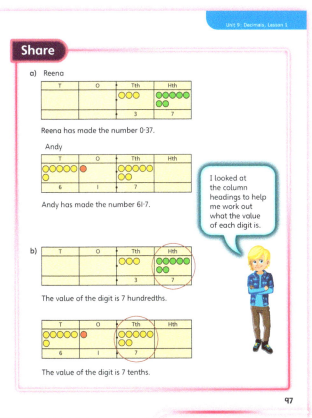

Think together

WAYS OF WORKING Whole class teacher led (I do, We do, You do)

ASK

- Question **1**: *What number is represented in a column that has no counters in it?*
- Question **2**: *What is new in this place value grid that you have not seen in previous questions?*
- Question **3**: *What might be confusing about the value of '7' in the number 2·107?*

IN FOCUS Question **1** uses place value grids to explore basic place value from 10s to hundredths. Children consider the fact that the '5' digit has a different value in each number. Question **2** works with place value up to thousandths and prompts children to investigate the role of placeholder 0s. Question **3** introduces the part-whole model to partition decimal numbers into their place value parts. Children also recombine partitioned numbers to find the whole. Children should recognise that the '0' in 2·107 means that there are zero hundredths, and the '7' is seven thousandths.

STRENGTHEN Encourage children to use counters on place value grids to copy and rehearse the numbers in each question. They can then transfer their counters to part-whole models to partition.

DEEPEN Ask: *What decimal numbers can you make using exactly five counters?* Challenge children to find as many different numbers as they can.

ASSESSMENT CHECKPOINT Question **2** assesses whether children can work with place value in a number with 3 decimal places and also with a placeholder 0.

ANSWERS

Question **1** a): 0·25
3·57
15·7

Question **1** b): The value of the digit '5' in each number is:
5 hundredths
5 tenths
5 ones

Question **2**: Emma is incorrect. She has made the number 0·307.

Question **3** a):

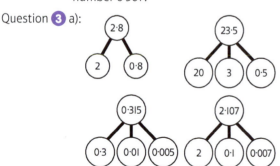

Question **3** b): 0·3 + 0·08 = 0·38
7 + 0·3 + 0·06 = 7·36
6 + 0·02 + 0·004 = 6·024

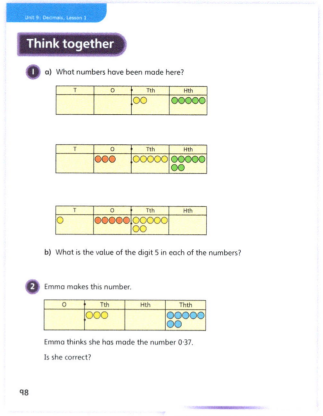

PUPIL TEXTBOOK 6B PAGE 98

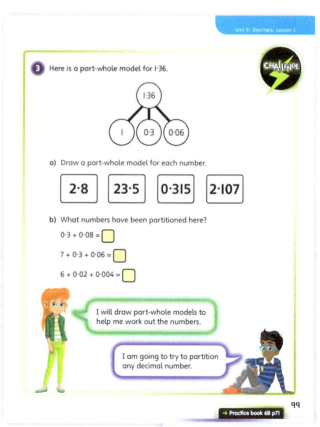

PUPIL TEXTBOOK 6B PAGE 99

Practice

WAYS OF WORKING Independent thinking

IN FOCUS Question **1** requires children to write decimal numbers that are shown with counters on place value grids, whereas in question **2**, children draw their own counters to construct given numbers.
In question **3**, children identify the value of a given digit in numbers with up to 3 decimal places.

Question **4** asks children to use the part-whole model to partition decimals into their place value parts and, in question **5**, they express partitioning as addition sentences.

Question **6** challenges children to consider the effect of an increase or decrease in one of the place value columns.

STRENGTHEN From question **3** onwards, supporting images of place value grids are not provided. Children should use counters on their own place value grids alongside these questions, explaining how they will make each number and what this represents.

DEEPEN Play 'I am thinking of a number'. Choose a mystery number with up to 3 decimal places that children try to identify. Allow them to ask yes/no questions only. For example, *Is there a 6 in the tenths column?*

ASSESSMENT CHECKPOINT Use question **3** to assess whether children can identify the place value of a specified digit in any written number with up to 3 decimal places.

ANSWERS Answers for the **Practice** part of the lesson can be found in the *Power Maths* online subscription.

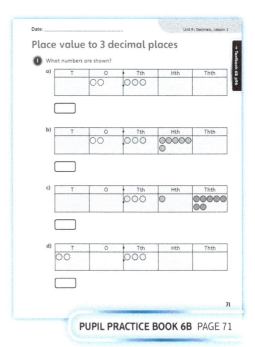

PUPIL PRACTICE BOOK 6B PAGE 71

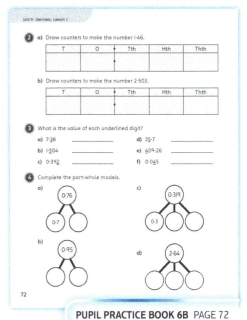

PUPIL PRACTICE BOOK 6B PAGE 72

Reflect

WAYS OF WORKING Pair work

IN FOCUS The **Reflect** part of the lesson prompts children to consider their own learning about decimals, in the context of this lesson. Look for children demonstrating an understanding of the place value in numbers that include tenths, hundredths and thousandths.

ASSESSMENT CHECKPOINT Assess whether children can accurately use key vocabulary to describe the main points from this lesson. For example, place value, decimal place, digit, tenth, hundredth, thousandth and partition.

ANSWERS Answers for the **Reflect** part of the lesson can be found in the *Power Maths* online subscription.

After the lesson ⏸

- Were children able to read and write numbers including decimals?
- Did children understand how to use the part-whole model to partition decimal numbers?

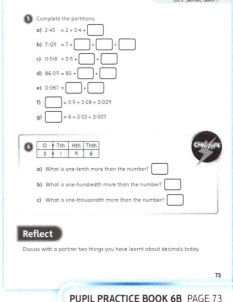

PUPIL PRACTICE BOOK 6B PAGE 73

Round decimals

Learning focus

In this lesson, children will round decimals to the nearest whole number and then to the nearest tenth or hundredth.

Before you teach ⏸

- Can children read and write decimal numbers and explain how to partition them by place value?
- Can children draw number lines to show the position of decimals in the linear number system?

NATIONAL CURRICULUM LINKS

Year 6 Number – fractions (including decimals and percentages)

Identify the value of each digit in numbers given to three decimal places and multiply and divide numbers by 10, 100 and 1,000 giving answers up to three decimal places.

Solve problems which require answers to be rounded to specified degrees of accuracy.

ASSESSING MASTERY

Children can round numbers to 1 or 2 decimals places, identifying when to round up and when to round down.

COMMON MISCONCEPTIONS

Children may ignore any digits that are to the left of the decimal place and not understand why they are important when rounding with decimals. Ask:

- *What whole number is this decimal near? How do you know?*

STRENGTHENING UNDERSTANDING

Give children opportunities to build strength in using number lines to locate decimal numbers. Draw number lines and ask children to estimate the position of given decimals.

GOING DEEPER

Challenge children to investigate which numbers round to a whole number, when rounding to the nearest tenth or hundredth. For example, 3·99 rounded to the nearest tenth is 4·0.

KEY LANGUAGE

In lesson: round, nearest, round up, whole number, decimal, decimal place, tenth, hundredth

Other language to be used by the teacher: half-way, greater, equal, between, digit

STRUCTURES AND REPRESENTATIONS

Number line

RESOURCES

Optional: tape measures, metre rulers, place value grids, number lines

 In the eTextbook of this lesson, you will find interactive links to a selection of teaching tools.

Quick recap

Challenge children to round the number 9,592 to the nearest 10, to the nearest 100 and to the nearest 1,000.

Discuss the methods that they used.

Discover

WAYS OF WORKING Pair work

ASK

- Question **1** a): *Can you explain the markings on the ruler?*
- Question **1** a): *Can you think of more than one way to work out the exact measurement?*
- Question **1** b): *Look at the length of the jump. What whole numbers does it fall between?*
- Question **1** b): *How do you know if it is closer to 2 metres or 3 metres?*

IN FOCUS This scenario introduces basic rounding with decimals. Children start by identifying a number with 1 decimal place and then consider how it can be rounded to the nearest whole number.

PRACTICAL TIPS Safely try out this activity as part of a PE lesson. Use real tape measures or metre rulers to measure and collect information about children's own long jumps. Place a marker to show the jump of the athlete in the **Discover** question. Point out that the tape measure looks like a number line and discuss how this can be used to round each jump to the nearest whole number of metres.

ANSWERS

Question **1** a): The athlete has jumped 2·8 m.

Question **1** b): 2·8 m to the nearest whole metre is 3 m.

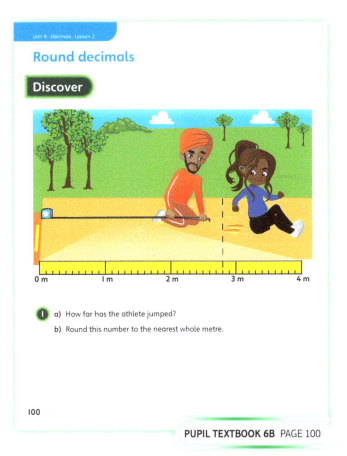

PUPIL TEXTBOOK 6B PAGE 100

Share

WAYS OF WORKING Whole class teacher led

ASK

- Question **1** a): *What would you say to help someone who thought the jump was 2·08 metres?*
- Question **1** a): *Can you show this jump on your own number line?*
- Question **1** b): *How can you justify the decision to round the jump to 3 metres?*
- Question **1** b): *Why does this number line now also show 2·5?*

IN FOCUS Children explore what information is needed in order to round a decimal to the nearest whole number. Agree that you first need to identify which two whole numbers the decimal is between and then you need to decide whether to round up or down. Look together at Sparks' comment and refer children to the number line. Agree that this number is more than half-way and so it should be rounded up.

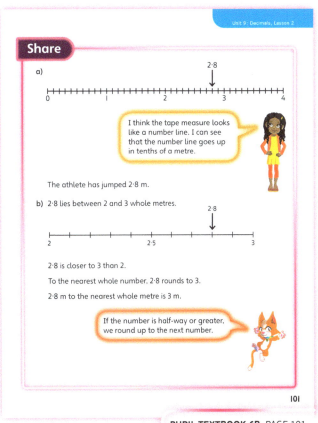

PUPIL TEXTBOOK 6B PAGE 101

Think together

WAYS OF WORKING Whole class teacher led (I do, We do, You do)

ASK

- Question **1**: *How can you estimate the position of each number on the number line? How accurate can you be?*
- Question **2**: *How would you explain what Jamie should do?*
- Question **3**: *How do you use the digits in a number to help you round to the nearest 10, 100 or 1,000? How could that thinking help you here?*

IN FOCUS In question **1**, children round decimals with up to 3 decimal places to the nearest whole number. In question **2**, they explore a misconception about how to round to 1 decimal place and, in question **3**, they consider possible methods for rounding to 1 or 2 decimal places.

STRENGTHEN Ask children to draw their own number lines and to use these to locate the decimals given in each question. This will build strength in representing decimals in the linear number system.

DEEPEN Challenge children to discuss and explain the similarities and differences between estimating, approximating and rounding.

ASSESSMENT CHECKPOINT Use question **3** to assess whether children can make links between their understanding of place value and their thinking about rounding decimals.

ANSWERS

Question **1** a): 6·2 rounds to 6.

Question **1** b): 6·75 rounds to 7.

Question **1** c): 6·5 rounds to 7.

Question **1** d): 6·415 rounds to 6.

Question **2** a): Jamie has rounded to the nearest whole number instead of to 1 decimal place.

Question **2** b): 3·3

Question **3** a): 4·37 rounds to 4·4.
16·14 rounds to 16·1.
5·349 rounds to 5·3.

Question **3** b): Children should explain that they look at the thousandths digit to round to 2 decimal places. 8 > 5, so 8·158 rounds up to 8·16.

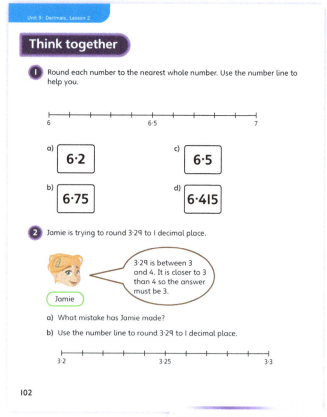

PUPIL TEXTBOOK 6B PAGE 102

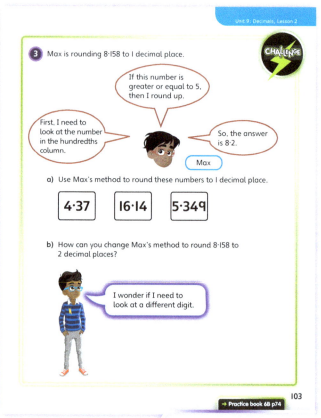

PUPIL TEXTBOOK 6B PAGE 103

Practice

WAYS OF WORKING Pair work

IN FOCUS In question ❶, children use number lines to help them round decimals to the nearest whole number. They then apply this with numbers that are not shown on a number line. In question ❷, number lines once again provide scaffolding, this time rounding numbers to 1 decimal place.

Question ❸ requires children to complete a table showing numbers rounded to different degrees of accuracy. They progress from rounding a given number to a whole number to then rounding the same number to 1 decimal place.

In question ❹, children round numbers to 2 decimal places and in question ❻, they explore possible ranges in rounding problems. In both instances, no scaffolding or visual representations are provided.

STRENGTHEN Children can explore ranges when rounding by using the number lines in question ❶ and ❷ to practise finding which numbers will round up and which will round down.

DEEPEN Ask children to discuss the use of rounding in the context of measures. For example, they can make estimates and approximations about the length, capacity or mass of different items.

THINK DIFFERENTLY In question ❺, children are shown a common misconception where a number with 2 decimal places is rounded based on the number of tenths rather than the total number of hundredths. This is presented as a plausible approach described in a logical way, however children should identify that it results in an incorrect answer. A number line can help to model this.

ASSESSMENT CHECKPOINT Use the table in question ❸ to assess whether children can use their understanding of place value to round numbers to different levels of accuracy.

ANSWERS Answers for the **Practice** part of the lesson can be found in the *Power Maths* online subscription.

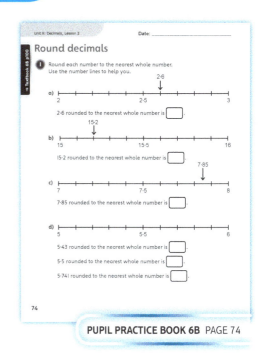

PUPIL PRACTICE BOOK 6B PAGE 74

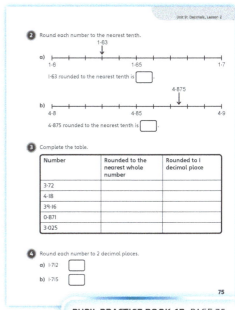

PUPIL PRACTICE BOOK 6B PAGE 75

Reflect

WAYS OF WORKING Pair work

IN FOCUS The **Reflect** part of the lesson prompts children to explore a possible misconception about which digit or digits you need to look at when rounding a decimal to the nearest whole number.

ASSESSMENT CHECKPOINT Assess whether children can suggest helpful and accurate advice about how to apply an understanding of place value when rounding a decimal.

ANSWERS Answers for the **Reflect** part of the lesson can be found in the *Power Maths* online subscription.

After the lesson ⏸

- Can children round decimals to different degrees of accuracy?
- Did children understand why the number line is a helpful model to use when rounding?

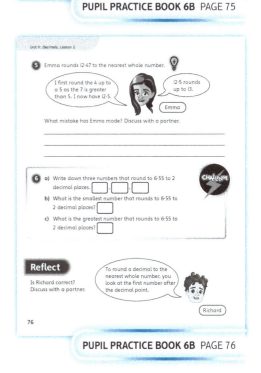

PUPIL PRACTICE BOOK 6B PAGE 76

Add and subtract decimals

Learning focus

In this lesson, children will revise and rehearse written methods for the addition and subtraction of decimals.

Before you teach

- Can children explain the place value of each digit in a number, including decimals?
- Can children accurately read and write decimal numbers with up to 3 decimal places?

NATIONAL CURRICULUM LINKS

Year 6 Number – fractions (including decimals and percentages)

Solve problems which require answers to be rounded to specified degrees of accuracy.

ASSESSING MASTERY

Children can accurately choose and use written methods to add or subtract decimal numbers when appropriate.

COMMON MISCONCEPTIONS

Children may not line up the digits correctly when setting out a written method of addition or subtraction with decimals. Ask:
- *Can you show these numbers on a place value grid? Does this look the same as or different to your written calculation? Why is it important to line up the decimal points?*

STRENGTHENING UNDERSTANDING

Focus on developing these addition and subtraction skills with decimals as an extension of children's existing fluency and arithmetic skills when working with whole numbers.

GOING DEEPER

Regularly give children opportunities to consider whether a mental method or a written method would be more suitable or efficient for a given calculation. For example, it is appropriate for the calculation $2·5 - 0·9$ to be solved using a mental method.

KEY LANGUAGE

In lesson: add, subtract, decimal, how much?, difference

Other language to be used by the teacher: method, calculation, number sentence, place value, tenth, hundredth, thousandth, column

STRUCTURES AND REPRESENTATIONS

Place value equipment, column methods

RESOURCES

Optional: place value equipment, measuring jugs

 In the eTextbook of this lesson, you will find interactive links to a selection of teaching tools.

Quick recap

Ask children to complete each of these calculations using a written method:

$2,354 - 236$ $598 + 3,772$

Discover

WAYS OF WORKING Pair work

ASK

- Question ❶ a): *What would be a good approximate answer? Could you use rounding to help you?*
- Question ❶ a): *How would you set out this calculation?*
- Question ❶ b): *What operations will you need to use?*
- Question ❶ b): *What will you need to do first? What will you need to do next?*

IN FOCUS This scenario shows a practical situation where it will be useful to add and subtract decimals in the context of measures in litres. The numbers involved have 2 decimal places and children may find they cannot easily add or subtract them using mental methods. Support them in concluding that written methods would be more appropriate here.

PRACTICAL TIPS Consider using real measuring jugs to represent these amounts of water. Then ask children to use place value equipment to make each number. Make links between this place value representation and the setting out of written addition and subtraction methods. Draw particular attention to the position of the decimal point.

ANSWERS

Question ❶ a): There are 9·38 litres in total.

Question ❶ b): 0·62 litres will be needed to fill the bottle.

PUPIL TEXTBOOK 6B PAGE 104

Share

WAYS OF WORKING Whole class teacher led

ASK

- Question ❶ a): *Why is there a small 1 underneath the 9?*
- Question ❶ a): *How could you check this answer?*
- Question ❶ b): *How are the two methods related?*
- Question ❶ b): *Can you think of another way to solve this?*

IN FOCUS A written column method has been used to first add, and then subtract decimals. Consider the similarities between the place value grids and the written methods. They both have place value column headings and both show the position of the decimal point. Agree that it is important to set these methods out accurately.

Children may also notice that subtracting 9·38 from 10·00 requires three exchanges and so makes the written method more complicated. Discuss why Flo's method gives the same answer (because we first subtract 0·01 from both 10 and 9·38) but makes the written calcluation easier (because no exchanges are needed).

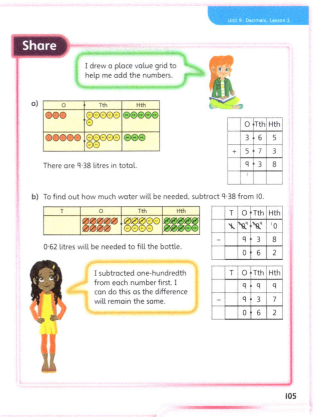

PUPIL TEXTBOOK 6B PAGE 105

Think together

WAYS OF WORKING Whole class teacher led (I do, We do, You do)

ASK

- Question ❶: *How could a mental method help you to estimate the answers first?*
- Question ❷: *Could you solve any of these using a mental method?*
- Question ❸: *Why is it important to line up the decimal points?*

IN FOCUS Questions ❶ and ❷ require children to complete additions, and then subtractions, of numbers with up to 3 decimal places. The written method for the first calculation in each question is shown, set out on a place value grid. This should help children use a similar written method in parts b) and c). Children may also find it helpful to model each calculation with place value counters on a place value grid.

In question ❸, children explore possible errors that can occur when using a written method for a calculation where the two numbers have a different number of decimal places. Reinforce the importance of correctly lining up the digits in place value columns.

STRENGTHEN Children should use place value equipment to model every calculation and describe the place value of each digit as they work through. For example, they say: *Six tenths add eight tenths, rather than just six add eight.*

DEEPEN Ask children to find or devise additions and subtractions with decimals where it will be more efficient to use a mental method rather than a written method, and vice versa.

ASSESSMENT CHECKPOINT Use question ❸ to assess whether children can work accurately when using written methods to add and subtract decimals.

ANSWERS

Question ❶ a): 3·6 + 4·9 = 8·5

Question ❶ b): 2·08 + 3·55 = 5·63

Question ❶ c): 16·8 + 29·5 = 46·3

Question ❷ a): 5·1 − 3·6 = 1·5

Question ❷ b): 0·964 − 0·183 = 0·781

Question ❷ c): 26·7 − 23·9 = 2·8

Question ❸ a): Emma has not written the digits for 6·5 in the correct columns.
6·5 is 6 ones and 5 tenths, not 6 tenths and 5 hundredths.

Question ❸ b): 6·5 + 3·84 = 10·34

Question ❸ c): 2·34 + 0·172 = 2·512
35·8 + 6·14 = 41·94
7·5 − 3·16 = 4·34
0·4 − 0·157 = 0·243

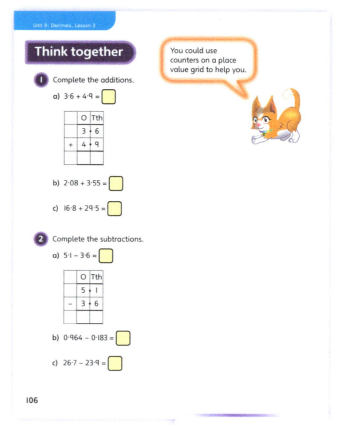

PUPIL TEXTBOOK 6B PAGE 106

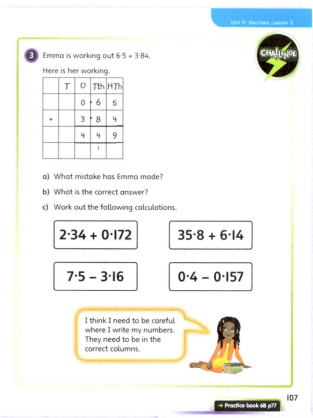

PUPIL TEXTBOOK 6B PAGE 107

Practice

WAYS OF WORKING Pair work

IN FOCUS In question **1**, children use basic written methods of addition with decimals. The first few calculations are set out in place value grids. Children will need to set out accurately the subsequent calculations themselves.

In question **3**, children set out and complete written subtraction methods for numbers with up to 3 decimal places and, in question **4**, they explore variations in subtractions where one of the numbers has a different number of decimal places each time.

Question **5** introduces missing number problems in the context of additions where the answer is known and a subtraction method is needed to find the missing information.

STRENGTHEN Encourage children to use place value equipment alongside each calculation. They should use it to support and justify their thinking and check their answers, rather than just using it to count and find totals.

DEEPEN Ask children to use rounding to produce a reasonable estimate for every calculation that will help them to check their answer each time.

THINK DIFFERENTLY Question **2** requires children to apply their learning to correct mistakes in a written subtraction which has been set out incorrectly. The mistakes have arisen because the two numbers in this calculation have a different number of decimal places.

ASSESSMENT CHECKPOINT Use question **3** to assess whether children can work accurately with written methods including when there are a different number of decimal places.

ANSWERS Answers for the **Practice** part of the lesson can be found in the *Power Maths* online subscription.

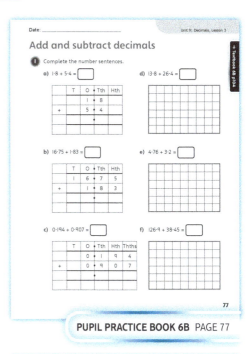

PUPIL PRACTICE BOOK 6B PAGE 77

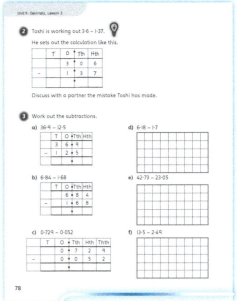

PUPIL PRACTICE BOOK 6B PAGE 78

Reflect

WAYS OF WORKING Pair work

IN FOCUS The **Reflect** part of the lesson prompts children to think about how the setting out of written methods can affect the accuracy of their answers.

ASSESSMENT CHECKPOINT Assess whether children can explain the importance of place value and the position of the decimal points when using written methods to add and subtract decimals.

ANSWERS Answers for the **Reflect** part of the lesson can be found in the *Power Maths* online subscription.

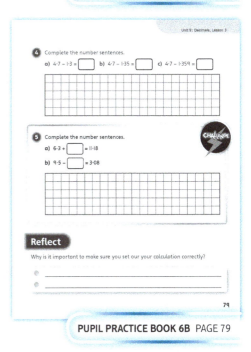

PUPIL PRACTICE BOOK 6B PAGE 79

After the lesson ⏸

- Can children explain possible mistakes that can be made with these methods, and how to avoid them?
- Did children set out calculations correctly?

Multiply by 10, 100 and 1,000

Learning focus

In this lesson, children will learn to multiply decimals by powers of 10. They will apply their knowledge from previous learning of multiplying whole numbers by 10 and 100.

Before you teach

- Can children multiply whole numbers by 10, 100 and 1,000?
- Do children have a secure understanding of place value in decimals?
- How can you use concrete equipment to model multiplying by 10, 100 and 1,000?

NATIONAL CURRICULUM LINKS

Year 6 Number – fractions (including decimals and percentages)

Identify the value of each digit in numbers given to three decimal places and multiply and divide numbers by 10, 100 and 1,000 giving answers up to three decimal places.

ASSESSING MASTERY

Children can multiply decimals by powers of 10, understanding how and why digits move to a higher place value column and apply their knowledge of multiplying whole numbers by 10 in order to multiply decimals by 10, 100 and 1,000. Secure understanding of place value will enable children to correctly use placeholders.

COMMON MISCONCEPTIONS

Children may not move digits the correct number of places when multiplying by powers of 10. They may omit placeholders or include them when they are not needed. Ask:

- *What would that look like on a place value grid? Which counters would you move?*

STRENGTHENING UNDERSTANDING

Use concrete equipment such as base 10 equipment or place value counters to help children's conceptual understanding of multiplying by powers of 10. Begin by multiplying whole numbers to secure understanding of how each digit becomes 10 or 100 times bigger, before multiplying numbers with one decimal place by powers of 10.

GOING DEEPER

Apply multiplying by powers of 10 to converting between units of measure. Children can convert kilometres into metres, centimetres and millimetres in a practical activity, such as measuring the perimeter of the playground.

KEY LANGUAGE

In lesson: multiply, place value, hundredths, tenths, ones, tens, exchange, kilogram, total, decimal

Other language to be used by the teacher: mass, placeholder

STRUCTURES AND REPRESENTATIONS

Place value grid

RESOURCES

Mandatory: place value grids, place value counters

Optional: base 10 equipment, measuring equipment, whiteboards, 10 plates

 In the eTextbook of this lesson, you will find interactive links to a selection of teaching tools.

Quick recap

Challenge children to multiply each of these numbers by 10, by 100 and by 1,000:

5   23   157

Then ask them to explain each of their answers in terms of place value.

Discover

Pair work

ASK

- Question **1** a): *What is the value of each digit in 0·3?*
- Questions **1** a) and **1** b): *What do you know that can help you find the solutions?*
- Question **1** b): *What calculation do you need to do?*

IN FOCUS Question **1** b) involves moving digits two places. This will reveal whether children have any misconceptions about what happens to the digits when multiplying by 100. It may also highlight if any children are not secure on the place value of decimals.

PRACTICAL TIPS Having real plates available may help children to visualise the problem. Label the mass of one plate.

Children may try to find the solutions by repeated addition. Allow them to carry this out and then ask them if they can see a relationship between the mass of one item and the mass of ten.

ANSWERS

Question **1** a): The mass of 10 plates is 3 kg.

Question **1** b): The mass of 100 plates is 30 kg.

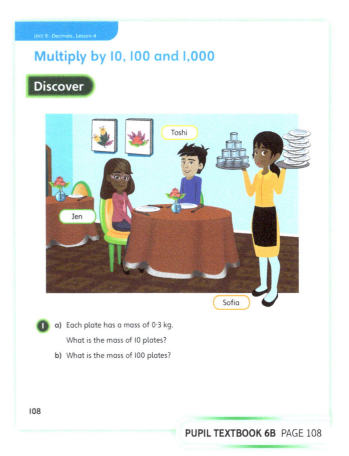

Multiply by 10, 100 and 1,000

Discover

1 a) Each plate has a mass of 0·3 kg.
What is the mass of 10 plates?

b) What is the mass of 100 plates?

108

PUPIL TEXTBOOK 6B PAGE 108

Share

Whole class teacher led

ASK

- Question **1** a): *How can you describe what happens when you multiply a number by 10? Why do the digits move one place to the left?*
- Question **1** b): *What happens to each digit when you multiply by 100?*

IN FOCUS Question **1** a) uses the place value grid to model how multiplying by 10 involves an exchange from tenths to ones. Make sure children are confident that 10 tenths make one so 30 tenths is the same as 3 ones. Make the link between the counters on the place value grid and the digits on the place value grid. Ensure children see each digit move one place to the left and understand how to write the answer correctly.

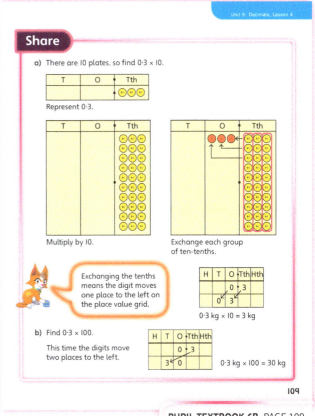

Share

a) There are 10 plates, so find 0·3 × 10.

Represent 0·3.

Multiply by 10.

Exchange each group of ten-tenths.

Exchanging the tenths means the digit moves one place to the left on the place value grid.

0·3 kg × 10 = 3 kg

b) Find 0·3 × 100.
This time the digits move two places to the left.

0·3 kg × 100 = 30 kg

109

PUPIL TEXTBOOK 6B PAGE 109

Think together

Whole class teacher led (I do, We do, You do)

ASK

- Question **1**: *In which direction do the digits move when you multiply by 10? By 100? By 1,000? How many place(s) do they move by?*
- Question **2**: *What happens to the place value of each digit when you multiply by 10? By 100? By 1,000?*
- Question **3**: *How would you multiply 2·3 by 1,000?*

IN FOCUS Question **3** requires children to understand that 'moving one place to the left twice' is the same as 'moving two places to the left'. Help children to then make the connection that multiplying by 10 twice is the same as multiplying by 100.

You can further reinforce this learning by modelling 2·3 using place value counters on a place value grid. Multiply by 10 to give 20 ones and 30 tenths, and then exchange for 2 tens and 3 ones. Repeat this process as you multiply by 10 twice.

STRENGTHEN Provide children with place value grids to support their calculations. If necessary, children can also use base 10 equipment to see how each digit becomes 10 or 100 times bigger.

DEEPEN Children explore what happens when they multiply a number with 3 decimal places by 10, 100 and 1,000. Can they first predict what each answer will be and describe how each answer can help them to find the next?

ASSESSMENT CHECKPOINT Check whether children are moving each digit the correct number of place value places. Take particular note of the questions that involve placeholders to ensure children are including them in the correct place value column or omitting them if necessary.

ANSWERS

Question **1**: Ambika: 1·5 × 10 = 15
1·5 × 100 = 150
1·5 × 1,000 = 1,500

Lee: 0·36 × 10 = 3·6
0·36 × 100 = 36
0·36 × 1,000 = 360

Children should notice that the digits stay the same but their values increase.

Question **2**: a): 5·2 × 10 = 52
5·2 × 100 = 520
5·2 × 1,000 = 5,200

Question **2**: b): 0·12 × 10 = 1·2
1·02 × 100 = 102
10·02 × 1,000 = 10,020

Question **2**: c): 50·2 × 10 = 502
5·02 × 1,000 = 5,200
0·502 × 1,000 = 502

Question **3**: Multiplying by 10 and then 10 again is the same as multiplying by 100 because 10 × 10 = 100. Both increase the value of each digit 100 times.

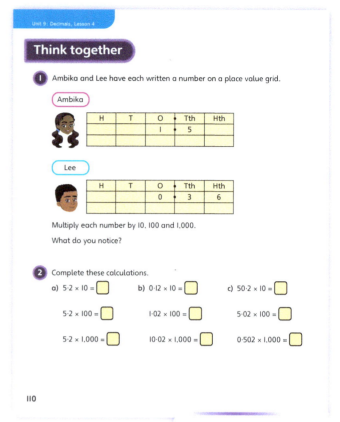

PUPIL TEXTBOOK 6B PAGE 110

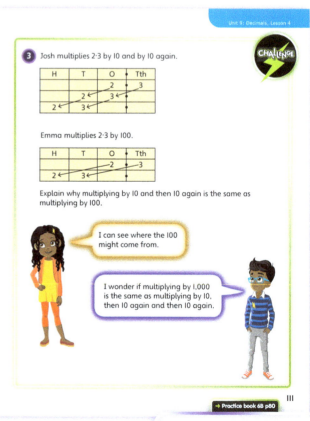

PUPIL TEXTBOOK 6B PAGE 111

Practice

WAYS OF WORKING Independent thinking

IN FOCUS Questions ❶, ❷ and ❸ give children plenty of practice at multiplying decimals by 10, 100 and 1,000 by moving the place value of digits to the left. The place value grids support the important learning principle that children should not simply 'add 0s to the end', but should change the place value of each digit.

STRENGTHEN Provide children with whiteboards where they can draw place value grids. They can then draw arrows to show how each digit will move along the place value grid.

DEEPEN Ask children to write missing number multiplication problems similar to question ❻ for a partner. How many possible solutions can they find to each problem? For example, if the number sentence is 2·3 × ☐ = 230, children could write 2·3 × 100 = 230, or they could write 2·3 × 10 × 10 = 230. Can they find a pattern to make it easier to find several solutions?

THINK DIFFERENTLY Question ❹ tackles the misconception that, when you multiply by 100, you simply 'write two 0s at the end of the number' instead of moving digits two places to the left on the place value grid. Writing two 0s at the end of 1·6 to make it 1·600 does not change the value of the number, as the 1 and the 6 still have the same place value. You may also want to reinforce that when multiplying 1·6 by 100 to become 160, for the 1 to be in the 100s place and the 6 to be in the 10s place, you need a 0 placeholder in the 1s place.

ASSESSMENT CHECKPOINT Assess whether children can move each digit the correct number of places along the place value grid. Are children moving placeholders correctly and omitting unnecessary placeholders (for example, 0·012 × 1,000 = 12, not 0012)?

ANSWERS Answers for the **Practice** part of the lesson can be found in the *Power Maths* online subscription.

Reflect

WAYS OF WORKING Independent thinking

IN FOCUS This question prompts children to articulate their understanding of what happens when multiplying decimals by powers of 10. They should include an explanation of how any placeholders move and whether or not they need to be included in the final answer.

ASSESSMENT CHECKPOINT This section will determine whether children have a secure understanding of how to multiply decimals by powers of 10. Encourage them to give and solve an example of a calculation to demonstrate their explanation.

ANSWERS Answers for the **Reflect** part of the lesson can be found in the *Power Maths* online subscription.

After the lesson ⏸

- Were the models and concrete equipment helpful in securing children's understanding of multiplying decimals by powers of 10?
- Are there opportunities to display models and prompts to further support children's understanding?

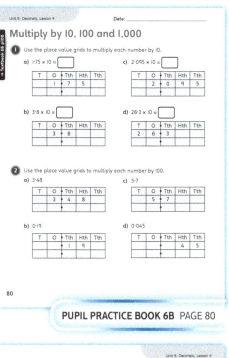

PUPIL PRACTICE BOOK 6B PAGE 80

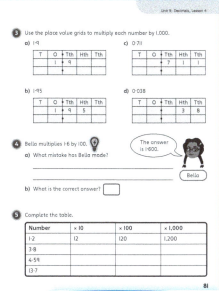

PUPIL PRACTICE BOOK 6B PAGE 81

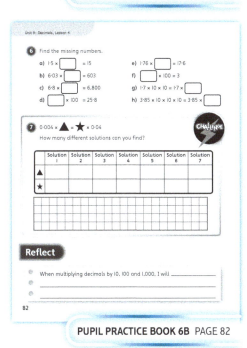

PUPIL PRACTICE BOOK 6B PAGE 82

Divide by 10, 100 and 1,000

Learning focus

In this lesson, children will divide by powers of 10. They will develop understanding of digits moving to the right when dividing by 10, 100 and 1,000.

Before you teach

- How will you model dividing by powers of 10?
- Can you explain and model why the digits move to the right when dividing by powers of 10?

NATIONAL CURRICULUM LINKS

Year 6 Number – fractions (including decimals and percentages)

Identify the value of each digit in numbers given to three decimal places and multiply and divide numbers by 10, 100 and 1,000 giving answers up to three decimal places.

ASSESSING MASTERY

Children can use their knowledge of multiplying by powers of 10 in order to divide by powers of 10, understanding the inverse relationship and explaining why the digits move to the right. They will be able to explain when placeholders are needed and when they can be omitted within decimal numbers.

COMMON MISCONCEPTIONS

Children may not move the digits the correct number of places to the right. They may be confused by placeholders – either not including them or including them when they are not needed. Ask:
- *Is there a placeholder 0 in the question? Is there one in the answer? What does it represent each time?*

STRENGTHENING UNDERSTANDING

Place value grids can help children to identify which place value column each digit needs to move from and to. Base 10 equipment can be used to model the division and give children a visual image of how it works.

GOING DEEPER

Pose questions such as 7·2 ÷ 300 to give children the opportunity to investigate different ways of solving a calculation, applying knowledge of dividing by powers of 10.

KEY LANGUAGE

In lesson: equal, share, multiply, divide, inverse, convert, exchange

Other language to be used by the teacher: place value, digit, tenths, hundredths, thousandths, placeholder

STRUCTURES AND REPRESENTATIONS

Place value grid, bar model

RESOURCES

Mandatory: place value grids, place value counters

Optional: base 10 equipment, whiteboards

 In the eTextbook of this lesson, you will find interactive links to a selection of teaching tools.

Quick recap

Challenge children to multiply each of these numbers by 10, 100 and 1,000:

0·5   2·3   0·157

Discover

Unit 9: Decimals, Lesson 5

WAYS OF WORKING Pair work

ASK

- Questions **1** a) and **1** b): *What calculation do you need to do? How do you know?*
- Questions **1** a) and **1** b): *How can you use what you learnt in the last lesson to help?*

IN FOCUS Question **1** a) requires children to identify that this is a sharing problem and so a division by 10 is needed. Agree that this is the inverse of multiplying by 10 which they encountered in the previous lesson. They can then consider what method they will use to divide by 100 in question **1** b).

PRACTICAL TIPS Draw a picture of the paper chain and label the length '12 m'. Ask children what they need to do to the chain to work out the length for each child. You could model dividing it into 10 equal parts if necessary. Children can represent the chain using a number line or a bar model to see that they are dividing the length by 10.

ANSWERS

Question **1** a): Each child makes 1·2 m of paper chain.

Question **1** b): 36 ÷ 100 = 0·36

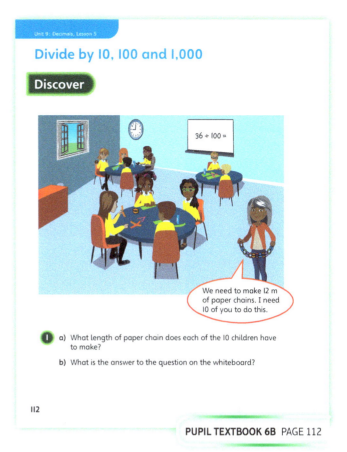

PUPIL TEXTBOOK 6B PAGE 112

Share

WAYS OF WORKING Whole class teacher led

ASK

- Question **1** a): *How can you describe what happens to the digits when you divide by 10?*
- Question **1** a): *What multiplication facts are you using to help you?*
- Question **1** b): *Can you think of another way to solve this?*

IN FOCUS Question **1** a) models the inverse relationship between multiplication and division. This allows children to draw on their learning from the previous lesson. By understanding that division is the inverse of multiplication, they can see that when they divide by 10, the digits will have to move in the opposite direction to when they multiply by 10.

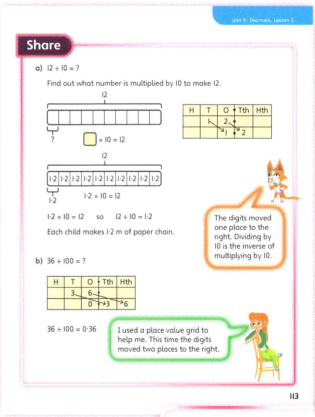

PUPIL TEXTBOOK 6B PAGE 113

Think together

WAYS OF WORKING Whole class teacher led (I do, We do, You do)

ASK

- Question **1**: *How does this compare to multiplying by 10?*
- Question **2**: *What patterns can you see?*
- Question **3** a): *How else would you write each of these calculations? What operation will you use to check your answers?*

IN FOCUS Question **1** gives a visual explanation of why digits move to the right when dividing by powers of 10. Children should be able to relate this to the previous lesson about multiplying by powers of 10. It illustrates the inverse relationship between multiplication and division, as the steps are reversed. It may help for children to model this using base 10 equipment. They could multiply by 10 and then divide by 10 to see how the steps are reversed.

STRENGTHEN Provide children with place value grids on whiteboards so they can move the digits to the right. Some children may need to reinforce this understanding with concrete equipment such as base 10 equipment or place value counters.

DEEPEN Can children explain why dividing by 100 is the same as dividing by 10 twice? They could use counters on a place value grid to help explain their thinking.

ASSESSMENT CHECKPOINT Check whether children are able to identify the relationship between multiplying and dividing by powers of 10. Are they moving the digits to the right the correct number of places? Are they using placeholders correctly?

ANSWERS

Question **1**: Reena is correct. Dividing by 10 moves each digit one place to the right.
Children should draw a diagram to show 12·3 ÷ 100 = 0·123. They should draw a place value table showing how the tens, ones and tenths move to tenths, hundredths and thousandths.

Question **2** a): 63 ÷ 10 = 6·3
63 ÷ 100 = 0·63
63 ÷ 1,000 = 0·063

Question **2** b): 717 ÷ 10 = 71·7
717 ÷ 100 = 7·17
717 ÷ 1,000 = 0·717

Question **3** a): Danny has divided 6·5 by 10 to find a whole when he needs to multiply 6·5 by 10 to find the missing part.

Question **3** b): 65 ÷ 10 = 6·5

Question **3** c): 40 ÷ 10 = 4   350 ÷ 100 = 3·5
5·8 ÷ 10 = 0·58   60 ÷ 100 = 0·6

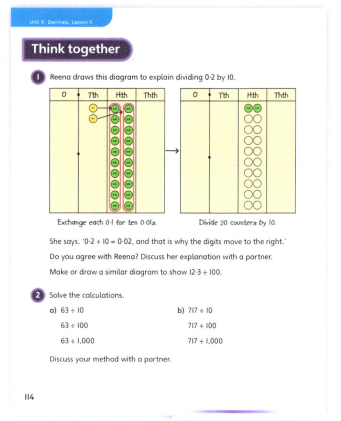

PUPIL TEXTBOOK 6B PAGE 114

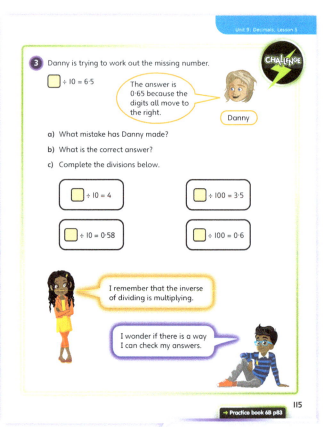

PUPIL TEXTBOOK 6B PAGE 115

Practice

WAYS OF WORKING Independent thinking

IN FOCUS Question ④ involves children completing a table to divide numbers by 10, then 100 and then 1,000. The placeholders may cause problems for some children. This could prompt a valuable discussion about 0 as a placeholder and when it is or is not necessary.

STRENGTHEN Provide children with place value grids to support dividing by powers of 10. If necessary, model the division using base 10 equipment. You could reinforce the link to the previous lesson by prompting children to check an answer by multiplying it by the divisor to see if they get back to the original number.

DEEPEN Ask children to write missing number division questions for a partner, like those in question ⑥, where the power of 10 is missing. Encourage them to include numbers with placeholders. What method does their partner use to find the answer? How can they check this is correct?

ASSESSMENT CHECKPOINT Check whether children are moving the digits the correct number of place value places to the right. Are they including placeholders where appropriate?

ANSWERS Answers for the **Practice** part of the lesson can be found in the *Power Maths* online subscription.

Reflect

WAYS OF WORKING Pair work

IN FOCUS This question requires children to think about the place value of digits when dividing by a power of 10. They should observe that dividing by 100 is the same as dividing by 10 and then 10 again and be able to justify that statement.

ASSESSMENT CHECKPOINT Do children draw on their learning from the lesson to give a sensible example that clearly demonstrates their explanation? Can they confidently divide by a power of 10, accounting for any placeholders and showing an understanding of the digits moving to the right?

ANSWERS Answers for the **Reflect** part of the lesson can be found in the *Power Maths* online subscription.

After the lesson

- Were children able to make links between this lesson and the last lesson?
- What concrete resources helped children to understand the concept of dividing by powers of 10?
- Were there any children who did not have a secure understanding of the place value of decimal numbers?

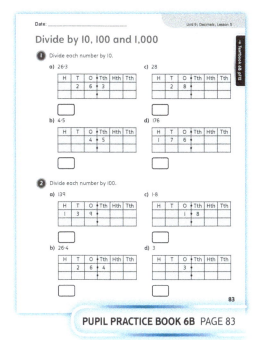

PUPIL PRACTICE BOOK 6B PAGE 83

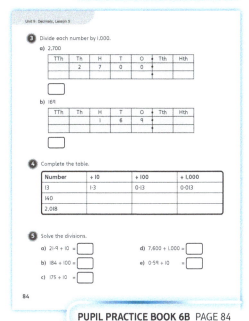

PUPIL PRACTICE BOOK 6B PAGE 84

PUPIL PRACTICE BOOK 6B PAGE 85

Multiply decimals by integers

Learning focus

In this lesson, children will multiply a decimal by a whole number where the product requires crossing into the next place up.

Before you teach

- What models and practical resources will you use to support understanding of place value?
- What problems or investigations can you use to deepen understanding of multiplying decimals?

NATIONAL CURRICULUM LINKS

Year 6 Number – fractions (including decimals and percentages)

Multiply 1-digit numbers with up to two decimal places by whole numbers.

ASSESSING MASTERY

Children can identify the multiplication fact needed to create known multiplication facts in order to multiply decimals by a whole number. Children understand that when the number you are multiplying by is less than 1, the product will be smaller than the number you are multiplying and vice versa. Their secure understanding of place value allows them to reason about the calculation and to estimate and/or check their answer.

COMMON MISCONCEPTIONS

Children may not realise that, when multiplying an integer by a decimal less than 1, that the product will always be less than what they started with. Ask:

- *What would happen if you multiplied a number by 1? So, what would happen if you multiplied it by 0·5? Remember, this is the same as multiplying it by $\frac{1}{2}$.*

STRENGTHENING UNDERSTANDING

Provide place value grids to help children determine the value of each digit in a multiplication with a decimal. Refer to lists of times-tables if children need support with finding suitable known facts to use. Then look closely at what happens during the exchange and what this will mean for the place value of the digits in the product.

GOING DEEPER

Children could explore what happens when both numbers in a multiplication are less than 1. Make this more investigative by looking at area in square metres and square centimetres. Show a 250 cm by 500 cm rectangle and ask children to find the area in square centimetres, then in square metres. Can they explain what happens?

KEY LANGUAGE

In lesson: fact, exchange, multiplication, area, product, decimal

Other language to be used by the teacher: tenths, hundredths, thousandths

STRUCTURES AND REPRESENTATIONS

Place value grid, bar model, number line, array

RESOURCES

Mandatory: place value grids

Optional: rectangle (250 cm × 500 cm), number line, times-table lists

 In the eTextbook of this lesson, you will find interactive links to a selection of teaching tools.

Quick recap

Ask children to describe and complete each of these patterns:

2 × 3 = 6	20 × 3 = 60	200 × 3 = ?
5 × 4 = 20	5 × 40 = 200	5 × 400 = ?

Discover

Unit 9: Decimals, Lesson 6

Multiply decimals by integers

Discover

WAYS OF WORKING Pair work

ASK

- Questions **1** a) and b): *What calculation do you need to do?*
- Questions **1** a) and b): *How did you go about finding the solution? Is there another way?*

IN FOCUS When multiplying a decimal by an integer, children will end up with a 2-digit product and will have to think carefully about the place value of each digit. For example, in question **1** a), a common error would be to say that $0.3 \times 6 = 0.18$. If this happens, talk about the height of 1 plank and how the height of 6 planks must be more, yet 0.18 is smaller than 0.3. Using the context of the problem will help children to reason about their answer.

PRACTICAL TIPS With the aid of a number line, use repeated addition to find the solution. Then ask children to solve 3×6. How does 3×6 relate to 0.3×6?

ANSWERS

Question **1** a): The fence panel is 1·8 m tall.

Question **1** b): The whole fence will be 5·6 m long.

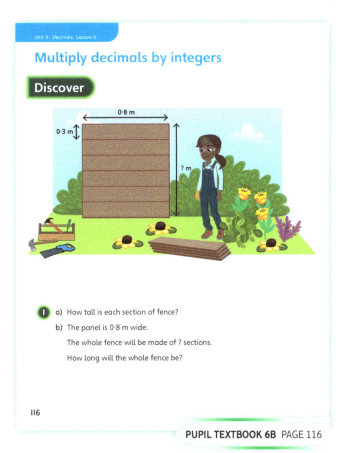

1 a) How tall is each section of fence?

b) The panel is 0·8 m wide.

The whole fence will be made of 7 sections.

How long will the whole fence be?

116

PUPIL TEXTBOOK 6B PAGE 116

Share

Unit 9: Decimals, Lesson 6

Share

WAYS OF WORKING Whole class teacher led

ASK

- Questions **1** a) and b): *What known facts can you use?*
- Questions **1** a) and b): *What happens if you convert the measurements to centimetres first?*
- Questions **1** a) and b): *What happens to the placeholders in these multiplications?*

IN FOCUS Children are multiplying a decimal number, which is less than 1 and has 1 decimal place, by a whole number. In both questions, children are asked to use a known multiplication fact with whole numbers to help them with this. Discuss which known fact has been used each time and why an exchange is needed to find the answer.

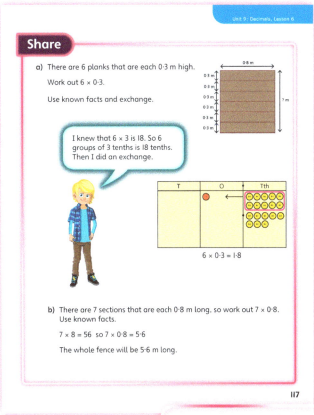

a) There are 6 planks that are each 0·3 m high.

Work out 6×0.3.

Use known facts and exchange.

I knew that 6 × 3 is 18. So 6 groups of 3 tenths is 18 tenths. Then I did an exchange.

$6 \times 0.3 = 1.8$

b) There are 7 sections that are each 0·8 m long, so work out 7×0.8. Use known facts.

$7 \times 8 = 56$ so $7 \times 0.8 = 5.6$

The whole fence will be 5·6 m long.

117

PUPIL TEXTBOOK 6B PAGE 117

Think together

WAYS OF WORKING Whole class teacher led (I do, We do, You do)

ASK

- Question **1**: *What multiplication facts will you use to find the solutions?*
- Question **2**: *What is the same and what is different about the first group of calculations and the second group?*

IN FOCUS Question **3** links multiplication with calculating area. In questions **1**, **2** and **3**, children should be able to solve the multiplications by multiplying the decimal number by a power of 10 to get a whole number, multiplying the whole numbers together and then adjusting the product by dividing it by the power of 10 they multiplied the decimal with at first.

(For example, 0.03×15 becomes $3 \times 15 = 45$ when you multiply 0.03 by 100. So, $0.03 \times 15 = 45 \div 100 = 0.45$.)

STRENGTHEN Encourage children to use place value grids to determine the value of each digit.

DEEPEN Ask: *If $0.4 \times 3 = 1.2$, what is 0.8×3? How do you know? Can you think of other related multiplications like this?*

ASSESSMENT CHECKPOINT Check whether children can identify a multiplication from a visual representation on a place value grid. Can children derive other multiplication facts where one or more numbers in a calculation are multiplied or divided by a power of 10? Can children multiply decimals by adjusting multiplication facts by powers of 10?

ANSWERS

Question **1** a): $0.2 \times 4 = 0.8$

Question **1** b): $0.4 \times 3 = 1.2$

Question **1** c): $0.7 \times 4 = 2.8$

Question **2** a): $0.4 \times 2 = 0.8$
$0.4 \times 3 = 1.2$
$0.4 \times 4 = 1.6$
$0.4 \times 5 = 2.0$

Question **2** b): $0.06 \times 2 = 0.12$
$0.06 \times 3 = 0.18$
$0.06 \times 4 = 0.24$
$0.06 \times 5 = 0.3$

Children should mention using multiplication tables to find the answers.

Question **3** a): 0.3 is ten times smaller than 3 so the answer to 32×0.3 is ten times smaller than 32×3.
$32 \times 0.3 = 96 \div 10 = 9.6$

Question **3** b): $12 \times 0.07 = 0.84$ m^2
$30 \times 0.5 = 15$ m^2
$4 \times 0.9 = 3.6$ m^2

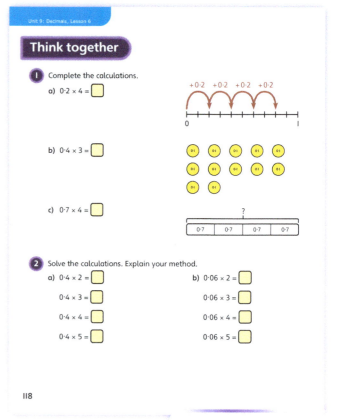

PUPIL TEXTBOOK 6B PAGE 118

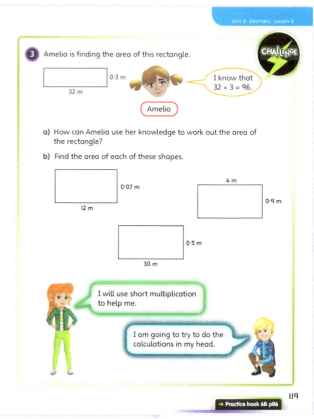

PUPIL TEXTBOOK 6B PAGE 119

Practice

WAYS OF WORKING Independent thinking

IN FOCUS Questions ③ and ⑤ both require children to explore how known multiplication facts can be used to help when multiplying by a decimal. Ensure they understand how to adjust the known fact each time based on the place value of the digits in each calculation.

STRENGTHEN Model the multiplications using place value grids to strengthen children's understanding of what happens when an exchange is needed.

DEEPEN Ask: *What is 0·5 × 0·5? Why is the product smaller than both of the numbers in the multiplication?* Can children explain what will happen with *0·5 × 0·5 × 0·5*?

THINK DIFFERENTLY In question ④, children explore a misconception that can occur when multiplying a decimal by an integer. Children should reason that 0·024 < 0·08, so a place value error has been made. Challenge children to find the correct answer.

ASSESSMENT CHECKPOINT Assess whether children are able to identify and solve the multiplication needed from a visual representation using place value grids. Can they apply multiplication facts of whole numbers and adjust by dividing by powers of 10 to solve multiplications involving decimals? Are children secure in their understanding of place value when multiplying decimals by whole numbers? Do children understand when to use or not use a placeholder when multiplying decimals?

ANSWERS Answers for the **Practice** part of the lesson can be found in the *Power Maths* online subscription.

Reflect

WAYS OF WORKING Independent thinking

IN FOCUS For this question, children consider the method they have learnt to multiply a decimal by a whole number by using a known multiplication fact such as 4 × 7 = 28. They should justify their choice of fact and describe how it will be helpful and what steps they will take to find the answer.

ASSESSMENT CHECKPOINT Assess whether children understand how known multiplication facts of whole numbers can be used to solve multiplications with decimals. This question will highlight if children have a secure understanding of place value when multiplying decimals.

ANSWERS Answers for the **Reflect** part of the lesson can be found in the *Power Maths* online subscription.

After the lesson ⏸

- Were children confident in selecting the most appropriate known facts to help them?
- Were children able to adjust the product correctly when using multiplication facts to help solve multiplications of decimals?

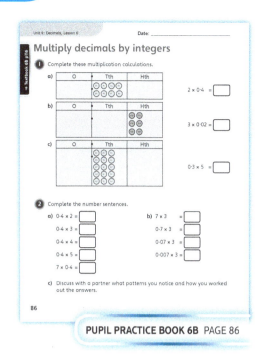

PUPIL PRACTICE BOOK 6B PAGE 86

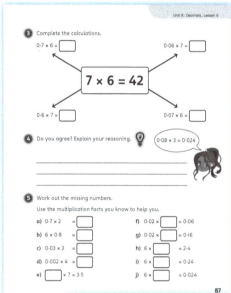

PUPIL PRACTICE BOOK 6B PAGE 87

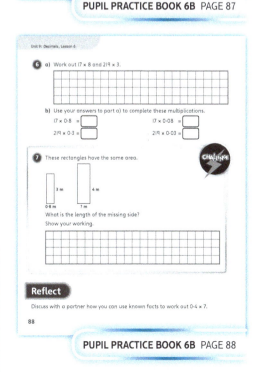

PUPIL PRACTICE BOOK 6B PAGE 88

155

Divide decimals by integers

Learning focus

In this lesson, children will divide decimals by using known multiplication facts and adjusting by powers of 10. They will understand how to exchange 1s to tenths in order to solve the division by sharing.

Before you teach

- Can children recall decimal multiplication facts?
- Do children have a secure understanding of the inverse relationship between multiplication and division?

NATIONAL CURRICULUM LINKS

Year 6 Number – fractions (including decimals and percentages)

Use written division methods in cases where the answer has up to two decimal places.

Solve problems which require answers to be rounded to specified degrees of accuracy.

ASSESSING MASTERY

Children can identify related division facts, explain how to divide decimals through exchanging and sharing, and apply these techniques to solve divisions involving decimals. Children can use the result of a divided decimal to generate other related divisions.

COMMON MISCONCEPTIONS

Children may try to apply grouping to dividing decimals, for example, seeing $1.2 \div 6$ as how many 6s make 1·2 and not being able to identify that you would need 0·2 lots of 6 to make 1·2. Ask:
- *Is there a fact that could help you? What is the relationship between $12 \div 6$ and $1.2 \div 6$?*

STRENGTHENING UNDERSTANDING

To aid children with exchanging and sharing, provide them with concrete resources such as base 10 equipment. This will enable them to physically divide by sharing and to count the number in each set. The use of place value grids will aid children in using known multiplication facts and adjusting by powers of ten correctly.

GOING DEEPER

Challenge children to solve a calculation such as $1.6 \div 0.4$. What do they notice?

KEY LANGUAGE

In lesson: multiplication, fact, share, equal, division, short division, decimal, exchange, tenths

Other language to be used by the teacher: divisor, hundredths, grouping

STRUCTURES AND REPRESENTATIONS

Bar model, place value grid

RESOURCES

Optional: place value grids, base 10 equipment, number lines

 In the eTextbook of this lesson, you will find interactive links to a selection of teaching tools.

Quick recap

Ask children to describe and complete each of these patterns:

$6 \div 3 = ?$	$60 \div 3 = ?$	$600 \div 3 = ?$
$24 \div 8 = ?$	$240 \div 8 = ?$	$2,400 \div 8 = ?$

Discover

WAYS OF WORKING Pair work

ASK

- Question ① a): *What multiplication facts could help you find this solution?*
- Question ① a): *What would the mass be if there were two small blocks? Eight small blocks?*

IN FOCUS Questions ① a) and b) require children to draw on known multiplication facts. They should now recognise that 0·8 = 4 × 0·2 without having to adjust from 8 = 4 × 2. Children may find it easier to think of this as a missing number from a multiplication as opposed to a division (0·8 = 4 × ☐ as opposed to 0·8 ÷ 4 = ☐). However, it is important for them to understand that they are carrying out a division here and that they can use their learning from the previous lessons in this unit to find the solution.

PRACTICAL TIPS The use of a number line or a bar model to represent the division can help children to identify what they need to do here. If the fact that the division involves decimals confuses some children, start with the fact that 2 × 4 = 8 and ask children to think about how they can use this fact to find the solution.

ANSWERS

Question ① a): The mass of each block is 0·2 kg.

Question ① b): 40 blocks will balance an 8 kg crate.

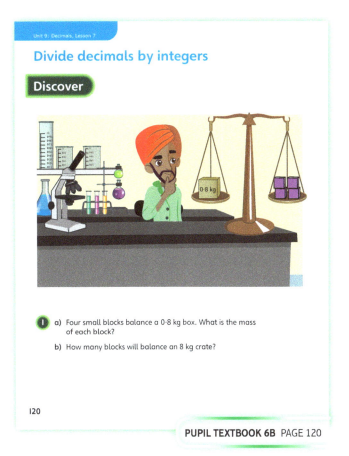

Divide decimals by integers

Discover

① a) Four small blocks balance a 0·8 kg box. What is the mass of each block?

b) How many blocks will balance an 8 kg crate?

120

PUPIL TEXTBOOK 6B PAGE 120

Share

WAYS OF WORKING Whole class teacher led

ASK

- Question ① a): *What if you convert the mass to grams? Does this make the calculation easier?*
- Question ① a): *Whose method do you prefer, Dexter's or Flo's?*
- Question ① a): *What is 0·8 ÷ 0·2?*

IN FOCUS In question ① a), Flo models sharing in order to find the solution. This replicates the context of the problem as you are distributing the 0·8 kg into four parts to represent the four blocks on the balance. The model of the shared counters provides a visual image of this. However, children need to understand that whether they think of it as 4 lots of *what* make 0·8 or as *what* is 0·8 shared between 4, the answer will be the same.

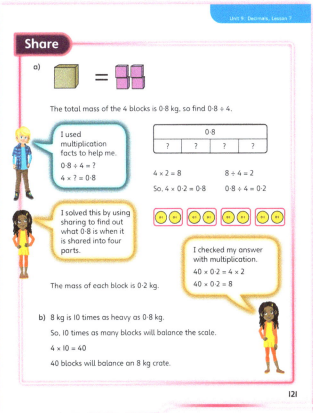

Share

a)

The total mass of the 4 blocks is 0·8 kg, so find 0·8 ÷ 4.

I used multiplication facts to help me.
0·8 ÷ 4 = ?
4 × ? = 0·8

0·8			
?	?	?	?

4 × 2 = 8   8 ÷ 4 = 2
So, 4 × 0·2 = 0·8   0·8 ÷ 4 = 0·2

I solved this by using sharing to find out what 0·8 is when it is shared into four parts.

I checked my answer with multiplication.
40 × 0·2 = 4 × 2
40 × 0·2 = 8

The mass of each block is 0·2 kg.

b) 8 kg is 10 times as heavy as 0·8 kg.

So, 10 times as many blocks will balance the scale.

4 × 10 = 40

40 blocks will balance an 8 kg crate.

121

PUPIL TEXTBOOK 6B PAGE 121

Think together

WAYS OF WORKING Whole class teacher led (I do, We do, You do)

ASK

- Question **1**: *What multiplication fact can you use to help you?*
- Question **2**: *What patterns do you notice? How could one answer help you with finding another?*
- Question **3** a): *What does Toshi's working show? What is missing?*
- Question **3** b): *How will you set out the short division?*

IN FOCUS In question **3**, children will be working with numbers where it is no longer helpful to use known facts. Instead they are prompted to use the formal written method of short division. This is partly scaffolded in question **3** a), whereas in question **3** b), children will need to identify how to correctly set it out themselves.

STRENGTHEN Provide children with counters that they can physically share into sets. When there is a need to exchange in order to share, you can use base 10 equipment where the hundred blocks are worth 1 and the rods of ten are worth 0·1.

DEEPEN Show children the missing number calculation 4·8 ÷ ☐ = ☐. Ask them to suggest possible number sentences to complete the statement.

ASSESSMENT CHECKPOINT Assess whether children can share counters in order to solve a division involving decimals. Are they able to identify how to solve a division with decimals through sharing? Can children solve multi-step problems involving dividing decimals?

ANSWERS

Question **1** a): $12 \div 3 = 4$

Question **1** b): $1·2 \div 3 = 0·4$

Question **1** c): $0·12 \div 3 = 0·04$

Question **2** a): $35 \div 5 = 7$
$350 \div 5 = 70$
$3·5 \div 5 = 0·7$
$0·35 \div 5 = 0·07$

Question **2** b): $2·4 \div 8 = 0·3$
$2·4 \div 3 = 0·8$
$2·4 \div 4 = 0·6$
$2·4 \div 6 = 0·4$

Question **3** a): $4·24 \div 8 = 0·53$ m

Question **3** b): $15·6 \div 2 = 7·8$
$15·6 \div 3 = 5·2$

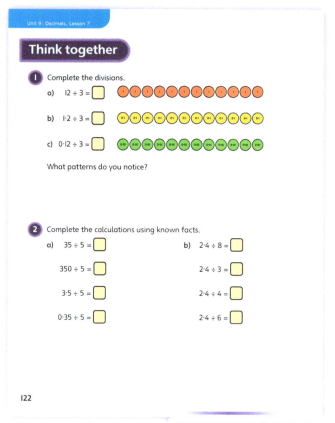

PUPIL TEXTBOOK 6B PAGE 122

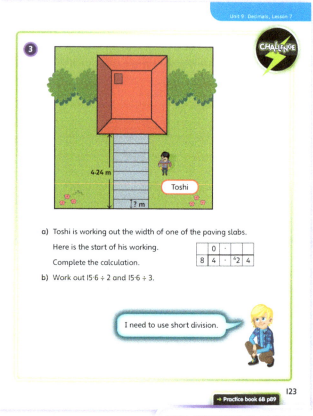

PUPIL TEXTBOOK 6B PAGE 123

158

Practice

WAYS OF WORKING Independent thinking

IN FOCUS Question **5** is a multi-step word problem involving measures. Children will first need to divide to calculate the mass of a single box, and then use this to find the mass of 5 boxes.

Question **6** requires children to use the formal written method of short division. The method is set out for them and they will need to recognise how this represents each number in a given calculation and what steps are needed to complete it. They should pay particular attention to the position of the decimal point in both the question and the answer.

STRENGTHEN Use base 10 equipment to support children in exchanging 1s for tenths and then sharing the tenths in a concrete way. Use place value grids to help children use known multiplication and division facts and then adjust by dividing by powers of 10.

DEEPEN Challenge children to come up with their own question in the style of the word problem in question **5**.

ASSESSMENT CHECKPOINT Can children share tenths and hundredths in order to divide decimal numbers? Can they use known multiplication facts to divide decimals? Can children exchange tenths for hundredths to divide decimals? Can they apply their knowledge of dividing by decimals to solve multi-step problems involving different operations?

ANSWERS Answers for the **Practice** part of the lesson can be found in the *Power Maths* online subscription.

Reflect

WAYS OF WORKING Independent thinking

IN FOCUS In this question, children have to identify the error in a calculation. They can refer back to similar calculations in previous questions. They may find it helpful to share out place value counters to identify where and how a place value error has been made. They may also describe a known division fact that could help and how it should be adjusted correctly.

ASSESSMENT CHECKPOINT Use this question to determine whether children have a secure understanding of the concept of dividing decimals by sharing or by using known division facts and adjusting.

ANSWERS Answers for the **Reflect** part of the lesson can be found in the *Power Maths* online subscription.

After the lesson ⏸

- Were children able to identify related division facts?
- Did children solve divisions both by exchanging and sharing, and by applying division facts and adjusting?

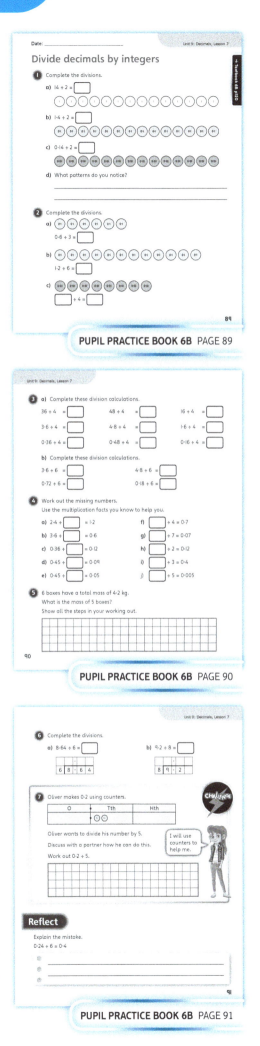

PUPIL PRACTICE BOOK 6B PAGE 89

PUPIL PRACTICE BOOK 6B PAGE 90

PUPIL PRACTICE BOOK 6B PAGE 91

Fractions to decimals

Learning focus

In this lesson, children will learn to convert fractions to decimals and decimals to fractions where the denominator is a power of 10, using equivalent fractions and simplification.

Before you teach

- How secure are children in their understanding of fractions?
- Are there any children who still need support in identifying the value of each digit in a decimal?

NATIONAL CURRICULUM LINKS

Year 6 Number – fractions (including decimals and percentages)

Associate a fraction with division and calculate decimal fraction equivalents [for example, 0·375] for a simple fraction [for example, $\frac{3}{8}$].

Identify the value of each digit in numbers given to three decimal places and multiply and divide numbers by 10, 100 and 1,000 giving answers up to three decimal places.

ASSESSING MASTERY

Children can use their knowledge of place value in decimal numbers to convert fractions to decimals and decimals to fractions, and can explain how to determine the numerator and the denominator when converting. They are able to identify common factors in order to write the corresponding fraction in its simplest form.

COMMON MISCONCEPTIONS

Children may incorrectly identify the value of each digit in a decimal, and so make mistakes in identifying the denominator and/or the numerator of the corresponding fraction. Ask:

- *How many tenths are there in the decimal? How many hundredths? How will you show this as a fraction?*

STRENGTHENING UNDERSTANDING

Use place value grids or base 10 equipment to support children's understanding of place value. Use this equipment alongside models of a whole square divided into tenths, hundredths and thousandths. Graph paper can be useful for this.

GOING DEEPER

Link the learning from this lesson to the context of measure. Children could work out the fraction of a unit of measure from a given measurement, through questions such as: *What fraction of a kilogram is 375 grams?*

KEY LANGUAGE

In lesson: fraction, decimal, equivalent, simplify, common factor, numerator, denominator

Other language to be used by the teacher: place value, tenths, hundredths, thousandths, placeholder

STRUCTURES AND REPRESENTATIONS

Place value grid, tenths / hundredths / thousandths grid, number line, fraction wall

RESOURCES

Optional: base 10 equipment, place value grids, graph paper, fraction walls

 In the eTextbook of this lesson, you will find interactive links to a selection of teaching tools.

Quick recap

Challenge children to describe the place value of the digit 4 in each of these numbers:

0·413   0·394   0·54

Discover

Unit 9: Decimals, Lesson 8

WAYS OF WORKING Pair work

ASK

- Question ❶ a): *What is the value of each digit?*
- Question ❶ a): *How do you know which fraction goes with which decimal number?*
- Question ❶ a): *Can you see a pattern between the fractions for each decimal?*

IN FOCUS Question ❶ b) asks children to simplify the fractions. Children should have experience of this from Unit 4. By simplifying the fractions, children can begin to relate decimals to fractions where the denominator is a factor or multiple of 10.

PRACTICAL TIPS Use graph paper to represent the drawings in the picture. Children could shade in the correct proportion for each decimal and/or fraction. This will help to secure a visual representation of decimals as well as fractions where the denominator is a power of 10.

ANSWERS

Question ❶ a): $\frac{6}{1,000}$ is equivalent to 0·006.

$\frac{6}{100}$ and $\frac{60}{1,000}$ are equivalent to 0·06.

$\frac{6}{10}$, $\frac{60}{100}$ and $\frac{600}{1,000}$ are equivalent to 0·6.

Question ❶ b): $\frac{6}{1,000}$ can be simplified to $\frac{3}{500}$.

$\frac{6}{100}$ and $\frac{60}{1,000}$ can be simplified to $\frac{3}{50}$.

$\frac{6}{10}$, $\frac{60}{100}$ and $\frac{600}{1,000}$ can be simplified to $\frac{3}{5}$.

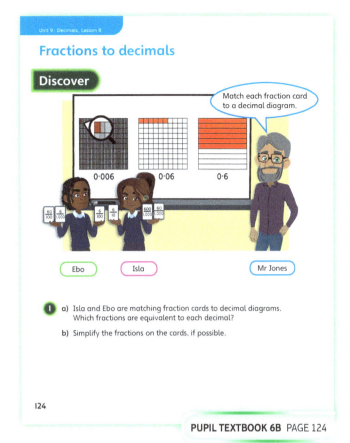

Fractions to decimals

Discover

Match each fraction card to a decimal diagram.

0·006   0·06   0·6

Ebo   Isla   Mr Jones

❶ a) Isla and Ebo are matching fraction cards to decimal diagrams. Which fractions are equivalent to each decimal?

b) Simplify the fractions on the cards, if possible.

124

PUPIL TEXTBOOK 6B PAGE 124

Share

WAYS OF WORKING Whole class teacher led

ASK

- Question ❶ a): *Can you see a relationship between the equivalent fractions?*
- Question ❶ a): *What helped you to work out which fraction went with which decimal?*

IN FOCUS In question ❶ a), children are shown that there is more than one fraction for 0·6 and 0·06. To help them see why this is the case, use a place value grid and put placeholders after the 6 digit, for example, 0·60 to represent $\frac{60}{100}$ and 0·600 to represent $\frac{600}{1,000}$. Ask: *Have you changed the value of the number by doing this? Why not?*

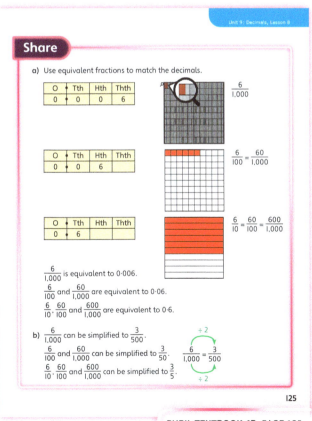

Share

a) Use equivalent fractions to match the decimals.

O	Tth	Hth	Thth
0	0	0	6

$\frac{6}{1,000}$

O	Tth	Hth	Thth
0	0	6	

$\frac{6}{100} = \frac{60}{1,000}$

O	Tth	Hth	Thth
0	6		

$\frac{6}{10} = \frac{60}{100} = \frac{600}{1,000}$

$\frac{6}{1,000}$ is equivalent to 0·006.

$\frac{6}{100}$ and $\frac{60}{1,000}$ are equivalent to 0·06.

$\frac{6}{10}$, $\frac{60}{100}$ and $\frac{600}{1,000}$ are equivalent to 0·6.

b) $\frac{6}{1,000}$ can be simplified to $\frac{3}{500}$.

$\frac{6}{100}$ and $\frac{60}{1,000}$ can be simplified to $\frac{3}{50}$.

$\frac{6}{10}$, $\frac{60}{100}$ and $\frac{600}{1,000}$ can be simplified to $\frac{3}{5}$.

$$\frac{6}{1,000} = \frac{3}{500} \quad \div 2$$

125

PUPIL TEXTBOOK 6B PAGE 125

Think together

Whole class teacher led (I do, We do, You do)

ASK

- Questions **1** and **2**: *What do you notice about the denominators?*
- Question **3**: *How would you explain how to simplify fractions?*
- Question **3** b): *Were you able to determine any of the fractions in their simplest form straight away?*

IN FOCUS In question **1**, children are asked to find decimals that are equivalent to common fractions including quarters and tenths. In question **1** a), children could first find an equivalent fraction with 100 as the denominator, for example, $\frac{1}{4} = \frac{25}{100}$ (multiplying the numerator and denominator by 25). From there, they should recognise that $\frac{25}{100} = 0.25$.

Children should consider how each answer might help them to work out the next. Flo prompts children to memorise these decimal equivalents as they will be helpful facts to recall and use in the future.

STRENGTHEN Use base 10 equipment or graph paper to model the decimals. This may help children to visualise how the 'whole' is divided up.

DEEPEN Incorporate a measures context by posing questions such as: *What fraction of 1 metre is 150 centimetres?*

ASSESSMENT CHECKPOINT Check whether children are secure in identifying the place value of the digits in decimals. Can they use this knowledge to represent a decimal as a fraction where the denominator is a power of 10?

ANSWERS

Question **1** a): $\frac{1}{4} = 0.25$ Question **1** b): $\frac{1}{10} = 0.1$
$\frac{2}{4} = 0.5$ $\frac{2}{10} = 0.2$
$\frac{3}{4} = 0.75$ $\frac{3}{10} = 0.3$
  $\frac{5}{10} = 0.5$
  $\frac{7}{10} = 0.7$

Question **2** a): 0.93, 0.12, 0.55, 0.347, 0.25, 0.073

Question **2** b): $0.6 = \frac{6}{10} = \frac{3}{5}$ $0.23 = \frac{23}{100}$
$0.06 = \frac{6}{100} = \frac{3}{50}$ $0.023 = \frac{23}{1,000}$
$0.006 = \frac{6}{1,000} = \frac{3}{500}$ $0.123 = \frac{123}{1,000}$

Question **3** a): $0.4 = \frac{4}{10} = \frac{2}{5}$ $1.2 = \frac{12}{10} = 1\frac{1}{5}$
$0.6 = \frac{16}{10} = \frac{3}{5}$ $1.4 = \frac{14}{10} = 1\frac{2}{5}$
$0.8 = \frac{8}{10} = \frac{4}{5}$ $1.6 = \frac{16}{10} = 1\frac{3}{5}$
$1.8 = \frac{18}{10} = 1\frac{4}{5}$

Question **3** b): $0.25 = \frac{25}{100} = \frac{1}{4}$ $0.125 = \frac{125}{1,000} = \frac{1}{8}$
$0.875 = \frac{875}{1,000} = \frac{7}{8}$ $0.35 = \frac{35}{100} = \frac{7}{20}$
$0.95 = \frac{95}{100} = \frac{19}{20}$

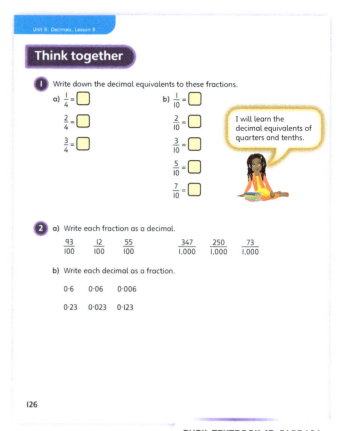

Think together

1 Write down the decimal equivalents to these fractions.

a) $\frac{1}{4} = \square$ b) $\frac{1}{10} = \square$

$\frac{2}{4} = \square$ $\frac{2}{10} = \square$

$\frac{3}{4} = \square$ $\frac{3}{10} = \square$

  $\frac{5}{10} = \square$

  $\frac{7}{10} = \square$

I will learn the decimal equivalents of quarters and tenths.

2 a) Write each fraction as a decimal.

$\frac{93}{100}$ $\frac{12}{100}$ $\frac{55}{100}$ $\frac{347}{1,000}$ $\frac{250}{1,000}$ $\frac{73}{1,000}$

b) Write each decimal as a fraction.

0.6   0.06   0.006

0.23   0.023   0.123

126

PUPIL TEXTBOOK 6B PAGE 126

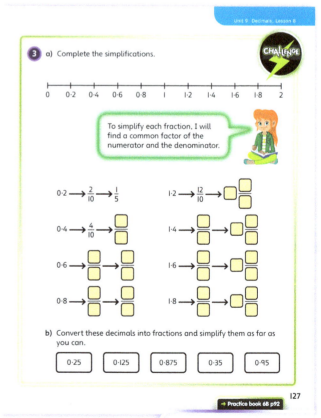

3 a) Complete the simplifications.

CHALLENGE

To simplify each fraction, I will find a common factor of the numerator and the denominator.

$0.2 \rightarrow \frac{2}{10} \rightarrow \frac{1}{5}$ $1.2 \rightarrow \frac{12}{10} \rightarrow \square$

$0.4 \rightarrow \frac{4}{10} \rightarrow \square$ $1.4 \rightarrow \square \rightarrow \square$

$0.6 \rightarrow \square \rightarrow \square$ $1.6 \rightarrow \square \rightarrow \square$

$0.8 \rightarrow \square \rightarrow \square$ $1.8 \rightarrow \square \rightarrow \square$

b) Convert these decimals into fractions and simplify them as far as you can.

| 0.25 | 0.125 | 0.875 | 0.35 | 0.95 |

127

→ Practice book 6B p92

PUPIL TEXTBOOK 6B PAGE 127

Practice

WAYS OF WORKING Pair work

IN FOCUS Question ③ introduces the fraction wall alongside the number line to support children in converting fractions to decimals. Each fraction has a denominator that is a factor or multiple of 10 and children can use equivalent fractions to help them find each answer.

STRENGTHEN Provide children with place value grids if they are not secure in their understanding of place value in decimals, as this is essential when converting decimals to fractions.

DEEPEN Provide children with a mix of decimals and fractions to place in order, such as 0·35, $\frac{5}{20}$, 0·125, $\frac{1}{4}$. They could then come up with their own similar problems for a partner to solve.

ASSESSMENT CHECKPOINT Assess whether children can convert a decimal into a fraction where the denominator is a power of 10, and simplify the fraction to its simplest form. Can children match decimals to their fraction equivalent, showing that they are secure in their understanding of place value in decimal numbers? Can children convert a fraction back into a decimal?

ANSWERS Answers for the **Practice** part of the lesson can be found in the *Power Maths* online subscription.

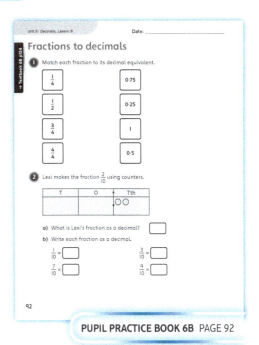

PUPIL PRACTICE BOOK 6B PAGE 92

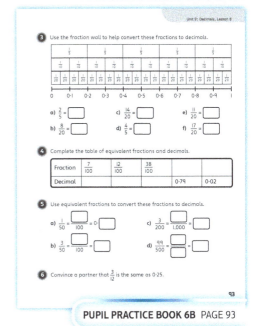

PUPIL PRACTICE BOOK 6B PAGE 93

Reflect

WAYS OF WORKING Independent thinking

IN FOCUS This section requires children to articulate the common fraction and decimal equivalents that they are familiar with. They need to have a secure conceptual understanding of decimals and how they relate to fractions in order to do this.

ASSESSMENT CHECKPOINT Check whether children are able to explain how to find decimal equivalents of fifths, tenths and quarters.

ANSWERS Answers for the **Reflect** part of the lesson can be found in the *Power Maths* online subscription.

After the lesson ⏸

- Are children secure in their understanding of place value and/or fractions?
- What models were successful in supporting children's understanding of converting decimals to fractions?

PUPIL PRACTICE BOOK 6B PAGE 94

Fractions as division

Learning focus

In this lesson, children will calculate the decimal equivalents of fractions by dividing the numerator by the denominator.

Before you teach

- Are children confident with formal division?
- How secure are children in their understanding of fractions and finding equivalent fractions?

NATIONAL CURRICULUM LINKS

Year 6 Number – fractions (including decimals and percentages)

Associate a fraction with division and calculate decimal fraction equivalents [for example, 0·375] for a simple fraction [for example, $\frac{3}{8}$].

ASSESSING MASTERY

Children understand that a fraction represents division where the numerator can be divided by the denominator to calculate the decimal equivalent. Children can carry out compact formal methods of division fluently where the answer is a decimal and can identify when it will be a recurring decimal.

COMMON MISCONCEPTIONS

Children may not notice the relationship between a familiar fraction and a fraction where the numerator is a multiple or factor of the familiar fraction. Ask:

- *Is this an equivalent fraction? What multiplication facts might help you to find out?*

Children may make errors in place value when carrying out formal division, particularly with placeholders. Ask:

- *What would this look like on a place value grid?*

STRENGTHENING UNDERSTANDING

Fraction walls can help children identify relationships between fractions with different denominators. Providing decimal equivalents of common fractions will give children a bank of facts to draw upon.

GOING DEEPER

Give children the opportunity to explore how multiplying or dividing the numerator or denominator affects the equivalent decimal. Ask them to summarise what happens.

KEY LANGUAGE

In lesson: decimal, fraction, convert, division, equivalence, **recurring decimals**

Other language to be used by the teacher: factor, multiple, place value, placeholder, numerator, denominator

STRUCTURES AND REPRESENTATIONS

Number line, short division

RESOURCES

Optional: fraction walls, place value grids, strips of paper

 In the eTextbook of this lesson, you will find interactive links to a selection of teaching tools.

Quick recap

Ask children to use a written division method to solve each of these calculations:

560 ÷ 5   364 ÷ 7   2,385 ÷ 5

Discover

Unit 9: Decimals, Lesson 9

WAYS OF WORKING Pair work

ASK

- Question ① a): *What would you say to explain how you found this fraction?*
- Question ① b): *Are there any points on the number line that you already know the decimal equivalent of?*
- Question ① b): *What do you need to do to help you complete this question?*

IN FOCUS $\frac{3}{8}$ is not the first fraction that children would identify. However, they can use their knowledge of $\frac{1}{4}$ and $\frac{1}{2}$ and their understanding of the relationship between $\frac{1}{4}$ and $\frac{1}{8}$ to find it. This highlights how being able to identify common unit fractions can help when finding other fractions.

PRACTICAL TIPS Provide children with three equal strips of paper. They can fold one into halves, a second into quarters and a third into eighths. They can then use the strips to create their own fraction walls.

ANSWERS

Question ① a): The arrow is pointing to $\frac{3}{8}$.

Question ① b): The arrow is pointing to 0·375.

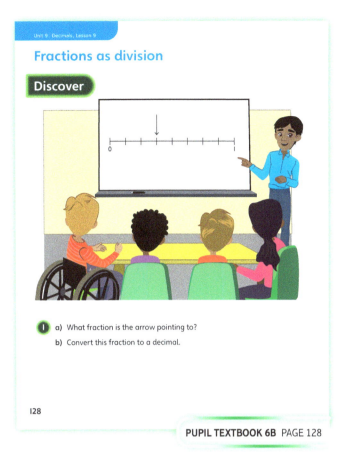

Fractions as division

Discover

① a) What fraction is the arrow pointing to?

b) Convert this fraction to a decimal.

128

PUPIL TEXTBOOK 6B PAGE 128

Share

WAYS OF WORKING Whole class teacher led

ASK

- Question ① a): *Which other fractions do you recognise on the number line? Could you simplify them?*
- Question ① b): *Why are there 0s after the decimal point?*

IN FOCUS Question ① b) shows how a fraction can be converted into a decimal by dividing the numerator by the denominator. Emphasise that a fraction is another way of writing division and that the horizontal line means 'divide.' Relate this to the division sign (÷), which resembles a fraction, with the two dots representing the numerator and denominator. If necessary, ask children to use division to convert known fractions, such as $\frac{1}{2}$, $\frac{1}{4}$ and $\frac{1}{5}$, into decimals.

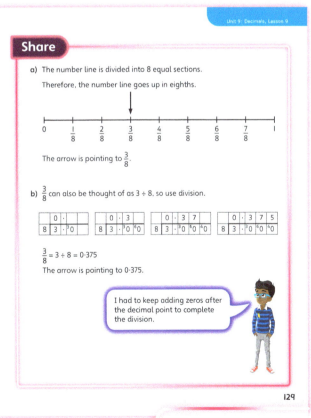

Share

a) The number line is divided into 8 equal sections.

Therefore, the number line goes up in eighths.

The arrow is pointing to $\frac{3}{8}$.

b) $\frac{3}{8}$ can also be thought of as 3 ÷ 8, so use division.

$\frac{3}{8}$ = 3 ÷ 8 = 0·375

The arrow is pointing to 0·375.

> I had to keep adding zeros after the decimal point to complete the division.

129

PUPIL TEXTBOOK 6B PAGE 129

Think together

WAYS OF WORKING Whole class teacher led (I do, We do, You do)

ASK

- Questions ❶ and ❷: *What previous learning can you use to help you?*
- Question ❸: *Does it help to simplify any of the fractions first?*

IN FOCUS Question ❸ requires children to look carefully at the numbers involved and choose the most efficient method or approach. If children use the same method for each calculation, it may be worthwhile to prompt them to use different methods. If they cannot use known fraction or decimal equivalents to solve some of these, it may highlight gaps in their understanding of fractions or their ability to find equivalent fractions.

STRENGTHEN Provide children with a fraction wall to help them find equivalent fractions. Providing a reference of common fraction or decimal equivalents can also help them to derive the decimals of some less familiar fractions. Looking back at the learning from Unit 3 may support them in carrying out formal divisions.

DEEPEN Ask children what happens to the decimal equivalent of a fraction if the denominator doubles. What about if the denominator is multiplied by 5? Can they explain why this is?

ASSESSMENT CHECKPOINT Check whether children are secure in formal methods of division and their understanding of fractions as a representation of division. Can they represent a division as a fraction and convert it to a decimal? Do children demonstrate understanding of fractions and use different methods to find decimal equivalents, choosing the most efficient?

ANSWERS

Question ❶:

$$3 \overline{)1 \cdot {}^1 0} = 0 \cdot$$

Children should notice that:
- Converting a proper fraction results in a decimal < 1.
- The denominator is the number to divide by.
- The numerator is the number to divide into.

Question ❷: $\frac{5}{8} = 0.625$ $\frac{1}{9} = 0.111$

$\frac{1}{6} = 0.166$ $\frac{2}{5} = 0.4$

Question ❸: $\frac{6}{9} = \frac{2}{3} = 0.667$ simplify then divide

$\frac{3}{25} = \frac{12}{100} = 0.12$ convert to equivalent fraction in hundredths

$\frac{3}{50} = \frac{6}{100} = 0.06$ convert to equivalent fraction in hundredths

$\frac{5}{12} = 0.417$ divide

$\frac{300}{450} = \frac{2}{3} = 0.667$ simplify then divide

$\frac{6}{90} = \frac{1}{15} = 0.067$ simplify then divide

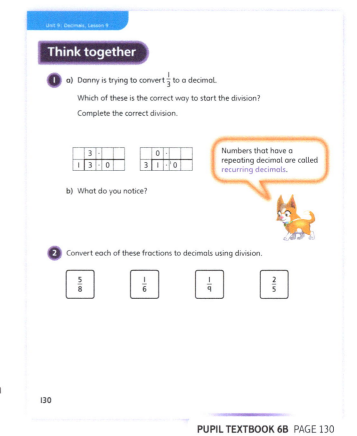

Unit 9: Decimals, Lesson 9

Think together

❶ a) Danny is trying to convert $\frac{1}{3}$ to a decimal.

Which of these is the correct way to start the division?

Complete the correct division.

Numbers that have a repeating decimal are called recurring decimals.

b) What do you notice?

❷ Convert each of these fractions to decimals using division.

$\frac{5}{8}$ $\frac{1}{6}$ $\frac{1}{9}$ $\frac{2}{5}$

130

PUPIL TEXTBOOK 6B PAGE 130

❸ Discuss with a partner different methods for converting these fractions into decimals.

CHALLENGE

$\frac{6}{9}$ $\frac{3}{25}$ $\frac{3}{50}$

$\frac{5}{12}$ $\frac{300}{450}$ $\frac{6}{90}$

Convert each fraction into a decimal using an efficient method.

Round any recurring decimals to three decimal places.

The phrase 'three decimal places' can also be shortened to 'three dp', which is quicker to write and say.

To round to three dp, I will look at the fourth decimal place and decide whether to round up or down.

→ Practice book 6B p95   131

PUPIL TEXTBOOK 6B PAGE 131

Practice

IN FOCUS Question **5** b) prompts children to estimate the decimal equivalents of given fractions. To do this, they need to consider the value of the fraction and to think where it would be in relation to other known fractions or where they would place it on a number line. This helps children to consider the numbers involved and provides them with a way of checking their answers through reasoning.

STRENGTHEN Provide children with a reference of known fraction or decimal equivalents as well as a fraction wall to support their reasoning and calculating.

DEEPEN Ask: *If $\frac{3}{8} = 0\cdot375$, what fraction is 3·75? 37·5? 0·0375? 0·1875? Can you derive any other fraction or decimal equivalents?*

ASSESSMENT CHECKPOINT Assess whether children are able to use known fraction or decimal equivalents to calculate other fraction or decimal equivalents. Can children calculate the decimal equivalent of a fraction by dividing the numerator by the denominator?

ANSWERS Answers for the **Practice** part of the lesson can be found in the *Power Maths* online subscription.

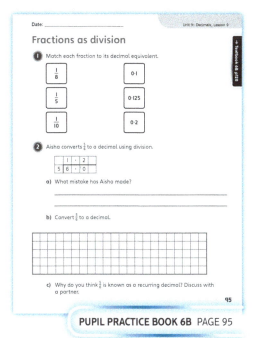

PUPIL PRACTICE BOOK 6B PAGE 95

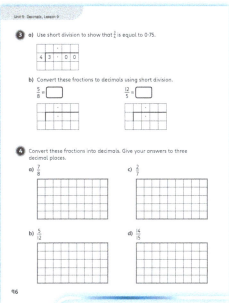

PUPIL PRACTICE BOOK 6B PAGE 96

Reflect

IN FOCUS This question prompts children to think about using division to convert fractions to decimals

ASSESSMENT CHECKPOINT In this question, look for children's ability to convert fractions into decimals and reason about the relationship between division, fractions and their decimal equivalents.

ANSWERS Answers for the **Reflect** part of the lesson can be found in the *Power Maths* online subscription.

After the lesson ⏸

- Do children now have an increased knowledge of fraction or decimal equivalents that they can draw upon?
- Do children understand the relationship between fractions and division?

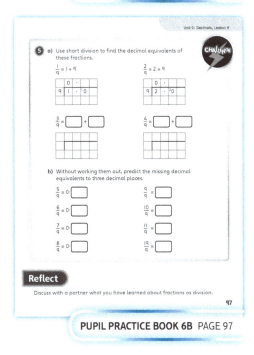

PUPIL PRACTICE BOOK 6B PAGE 97

End of unit check

Don't forget the unit assessment grid in your *Power Maths* online subscription.

WAYS OF WORKING Group work adult led

IN FOCUS This **End of unit check** will allow you to focus on children's understanding of decimals. The questions are designed to draw out misconceptions. Question **1** assesses children's ability to divide by a power of 10. Question **2** assesses children's ability to convert a fraction to a decimal. Questions **3** and **5** assess children's understanding of place value.

ANSWERS AND COMMENTARY By the end of this unit, children should be able to add and subtract decimals with up to 3 decimal places, and round them to a specified degree of accuracy. They should also be confident multiplying and dividing decimals by powers of 10. They should be able to convert a fraction to a decimal either through division or by applying known fraction decimal equivalents. They should be able to carry out formal short division with decimals, understand the place value of decimals and how it is applied in multiplication, and be able to apply known multiplication facts to dividing and multiplying decimals.

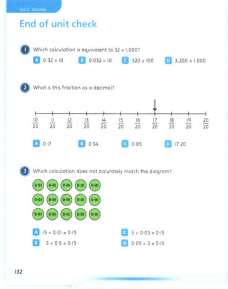

PUPIL TEXTBOOK 6B PAGE 132

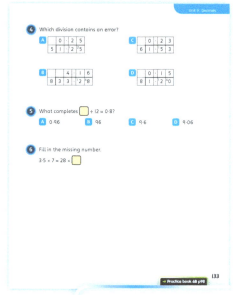

PUPIL TEXTBOOK 6B PAGE 133

Q	A	WRONG ANSWERS AND MISCONCEPTIONS	STRENGTHENING UNDERSTANDING
1	A	B or C suggest an error in place value. D suggests children do not understand how to multiply or divide by powers of 10.	Have place value grids available to support children with determining the value of each digit.
2	C	A suggests children have divided by 100 rather than by 20. B suggests children have divided by 10 and then multiplied by 2. D suggests children do not understand how to convert fractions to decimals.	Children could use base 10 equipment to support their understanding of calculating with decimals.
3	B	A, C or D indicate an error in place value.	
4	C	A, B, or D indicate children do not fully understand how to carry out formal division with decimals.	Resources can also be used by the teacher to help model comparing decimals, as well as exchanging when multiplying or dividing.
5	C	A, B or D indicate children do not fully understand place value of decimals.	
6	0·875	If children answer 14, this suggests they have understood that 28 is four times bigger than 7 but have multiplied 3·5 by 4, rather than dividing it by 4.	

My journal

WAYS OF WORKING Independent thinking

ANSWERS AND COMMENTARY

Children have to carry out a multiplication and a division with each of the inputs. However, they may realise they can work out $0.8 \div 20$ first, and then multiply each input by that answer. Ask: *Is there more than one way of doing this?* Another way to look at this problem is to think of $0.8 \div 20$ as a fraction, $\frac{0.8}{20}$ or $\frac{8}{200}$ or $\frac{4}{100}$ or $\frac{1}{25}$. Children could then multiply each input by 4 and divide by 100.

The answers are:

$3 \times 0.8 \div 20 = 0.12$
$6 \times 0.8 \div 20 = 0.24$
$20 \times 0.8 \div 20 = 0.8$
$100 \times 0.8 \div 20 = 4$

Power check

WAYS OF WORKING Independent thinking

ASK

- *How confident are you in identifying the value of each digit in a decimal number?*
- *Can you explain how to multiply and divide a decimal by 100?*
- *Can you explain the relationship between a decimal and a fraction?*
- *How confident are you in multiplying a decimal by a whole number?*
- *How confident are you in dividing a decimal by a whole number?*

Power play

WAYS OF WORKING Pair work

IN FOCUS This activity will show whether children have a secure understanding of place value as well as determining if they can multiply decimal numbers. Throughout the activity, ask children to comment on their decisions about where they put the digits in their multiplication, as this will give you an insight into their thinking and reasoning.

ANSWERS AND COMMENTARY Answers will vary. If children are able to make decisions about where to place a digit in their multiplication based on what numbers they have already plotted on the number line, this shows that they have a secure understanding of place value in decimals and how to compare and order decimals. Look at how they carry out the multiplication. Are they using known multiplication facts and adjusting correctly?

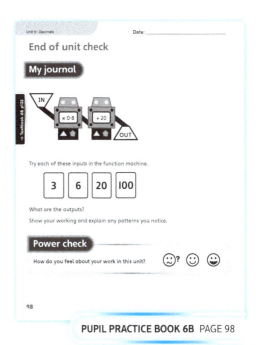

PUPIL PRACTICE BOOK 6B PAGE 98

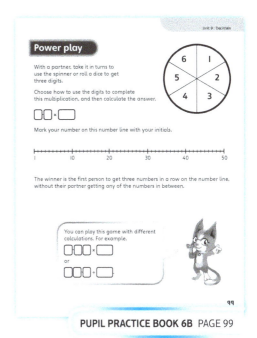

PUPIL PRACTICE BOOK 6B PAGE 99

After the unit ⏸

- Were children able to explain clearly about the place value of each digit and the implications of these when calculating with decimals?
- The easiest application of the learning from this unit is with measures, particularly converting between different units of measure. Can you provide opportunities for children to apply their learning in other curriculum areas such as PE, Design and Science?

Strengthen and **Deepen** activities for this unit can be found in the *Power Maths* online subscription.

Unit 10
Percentages

Don't forget to watch the Unit 10 video!

Mastery Expert tip! 'In my experience of teaching this unit, it is beneficial to use lots of representations, such as a hundredths grid, bar models and number lines, so children get a deeper understanding of percentages, decimals and fractions.'

WHY THIS UNIT IS IMPORTANT

This unit focuses on strengthening children's knowledge of percentages. Children will learn a range of strategies to find percentages of amounts. They will then apply these strategies to convert between percentages, decimals and fractions. They will develop their understanding throughout the unit and ultimately use their knowledge to solve related puzzles and multi-step problems.

WHERE THIS UNIT FITS

→ Unit 9: Decimals

→ **Unit 10: Percentages**

→ Unit 11: Measure – perimeter, area and volume

Before they start this unit, it is expected that children:

- understand that 'per cent' relates to 'number of parts per hundred'
- can represent a percentage on a hundredths grid
- have a firm grasp of decimals and fractions (up to thousandths)
- can confidently convert between and solve problems involving decimals and fractions
- are able to convert fractions (with a denominator of 100) to percentages
- are able to convert decimals (up to two decimal places) to percentages.

ASSESSING MASTERY

Assess mastery in this unit by observing which children have a deeper understanding of percentages. They should be able to efficiently convert between decimals, percentages and fractions, including when the denominator of the fraction is not 100 or a factor of 100. They should be comfortable with finding percentages of amounts – even when there is a missing value – such as '40% of ☐ = 25'. Finally, children will be able to solve multi-step problems and confidently reason why the solution they found is correct.

COMMON MISCONCEPTIONS	STRENGTHENING UNDERSTANDING	GOING DEEPER
Children may convert a decimal, fraction or percentage incorrectly; this is particularly common with fractions which do not have a denominator of 100.	Encourage children to represent percentages on a hundred grid.	Solve problems involving a combination of percentages, fractions and decimals.
Children may work out percentages of amounts with missing values incorrectly; for example, to find the answer to '10% of ☐ = 25', they may just find 10% of 25.	Practise finding percentages of given amounts first. Afterwards, children can draw diagrams to support their understanding of missing value problems. If, for example, they knew that 10% of the total was 25, how could they represent this on a diagram and then use the diagram to find the total?	Challenge children to find percentages of amounts in which there are missing numbers.
Children may solve word problems incorrectly by doing the wrong calculations.	Ask children to represent multi-step word problems on a bar model.	Can children come up with their own multi-step problems involving mixed percentages, fractions or decimals?

Unit 10: Percentages

Use these pages to introduce the unit to children. Focus on the number line and discuss how it shows decimals, fractions and percentages.

STRUCTURES AND REPRESENTATIONS

Number line: This model helps children to visualise the order of numbers. In this unit, it will help children to understand and order decimals, fractions and percentages, and to find equivalent values.

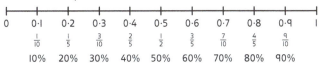

Bar model: This is a powerful representation that allows children to organise information visually. It helps children to find the fraction, decimal or percentage left over in problem-solving questions. It is also used to find the total, or the difference between amounts, in fractions, decimals or percentages.

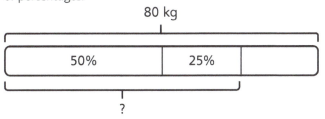

KEY LANGUAGE

There is some key language that children will need to know as part of the learning in this unit:

➜ per cent (%), percentage

➜ parts, whole

➜ decimal

➜ fraction, equivalent fraction, tenth, hundredth, half, quarter

➜ less than (<), greater than (>)

➜ divide (÷), share, multiply (×)

➜ convert, compare, order, simplify

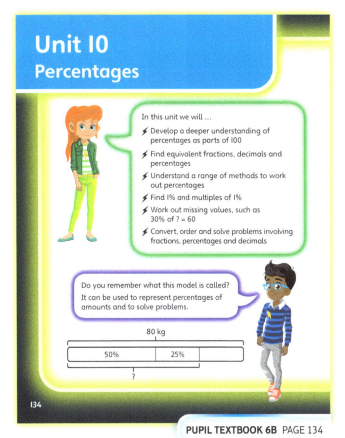

PUPIL TEXTBOOK 6B PAGE 134

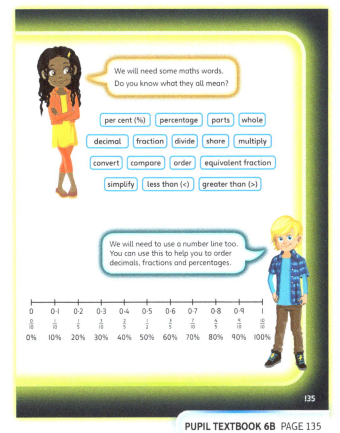

PUPIL TEXTBOOK 6B PAGE 135

Understand percentages

Learning focus

In this lesson, children will work with fractions that are shown as 'out of 100' and will express these as percentages. They will use the % sign to represent per cent.

Before you teach

- Can children recognise and write the percentage sign?
- Can children recognise and write fractions as hundredths?

NATIONAL CURRICULUM LINKS

Year 6 Number – fractions (including decimals and percentages)

Recall and use equivalences between simple fractions, decimals and percentages, including in different contexts.

ASSESSING MASTERY

Children can understand that a fraction with a denominator of 100 represents an amount out of 100 and can use this to convert it to a percentage.

COMMON MISCONCEPTIONS

Children may think that the total number of shaded parts on any diagram is always the same as the percentage. Ask:
- *How many parts are shaded? How many total parts are there? Can you write this as a fraction? How can you find the equivalent fraction if there are 100 parts? What is that as a percentage?*

STRENGTHENING UNDERSTANDING

Ask children to shade different amounts of numbers on 100 squares to support them in making the link with percentage as the number of parts out of 100.

GOING DEEPER

Challenge children to explore percentages such as 99%. Ask: *How else could you show this percentage? How does this percentage relate to the whole?*

KEY LANGUAGE

In lesson: out of, percentage, hundredths, 100, total, fraction, per cent (%)

Other language to be used by the teacher: denominator

STRUCTURES AND REPRESENTATIONS

Hundred grid

RESOURCES

Mandatory: hundred grids, 100 squares, bead strings

Optional: counters, base 10 equipment

 In the eTextbook of this lesson, you will find interactive links to a selection of teaching tools.

Quick recap

Challenge children to represent fractions with a denominator of 100 in different ways, for example by using place value equipment, number lines or shading on a grid.

Discover

ASK

- Question **1** a): *How many circles are there in total?*
- Question **1** a): *How many circles are shaded?*
- Question **1** b): *What does 'per cent' mean?*
- Question **1** b): *Can you explain your way of understanding per cent?*

IN FOCUS The scenario shows a visual representation of a number of parts 'out of 100'. Discuss why it is important to establish the total number of circles and to find how many of those circles are painted. Agree that this can be expressed as a fraction with hundredths and it can also be expressed as a percentage.

PRACTICAL TIPS Use counters on hundred grids to explore this scenario together as a class. Repeat with other amounts of counters, expressing these first as *x* parts out of 100 parts, then as a fraction with hundredths and finally as a percentage.

ANSWERS

Question **1** a): Mr Jones has painted $\frac{30}{100}$ or $\frac{3}{10}$ of the circles.

Question **1** b): Mr Jones has painted 30% of the circles

Understand percentages

Discover

My picture has 100 circles in total.

Mr Jones

1 a) What fraction of the circles has Mr Jones painted?

b) What percentage of the circles has Mr Jones painted?

136

PUPIL TEXTBOOK 6B PAGE 136

Share

ASK

- Question **1** a): *Can you explain why the denominator is 100?*
- Question **1** a): *Can you explain why the numerator is 30?*
- Question **1** b): *Why is the answer not 3%?*
- Question **1** b): *What would the percentage be if one more circle was painted?*
- Question **1** b): *What percentage of the circles are not painted?*

IN FOCUS Look together at the fraction of circles painted and link this to the percentage of circles painted. The numerator is the number of circles painted and the denominator is the total number of circles. This represents 30 circles out of 100, which is the same as 30% of all the circles.

Refer to Dexter's comment and read the fraction aloud together. Agree that Dexter has simplified the fraction to its simplest form (tenths) but that this still represents a number of parts out of 100 and so it can still be expressed as a percentage.

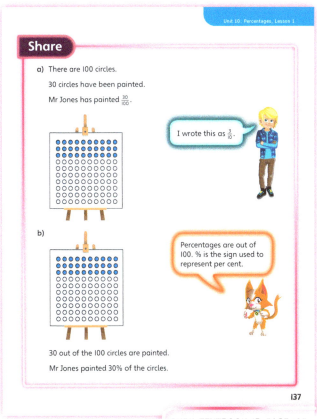

Share

a) There are 100 circles.

30 circles have been painted.

Mr Jones has painted $\frac{30}{100}$.

I wrote this as $\frac{3}{10}$.

b)

Percentages are out of 100. % is the sign used to represent per cent.

30 out of the 100 circles are painted.

Mr Jones painted 30% of the circles.

137

PUPIL TEXTBOOK 6B PAGE 137

Think together

WAYS OF WORKING Whole class teacher led (I do, We do, You do)

ASK

- Question **1**: *How will you count efficiently?*
- Question **2**: *Can you say these percentages as fractions 'out of 100'?*
- Question **3**: *How could you change this to show 'out of 100'?*

IN FOCUS Question **1** requires children to recognise basic percentages from representations where different amounts of squares are shaded on hundred grids.

In question **2**, children are asked to use their understanding of per cent as parts out of 100 to create models or diagrams that show given percentages.

Question **3** introduces children to a situation where the total number of parts is not 100. They explore how this can be converted to a percentage.

STRENGTHEN Children can use hundred grids or bead strings alongside their working in order to discuss and justify their reasoning. They should describe how their chosen model represents a given number of parts out of 100.

DEEPEN Challenge children to find as many different ways as they can to shade 99% of the squares on a hundred grid. Ask: *Is there a quick way to do this? What is the pattern? How many squares are not shaded?* To follow on from question **3**, you could present students with other grids in which the number of squares is a factor or multiple of 100. You could ask them to shade in a given percentage.

If the number of squares is a factor of 100 (for example, 25, because 100 = 25 × 4), then to shade 80% you must divide 80 by 4 to give 20 squares.

If the number of squares is a multiple of 100, you need to multiply rather than divide.

ASSESSMENT CHECKPOINT Question **2** assesses whether children can create a model or diagram to accurately represent a given percentage.

ANSWERS

Question **1** a): 45%

Question **1** b): 97%

Question **1** c): 6%

Question **1** d): 90%

Question **2**: Children should shade empty hundred grids to show:
18%: 1 complete row (or column) and 8 cells in adjoining row (or column).
40%: 4 complete rows (or columns).
7%: first 7 cells of top row (or column).

Question **3**: 64% of the grid is shaded. There are 50 sections in the whole grid, so each section is worth 2%.

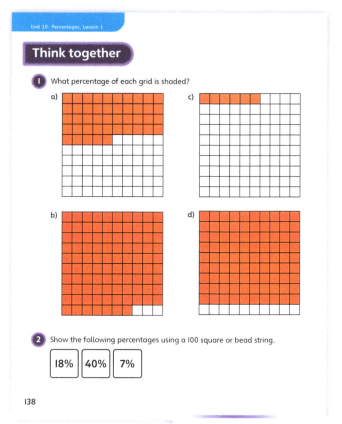

PUPIL TEXTBOOK 6B PAGE 138

PUPIL TEXTBOOK 6B PAGE 139

Practice

WAYS OF WORKING Pair work

IN FOCUS Question ❶ requires children to recognise percentages represented with shaded squares on a hundred grid, whereas in question ❷, they are asked to represent a given percentage by shading squares on hundred grids themselves.

Question ❸ uses a 100 square to represent the whole and asks children to break it up into several different parts which are each given as percentages. In question ❹, children use a numbered 100 square to explore number patterns in the context of percentages. In question ❺, children discuss the use of percentages in the context of a story problem.

Question ❻ explores the generation of percentages where the denominator of the corresponding fraction is not 100. Children should identify that the parts need to be multiplied by 2 to find the number of parts out of 100.

STRENGTHEN Provide hundred grids for children to shade and create further questions in the style of question ❸ to give practice in identifying several different percentages from one diagram.

DEEPEN Refer children to the grid in question ❻. Ask: *How many different ways could you find to shade 1% of this grid? Can you explain what you found?*

ASSESSMENT CHECKPOINT Assess children on their answers to question ❹. If children can confidently work with both percentages and number patterns on the 100 square, they are likely to be confident in their understanding of basic percentages.

ANSWERS Answers for the **Practice** part of the lesson can be found in the *Power Maths* online subscription.

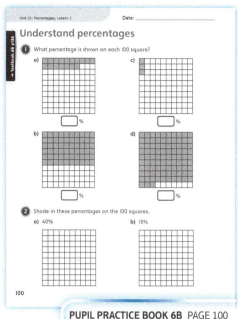

PUPIL PRACTICE BOOK 6B PAGE 100

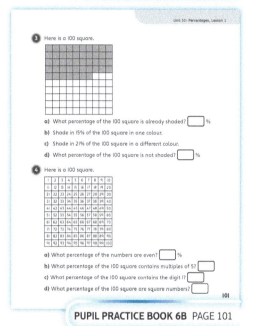

PUPIL PRACTICE BOOK 6B PAGE 101

Reflect

WAYS OF WORKING Pair work

IN FOCUS The **Reflect** part of the lesson prompts children to discuss the concept of percentages. They can explore what 'per cent' means and how it is linked to other representations of a number of parts out of 100.

ASSESSMENT CHECKPOINT Assess whether children can explain what 'per cent' means and how it is related to the number 100.

ANSWERS Answers for the **Reflect** part of the lesson can be found in the *Power Maths* online subscription.

After the lesson ⏸

- Were children able to identify and represent basic percentages out of 100?
- Are children confident with questions where the total number of parts is a factor of 100?
- Can children think of any other story problem contexts where percentages might be helpful?

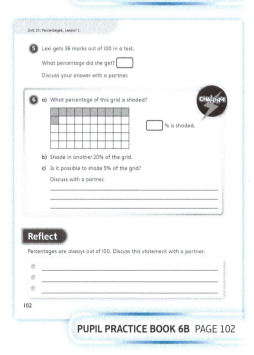

PUPIL PRACTICE BOOK 6B PAGE 102

Fractions to percentages

Learning focus

In this lesson, children will apply their understanding of equivalent fractions and parts out of 100 to convert fractions to percentages.

Before you teach

- Can children find equivalent fractions of a given fraction?
- Can children identify basic percentages as the number of parts 'out of 100'?

NATIONAL CURRICULUM LINKS

Year 6 Number – fractions (including decimals and percentages)

Recall and use equivalences between simple fractions, decimals and percentages, including in different contexts.

ASSESSING MASTERY

Children can use equivalent fractions to find the number of parts out of 100 in order to convert fractions to percentages.

COMMON MISCONCEPTIONS

Children may think that only a fraction with hundredths can be converted to a percentage. Ask:
- *How could you make this into a fraction with 100 as the denominator? What fraction of a whole is 50%? How could that help you?*

STRENGTHENING UNDERSTANDING

Build children's understanding of the role of equivalent fractions in percentages using representations of halves, quarters and tenths.

GOING DEEPER

Challenge children to explore how a fraction can be converted to a percentage when it has a denominator that is not a multiple or a factor of 100, for example, $\frac{24}{40}$.

KEY LANGUAGE

In lesson: fraction, percentage, equal, parts, whole, equivalent fraction, denominator, convert, multiply, divide

STRUCTURES AND REPRESENTATIONS

Hundred grid

RESOURCES

Optional: hundred grids, 100 squares, counters

 In the eTextbook of this lesson, you will find interactive links to a selection of teaching tools.

Quick recap

Ask children to represent the percentage 35% using a diagram of their choosing.

Discover

WAYS OF WORKING Pair work

ASK

- Question ① a): *How many rectangles make up the whole wall? How many rectangles are painted?*
- Question ① a): *Can you think of any other fractions that are equivalent to this one?*
- Question ① b): *Can you find an equivalent fraction with a denominator of 100?*
- Question ① b): *How do equivalent fractions help you here?*

IN FOCUS Work with children to make the link between equivalent fractions and percentages. Children should notice that the number of rectangles that make up the whole wall in this scenario is not 100. They may feel that it is therefore not possible to convert this fraction to a percentage. Remind them of previous work on equivalent fractions and discuss how they could use that here.

PRACTICAL TIPS Provide small grids for children to shade or cover with counters to represent given fractions. They can then use hundred grids to find the equivalent fraction with a denominator of 100.

ANSWERS

Question ① a): $\frac{10}{25}$ or $\frac{2}{5}$ of the wall is painted.

Question ① b): 40% of the wall is painted.

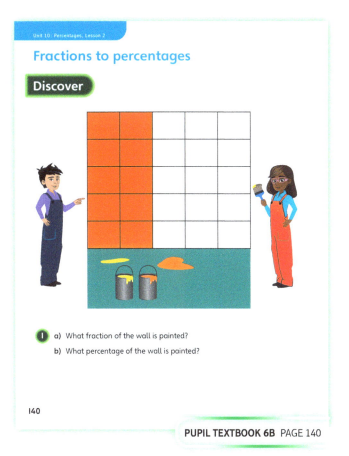

Fractions to percentages

Discover

① a) What fraction of the wall is painted?

b) What percentage of the wall is painted?

140

PUPIL TEXTBOOK 6B PAGE 140

Share

WAYS OF WORKING Whole class teacher led

ASK

- Question ① a): *How does the fraction $\frac{10}{25}$ relate to the diagram?*
- Question ① a): *Why is $\frac{2}{5}$ a possible answer?*
- Question ① b): *Can you explain why the diagram shows that each part is 4% of the whole?*
- Question ① b): *Why does Dexter write a fraction with a denominator of 100?*

IN FOCUS Look together at Flo's statement and agree that she has simplified in order to find an equivalent fraction. Ask: *Can you think of any other equivalent fractions, or find any on the page?* Then look at the two different methods that are shown to convert from fractions to percentages, using division or multiplication. Discuss which method children prefer.

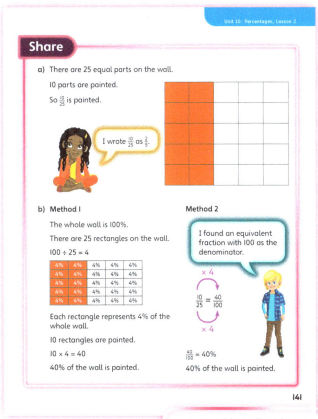

Share

a) There are 25 equal parts on the wall.

10 parts are painted.

So $\frac{10}{25}$ is painted.

I wrote $\frac{10}{25}$ as $\frac{2}{5}$.

b) **Method 1**

The whole wall is 100%.

There are 25 rectangles on the wall.

$100 \div 25 = 4$

Each rectangle represents 4% of the whole wall.

10 rectangles are painted.

$10 \times 4 = 40$

40% of the wall is painted.

Method 2

I found an equivalent fraction with 100 as the denominator.

$\times 4$

$\frac{10}{25} = \frac{40}{100}$

$\times 4$

$\frac{40}{100} = 40\%$

40% of the wall is painted.

141

PUPIL TEXTBOOK 6B PAGE 141

Think together

WAYS OF WORKING Whole class teacher led (I do, We do, You do)

ASK

• Question ❶: *How could you use equivalent fractions here?*
• Question ❷: *What denominator will you use each time? Why?*
• Question ❸: *Do you need to do more than one step to answer this?*

IN FOCUS Question ❶ uses shading on hundred grids to support children with basic conversions from fractions with denominators that are factors of 100 to percentages. In question ❷, children apply this to convert given written fractions by first finding equivalent fractions with denominators of 100.

Question ❸ requires children to first determine how many squares are in each grid and express the number of shaded squares as a fraction of the total. Children should then find an equivalent fraction with 100 as the denominator. In ❸ a), 20 squares is a factor of 100 and, in ❸ c), 200 squares is a multiple of 100. However, in question ❸ b), '30 squares' is not a factor of 100, so it is harder to express it as a percentage. Children should simplify $\frac{3}{30}$ to $\frac{1}{10}$ and then convert this to $\frac{10}{100}$.

STRENGTHEN Start by working with shaded squares on grids that represent tenths, fifths and quarters in order to build children's confidence with finding equivalents.

DEEPEN Challenge children to explore how they could shade 10% of the squares on any given grid, and to justify their reasoning.

ASSESSMENT CHECKPOINT Question ❷ assesses whether children can work with written fractions, identifying the steps needed to convert each one to a percentage.

ANSWERS

Question ❶ a): $\frac{2}{10}$ = 20%

Question ❶ b): $\frac{1}{4}$ = 25%

Question ❷ a): $\frac{7}{10} = \frac{70}{100}$ = 70%

Question ❷ b): $\frac{7}{20} = \frac{35}{100}$ = 35%

Question ❷ c): $\frac{7}{25} = \frac{28}{100}$ = 28%

Question ❷ d): $\frac{7}{50} = \frac{14}{100}$ = 14%

Question ❸ a): $\frac{6}{20} = \frac{3}{10}$ = 30%

Question ❸ b): $\frac{120}{200} = \frac{60}{100}$ = 60%

Question ❸ c): $\frac{3}{30} = \frac{1}{10}$ = 10%

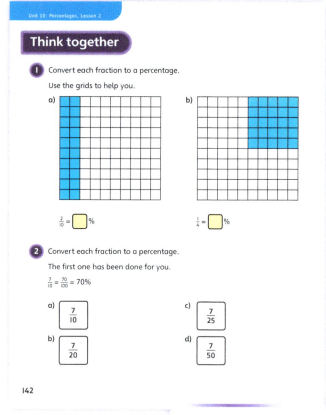

PUPIL TEXTBOOK 6B PAGE 142

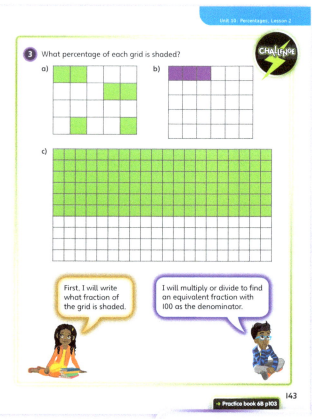

PUPIL TEXTBOOK 6B PAGE 143

Practice

WAYS OF WORKING Independent thinking

IN FOCUS Question ① requires children to do basic conversions of fractions to percentages, where the fractions all have denominators that are factors of 100. This is scaffolded with visual representations of shading on hundred grids.

In questions ② and ③, children use their knowledge of equivalent fractions to convert key fractions to percentages, and observe patterns in their answers.

Question ④ requires children to work with fractions that have a denominator less than 100, with scaffolding from shaded grids, and in question ⑤, they carry out a multi-step conversion to solve a word problem.

STRENGTHEN Provide children with more questions in the style of question ③ to give them practice with working through the steps needed to convert a fraction where the denominator is a factor or multiple of 100 to a percentage.

DEEPEN Challenge children to explore conversions of fractions to percentages where the denominators are greater than 100, for example $\frac{140}{200}, \frac{450}{500}, \frac{60}{150}$.

ASSESSMENT CHECKPOINT Use question ③ to assess whether children can convert to percentages using equivalent fractions.

ANSWERS Answers for the **Practice** part of the lesson can be found in the *Power Maths* online subscription.

Reflect

WAYS OF WORKING Independent thinking

IN FOCUS The **Reflect** part of the lesson prompts children to consider the methods they have used when converting a fraction to a percentage.

ASSESSMENT CHECKPOINT Assess whether children can compare and contrast different methods of conversion and can describe the steps that are needed to carry out a conversion.

ANSWERS Answers for the **Reflect** part of the lesson can be found in the Power Maths online subscription.

After the lesson ⏸

- Can children confidently find equivalent fractions?
- Are children able to use equivalent fractions to convert to percentages?

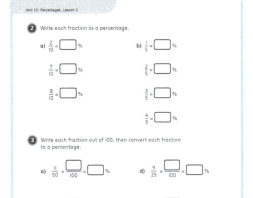

PUPIL PRACTICE BOOK 6B PAGE 103

PUPIL PRACTICE BOOK 6B PAGE 104

PUPIL PRACTICE BOOK 6B PAGE 105

Equivalent fractions, decimals and percentages

Learning focus

In this lesson, children will find equivalent fractions, decimals and percentages, and convert between them.

Before you teach

- Are children confident when converting fractions to percentages and percentages to fractions?
- Do they have a solid understanding of place value in decimals?

NATIONAL CURRICULUM LINKS

Year 6 Number – fractions (including decimals and percentages)

Recall and use equivalences between simple fractions, decimals and percentages, including in different contexts.

ASSESSING MASTERY

Children can find equivalent fractions, decimals and percentages following the learnt method. They have a deep understanding of place value in decimals, for example $0·4 = \frac{40}{100} = 40\%$, and $0·04 = \frac{4}{100} = 4\%$.

COMMON MISCONCEPTIONS

Children may assume that $0·4 = 4\%$. Ask:
- *Can you use a place value grid and convert the amount to a fraction first?*

Children may not write fractions in their simplest form when converting from a percentage or decimal. Ask:
- *Are there any smaller equivalent fractions?*

STRENGTHENING UNDERSTANDING

Strengthen understanding of converting decimals, fractions and percentages by using a 10-sided dice. Children roll a percentage or decimal and then convert.

GOING DEEPER

Deepen learning in this lesson by providing children with a bar model with part of it shaded in. Ask children to estimate the decimal, percentage and fraction of the shaded (and non-shaded) sections.

KEY LANGUAGE

In lesson: per cent (%), percentage, decimal, equivalent, estimate

Other language to be used by the teacher: hundredths, divide, multiply, convert, tenths, equivalent fraction

STRUCTURES AND REPRESENTATIONS

Bar model, number line, hundred grid

RESOURCES

Optional: 10-sided dice, chalk

 In the eTextbook of this lesson, you will find interactive links to a selection of teaching tools.

Quick recap

Challenge children to convert these fractions into percentages:

$\frac{3}{20} = \frac{?}{100} = ?\%$

$\frac{15}{25} = \frac{?}{100} = ?\%$

Discover

WAYS OF WORKING Pair work

ASK

- Question **1** a): *How many intervals are there on the number line? How do you convert a fraction to a decimal? How do you convert a decimal to a percentage?*
- Question **1** b): *What is $\frac{19}{20}$ equivalent to?*

IN FOCUS Question **1** is focused around children needing to work out each interval on the number line (0·1). They must then convert 70% and $\frac{2}{5}$ to decimals to place them on the number line.

PRACTICAL TIPS Recreate a similar activity to question **1** by drawing chalk number lines in the playground. Give children pieces of chalk, shout out decimals, percentages and fractions and ask children to mark them on the number lines.

ANSWERS

Question **1** a):

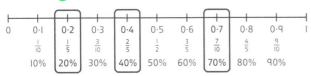

Question **1** b): $\frac{19}{20} = \frac{95}{100} = 0.95 = 95\%$

Equivalent fractions, decimals and percentages

Discover

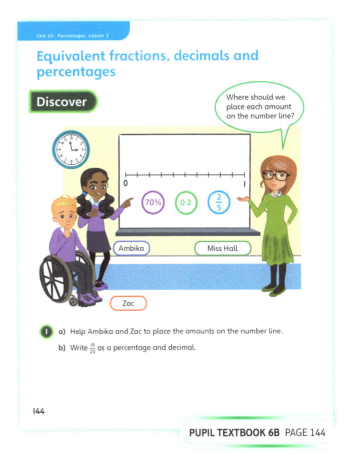

Where should we place each amount on the number line?

Ambika

Miss Hall

Zac

1 a) Help Ambika and Zac to place the amounts on the number line.

b) Write $\frac{19}{20}$ as a percentage and decimal.

144

PUPIL TEXTBOOK 6B PAGE 144

Share

WAYS OF WORKING Whole class teacher led

ASK

- Question **1** a): *Why aren't all the fractions in tenths? Does Sparks' comment help to explain this?*
- Question **1** b): *Could you multiply the fraction so that the denominator equals 100?*
- Question **1** b): *Could you convert the fraction to a decimal to help you?*

IN FOCUS In question **1** b), children should multiply $\frac{19}{20}$ by 5 in order to find $\frac{95}{100}$. They can then convert this to a decimal, 0·95. You may want to discuss with children that the interval is not marked on the number line. Where do they think it needs to go?

Share

a) Decimals, fractions and percentages can all represent equivalent numbers or amounts.

Each fraction is in its simplest form.

Ambika and Zac should place the numbers as shown below.

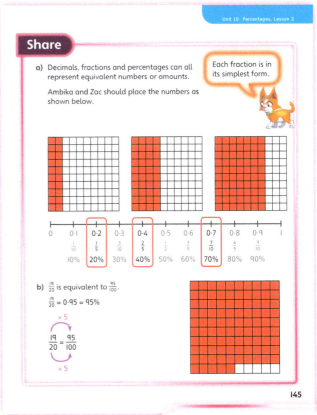

b) $\frac{19}{20}$ is equivalent to $\frac{95}{100}$.

$\frac{19}{20} = 0.95 = 95\%$

$\frac{19}{20} = \frac{95}{100}$ ×5

145

PUPIL TEXTBOOK 6B PAGE 145

Think together

WAYS OF WORKING Whole class teacher led (I do, We do, You do)

ASK

- Question **2**: *Can you convert all the numbers to a fraction, a decimal or a percentage so you can see which is the odd one out? What would you find it easier to convert everything to? Can you explain why?*
- Question **3**: *Is 6% equivalent to 0·6? Why not?*

IN FOCUS Question **1** provides the scaffolding of a shaded hundred grid to support children in converting a decimal to a percentage and then a fraction. Children may first write the fraction with a denominator of 100, but they should realise that it is also possible to simplify it further.

For question **2**, children have to find equivalent fractions, decimals and percentages to conclude that the only amount that is not equal to $\frac{1}{10}$ is 0·01. They should aim to convert all the numbers to the same form (fractions, decimals or percentages) in order to do this. Which do they find it easier to convert to? Can they explain why?

STRENGTHEN When completing question **3**, children may become confused about how to convert percentages to decimals (for instance, they may write 6% as 0·6). Support them with a place value grid and show them how to convert using their knowledge of tenths and hundredths.

DEEPEN For question **2**, ask children to convert each of the numbers to a different form (for example, if they converted to fractions the first time, can they now convert to percentages?). You could also challenge children to create a similar problem of their own for 60%.

ASSESSMENT CHECKPOINT Assess children on their answer to question **2**. Can they spot the odd one out? Can they explain why it is the odd one out, using the correct mathematical terminology?

ANSWERS

Question **1** a): 0·55 = 55%

Question **1** b): 0·55 = $\frac{55}{100} = \frac{11}{20}$

Question **2**: 0·01 is not equivalent to the others. It is equivalent to $\frac{1}{100}$ and 1%. All the others are equivalent to $\frac{1}{10}$, 10% and 0·1.

Question **3**:

Decimal	Percentage	Fraction
0·25	25%	$\frac{1}{4}$
0·5	50%	$\frac{1}{2}$
0·65	65%	$\frac{13}{20}$
0·6	60%	$\frac{3}{5}$
0·3	30%	$\frac{3}{10}$
0·07	7%	$\frac{7}{100}$

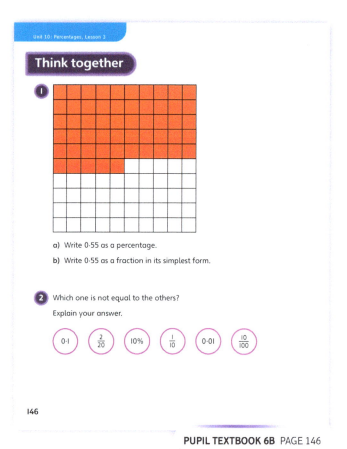

Unit 10: Percentages, Lesson 3

Think together

1

a) Write 0·55 as a percentage.

b) Write 0·55 as a fraction in its simplest form.

2 Which one is not equal to the others?
Explain your answer.

0·1 $\frac{2}{20}$ 10% $\frac{1}{10}$ 0·01 $\frac{10}{100}$

146

PUPIL TEXTBOOK 6B PAGE 146

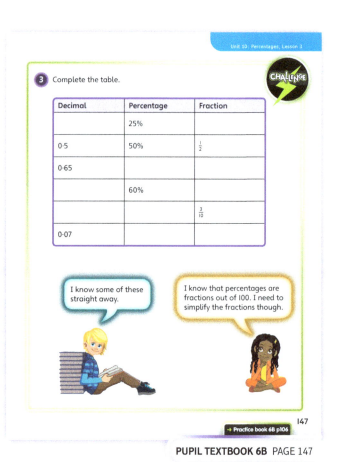

3 Complete the table.

CHALLENGE

Decimal	Percentage	Fraction
	25%	
0·5	50%	$\frac{1}{2}$
0·65		
	60%	
		$\frac{3}{10}$
0·07		

I know some of these straight away.

I know that percentages are fractions out of 100. I need to simplify the fractions though.

→ Practice book 6B p106

147

PUPIL TEXTBOOK 6B PAGE 147

Practice

WAYS OF WORKING Independent thinking

IN FOCUS Question ③ probes children's understanding of place value when converting between percentages, decimals and fractions. Many of the same digits are used, so children must be confident with their choices. A place value grid may provide useful support here.

STRENGTHEN Once children have correctly completed question ①, they should make a copy of the number line and stick it in the front or back of their books. This will be great for revision and support in further lessons. Encourage them to refer to it as and when needed.

DEEPEN To extend this activity, give children a variety of blank number lines and hundredths grids and ask them to create their own diagrams. They may then swap diagrams with a partner and write the equivalent decimals, fractions and percentages.

ASSESSMENT CHECKPOINT Use question ① to see if children can convert between decimals, percentages and fractions confidently. Assess whether there are any patterns in the areas that need further work or support. If children can read a diagram and find the equivalent fraction, decimal and percentage as in question ②, they are likely to have mastered the lesson.

ANSWERS Answers for the **Practice** part of the lesson can be found in the *Power Maths* online subscription.

Reflect

WAYS OF WORKING Pair work, independent thinking

IN FOCUS For this question, children may work together to measure the unshaded part. They should conclude that the shaded part represents approximately $\frac{2}{3}$ of the bar model (that one more third will fit in). They should then work independently or in pairs to convert this to a percentage and a decimal.

ASSESSMENT CHECKPOINT Assess children on whether they can read the bar model and write a fraction from it. Following this, observe how they convert the fraction to a decimal and percentage, bearing in mind that 3 is not a factor of 100. Remind them that they are only working out an estimate, so they can find the nearest whole decimal and percentage.

ANSWERS Answers for the **Reflect** part of the lesson can be found in the *Power Maths* online subscription.

After the lesson ⏸

- Can children read a diagram and write down the equivalent decimal, fraction and percentage?
- Can children explain the methods they use to find equivalent decimals, fractions and percentages?

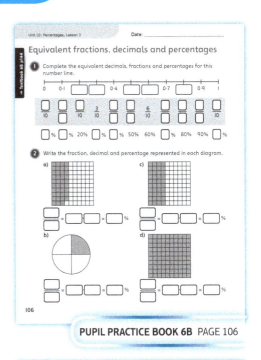

PUPIL PRACTICE BOOK 6B PAGE 106

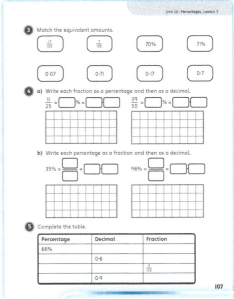

PUPIL PRACTICE BOOK 6B PAGE 107

PUPIL PRACTICE BOOK 6B PAGE 108

Order fractions, decimals and percentages

Learning focus

In this lesson, children will order and compare decimals, percentages and fractions, including those that are greater than 1.

Before you teach

- Can children find equivalent fractions, decimals and percentages?

NATIONAL CURRICULUM LINKS

Year 6 Number – fractions (including decimals and percentages)

Compare and order fractions, including fractions > 1.

Recall and use equivalences between simple fractions, decimals and percentages, including in different contexts.

ASSESSING MASTERY

Children can compare fractions, decimals and percentages and explain the methods they use to do so. They use learnt strategies to spot equivalents, including those which are greater than 1.

COMMON MISCONCEPTIONS

Children may get stuck when dealing with fractions, decimals or percentages which are greater than 1. Ask:
- *Could you use the strategies you have learnt previously and apply them to amounts greater than 1?*

Children may not be able to find more than one amount between close fractions, decimals and percentages, such as $\frac{6}{10}$ and $\frac{8}{10}$. Ask:
- *Could finding an equivalent fraction help you to solve the problem?*

STRENGTHENING UNDERSTANDING

Strengthen understanding of converting between decimals, fractions and percentages by encouraging children to draw or use bar models, place value grids and number lines, as needed, to model and support their understanding of each question.

GOING DEEPER

Deepen learning in this lesson by asking children to find mid-points between two fractions, decimals or percentages (or a mixture of two).

KEY LANGUAGE

In lesson: per cent (%), percentage, equivalent, equivalent fraction, decimal, fraction, simplify, order, compare, less than, greater than

Other language to be used by the teacher: convert

STRUCTURES AND REPRESENTATIONS

Number line, fraction strips

RESOURCES

Optional: base 10 equipment, bean bags, boxes or buckets

 In the eTextbook of this lesson, you will find interactive links to a selection of teaching tools.

Quick recap

As a class, collect as many common fraction, decimal and percentage families as you can. For example, $\frac{1}{10}$, 10% and 0·1.

Discover

WAYS OF WORKING Pair work

ASK

- Question **1** a): *Why can't you directly compare the fractions? What do you need to change the denominators to in order to compare them?*

IN FOCUS In question **1** a), children have to directly compare two fractions with different denominators. Start by asking if they can compare the two given fractions. Children may guess the answer. Work with them to ensure that they find equivalent fractions in which the denominator is the same. You could also show them that there are more ways to work out the correct answer, for example by converting the amounts to decimals.

PRACTICAL TIPS Play some games with the class in which the scores are recorded; for example, ask them to throw bean bags into a box or basket. Gather decimals, fractions and percentages from the scores and pose questions about the results for children to answer.

ANSWERS

Question **1** a): Lee: 6 out of 20 = $\frac{6}{20} = \frac{30}{100}$ = 30%.

Kate: 7 out of 25 = $\frac{7}{25} = \frac{28}{100}$ = 28%.
Lee was more accurate at the coconut shy.

Question **1** b): A possible fraction between 28% and 30% is 29% = $\frac{29}{100}$.
A fraction made from a decimal between 0·28 and 0·3 also works, for example, 0·295 = $\frac{295}{1,000}$, 0·281 = $\frac{281}{1,000}$ or 0·299 = $\frac{299}{1,000}$.

Share

WAYS OF WORKING Whole class teacher led

ASK

- Question **1** b): *What other fractions are between $\frac{28}{100}$ and $\frac{30}{100}$?*
- Question **1** b): *How does the number line help you to solve the problem?*

IN FOCUS Question **1** b) is significant because children have to compare two fractions that are very close. Offer the prompt that equivalent fractions may help. It is important to note that children may use different methods. For example, the numerators and denominators of both fractions can been multiplied by 10, so any fraction between $\frac{280}{1,000}$ and $\frac{300}{1,000}$ would work.

PUPIL TEXTBOOK 6B PAGE 148

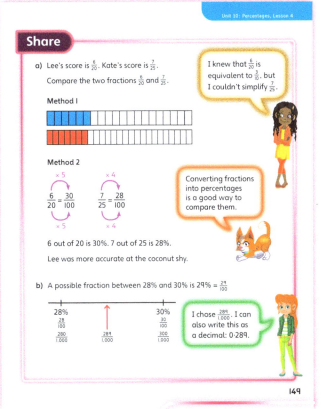

PUPIL TEXTBOOK 6B PAGE 149

Think together

WAYS OF WORKING **WAYS OF WORKING** Whole class teacher led (I do, We do, You do)

ASK

- Questions ① and ②: *What method can you use to compare and order these amounts? Can you convert them all to percentages?*
- Question ③: *Can you convert both of Lexi's numbers to fractions? To percentages? How does that help you to compare them?*

IN FOCUS In questions ① and ②, children will need to recall their learning from previous lessons to order and compare sets of numbers that are expressed as a mixture of fractions, decimals and percentages. Children will find that it is necessary to convert the numbers in each set to the same form before they can be compared. Ask: *Why did you choose to convert them all to fractions/decimals/percentages this time?*

Question ③ involves an important learning point: it does not matter if the denominator of a fraction is not a factor of 100, it can still be converted to a percentage by using multiplication, division and equivalence.

STRENGTHEN To support children with exploring Luis's statement in question ③, offer them an answer scaffold to structure their thinking, such as $\frac{32}{80} = \frac{?}{?} = \frac{?}{100}$.

DEEPEN Use question ② to deepen learning by discussing how percentages can help when solving problems in a real-life context where the total number is not known. Ask: *Can we work out how many questions were in Aki's second test?* (No) *Does this matter?* (No, if we express both scores as a percentage they can be compared.) Challenge children to write their own story problems in this style.

ASSESSMENT CHECKPOINT Assess children on their answers to question ①. This will show which children can find equivalents to compare and order percentages, decimals and fractions.

ANSWERS

Question ① a): 73% is greater than 0·55 (55%).

Question ① b): $\frac{17}{50}$ ($\frac{17}{50} = \frac{34}{100} = 34\%$) is greater than 29%.

Question ① c): $\frac{7}{20}$ ($\frac{7}{20} = \frac{35}{100} = 0·35$) is greater than 0·34.

Question ② a): Smallest to largest: $\frac{7}{25}$, 0·38, 45%.

Question ② b): $\frac{9}{25} = \frac{36}{100} = 36\%$. 40% > 36% so Aki has improved.

Question ③: Lexi is not correct: $0·5 = \frac{5}{10} = \frac{50}{100} = 50\%$
$\qquad$ $0·45 = 45\%$
$\qquad$ $50\% > 45\%$
$\qquad$ Or 0·5 has 5 tenths but 0·45 only has 4 tenths.
$\qquad$ Luis is not correct: $\frac{32}{80} = \frac{4}{10} = 40\%$.

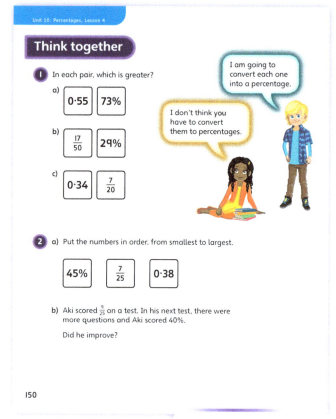

PUPIL TEXTBOOK 6B PAGE 150

PUPIL TEXTBOOK 6B PAGE 151

Practice

WAYS OF WORKING Independent thinking

IN FOCUS The focus of question ❷ is on children comparing a percentage with a fraction. Children convert a fraction to a percentage in question ❷ a) and then use this to compare with another percentage in question ❷ b). Children may notice, however, that these numbers are easy to compare because they already know that $\frac{27}{50}$ is more than half and 48% is less than half.

STRENGTHEN Strengthen understanding of question ❺ by asking children to first compare small whole numbers using the < or > signs. They can then move on to comparing given pairs of decimals, percentages or fractions with the same denominator, before doing the necessary conversions to compare numbers that are written in different forms.

DEEPEN Question ❼ will deepen learning. Children have to compare two numbers written in different forms, where the total amount also changes. Children draw a diagram to represent this. Challenge them to justify their reasoning and to describe other key variables in this context. Can children make up their own problems like this?

THINK DIFFERENTLY The focus of question ❻ is on children comparing a decimal with a fraction where both are greater than 1. Encourage children to draw the decimal and the fraction to show what they look like (they could also model this with base 10 equipment). Next, ask them to convert one amount; for example, $1·8 = 1\frac{8}{10} = 1\frac{16}{20}$. Highlight that the whole is kept separate from the fraction.

ASSESSMENT CHECKPOINT Question ❷ will tell you if children can apply their learning from this lesson to solve a problem involving the comparison of a percentage with a fraction. Check that children realise that it is 87% of *one* apple and $\frac{4}{9}$ of *two* apples. Review their reasoning in question ❷ b) to assess the depth of their understanding.

ANSWERS Answers for the **Practice** part of the lesson can be found in the *Power Maths* online subscription.

Reflect

WAYS OF WORKING Independent thinking

IN FOCUS This reflection is important because children need to draw on their knowledge from the lesson and summarise it in concise terms. You may want to encourage children to write in numbered steps. You may also choose to display key vocabulary for support.

ASSESSMENT CHECKPOINT Assess children on the language they use and the accuracy of the explanation. If children find this challenging, encourage them to work through an example and write down what they are doing at each step.

ANSWERS Answers for the **Reflect** part of the lesson can be found in the *Power Maths* online subscription.

After the lesson ⏸

- Can children compare two fractions (including ones that are close, such as $\frac{3}{10}$ and $\frac{5}{10}$)?
- Can they compare more than two fractions on a number line?

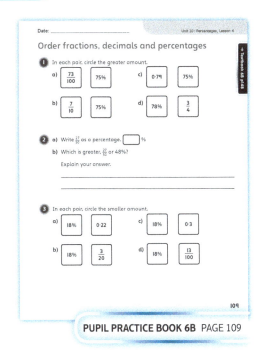

PUPIL PRACTICE BOOK 6B PAGE 109

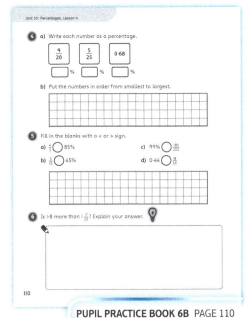

PUPIL PRACTICE BOOK 6B PAGE 110

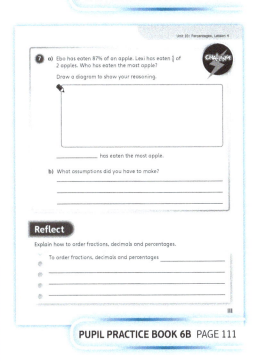

PUPIL PRACTICE BOOK 6B PAGE 111

Simple percentage of an amount

Learning focus

In this lesson, children will learn two methods of finding 20%. They understand that $20\% = \frac{20}{100} = \frac{2}{10} = \frac{1}{5}$, so they can find $\frac{1}{5}$. They will also learn that 20% is a compound of 10% and 10% and will use this to find other simple percentages of amounts.

Before you teach

- Can children confidently identify 10%, 25% and 50% of a number?

NATIONAL CURRICULUM LINKS

Year 6 Number – fractions (including decimals and percentages)

Recall and use equivalences between simple fractions, decimals and percentages, including in different contexts.

Solve problems involving the calculation of percentages [for example, of measures and such as 15% of 360] and the use of percentages for comparison.

ASSESSING MASTERY

Children can confidently apply both methods of finding 20%. They can also identify when it is more efficient to use one method than the other. Children can then work out other simple percentages, for example finding 90% by doing 100% – 10%.

COMMON MISCONCEPTIONS

Children may work out 20% by finding 10% and then halving (rather than doubling). Ask:
- *Why do you need to double after finding 10% in order to find 20%?*

Some children may think that to find 20% you divide by 20. Ask:
- *How many lots of 20% make 100%?*

STRENGTHENING UNDERSTANDING

Children could practise finding 20% of amounts by finding 10% and then doubling. They should check their answer by dividing the amount by 5.

GOING DEEPER

Deepen learning by asking children to challenge each other to find 20% of amounts of their choosing and then to make a list of other simple percentages they will be able to work out if they know 20%.

KEY LANGUAGE

In lesson: per cent (%), percentage, divide, difference, double, method

Other language to be used by the teacher: parts, decimal, fraction, tenth, hundredth, half, quarter, share, convert, order

STRUCTURES AND REPRESENTATIONS

Bar model, number line, hundred grid

RESOURCES

Mandatory: counters, cubes

 In the eTextbook of this lesson, you will find interactive links to a selection of teaching tools.

Quick recap

Challenge children to find $\frac{1}{2}$ of each of these numbers:

300   1,500   195

Discover

Unit 10: Percentages, Lesson 5

Simple percentage of an amount

WAYS OF WORKING Pair work

ASK

- Question **1** a): *How many vehicles are there on the ferry in total? How can you find 20%? Can you think of more than one method?*

IN FOCUS Question **1** a) is the first time that children are asked to find 20%. Prompt them to think of the relationship between 10 and 20 and how this might relate to 10% and 20%.

PRACTICAL TIPS Cut out some cardboard rectangles and write either 10% or 20% on each card. Ask children to put the cards together into a long row to make 100%, using just 10% cards, just 20% cards, or a combination of both. This will help children to understand how many of each amount make a whole.

ANSWERS

Question **1** a): There are 12 motorbikes on the ferry.

Question **1** b): There are 15 vans on the ferry.

15 – 12 = 3

There are 3 more vans than motorbikes on the ferry.

Discover

1 a) How many motorbikes are on the ferry?

b) 25% of the vehicles on the ferry are vans.

How many more vans than motorbikes are there?

152

PUPIL TEXTBOOK 6B PAGE 152

Share

WAYS OF WORKING Whole class teacher led

ASK

- Question **1** b): *How many steps are there to this problem? Do you remember how to find 25%?*

IN FOCUS Question **1** b) challenges children to compare percentages of amounts. Some children may give the answer as a percentage: for example, there are 5% more vans than motorbikes. Encourage them to read the question carefully and then work out the number of motorbikes and vans first. Ask children to focus on the bar model and explain how it shows the amounts of the two types of vehicle, and that the question is trying to get them to find the difference between them.

Share

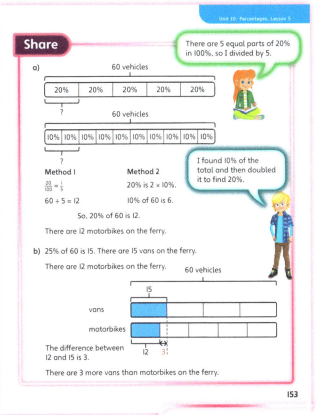

153

PUPIL TEXTBOOK 6B PAGE 153

Think together

WAYS OF WORKING Whole class teacher led (I do, We do, You do)

ASK

• Question **1** b): *If you know 10%, how can you work out 20% of a number?*

• Question **3** b): *Which of Luis's answers will you use to help you? Why?*

IN FOCUS Question **3** asks children to break down how to use a known percentage of an amount to work out other simple percentages, for example 10% ÷ 2 = 5% and 25% × 2 = 50%. They then apply this to further examples of simple percentages that can be worked out.

STRENGTHEN Question **1** can be used to strengthen children's learning. Repeat the exercise with different-sized grids. You could also change the grid to different shapes so children understand that it is not only boxes which you can find a percentage of. Alternatively, use counters and challenge children to find 10% and 20% of a group of counters.

DEEPEN In question **2**, go deeper by asking children how 20% of 150 and 20% of 75 are linked. They should realise that because 75 is half of 150, 10% of 150 is equal to 20% of 75.

ASSESSMENT CHECKPOINT Assess children on their work during question **2**. Can they work out the answers and explain their methods? Are they starting to make links between different percentages, such as realising that '20% of 80 = 16' can help them to work out '10% of ☐ = 16'?

ANSWERS

Question **1** a): 10% of 30 = 3 squares covered.

Question **1** b): 20% of 30 = 6 squares covered.

Question **2** a): 10% of 120 = 12
20% of 120 = 24
20% of a number is double 10% of that same number.

Question **2** b): 10% of 150 = 15
20% of 75 = 15
75 is half of 150, so 20% of 75 is the same as 10% of 150.

Question **2** c): 10% of 80 = 8
90% of 80 = 72
90% of 80 is 9 x 10% of 80 or 100% − 10%.

Question **3** a): Various responses are possible. Children might explain:
$10\% = \frac{1}{10}$ so divide 60 by 10
5% is half of 10%
$50\% = \frac{1}{2}$ so half 60
25% is half of 50% or $\frac{1}{4}$ of 60.

Question **3** b): There are several ways children could work these out, for example:
15% of £60 = 10% + 5% = 6 + 3 = £9
55% of £60 = 50% + 5% = 30 + 3 = £33
70% of £60 = 10% × 7 = 6 × 7 = £42
95% of £60 = 100% − 5% = 60 − 3 = £57

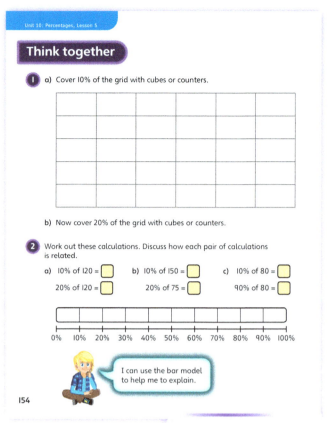

PUPIL TEXTBOOK 6B PAGE 154

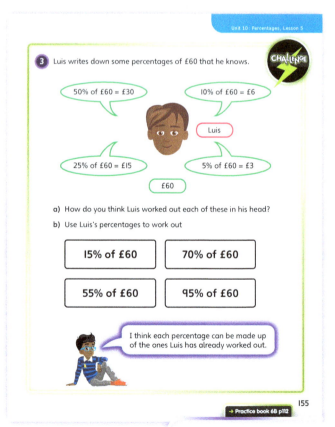

PUPIL TEXTBOOK 6B PAGE 155

190

Practice

WAYS OF WORKING Independent thinking

IN FOCUS Question **1** requires children to apply their learning by finding simple percentages of different amounts, including some in the context of measures and money. Children should be able to describe which method they have chosen to use each time. Ensure they include the correct unit of measure in their answers, where relevant.

STRENGTHEN Question **3** will strengthen learning. For each part of the table, ask children to explain what they are doing and why. If they cannot (some may just be following the learnt formula), help them to draw bar models for each row of the table to cement their understanding.

DEEPEN Challenge children by giving them an extension to question **4**. Ask them to write their own percentage word problems and solve them. They can then swap their word problems with a partner. Did they reach the same answer? Did they use the same method to find the answer?

THINK DIFFERENTLY Question **2** tackles a common misconception that to find 20% you divide by 20. Encourage children to use bar models to support their explanation of why Zac is mistaken.

ASSESSMENT CHECKPOINT Assess children on question **5**. They are likely to have mastered the lesson if they can apply their learning to a measure problem. Question **4** will show whether children can apply their learning when working with bigger numbers.

ANSWERS Answers for the **Practice** part of the lesson can be found in the *Power Maths* online subscription.

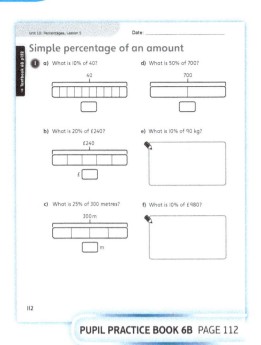

PUPIL PRACTICE BOOK 6B PAGE 112

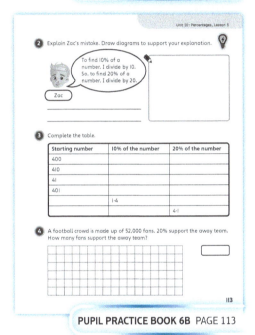

PUPIL PRACTICE BOOK 6B PAGE 113

Reflect

WAYS OF WORKING Pair work, Independent thinking

IN FOCUS This task requires children to use their knowledge from the lesson to move their learning forwards. They should recognise that if they know 10%, they cannot work out any percentage, but they can work out any percentage that is a factor or multiple of 10.

ASSESSMENT CHECKPOINT This reflective exercise will demonstrate whether children can apply their learning in the lesson to work with other percentages.

ANSWERS Answers for the **Reflect** part of the lesson can be found in the *Power Maths* online subscription.

After the lesson ⏸

- Can children confidently use both methods to find 20%?
- Do all children know which method to select?
- Can children apply their learning to solve percentage problems with other simple percentages?

PUPIL PRACTICE BOOK 6B PAGE 114

Percentage of an amount – 1%

Learning focus

In this lesson, children will find 1% and then use this to work out multiples of 1%.

Before you teach

- Can children find 10% of an amount?
- Do children fully understand how to use a hundredths grid to represent percentages?

NATIONAL CURRICULUM LINKS

Year 6 Number – fractions (including decimals and percentages)

Recall and use equivalences between simple fractions, decimals and percentages, including in different contexts.

Solve problems involving the calculation of percentages [for example, of measures and such as 15% of 360] and the use of percentages for comparison.

ASSESSING MASTERY

Children can confidently work out any percentage from 0 to 100 and can use this knowledge to solve problems – including those which compare two percentages of amounts.

COMMON MISCONCEPTIONS

Children may not be confident with dividing by 100 (especially if the answer is a decimal). Ask:
- *Could you use a place value grid to help you?*

When children are working out 10% in this lesson, they may find 1% and then multiply by 10. Ask:
- *Think back to previous lessons. Is there a more efficient method?*

STRENGTHENING UNDERSTANDING

Ask children to practise dividing by 100 and then multiplying the answer by a number between 1 and 10. Use function machines, select numbers to input and then, for example, divide by 100 and multiply by 3. Discuss the outputs.

GOING DEEPER

Deepen learning in this lesson by challenging children to compare percentages of amounts. For example, ask: *Is 25% of 40 greater than 3% of 300?*

KEY LANGUAGE

In lesson: per cent (%), percentage, whole, tenth ($\frac{1}{10}$), hundredth ($\frac{1}{100}$), divide, multiply, least, greatest

Other language to be used by the teacher: efficient, method, compare

STRUCTURES AND REPRESENTATIONS

Bar model, hundred grid, place value table

RESOURCES

Optional: counters, base 10 equipment

 In the eTextbook of this lesson, you will find interactive links to a selection of teaching tools.

Quick recap

Challenge children to find $\frac{1}{100}$ of each of these numbers:

300   1,500   1,950

Discover

WAYS OF WORKING Pair work

ASK

- Question **1** a): *How many chocolate bars are in the boxes? How can you work out 1%? How would you write 1% as a fraction? Could this help you to work out what you have to do to find 1%?*

IN FOCUS Question **1** a) introduces children to finding 1% of a number. Encourage them to think about what they have to do to work out 10% and then ask what they think they must do to work out 1%. Ask children to convert 1% to a fraction – this might prompt them to realise that they need to divide by 100.

PRACTICAL TIPS It is a good idea to show children what 1% of something looks like. For example, you could show them: 1 cm compared to 1 m; 1 base 10 cube compared to a base 10 hundred flat; or 1 marble out of 100.

ANSWERS

Question **1** a): 1% of 500 = 5
In a box of 500 bars, there are 5 winning rainbow tickets.

Question **1** b): In a box of 200 bars, there are 2 winning rainbow tickets.
In a box of 1,000 bars, there are 10 winning rainbow tickets.
In a box of 2,500 bars, there are 25 winning rainbow tickets.

PUPIL TEXTBOOK 6B PAGE 156

Share

WAYS OF WORKING Whole class teacher led

ASK

- Question **1** a): *What is Dexter's method showing? What can you see on the shaded grids? What is 1% of 100?*
- Question **1** b): *How can you work out 1% of 1,000? Can you explain why you should divide by 100 when finding 1%?*

IN FOCUS In question **1** b), children can see that finding $\frac{1}{100}$ is the same as finding 1%: they need to divide by 100. Some children may need support when tackling the larger numbers such as 1,000 and 2,500. Encourage children to explain their method to check that they fully understand the reasoning behind finding 1%.

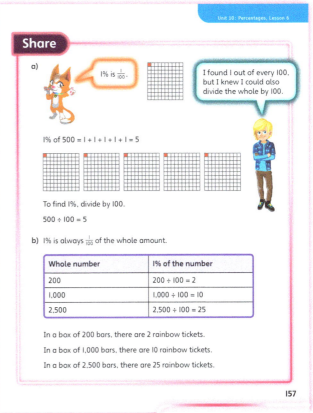

PUPIL TEXTBOOK 6B PAGE 157

Think together

Whole class teacher led (I do, We do, You do)

ASK

- Question **1**: *What is 1% of 400?*
- Question **3**: *How does the table help you to identify the strategy you need to use to find percentages? Which percentage did you find the trickiest to find?*
- Question **3**: *Were Emma's and Isla's methods more efficient or less efficient for different calculations? What do you notice about their methods for finding 2%, 5% and 9%?*

IN FOCUS Question **1** requires children to first find 1% of each amount and then to multiply by the given number in order to find that percentage of each amount. Ensure that they are confident in dividing by 100 to find 1%.

STRENGTHEN Some children will need practice dividing by 100 in this section. Use a place value table to help – particularly in question **2**, which involves decimals.

DEEPEN Following question **3**, challenge children to work out 97% of a number. Ask them if dividing by 100 and then multiplying by 97 is a good strategy. You may want to hint that 3% might help. Also for question **3**, children can explore whether it is easier to convert the pounds to pence when finding the percentages.

ASSESSMENT CHECKPOINT Assess children's answers to question **3**. Did they get every answer correct? Can they explain the method they used? Did they use any other strategies, such as halving 10% to find 5%?

ANSWERS

Question **1**: 3% of 700 kg = 21 kg, 7% of £800 = £56, 8% of 1,200 km = 96 km, 22% of £400 = £88

Question **2** a): Yes, Reena is correct. $\frac{40}{100}$ means $40 \div 100 = 0.4$. 1% of 40 = 0.4

Question **2** b): 7% of 40 = 0.4 × 7 = 2.8

Question **2** c): 17% of 40 = 10% of 40 + 7% of 40 = 4 + 2.8 = 6.8 or 17% of 40 = 17 × 1% of 40 = 17 × 0.4 = 6.8

Question **3**:

	Emma's method	Isla's method	Percentage of £40
50%	Divide the whole by 2.	Find 1% and then multiply by 50.	£20
25%	Divide the whole by 4.	Find 1% and then multiply by 25.	£10
20%	Divide the whole by 5.	Find 1% and then multiply by 20.	£8
10%	Divide the whole by 10.	Find 1% and then multiply by 10.	£4

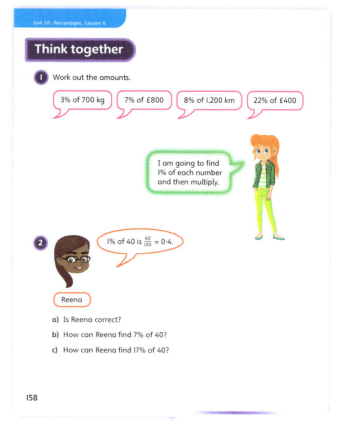

PUPIL TEXTBOOK 6B PAGE 158

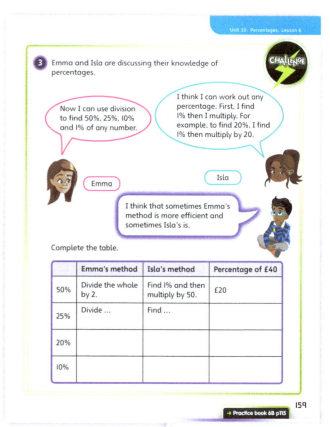

PUPIL TEXTBOOK 6B PAGE 159

Practice

WAYS OF WORKING Independent thinking

IN FOCUS Question **2** encourages children to apply their knowledge of percentages and place value to find 1% and 10% of related numbers. Offer children physical apparatus such as base 10 equipment or counters to allow them to model the calculations and prove that they match.

STRENGTHEN Following question **6**, strengthen learning by challenging children to think of pairs of percentages of amounts that are equal, such as 1% of 500 and 10% of 50.

DEEPEN For question **4**, encourage children to start thinking of some different, more efficient strategies to work out some of the percentages. For example, if they have worked out 3%, they can double it to find 6%. Question **6** will deepen learning, as children will need to work out the percentages and compare the two amounts.

ASSESSMENT CHECKPOINT Assess children on question **5**. If they can use efficient methods to work out percentages of amounts, they are ready for some deeper learning.

ANSWERS Answers for the **Practice** part of the lesson can be found in the *Power Maths* online subscription.

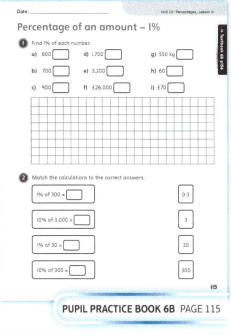

PUPIL PRACTICE BOOK 6B PAGE 115

PUPIL PRACTICE BOOK 6B PAGE 116

Reflect

WAYS OF WORKING Independent thinking

IN FOCUS This is an important question because children must visually represent 3% of a number. They may want to use a hundred grid to support them. They may also want to write down the steps.

ASSESSMENT CHECKPOINT Assess children on whether they can show how to work out 3% of a number visually. Often, children can follow instructions, but by using a diagram they can demonstrate their deeper understanding.

ANSWERS Answers for the **Reflect** part of the lesson can be found in the *Power Maths* online subscription.

After the lesson ⏸

- Are children clear on how to find 1% and then use this to work out multiples of 1%?
- Are children beginning to identify which method might be more efficient to solve different calculations?
- Are children ready to move on to the next lesson, in which 75% is found by working out 50% and 25%?

PUPIL PRACTICE BOOK 6B PAGE 117

Percentages of an amount

Learning focus

In this lesson, children will find 75% by working out 50% and 25% and then adding them together. They will explore other compounds as well, such as 15% and 99%.

Before you teach ⏸

- Are children confident with partitioning numbers up to 100?
- Are they confident with finding 1%, 10%, 20%, 25% and 50% of a number?

NATIONAL CURRICULUM LINKS

Year 6 Number – fractions (including decimals and percentages)

Recall and use equivalences between simple fractions, decimals and percentages, including in different contexts.

Solve problems involving the calculation of percentages [for example, of measures and such as 15% of 360] and the use of percentages for comparison.

ASSESSING MASTERY

Children can find the percentages of amounts for a range of different numbers, without being told what the compounds are. For instance, if they are asked to work out 60% of an amount, they know to find 50% and another 10% (or they may do 3 lots of 20%).

COMMON MISCONCEPTIONS

Children may work out the compounds, but neglect to add them together. Ask:
- *Have you found the final answer? Is there another step you have missed?*

Children may be unsure which compounds to use, for example not knowing how to break down 65%. Ask:
- *Can you partition 65% using a part-whole model?*

STRENGTHENING UNDERSTANDING

Children could practise partitioning percentages into 1%, 5%, 10%, 20%, 25% and 50%: for example, 65% = 50% + 10% + 5%.

GOING DEEPER

Deepen learning in this lesson by asking children to discuss a range of methods by which to find percentages of numbers. For example, to find 65% of 200 they could do:

50% + 10% + 5%

20% + 20% + 20% + 5%

100% − (20% + 10% + 5%)

KEY LANGUAGE

In lesson: per cent (%), percentage, bar chart, whole, kilogram (kg), kilometre (km), centimetre (cm)

Other language to be used by the teacher: parts, partition, decimal, fraction, tenth, hundredth, divide, share, convert

STRUCTURES AND REPRESENTATIONS

Bar model, part-whole model

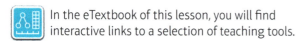 In the eTextbook of this lesson, you will find interactive links to a selection of teaching tools.

Quick recap 🔄

Challenge children to find 1% and 50% of each of these numbers:

| 900 | 250 | 880 |

Discover

Pair work

ASK

- Question **1** a): *What does the bar chart show? What percentage is paper? What percentage is plastic? What does 100% represent in terms of the total weight of recycling Class 1 collected? How can you work out 75% of 80 kg? Could working out 50% and 25% help you?*
- Question **1** b): *What does 'more … than' mean? What operation must you use to work out the answer?*

IN FOCUS Question **1** a) will encourage children to think carefully about how to find 75%. They cannot just divide by a number as they could with 50% or 10%. Prompt children to break down 75% to help them solve the problem. Spend some time discussing the bar chart with children and ensure they are able to identify what information is being presented. In question **1** b), children will have to apply their knowledge of percentages to solve a word problem. Be wary of children adding the 60 kg and 20 kg: they may assume that 'more' means add. Explain the language to them with the support of the bar model.

Some children may realise that they can subtract 60 kg from 80 kg to find 20 kg and then subtract 20 kg from 60 kg to find 40 kg. However, encourage them to use a method that allows them to practise working out percentages.

PRACTICAL TIPS Set children their own recycling challenge. Each child could bring paper and plastics (or items the school can easily recycle) to school one day. Weigh (or estimate the weight of) the materials they have collected and then find the percentage differences.

ANSWERS

Question **1** a): 75% of 80 kg is 60 kg. Class 1 recycled 60 kg of paper.

Question **1** b): Class 1 recycled 40 kg more paper than plastic.

Share

Whole class teacher led

ASK

- Question **1** a): *Which do you think is the most effective method to work out the answer?*
- Question **1** b): *Can you explain how the bar model shows how you can find the answer?*

IN FOCUS Question **1** a) shows that there are several ways to work out the answer and it provides a good opportunity to discuss which method is the most efficient and why.

The bar model in question **1** b) shows children that they need to work out the two amounts and then subtract.

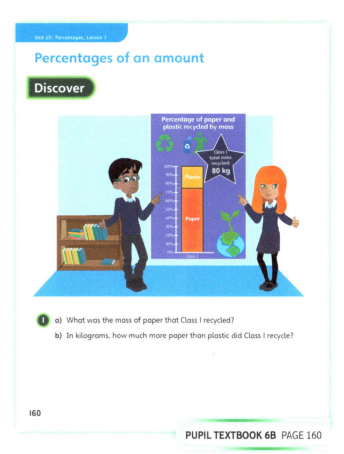

PUPIL TEXTBOOK 6B PAGE 160

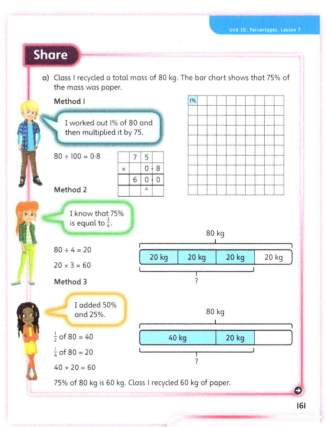

PUPIL TEXTBOOK 6B PAGE 161

Think together

WAYS OF WORKING Whole class teacher led (I do, We do, You do)

ASK

• Question **1**: *Is there more than one way to work out the answer? How many parts has the first bar model been split into? Look at the second bar model. What two percentages have been used to work out 60%? How can you work out the 40%?*

IN FOCUS Question **3** provides a good opportunity for children to think carefully about finding a range of percentages of the same number. Ask them to compare and discuss their strategies. Sharing in this way will help children to see that there are different ways in which mathematical problems can be solved. Do they use different strategies to find different percentages?

STRENGTHEN Some children may need support with identifying efficient strategies. For instance, in question **2**, they must work out 95% of 300 km. Some children may find 50% + 10% + 10% + 10% +10% + 5%. Ask them if they can think of a more efficient method. They should see that it is easier to find 5% and then subtract this from 100%. If they do not reach this conclusion, show them on a bar model how this would work.

DEEPEN Following question **1**, explore a different way in which children could work out the solution. They could find 60% and then 40%; or they could work out 60% and then take that amount away from the total (100%) to leave 40%.

ASSESSMENT CHECKPOINT Assess children when they are completing question **2**. Are they using efficient strategies to find the percentages?

ANSWERS

Question **1**: 60% of 120 kg = 72 kg of paper
40% of 120 kg = 48 kg of plastic

Question **2** a): 5% of £300 = £15

Question **2** b): 55% of 300 kg = 165 kg

Question **2** c): 15% of 300 cm = 45 cm

Question **2** d): 95% of 300 km = 285 km

Question **3**: Children should discuss various methods to find percentages of 320 and their efficiency. They should draw bar models and grids to help them explain their methods.

Methods might include:
11% = 10% + 1% = 32 + 3·2 = 35·2
11% = 11 × 1% = 11 × 3·2 = 35·2
51% = 50% + 1% = 160 + 3·2 = 163·2
9% = 9 × 1% = 9 × 3·2 = 28·8
9% = 10% − 1% = 32 − 3·2 = 28·8
19% = 20% − 1% = 64 − 3·2 = 60·8
49% = 50% − 1% = 160 − 3·2 = 156·8

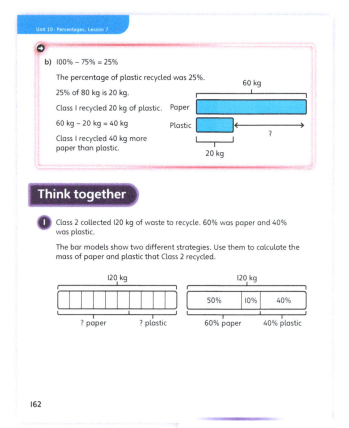

PUPIL TEXTBOOK 6B PAGE 162

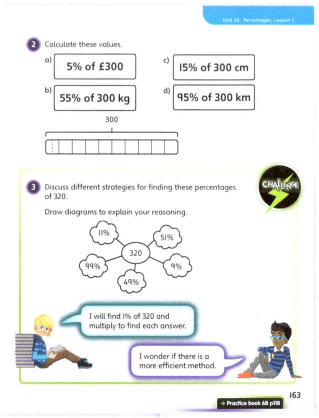

PUPIL TEXTBOOK 6B PAGE 163

Practice

WAYS OF WORKING Independent thinking

IN FOCUS Question **2** is important because children not only have to work out percentages of amounts, but they also have to calculate the missing percentage for the pink tulips. Encourage children to draw a bar model in which the percentages are labelled (mark the missing percentage with a question mark) and label 100% across the whole of the bar. This should help them to reason effectively.

STRENGTHEN To strengthen learning, suggest that children draw a bar model to support them with question **4**. It should have the parts labelled: 11%, 29% and ☐%. This should help children to visualise that they need to start with 100%, subtract 11% and then subtract 29%. The missing part will be the percentage they need to find, namely 60% of 32,500 (19,500). Discuss the various strategies they could use to find the answer and which is most efficient.

DEEPEN Question **5** challenges children to calculate percentages in the context of area. Present children with more multi-step problems similar to questions **4** and **5** and ask them to draw bar models to represent the problems. You can increase the complexity by adding more percentages for them to find.

ASSESSMENT CHECKPOINT Question **4** will help you to assess whether children can work out a multi-step problem involving percentages.

ANSWERS Answers for the **Practice** part of the lesson can be found in the *Power Maths* online subscription.

Reflect

WAYS OF WORKING Independent thinking

IN FOCUS This is an excellent way to consolidate learning from the lesson. Children should find 50% + 10% + 10% + 10% + 5%, or 50% + 25% + 10%, or they could do 10% + 5% and then take the total away from 100%.

ASSESSMENT CHECKPOINT Assess children on the two ways they use to find the answer. Deeper thinkers may find answers such as 50% + 25% +10%. Some children may be able to do the calculation mentally too, which shows a fluency with numbers.

ANSWERS Answers for the **Reflect** part of the lesson can be found in the *Power Maths* online subscription.

After the lesson ⏸

- Can children choose an efficient strategy to work out a percentage of an amount? Are any children still doing 10% + 10% + 10% + 10% + 10% + 10% + 1% to work out 61% of a number, for instance?
- Can children effectively draw bar models to support their understanding of the information given in the questions?

PUPIL PRACTICE BOOK 6B PAGE 118

Unit 10: Percentages, Lesson 7   Date: _____

Percentages of an amount

1 Calculate these percentages.

a) 30% of £400 = £ ☐
£400
☐☐☐☐☐☐☐☐☐☐
400 ÷ 10 = ☐
☐ × 3 = ☐

c) 75% of £60 = £ ☐

b) 60% of 400 g = ☐ g

d) 15% of £120 = £ ☐

2 Toshi plants 240 tulip bulbs. 10% are red tulips and 5% are yellow. The rest are pink. How many of each colour are there?

☐ red ☐ yellow and ☐ pink tulips.

118

PUPIL PRACTICE BOOK 6B PAGE 119

Unit 10: Percentages, Lesson 7

3 a) Complete these percentages.

50% of 700 = ☐   10% of 700 = ☐   1% of 700 = ☐

b) Now find these percentages of 700.

11%   51%   9%
33%   700   49%
30%   99%
6%   5%

4 32,500 people signed up to run a marathon.

11% dropped out before race day. 29% did not complete the course.

How many people finished the marathon?

☐

119

PUPIL PRACTICE BOOK 6B PAGE 120

Unit 10: Percentages, Lesson 7

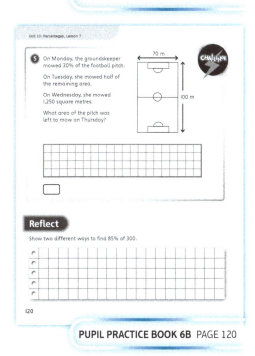

5 On Monday, the groundskeeper mowed 30% of the football pitch.

On Tuesday, she mowed half of the remaining area.

On Wednesday, she mowed 1,250 square metres.

What area of the pitch was left to mow on Thursday?

70 m
100 m
CHALLENGE

☐

Reflect

Show two different ways to find 85% of 300.

120

Percentages (missing values)

Learning focus

In this lesson, children will find missing values in problems involving percentages.

Before you teach

- Are children confident identifying the whole and part to solve percentage questions?
- Can they apply a range of strategies, such as multiplying or dividing the whole to find a percentage?
- Are children confident in drawing and using bar models to break down a percentage question?

NATIONAL CURRICULUM LINKS

Year 6 Number – fractions (including decimals and percentages)

Recall and use equivalences between simple fractions, decimals and percentages, including in different contexts.

Multiply 1-digit numbers with up to two decimal places by whole numbers.

ASSESSING MASTERY

Children can confidently solve percentage problems involving missing numbers. They have a firm grasp of the numbers involved, are able to represent a problem using a bar model, and can explain their answers effectively.

COMMON MISCONCEPTIONS

Children may simply work out the percentage of a number. For instance, for '20% of ⬜ = 50', they think the answer is 10 as they have mistakenly worked out 20% of 50. Ask:
- *Could you use a bar model to represent the problem?*

Children may misinterpret word problems. Ask:
- *Can you write a number sentence which matches the word problem?*

STRENGTHENING UNDERSTANDING

Give children a range of percentage problems and ask them to draw diagrams (such as bar models) to represent them. This should reinforce their understanding of problem solving with percentages.

GOING DEEPER

Deepen learning in this lesson by challenging children to create their own missing word problems involving percentages. Ask them to swap their problems with a partner and compare and discuss strategies and answers.

KEY LANGUAGE

In lesson: per cent (%), percentage, equivalent, parts, whole, multiply

Other language to be used by the teacher: parts, fraction, hundredth, divide, factor

STRUCTURES AND REPRESENTATIONS

Bar model

 In the eTextbook of this lesson, you will find interactive links to a selection of teaching tools.

Quick recap ↺

Ask: *What is the same and what is different in each of these pairs of calculations?*

3 + 5 = ?	3 + ? = 5
50 − 20 = ?	? − 50 = 20
3 × 12 = ?	3 × ? = 12

Discover

WAYS OF WORKING Pair work

ASK

- Question **1** a): *Can you draw a diagram of the problem to help you? What information do you have and what do you need to work out? What is the whole and what is the part?*
- Question **1** b): *What fraction is 20% equivalent to? How does that help you to work out the answer?*

IN FOCUS Question **1** a) introduces missing percentage problems to children. They will have to think carefully about the part and the whole, particularly when identifying which one they need to work out. Encourage children to draw a diagram of the problem to reinforce their understanding. What information do they already have? How can they use it to work out the missing information?

PRACTICAL TIPS Ask children to take it in turns to do some standing jumps. They should measure their jump and then pretend it is 50% (or a different percentage) of the world record. They should then work out what the world record would be.

ANSWERS

Question **1** a): The world record for women's long jump is 7·5 m.

Question **1** b): The world record for men's high jump is 245 cm.

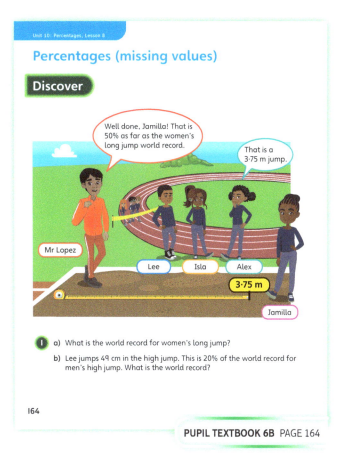

PUPIL TEXTBOOK 6B PAGE 164

Share

WAYS OF WORKING Whole class teacher led

ASK

- Question **1** a): *What is the whole and what is the part in this situation? If you know that the part is 3·75 m how can you use this information to find the whole/world record?*
- Question **1** b): *Why do you need to multiply by 5?*

IN FOCUS Question **1** a) offers an opportunity to address some misconceptions. Astrid thinks she has to work out 50% of 3·75 m. Discuss Astrid's mistake with children. Draw attention to the bar model, showing children that they are given the part and they need to find the whole.

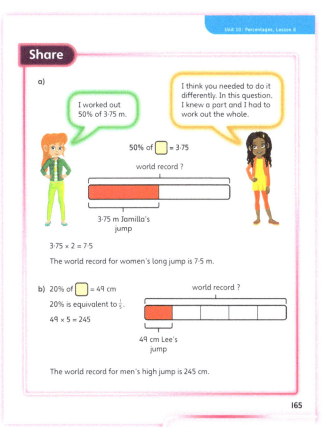

PUPIL TEXTBOOK 6B PAGE 165

201

Think together

WAYS OF WORKING Whole class teacher led (I do, We do, You do)

ASK

• Question **2**: *Is 40 a factor of 100? How many steps are required to solve this problem? How might it help to find 10% first?*

• Question **3** c): *How can you find the area of the shaded part of the rectangle? How can you use this to find the whole area?*

IN FOCUS Question **3** explores whether children can use the strategies they have learnt in previous questions and lessons to solve problems. Question **3** a) is particularly challenging because 75 is not a factor of 100. You may want to draw a bar model on the board to provide additional support. For question **3** c), some children may need a brief reminder of how to work out the area of a rectangle.

STRENGTHEN For question **2**, children should realise that 40 is not a factor of 100. Explain that they need to work out 10% and why this will help them to find the answer. Ask them to draw their own bar model with a focus on finding 10%. What should they divide 120 by to find 10%? What do they then need to do to find 100%?

DEEPEN Question **2** will deepen learning as, in this multi-step problem, children are required to first find 10% by dividing 40% by 4, and then multiply by 10 to find 100%. For additional practice, see if children can solve similar problems without the support of a bar model. After completing question **3**, challenge children to think up another percentage problem that uses similar skills.

ASSESSMENT CHECKPOINT Assess children on question **3**. Can they use the strategies learnt to solve the problems effectively? Do they rely on a bar model?

ANSWERS

Question **1** a): 10% of 30 = 3

Question **1** b): 20% of 25 = 5

Question **1** c): 25% of 120 = 30

Question **2**: There are 300 spectators in total.

Question **3**: Here are some possible methods. Parts a) and c) involve working out the whole (100%) from a given percentage. Part b) is simply finding a percentage of the whole.

Question **3** a): If 75% = 30, 25% = 10, 100% = 40
The number is 40.

Question **3** b): 30% of 120 = 3 × 10% = 3 × 12 = 36 miles
Jen has completed 36 miles of the 120 mile journey.

Question **3** c): 15% of the rectangle = 5 m × 12 m = 60 m^2
1% of the rectangle = 60 m^2 ÷ 15 = 4 m^2
100% of the rectangle = 400 m^2

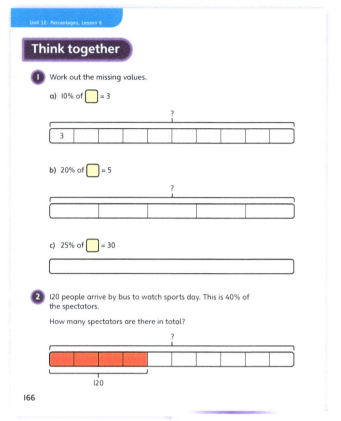

PUPIL TEXTBOOK 6B PAGE 166

PUPIL TEXTBOOK 6B PAGE 167

Practice

WAYS OF WORKING Independent thinking

IN FOCUS In question **3**, children will need to think carefully about what steps are required to solve the problem. In question **3** a), for example, they should realise that 70% of the sweets are lemon and then use this information to work out how many are orange. Prompt children to find 10% by dividing 63 by 7. They then multiply by 10 to find the whole.

STRENGTHEN Matching a bar model with a percentage problem (as in question **2**) will strengthen learning. If necessary, provide children with similar activities where they need to consider what information they have and what they need to work out. This may be particularly helpful in preparation for question **6**, where children may also need reminding how to find the perimeter of a shape.

DEEPEN Following question **6**, challenge children to make up their own similar problems. They could change the length and width, or the percentage, or they could even look at different areas and perimeters.

THINK DIFFERENTLY Question **4** requires children to work backwards. They will have to think carefully about their starting point and how they can use the inverse to solve the problem. If children are finding this difficult, support them by drawing a bar model (or by encouraging them to do so).

ASSESSMENT CHECKPOINT Question **6** is a challenging question. If children can successfully solve it, they are likely to have mastered the lesson. Note that the question asks for the perimeter, not the area.

Question **5** is also useful for assessing children's understanding, as it requires them to identify relationships between numbers and percentages. For example, if they know that 30% of 300 is 90, they can work out '30% of ☐ = 180' without having to calculate 10% and multiply by 10 to find the whole – the missing number must be double 300.

ANSWERS Answers for the **Practice** part of the lesson can be found in the *Power Maths* online subscription.

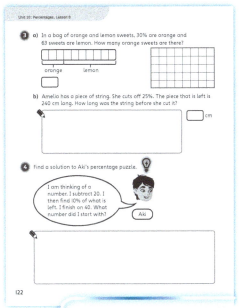

PUPIL PRACTICE BOOK 6B PAGE 121

PUPIL PRACTICE BOOK 6B PAGE 122

Reflect

WAYS OF WORKING Independent thinking

IN FOCUS This is an important reflection as it encourages children to focus on the difference between finding a percentage of an amount and finding a known percentage of a missing amount. Drawing diagrams will help children to clarify and cement this difference.

ASSESSMENT CHECKPOINT To assess children's understanding, consider whether they can represent the two problems with a diagram (preferably a bar model). Can they explain how they are different? Do they use the correct terminology, such as 'part' and 'whole'?

ANSWERS Answers for the **Reflect** part of the lesson can be found in the *Power Maths* online subscription.

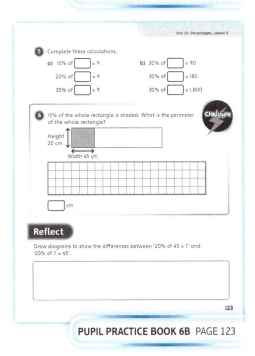

PUPIL PRACTICE BOOK 6B PAGE 123

After the lesson ⏸

- Do children understand missing number problems?
- Can they confidently identify whether they are being asked to find the total or part of a percentage?

End of unit check

Don't forget the unit assessment grid in your *Power Maths* online subscription.

IN FOCUS This **End of unit check** will allow you to focus on children's understanding of percentages and whether they can apply their knowledge to solve problems. The questions cover the range of questions they will encounter in this unit. Look carefully at the answer that is given for question **6**. It is a SATs-style question and will inform you as to whether children can use information to interpret a problem. It also involves finding a fraction and percentage of a large number.

ANSWERS AND COMMENTARY

By the end of this unit, children should be able to represent percentages on a grid and find percentages of given amounts. They should be confident in converting between fractions, decimals and percentages and they should know how to apply different strategies and check their strategies are suitable. They can use these skills to calculate answers to problems involving missing numbers. They can also apply their knowledge to solve multi-step problems.

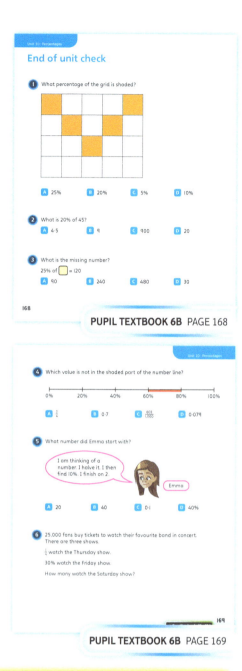

PUPIL TEXTBOOK 6B PAGE 168

PUPIL TEXTBOOK 6B PAGE 169

Q	A	WRONG ANSWERS AND MISCONCEPTIONS	STRENGTHENING UNDERSTANDING
1	A	C suggests children have counted the number of shaded squares and assumed that this is the percentage.	Give children support with representing percentages on hundredths grids.
2	B	Choosing C suggests children do not have a firm grasp of place value.	
3	C	D suggests children have misinterpreted the question: they have found 25% of 120. Choosing A suggests the child has found 25% and then subtracted it from 120.	Try giving children different amounts of counters. They must find percentages of the counters. Then move on to problems with missing numbers such as: 20% of ☐ = 40.
4	D	Any other answer suggests children cannot convert between decimals, percentages and fractions.	
5	B	A suggests children have forgotten to reverse the halve and are just focusing on the fact that 10% of 20 is 2.	Display the key vocabulary for the unit in your classroom.
6	11,250	Look carefully at how children find $\frac{1}{4}$ of 25,000 (they may halve it, then halve again; or divide by 4) and 30% of 25,000 (the easiest way is to find 10%, then multiply by 3).	Ask children to match word problems with representations on bar models or number lines.

My journal

WAYS OF WORKING Independent thinking

ANSWERS AND COMMENTARY

Question **1** a): First, children need to find out how many of the smallest rectangles make up the total shape. They may divide it up by drawing lines on the shape in the journal. When they have done this, they can see that there are 24 rectangles. 25% of 24 is 6 (children may halve and then halve again, or simply divide by 4). So, 6 rectangles should be shaded.

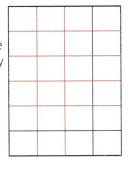

Question **1** b): For this question, children may be unsure of how to find 35% (they cannot simply divide by 35% as it is not a factor of 100). Help children by drawing this on the shape:

20%	10%	5%	5%			

Following this, children should be able to shade 35% by adding 20%, 10% and 5%.

Power check

WAYS OF WORKING Independent thinking

ASK

- *Can you write down some new words you have learnt and what they mean?*
- *Which visual representation helped you in this unit? Why?*
- *What do you know now that you did not at the start of the unit?*
- *How confident do you feel with solving problems involving percentages?*

Power play

WAYS OF WORKING Pair work

IN FOCUS Use this **Power play** to assess children's ability to work out percentages of amounts. Can they explain their methods or any strategies they used?

ANSWERS AND COMMENTARY If children can complete the **Power play**, this means they can find percentages of amounts – including those with missing numbers. Listen to their discussions about strategy and note any children who may need further support. Note that there are some squares that are completely blank. Children can make up their own problem (encourage them to extend their learning by choosing a more 'tricky' one). They should be encouraged to extend this **Power play** by creating their own similar puzzle.

End of unit check

My journal

1 a) Shade in 25% of the diagram. Explain your decisions.

b) Shade in 35% of this diagram.

Power check

How do you feel about your work in this unit?

124

PUPIL PRACTICE BOOK 6B PAGE 124

Power play

- Play in pairs with two different sets of counters.
- Take it in turns to choose a problem to solve (for example, 10% of 900 = ?). If your answer is correct, place one of your counters on the square where the answer would go.
- The first person to get a full row of counters wins!

of	900		260		1
10%		17			
		9			
75%					
			170	25	
99%					

Try creating your own game and then swap with a partner.

125

PUPIL PRACTICE BOOK 6B PAGE 125

After the unit ⏸

- Can children convert between fractions, decimals and percentages, including when the denominator is not 100?
- Can they confidently find percentages of amounts, even when there is a missing number?
- Can they apply the strategies they have learnt to solve multi-step problems?

Strengthen and **Deepen** activities for this unit can be found in the *Power Maths* online subscription.

Unit 11
Measure – perimeter, area and volume

Don't forget to watch the Unit 11 video!

Mastery Expert tip! 'When I taught this unit to my class, we spent a lot of time outside – we used chalk to draw parallelograms, rectangles and triangles, used a metre stick to measure the lengths of the shapes we drew and calculated their area. We drew different shapes with equal areas and different shapes with equal perimeters. My class then created their own investigative questions and we played "What would happen if …?". For example, "What would happen to the perimeter of a shape if the area increased?".'

WHY THIS UNIT IS IMPORTANT

This unit provides children with opportunities to explore the relationship between the area and perimeter of different 2D shapes. Children generate the formulae for the area of triangles and parallelograms and the volume of cubes and cuboids and use them to calculate areas, volumes and missing lengths. This is very important for their future learning as it enables them to understand their calculations rather than memorise steps. Children will apply their knowledge of perimeter, area and volume to solve problems, in particular when calculating unknown lengths, perimeters and areas of composite rectilinear shapes.

WHERE THIS UNIT FITS

→ Unit 10: Percentages
→ **Unit 11: Measure – perimeter, area and volume**
→ Unit 12: Statistics

This unit builds on the concepts of area and perimeter learned in Year 5. Previous methods (including doubling of the length and width to calculate perimeter, or multiplying the width and length of a rectangle to calculate its area) will be used as a starting point.

Before they start this unit, it is expected that children:
• can define the concepts of area, perimeter and volume
• can make links between the length and width of a rectangle and its area
• can find the perimeter of shapes when all side lengths are given.

ASSESSING MASTERY

Children who have mastered this unit will be able to accurately find and draw shapes with the same area but different perimeters and vice versa. Children will also be able to apply their knowledge of perimeter, area and volume to work backwards to calculate missing lengths. Children will confidently work out the area of triangles and parallelograms by turning them into rectangles. Children will use their knowledge of formulae and the properties of composite shapes to calculate their areas.

COMMON MISCONCEPTIONS	STRENGTHENING UNDERSTANDING	GOING DEEPER
Children may multiply the two sides of a parallelogram to find its area.	Present parallelograms drawn on squared paper and model transforming them into rectangles. Children can count the squares inside each shape and establish that *area = base × height*.	Challenge children to explore how the areas differ between a parallelogram and a rectangle with sides of equal length. Children could investigate dimensions for each shape that would produce equal areas.
Children may use side lengths as the base and height of a triangle and multiply them. They may assume that the triangle is right-angled when it is not.	Present children with different triangles and ask them to identify the base and height in each one. Ask: *How can you check whether these sides are perpendicular? How can you check that this is a right angle? Which side should you use to find the area?*	Challenge children to draw their own triangles and calculate the area or, if the area is given, to find the missing base length or height. Ask children to draw triangles with a given area. Ask: *How many different triangles with the same area can you draw?*

Unit 11: Measure – perimeter, area and volume

UNIT STARTER PAGES

Introduce the unit using whole-class discussion. Ask children to describe perimeter, area and volume and suggest situations where they may encounter these terms. Ascertain children's understanding and recognition of the key language.

STRUCTURES AND REPRESENTATIONS

2D rectilinear shapes represented on squared grids: This model allows children to count the side lengths of a shape and the number of squares that fit inside a shape.

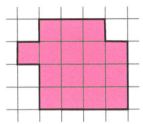

3D shapes made of 1 cm cubes: This model allows children to count the number of cubic centimetres in a solid shape.

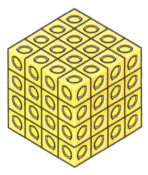

KEY LANGUAGE

There is some key language that children will need to know as part of the learning in this unit:

➔ perimeter, distance, area, space, volume

➔ centimetres (cm), metres (m), square centimetres (cm^2), square metres (m^2), cubic centimetres (cm^3), cubic metres (m^3), dimensions

➔ rectangle, square, triangle, rectilinear shape, compound shapes, sides, base, length, height, width, perpendicular, parallelogram, cube, cuboid

➔ measure, combine, total, double, estimate, formula

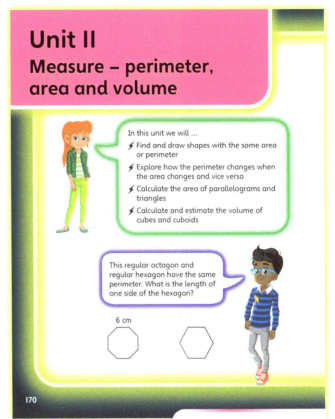

PUPIL TEXTBOOK 6B PAGE 170

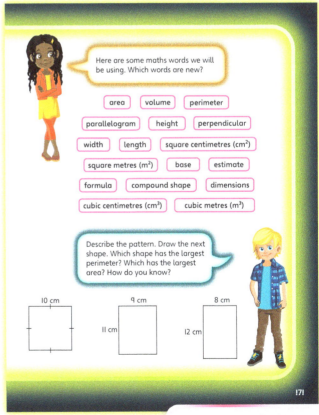

PUPIL TEXTBOOK 6B PAGE 171

Shapes – same area

Learning focus

In this lesson, children will find the areas of shapes by counting individual squares. They will draw different shapes with the same area.

Before you teach

- Can you link any practical measurement activities to your own school context?
- How sound is children's understanding of the term 'area'?

NATIONAL CURRICULUM LINKS

Year 6 Measurement

Recognise that shapes with the same areas can have different perimeters and vice versa.

ASSESSING MASTERY

Children can find and draw shapes with the same area. Children recognise that two shapes can have the same area but different perimeters.

COMMON MISCONCEPTIONS

Children may think that if two shapes have equal areas, they must be identical. Ask:

- *How do you measure area? Do you have enough information to find the area? What else do you need to measure?*

STRENGTHENING UNDERSTANDING

Provide children with rectangles and squares of different perimeters that have equal areas. Help children measure and find the perimeter and area of each shape.

GOING DEEPER

Challenge children to measure the width and length of the classroom floor and calculate the area. Can they draw two rooms that have different dimensions but the same area? Ask children to draw their floor plans to scale.

KEY LANGUAGE

In lesson: area, centimetres (cm), centimetre squared (cm^2), rectangle, square, dimensions, compound shape

Other language to be used by the teacher: perimeter, 2D, sides, measure, rectilinear, distance, combine

STRUCTURES AND REPRESENTATIONS

Diagrams (actual size) of rectangles and squares of different dimensions

RESOURCES

Mandatory: rulers, measuring tapes

Optional: squared paper

 In the eTextbook of this lesson, you will find interactive links to a selection of teaching tools.

Quick recap

As a class, discuss estimates for the area of the classroom carpet. Use approximate measures to test out these estimates.

Discover

WAYS OF WORKING Pair work

ASK

• Question ① a): *What is the same and what is different about the two rooms?*
• Question ① a): *Do you need to find the areas of the rooms to know if Jen is correct?*
• Question ① a): *How can you find the area?*

IN FOCUS When considering question ① a), use the practical activity described below in Practical tips to help children find the area and perimeter of each room. Ask them to consider how to determine if the two rooms have the same area by looking at the blocks of squares that make up each room. In question ① b), children are asked to find the areas of the rooms they have drawn. Encourage them to think of a quick way to calculate the number of squares rather than counting them individually. Ask them to relate the area of a rectangle to its width and length.

PRACTICAL TIPS Give children squared paper on which to draw the rooms. Ask children to shade each room a different colour before cutting them out. Some children may cut the rooms further into tiles and rearrange these to prove that the two rooms have the same area.

ANSWERS

Question ① a): Jen is correct.
Area of Room A = 4 m × 6 m = 24 m^2
Area of Room B = 3 m × 8 m = 24 m^2

Question ① b): Various arrangements are possible. The dimensions will change (for example, 2 m × 12 m) but the area will still be 24 m^2.

Share

WAYS OF WORKING Whole class teacher led

ASK

• Question ① a): *What do you notice about the two rooms? How can you work out if the areas of the two rooms are the same?*
• Question ① b): *How many different rectangular rooms with the same area can you draw? Can you draw rooms that are not rectangles but have the same area? How can you be sure all the rooms have the same area?*

IN FOCUS In question ① a), justify to children that the areas of the two rectangles are the same by looking at the number of strips that make up each rectangle. Because there are 3 × 4 m strips (12 squares in total) and 4 × 3 m strips (another 12 squares in total) the area of each square is 24 cm^2 altogether. You could model this by taking strips of paper to scale, and ask children to rearrange one rectangle to make the other. Since the strips of paper have not changed, the areas of both must be the same. When completing question ① b), prompt children to connect the length and width of a rectangle with its area, making them aware that multiplying width by length will give the area of a rectangle. Children should recognise that the rows and columns represent width and length in these rectangles and should use their knowledge of factors when they draw their own rooms (if these rooms are rectangular).

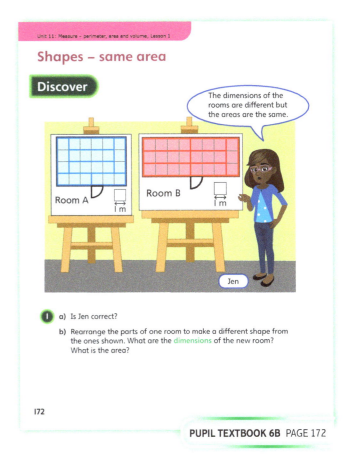

Shapes – same area

Discover

The dimensions of the rooms are different but the areas are the same.

Room A
Room B
1 m
1 m
Jen

① a) Is Jen correct?

b) Rearrange the parts of one room to make a different shape from the ones shown. What are the dimensions of the new room? What is the area?

172

PUPIL TEXTBOOK 6B PAGE 172

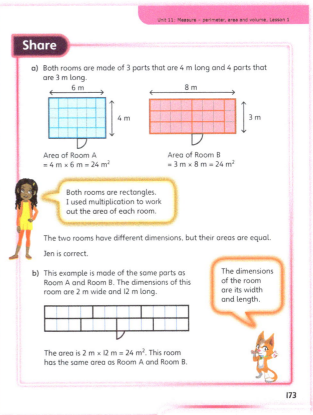

Share

a) Both rooms are made of 3 parts that are 4 m long and 4 parts that are 3 m long.

6 m
4 m
8 m
3 m

Area of Room A
= 4 m × 6 m = 24 m^2

Area of Room B
= 3 m × 8 m = 24 m^2

Both rooms are rectangles. I used multiplication to work out the area of each room.

The two rooms have different dimensions, but their areas are equal.

Jen is correct.

b) This example is made of the same parts as Room A and Room B. The dimensions of this room are 2 m wide and 12 m long.

The dimensions of the room are its width and length.

The area is 2 m × 12 m = 24 m^2. This room has the same area as Room A and Room B.

173

PUPIL TEXTBOOK 6B PAGE 173

Think together

WAYS OF WORKING Whole class teacher led (I do, We do, You do)

ASK

- Question **1**: *Can you spot a more efficient way to find the answer than counting the squares individually? How will you calculate the areas of shapes B and D?*
- Question **3**: *What do you know about a square that can help you find its length?*

IN FOCUS In question **1**, ensure children can explain how they found the width and length of each shape. For shapes A and C, discuss as a class the strategies used to find the area. Did children use their workings in D to find the area of C?

STRENGTHEN For question **3**, ensure children have an opportunity to model the problem. Provide children with squared paper or square counters to explore solutions. Discuss the number 16 and its factors: numbers that multiply to give 16. Provide scaffolding through questions such as: *What do you need to know to draw a square? What is special about the width and length of the rectangle? What could the values be?*

DEEPEN When answering question **2**, encourage children to conclude that the length and width of the rectangles are factor pairs of 30. Ask children to write all the factor pairs of 30 and use them to draw all the possible rectangles with an area of 30 cm^2 that have whole number dimensions.

ASSESSMENT CHECKPOINT Assess whether children understand that rectangles can have different widths and lengths but the same area. Do they display confidence in identifying the side lengths of shapes with the same area?

ANSWERS

Question **1**: A and D are both 8 m^2.
B and C are both 12 m^2.

Question **2** a): Luis is correct. Both shapes have an area of 30 m^2.

Question **2** b): Children should draw rectangles that are 15 cm by 2 cm or 30 cm by 1 cm.

Question **3** a): A: 4 cm by 4 cm
B: 2 cm by 8 cm
C: Various options are possible. Children should split the composite shape into two rectangles with a combined area of 16 cm^2.

For example, Rectangle 1: 12 cm^2 (2 cm × 6 cm); Rectangle 2: 4 cm^2 (2 cm × 2 cm).
The dimensions could then be (clockwise from top): 2 cm, 2 cm, 4 cm, 2 cm, 6 cm, 4 cm.

Question **3** b): Children should draw the shapes accurately on cm squared paper using the dimensions they worked out in part a).

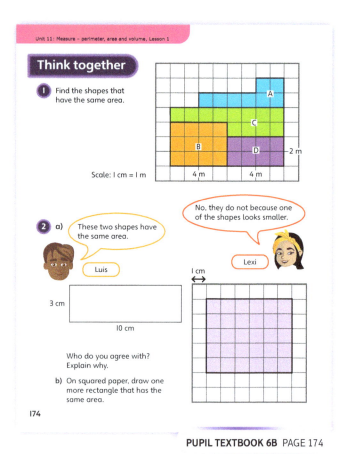

PUPIL TEXTBOOK 6B PAGE 174

PUPIL TEXTBOOK 6B PAGE 175

Practice

WAYS OF WORKING Independent thinking

IN FOCUS Questions **1** a) and b) involve children finding the areas of pairs of rectangles. Children will discover that the shapes have the same areas, even though they have different dimensions. This question can be used to address the misconception that shapes with equal areas have to be identical. Ask children to explain and demonstrate why this is incorrect. Encourage them to use the questions and give their own examples to support their discussion.

STRENGTHEN Question **3** requires children to problem solve to find the missing measurements. Some children may have difficulties starting the question as they are uncertain what the areas of the shapes can be. Encourage them to determine the area of shape A first. They can then use the known area to find the factor pairs of that number and find the other missing lengths. To strengthen children's understanding of the formula *area = width × length*, ask them to draw the three shapes on squared paper. This strategy will help children to see the individual squares as well as how the shape can be divided into rows or columns.

DEEPEN Question **4** challenges children to find the possible dimensions of a rectangle. Extend the challenge by asking children to investigate this statement: *Is it always true, sometimes true or never true that the area of a rectangle is a multiple of its width and length?*

ASSESSMENT CHECKPOINT Can children recognise that rectangles can have the same area but different dimensions? Can they draw a variety of rectangles with the same area and understand that, when drawing rectangles with the same area, the product of the width and length is always equal to the same number (the area of the rectangles)?

ANSWERS Answers for the **Practice** part of the lesson can be found in the *Power Maths* online subscription.

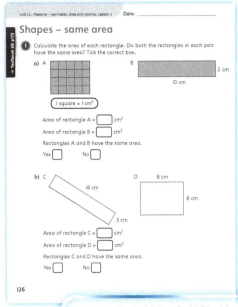

PUPIL PRACTICE BOOK 6B PAGE 126

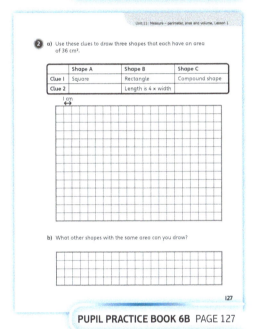

PUPIL PRACTICE BOOK 6B PAGE 127

Reflect

WAYS OF WORKING Independent thinking

IN FOCUS The aim of the question is for children to explain in words how to find the area of a rectangle. This question reveals children's understanding of strategies for measuring and calculating area. Encourage children to use full sentences to describe their strategy.

ASSESSMENT CHECKPOINT Can children describe how they would find the area of the room by multiplying the dimensions, or by repeated addition?

ANSWERS Answers for the **Reflect** part of the lesson can be found in the *Power Maths* online subscription.

After the lesson ⏸

- How many opportunities were children given to explore shapes with the same area but different perimeters?
- Are children confident in drawing shapes that have equal areas but different perimeters?

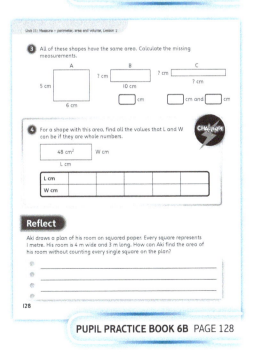

PUPIL PRACTICE BOOK 6B PAGE 128

Area and perimeter

Learning focus

In this lesson, children will explore simple shapes that have the same area but different perimeters. They will explore this in shapes other than rectangles.

Before you teach

- Are children confident about what 'area' measures?
- Are children confident about what 'perimeter' measures?

NATIONAL CURRICULUM LINKS

Year 6 Measurement

Recognise that shapes with the same areas can have different perimeters and vice versa.

ASSESSING MASTERY

Children can apply their knowledge of area and perimeter to work backwards to suggest the dimensions of shapes with the same given area but different perimeters.

COMMON MISCONCEPTIONS

Children may confuse 'area' and 'perimeter'. Ask:
- *Can you tell me a rule for working out the perimeter of a rectangle? What about its area? Will this work for all rectangles?*

STRENGTHENING UNDERSTANDING

Ask children to make a rectangle with a given area on a geoboard. Explain that the perimeter is the length of the elastic band – it is the length around the shape. The area is the number of squares the band encloses and is measured in squares (that is, cm^2). Ask: *Which lengths do you need to work out the perimeter? Can you use these lengths to find the area?*

GOING DEEPER

Challenge children to make two rectangles that have the same area on a geoboard and calculate their perimeters. Ask: *Can you make another rectangle with the same area? Will the perimeter be different?*

KEY LANGUAGE

In lesson: perimeter, area, equal, length, width, side

Other language to be used by the teacher: rectilinear shape, total, double, differ, compound shape

STRUCTURES AND REPRESENTATIONS

2D shapes drawn on squared paper, 2D shapes drawn on normal paper

RESOURCES

Mandatory: geoboards, elastics for geoboards

Optional: cardboard shapes, rulers, coloured pencils

 In the eTextbook of this lesson, you will find interactive links to a selection of teaching tools.

Quick recap

As a class, discuss estimates for the perimeter of the school hall. Use approximate measures to test out these estimates.

Discover

WAYS OF WORKING Pair work

ASK

• Question **1** a): *How can you find the areas of these shapes? How can you find their perimeters?*

IN FOCUS For question **1** a), help children describe the properties of each shape, such as equal side lengths, equal angles and the name of each shape. Discuss how knowing the properties of a shape can help them to find the perimeter and area of the shape.

PRACTICAL TIPS Provide children with geoboards and ask them to make the shapes, then determine their width and length. Discuss whether they will need to know all sides to calculate the area and the perimeter, or just two. Discuss other ways of calculating the area and perimeter of a rectangle. Ask children to consider the different strategies suggested and decide which method they think is the easiest and which method they think is the quickest.

ANSWERS

Question **1** a): Both shapes have the same area (36 cm^2) but different perimeters (Lexi 24 cm, Max 26 cm).

Question **1** b): There are two possible rectangles:
12 cm × 3 cm (perimeter of 30 cm or
18 cm × 2 cm (perimeter of 40 cm).

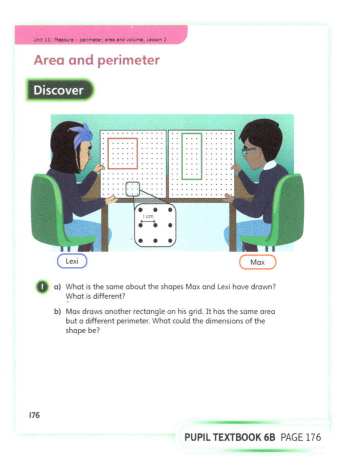

PUPIL TEXTBOOK 6B PAGE 176

Share

WAYS OF WORKING Whole class teacher led

ASK

• Question **1** a): *What shapes are in the picture? What measurements do you need to know to compare the shapes? How can you use the dimensions of the shapes to find their area and perimeter?*

• Question **1** b): *What other dimensions will give a shape with the same area?*

IN FOCUS Question **1** b) asks children to apply their knowledge of factor pairs to find the dimensions of other rectangles that have the same area. Revisit the strategies that children can use to find the area and perimeter, including the formulae, and clarify any misconceptions that children may have about the differences between area and perimeter.

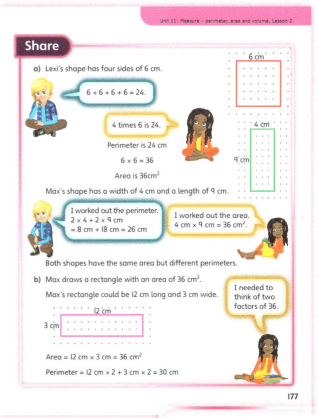

PUPIL TEXTBOOK 6B PAGE 177

Think together

WAYS OF WORKING Whole class teacher led (I do, We do, You do)

ASK

- Question **1** a): *How can you divide the compound shape (shape C) into two to help you find its area?*
- Question **2**: *Look carefully at the shapes. What do you notice? Without doing any calculations, can you predict which shape has the largest/smallest area? What about the largest/smallest perimeter?*

IN FOCUS In question **2**, children are asked to consider three shapes, each constructed with two 2 × 7 rectangles. Children should recognise that the shapes have equal areas by observation. Encourage children to speculate about the perimeter of each shape before performing the working out. Discuss all observations and speculations (including incorrect responses) and encourage children to explain their reasoning.

STRENGTHEN For further practice, provide children with cut-out shapes, such as four congruent rectangles and four congruent squares, each produced on squared paper. Have children work in small groups to explore shapes with equal areas by putting two or more shapes together. Children can draw the shapes they create and describe what they discover when finding the perimeter.

DEEPEN Use question **3** to deepen children's understanding of area and perimeter. Encourage them to draw shapes as Astrid and Ash suggest, to see how changing the area of a shape may affect its perimeter. Ask children to discuss Max's statement, referring to their drawings to explain why they think it is correct or incorrect.

ASSESSMENT CHECKPOINT Can children confidently describe how 2D shapes can have the same area but different perimeters? Can they explain that a larger area does not necessarily mean a larger perimeter and vice versa?

ANSWERS

Question **1** a):

Shape	Area	Perimeter
A	3 × 8 = 24 cm²	3 × 2 + 8 × 2 = 22 cm
B	6 × 4 = 24 cm²	6 × 2 + 4 × 2 = 20 cm
C	3 × 2 + 6 × 3 = 24 cm²	5 + 6 + 3 + 3 + 2 + 3 = 22 cm

Question **1** b): Various answers are possible. For example, children could draw a rectangle with dimensions 2 cm × 12 cm and perimeter 26 cm, or a range of different composite shapes.

Question **2**: The areas are all the same: 28 squares in total, 14 red and 14 yellow.
The perimeters are all different: A 22 cm, B 26 cm, C 32 cm.

Question **3**: Max is not correct. Children should show a counter example. For example, a 6 × 4 rectangle has an area of 24 cm² and perimeter of 20 cm. An 11 × 2 rectangle has a smaller area of 22 cm² but a greater perimeter of 26 cm.

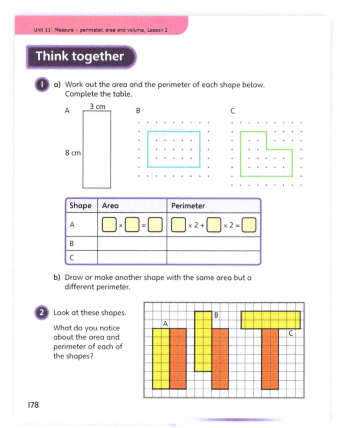

PUPIL TEXTBOOK 6B PAGE 178

PUPIL TEXTBOOK 6B PAGE 179

Practice

WAYS OF WORKING Independent thinking

IN FOCUS Questions **2** and **3** provide the opportunity for children to explore shapes that have the same area but different perimeters. In question **1**, ask children to pay attention to the first two shapes, which are oriented differently. Ensure children realise that the strategies for finding the area and perimeter of a shape do not change when the shape is rotated.

STRENGTHEN If children are finding it difficult to identify the dimensions of the shapes they will draw in question **2**, provide four square counters or four square pieces of paper. Children can move the squares around to explore different shapes, finding the perimeters as they go.

DEEPEN In question **5**, children explore the effect on the perimeter when the area of a shape changes. Until now, children have worked with shapes that have the same area, so give them time to see what happens when the area is reduced by one square. Extend the investigation by looking at a 3 × 3 square.

ASSESSMENT CHECKPOINT Assess whether children can confidently draw shapes that have the same area but different perimeters. Do they investigate, explore and draw accurate conclusions about how the area and perimeter can change and how changes in area may or may not affect the perimeter?

ANSWERS Answers for the **Practice** part of the lesson can be found in the *Power Maths* online subscription.

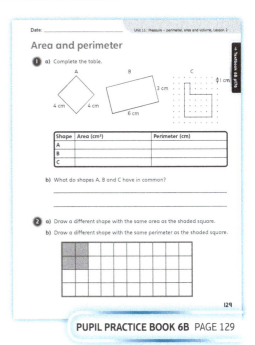

PUPIL PRACTICE BOOK 6B PAGE 129

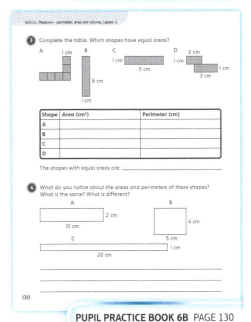

PUPIL PRACTICE BOOK 6B PAGE 130

Reflect

WAYS OF WORKING Independent thinking

IN FOCUS Use this question to check children's understanding of the connection between area and perimeter and their ability to prove and generalise.

ASSESSMENT CHECKPOINT Look for children to explain clearly that if two shapes have equal areas, they do not always have equal perimeters.

ANSWERS Answers for the **Reflect** part of the lesson can be found in the *Power Maths* online subscription.

After the lesson ⏸

- Do children understand that shapes can have the same area but different perimeters?
- Are they ready to move on to consider the area of shapes that have the same perimeter?

PUPIL PRACTICE BOOK 6B PAGE 131

Area and perimeter – missing lengths

Learning focus

In this lesson, children will explore how shapes with the same perimeter can have different areas. They will apply their knowledge of perimeter to find missing lengths and will calculate the area of squares, rectangles and rectilinear shapes.

Before you teach

- Are children confident calculating the area and perimeter of rectilinear shapes?

NATIONAL CURRICULUM LINKS

Year 6 Measurement

Recognise that shapes with the same areas can have different perimeters and vice versa.

ASSESSING MASTERY

Children understand that shapes with the same perimeter can have different areas, and apply their knowledge to work backwards to find the dimensions of shapes with the same given perimeter but different areas.

COMMON MISCONCEPTIONS

Children may think that if one pair of sides is lengthened and the other pair is shortened in a square or rectangle, both the perimeter and the area of the new rectangle are equal to the perimeter and area of the original shape. Ask:
- *How can you find the area? What happens to the perimeter? What happens to the area?*

STRENGTHENING UNDERSTANDING

Ask children to draw a rectangle on squared paper. Then ask them to draw a new rectangle with one pair of sides 2 cm longer and the other 2 cm shorter than the original, and to calculate the area of each shape. Discuss their findings.

GOING DEEPER

Give children some string or tape of a certain length and explore all the different shapes they can enclose with it. Encourage children to find the shapes with the largest and smallest perimeters and then make general statements about them. Encourage children to draw shapes to support their findings.

KEY LANGUAGE

In lesson: perimeter, area, length, width, square, rectangle

Other language to be used by the teacher: rectilinear shape, total, double, sides, distance

STRUCTURES AND REPRESENTATIONS

Representations of 2D rectilinear shapes

RESOURCES

Mandatory: rulers

Optional: string, tape, rods, straws or strips of paper

 In the eTextbook of this lesson, you will find interactive links to a selection of teaching tools.

Quick recap

Ask children to calculate the area and the perimeter of:
- A square with sides of length 10 cm.
- A rectangle with dimensions 10 cm by 5 cm.

Discover

ASK

• Question ① a): *If you are putting ribbon around a card, how can you work out how much ribbon you need?*
• Question ① a): *How many lengths does a rectangle have? How many widths?*
• Question ① a): *If you know the perimeter of a rectangle, and the length, how can you find the width?*

IN FOCUS Question ① a) presents an example of shapes with the same perimeter but different areas. The ribbon around the edge of each card gives a visual representation of perimeter as a length. Children need to recognise the perimeter as the sum of the length and width multiplied by 2. Question ① b) involves children finding all possible whole number dimensions for a rectangle with a given perimeter. This will reinforce the idea that shapes with the same perimeter can have different areas.

PRACTICAL TIPS Give children a 32 cm long ribbon or tape and a copy of the shapes in the Textbook (an 8 cm × 8 cm square and a 10 cm × 6 cm rectangle). Ask children to place the tape around each card and consider what the shapes have in common, and how they differ. Ask: *Which of the shapes has the greater area?*

ANSWERS

Question ① a): The area of Lee's card is 64 cm^2.
The area of Jamilla's card is 60 cm^2.

Question ① b): Perimeter = 32 cm so, length + width = 16 cm.
Some possible areas of Mrs Dean's card are:
Area = 13 × 3 = 39 cm^2
Area = 12 × 4 = 48 cm^2
Area = 11 × 5 = 55 cm^2
Area = 7 × 9 = 63 cm^2

Share

ASK

• Question ① a): *What do you divide 32 by to find the length of a square's sides? What do you need to divide and subtract to find the width of Jamilla's card?*
• Question ① b): *How can you work out the length and width?*

IN FOCUS In question ① a), children will need to understand how to use the information they are given to derive the unknown dimensions. Children may write a missing number sentence and then work backwards to find the unknown lengths. For example, when working out the length of the square, they could write 4 × ☐ = 32. At all times, make sure the links between sides are made explicit.

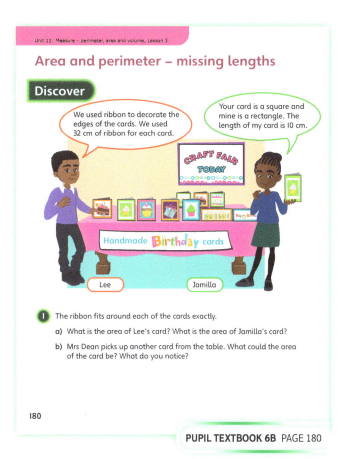

Area and perimeter – missing lengths

Discover

We used ribbon to decorate the edges of the cards. We used 32 cm of ribbon for each card.

Your card is a square and mine is a rectangle. The length of my card is 10 cm.

CRAFT FAIR TODAY

Handmade **Birthday** cards

Lee   Jamilla

① The ribbon fits around each of the cards exactly.

a) What is the area of Lee's card? What is the area of Jamilla's card?

b) Mrs Dean picks up another card from the table. What could the area of the card be? What do you notice?

180

PUPIL TEXTBOOK 6B PAGE 180

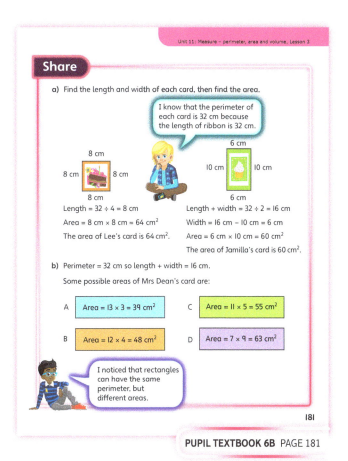

Share

a) Find the length and width of each card, then find the area.

I know that the perimeter of each card is 32 cm because the length of ribbon is 32 cm.

8 cm
8 cm 8 cm
8 cm
Length = 32 ÷ 4 = 8 cm
Area = 8 cm × 8 cm = 64 cm^2
The area of Lee's card is 64 cm^2.

6 cm
10 cm 10 cm
6 cm
Length + width = 32 ÷ 2 = 16 cm
Width = 16 cm – 10 cm = 6 cm
Area = 6 cm × 10 cm = 60 cm^2
The area of Jamilla's card is 60 cm^2.

b) Perimeter = 32 cm so length + width = 16 cm.

Some possible areas of Mrs Dean's card are:

A   Area = 13 × 3 = 39 cm^2

B   Area = 12 × 4 = 48 cm^2

C   Area = 11 × 5 = 55 cm^2

D   Area = 7 × 9 = 63 cm^2

I noticed that rectangles can have the same perimeter, but different areas.

181

PUPIL TEXTBOOK 6B PAGE 181

Think together

WAYS OF WORKING Whole class teacher led (I do, We do, You do)

ASK

- Question ❶: *What lengths do you need to know to find the area of each garden?*
- Question ❷: *How can you find the perimeter of the second shape in each pair? What does '1 cm' mean?*
- Question ❸: *If the perimeter is 30 m, what is the sum of one length and one width?*

IN FOCUS Question ❸ challenges children to apply their reasoning skills. They will use what they have learned to identify all the sides the rectangle could have. Children need to be systematic in their approach and use a table.

STRENGTHEN To strengthen understanding, give children the opportunity to explore shapes with the same perimeter by providing ribbon or tape of a given length and allowing them to enclose different areas with it. Children will benefit from the visual representation and manipulation of concrete resources and will see that shapes with the same perimeter can have different areas.

DEEPEN Prompt reasoning in question ❸ a) by asking children how they know they have found all the values. Discuss Flo's advice and encourage children to consider why the width has to be a prime number less than 15.

ASSESSMENT CHECKPOINT Are children confident identifying unknown side lengths when the perimeter is given. Do they understand that shapes with the same perimeter can have different areas and can they explain why?

ANSWERS

Question ❶ a): A: 9 m   B: 5 m   C: 6 m

Question ❶ b): A: 9 m²   B: 25 m²   C: 24 m²

Question ❶ c): The gardens have the same perimeter but different areas.

Question ❷ a):
A	B
Area = 15 cm²	Area = 13 cm²
Perimeter = 16 cm	Perimeter = 16 cm

They have the same perimeter but a different area.

Question ❷ b):
C	D
Area = 12 cm²	Area = 10 cm²
Perimeter = 14 cm	Perimeter = 14 cm

They have the same perimeter but a different area.

Question ❸ a):
Width	Length	Area
2 m	13 m	26 m²
3 m	12 m	36 m²
5 m	10 m	50 m²
7 m	8 m	56 m²
11 m	4 m	44 m²
13 m	2 m	26 m²

Question ❸ b): Smallest area = 26 m²
Largest area = 56 m²

Question ❸ c): Yes, Isla is correct. The length + width = 20 cm (half of 40 cm). A dimension cannot be zero, so both dimensions have to be 0 > and < 20.

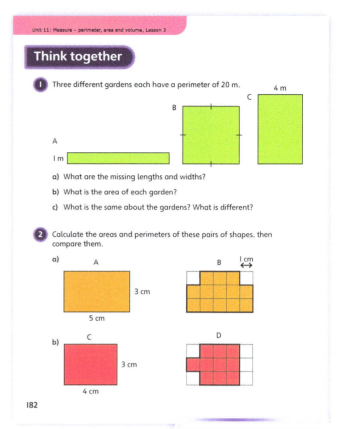

PUPIL TEXTBOOK 6B PAGE 182

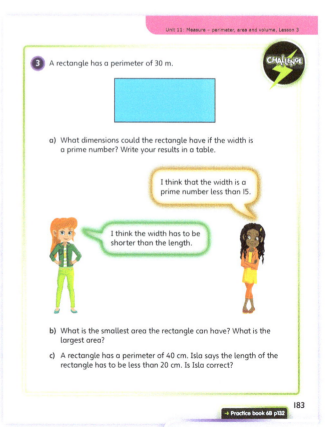

PUPIL TEXTBOOK 6B PAGE 183

218

Practice

WAYS OF WORKING Independent thinking

IN FOCUS In question ③, children problem solve to determine the dimensions of three shapes with the same perimeter and different areas. All shapes can be rectangles, however children should be encouraged to be curious and investigate the different compound shapes they can draw.

STRENGTHEN If children are unsure of where to start in question ④, encourage them to make a table to show all of the possible number pairs that add to 15 and then to find the areas of rectangles with these dimensions. Working systematically will help them to find the dimensions of garden A and garden B.

DEEPEN Provide children with rods, straws or strips of paper in question ⑥ so that they can make the shape before they draw it on the grid. Allow time for children to explore the shapes they can make.

THINK DIFFERENTLY In question ⑤, children need to think about how they can change the area of a shape without changing the perimeter. Provide nine identical square tiles so that children can physically move them to see what happens. Ask children to sketch the new shape and explain how they found its perimeter and area. Put the answers on the board for everyone to see and discuss.

ASSESSMENT CHECKPOINT Are children secure in their knowledge of shapes with the same perimeter but different areas? Can they use their knowledge to problem solve? Do they provide reasoning for why the area can change while the perimeter remains the same?

ANSWERS Answers for the **Practice** part of the lesson can be found in the *Power Maths* online subscription.

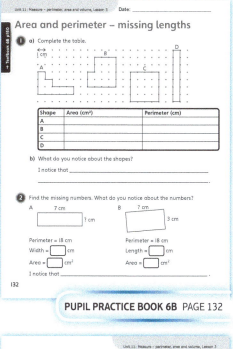

PUPIL PRACTICE BOOK 6B PAGE 132

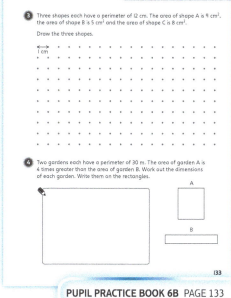

PUPIL PRACTICE BOOK 6B PAGE 133

Reflect

WAYS OF WORKING Independent thinking

IN FOCUS Children should use a variety of shapes to support their answers. Ask: *Is it always, sometimes or never true that shapes with the same perimeter have the same area? Can you always work out the area of a shape if the perimeter is given, or do you need more information? Does it depend on the shape?*

ASSESSMENT CHECKPOINT Assess whether children can give clear, reasoned answers and can make shapes and draw diagrams to support their answers.

ANSWERS Answers for the **Reflect** part of the lesson can be found in the *Power Maths* online subscription.

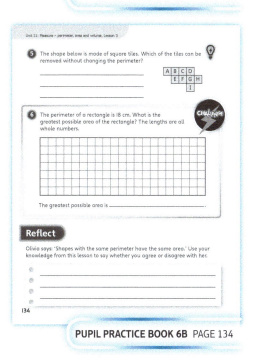

PUPIL PRACTICE BOOK 6B PAGE 134

After the lesson ⏸

- How well do you feel children have achieved the curriculum objective of being able to 'recognise that shapes with the same areas can have different perimeters and vice versa'?

Area of a triangle – counting squares

Learning focus

In this lesson, children will apply their knowledge of area to estimate and find the area of triangles by counting squares.

Before you teach

- How confident are children with the concept of estimation?
- How will you link their prior knowledge with the concept of estimation of area?

NATIONAL CURRICULUM LINKS

Year 6 Measurement

Calculate the area of parallelograms and triangles.

ASSESSING MASTERY

Children can confidently estimate the area of triangles by counting the number of complete squares and part squares.

COMMON MISCONCEPTIONS

Children may see estimating as a form of calculation, giving the actual area, because it involves counting. It is important to use correct vocabulary and compare the estimated area with the exact area of the triangle. Ask:

- *Can you describe whether you have estimated or calculated the actual area?*

STRENGTHENING UNDERSTANDING

It is important for children to understand that, when estimating, answers can vary. Children can gauge whether they have estimated an acceptable answer by placing the triangle inside a rectangle with the same length and width, so they can see that the triangle has half the area of this rectangle.

GOING DEEPER

Challenge children to predict the areas of compound shapes made with rectangles and triangles by counting squares.

KEY LANGUAGE

In lesson: triangle, area, square centimetres (cm^2), estimate, whole, part, almost-whole, half, less than, more than, rectangle, square

Other language to be used by the teacher: rotate

STRUCTURES AND REPRESENTATIONS

2D shapes drawn on squared paper

RESOURCES

Mandatory: coloured pencils, scissors

Optional: transparent squared overlay, square sheets of paper with area of 100 cm^2

 In the eTextbook of this lesson, you will find interactive links to a selection of teaching tools.

Quick recap

Challenge children to draw or sketch three different examples of a triangle that has one side length equal to 5 cm.

Discover

ASK

- Questions **1** a) and b): *How will the squared grid help you to find the areas of these triangles?*
- Questions **1** a) and b): *How many whole squares can you see? How many part squares can you see?*

IN FOCUS When looking at the picture, ask children to suggest strategies for finding the area of a triangle. Encourage children to identify the number of whole squares contained within Jamie's triangle. Then discuss that there are also some half squares in this triangle and agree that you would need to count up in 1s and then in halves to find the total.

PRACTICAL TIPS Provide children with squared paper to recreate Jamie and Andy's triangles. By exploring the number of whole squares and part squares in each triangle with concrete materials, children can develop a better understanding of how to count squares to find the total area.

ANSWERS

Question **1** a): The area of Jamie's triangle is approximately 9 cm^2.

Question **1** b): The area of Andy's triangle is approximately 6 cm^2.

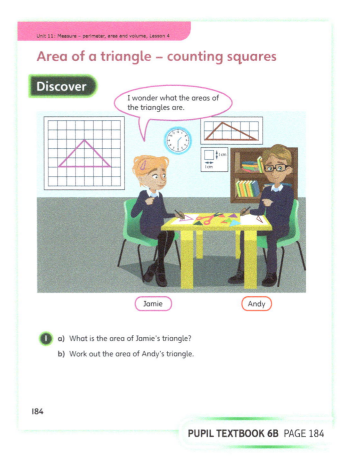

PUPIL TEXTBOOK 6B PAGE 184

Share

ASK

- Question **1** a): *Why do you think it is important to find all the whole squares first?*
- Question **1** b): *What part squares can you see in this triangle? What fraction of the square is inside the triangle? What fraction is not?*

IN FOCUS In question **1** b), the method for calculating the area of Andy's triangle is shown with illustrated steps. Children will see they can count the whole squares and then the part squares before adding them to find the total. They could also follow Dexter's advice from question **1** a) to find the part squares which could be combined to make whole squares.

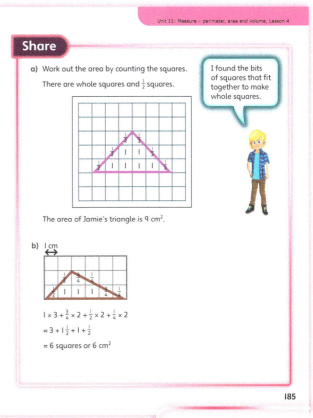

PUPIL TEXTBOOK 6B PAGE 185

Think together

WAYS OF WORKING Whole class teacher led (I do, We do, You do)

ASK

- Question **1**: *What are you basing your estimation on? Can you add any part squares together to make whole squares?*
- Question **3**: *Do you think the estimated area will be greater or smaller than the exact area of the triangle?*

IN FOCUS Question **1** requires children to estimate areas by classifying the different types of square that make up the area of each shape. Encourage children to be systematic in their approach and to think of ways to record the information. Remind them that they have been asked to estimate rather than calculate, so answers may vary. Acceptable answers should be sensible but do not need to be exact.

STRENGTHEN To support children initially, ask them to draw the triangles on a square grid. When estimating, children could use coloured pencils to shade the squares: one colour for whole squares, a different colour for half squares, a third colour for quarter squares and so on.

DEEPEN Question **3** uses one method of estimating and one of calculating area to prompt children to think more deeply about what it means to estimate the area covered by a shape. The question is also very useful in providing experience of working with triangles that do not have a horizontal base.

ASSESSMENT CHECKPOINT Assess whether children can estimate the area of a triangle by counting squares and work out the exact area by changing the triangle to a rectangle.

ANSWERS

Question **1** a): Approximately 13 cm^2

Question **1** b): Approximately 13 cm^2

Question **2** a): Approximately 3 cm^2

Question **2** b): Approximately 3 cm^2

Question **3**: Answers may vary for half/quarter/less than a quarter depending on children's estimations but the total number of part and whole squares should total to 12.

Whole squares	1
Almost-whole squares	1
Half squares	4
Quarter squares	3
Less than a quarter squares	3

Area: 5

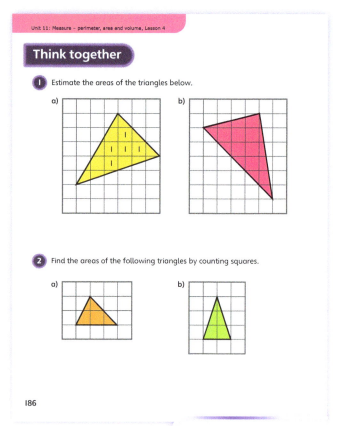

Unit 11: Measure – perimeter, area and volume, Lesson 4

Think together

1 Estimate the areas of the triangles below.

a)   b)

2 Find the areas of the following triangles by counting squares.

a)   b)

186

PUPIL TEXTBOOK 6B PAGE 186

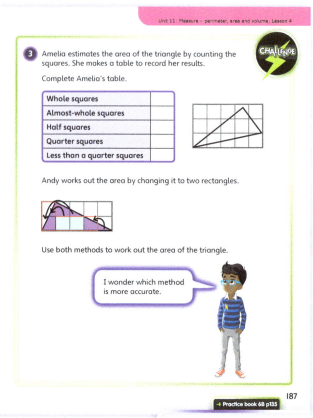

Unit 11: Measure – perimeter, area and volume, Lesson 4

3 Amelia estimates the area of the triangle by counting the squares. She makes a table to record her results.

Complete Amelia's table.

Whole squares	
Almost-whole squares	
Half squares	
Quarter squares	
Less than a quarter squares	

Andy works out the area by changing it to two rectangles.

Use both methods to work out the area of the triangle.

I wonder which method is more accurate.

CHALLENGE

187

→ Practice book 6B p135

PUPIL TEXTBOOK 6B PAGE 187

Practice

WAYS OF WORKING Independent thinking

IN FOCUS Question ② develops children's ability to estimate area and provides an opportunity for them to spot pairs of squares that can be combined to make one whole.

STRENGTHEN Provide children with enlarged copies of the triangles in question ②. Children could shade the squares, using different colours for whole squares, almost-whole squares, half squares and less-than-half squares. Encourage children to look for part-squares that will match up to make whole squares.

DEEPEN Question ⑥ challenges children to find the area of a shape on a cm grid. They should use the same method of counting squares as they did for triangles.

THINK DIFFERENTLY In question ⑤, children compare the areas of two triangles. The triangles are not symmetric, but children can employ a similar method to that used by Andy in the **Textbook**, **Think together** question 3. It is helpful to rearrange squares to turn each triangle into three rectangles, and use this to estimate the area of triangle B. You will see that Jess's statement is correct.

This is perhaps a question to return to when children know the formula area = $\frac{1}{2}$ × base × perpendicular height, as it is clear that since the base doubles but the height remains the same, the area of B is twice that of A.

ASSESSMENT CHECKPOINT Check whether children can estimate and calculate the area of a triangle. Are they secure in the strategies they use? Can they differentiate between an estimated area and an exact area and explain why both methods can be used in everyday life?

ANSWERS Answers for the **Practice** part of the lesson can be found in the *Power Maths* online subscription.

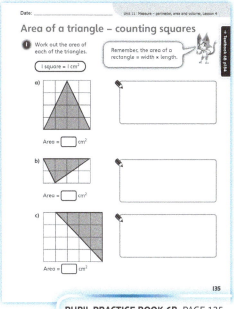

PUPIL PRACTICE BOOK 6B PAGE 135

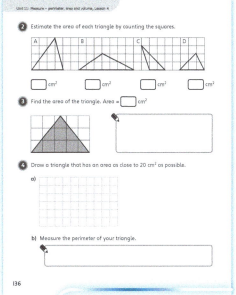

PUPIL PRACTICE BOOK 6B PAGE 136

Reflect

WAYS OF WORKING Independent thinking

IN FOCUS This question helps children look back on the strategies used so far to estimate and calculate the area of triangles. Discuss with children which method they think is easier and ask them to explain why. Discuss what mistakes someone may make when estimating and the errors that may occur when someone rearranges parts of a triangle into a rectangle.

ASSESSMENT CHECKPOINT Can children describe both methods of finding the area of a triangle? Do they know the difference between finding an estimate and finding an exact answer?

ANSWERS Answers for the **Reflect** part of the lesson can be found in the *Power Maths* online subscription.

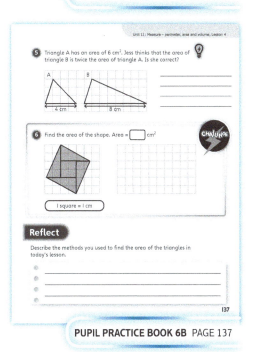

PUPIL PRACTICE BOOK 6B PAGE 137

After the lesson ⏸

- How well do you feel children understand what they have learnt about how to find the area of a triangle?

Area of a right-angled triangle

Learning focus

In this lesson, children will find the area of right-angled triangles. They will understand that the area of a triangle is half the area of a rectangle with the same height and width.

Before you teach

- How confident are children in drawing rectangles in different positions?
- How confident are children in calculating the area of a triangle by changing it to a rectangle?

NATIONAL CURRICULUM LINKS

Year 6 Measurement

Calculate the area of parallelograms and triangles.

ASSESSING MASTERY

Children can find the area of right-angled triangles. They derive the formula for the area of a triangle (*base × height ÷ 2*) by noticing that the area of a triangle is half that of a rectangle with the same height and width.

COMMON MISCONCEPTIONS

Children can find the area of a right-angled triangle with a horizontal base and vertical height, but when faced with a right-angled triangle in a rotated position, they may use the bottom line as the base and the line upwards from the bottom line as the height. Ask:

- *Can you show me the right angle in your triangle? Can you draw a rectangle around this triangle? How do you know that it is a rectangle? How many right angles are there?*

STRENGTHENING UNDERSTANDING

Encourage children to work backwards by drawing a rectangle first, labelling the length and width. Ask them to draw a diagonal line across the rectangle, shade one of the resulting triangles and find the area. This gives them a visual representation of the formula they will use to find the area of a triangle and allows them to link this concept with previous learning.

GOING DEEPER

Challenge children to draw five right-angled triangles in different positions, with perpendicular sides of 5 cm and 8 cm. Ask children to draw a rectangle that encloses each triangle, stating the length and width of the triangle. Ask: *Is it always, sometimes or never true that there are two equal triangles in every rectangle?*

KEY LANGUAGE

In lesson: area, triangle, rectangle, square centimetres (cm²), square metres (m²), **base**

Other language to be used by the teacher: largest/larger

STRUCTURES AND REPRESENTATIONS

Rectangles and right-angled triangles drawn on squared paper in different positions

RESOURCES

Mandatory: squared paper

Optional: rulers, paper squares

 In the eTextbook of this lesson, you will find interactive links to a selection of teaching tools.

Quick recap

Ask children to draw a sketch showing an example of:
- an equilateral triangle
- an isosceles triangle
- a scalene triangle
- a triangle with a right-angle.

Discover

WAYS OF WORKING Pair work

ASK

- Question ① a): *How can you cut a rectangular piece of paper to make two right-angled triangles? Is there only one way to do this? How can you check whether both triangles have the same area?*
- Question ① b): *What could you do to make it easier to work out the area of the triangle?*

IN FOCUS In question ① a), children are introduced to the formula for finding the area of a triangle ($A = b \times h \div 2$) with a simple example of cutting a rectangular piece of paper to make two right-angled triangles. Encourage children to be curious and to question what would happen if they cut the rectangular piece in a different way. Ask: *Will there always be two triangles? Will the triangles always be equal?*

PRACTICAL TIPS Provide children with rectangles of different sizes and ask them to split them in half. Allow children to explore the shapes that they make. If they make triangles, ask them to check whether the size of the rectangle determines the size of each triangle. Place two identical triangles one above the other and ask children to discuss what they see. Children should notice that the triangles have the same area.

ANSWERS

Question ① a): The area of the rectangle is twice the area of each triangle.

Question ① b): The area of Reena's triangle is 20 cm².

Share

WAYS OF WORKING Whole class teacher led

ASK

- Question ① a): *How can you find the area of the rectangle? How can you compare the area of each triangle with the area of the rectangle? Is there only one way to split the rectangle in half?*
- Question ① b): *What are the dimensions of the rectangle that would enclose Reena's triangle? How will you find the area of the triangle once you know the area of the rectangle?*

IN FOCUS In question ① b), children will need to find the area of the rectangle that the triangle would fit into. They will realise that the right-angled triangle has the same dimensions as the rectangle – the triangle's base and height are the same as the rectangle's length and width. Ensure children are able to explain that the area of a rectangle is double the area of a triangle, so they need to divide the area of the rectangle by two.

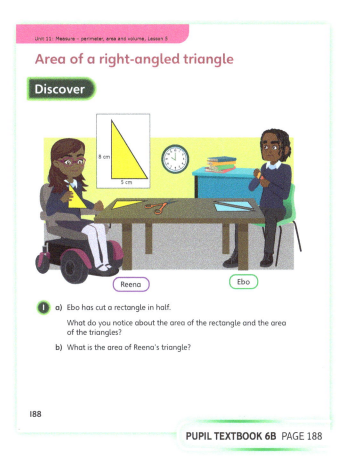

PUPIL TEXTBOOK 6B PAGE 188

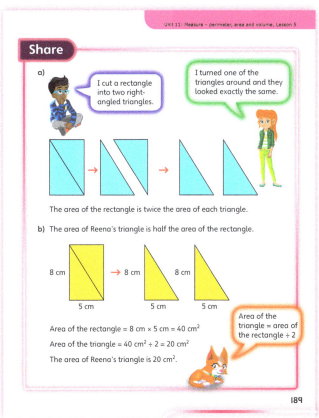

PUPIL TEXTBOOK 6B PAGE 189

Think together

Whole class teacher led (I do, We do, You do)

ASK

- Question **1**: *Which shape has the larger area, the rectangle or the triangle? How do you know? How can you check that the area of two triangles equals the area of a rectangle?*
- Question **1**: *Explain how you know which two numbers to multiply to find the area of the rectangle? Which sides do the rectangle and triangle have in common?*

IN FOCUS In question **2**, discuss which sides of the triangle are the *width* and *length* of the rectangle. Ensure children understand how the areas of the triangles and rectangles relate to each other.

STRENGTHEN Provide children with photocopies of the rectangles in questions **1** and **2** and ask them to split them in half along the diagonal. Children can place the triangles together when determining the area of the rectangle and move them apart when finding the area of the triangle. Ask questions such as: *Does it matter what the length and the width of the rectangle are? Will the area of the triangle always be half the area of the rectangle? If you know the area of the triangle, what will the width and the length of the rectangle be?*

DEEPEN Question **3** deepens children's understanding of the method for finding the area of a triangle by asking them to generalise about the formula. Point them back to the triangles they have worked with in questions **1** and **2** and ask them to replace the values with *b* for base and *h* for height in the working out, to attain the formula.

ASSESSMENT CHECKPOINT Assess whether children can correctly identify the base and height of triangles. Are they secure in finding the area of a right-angled triangle by dividing the area of a rectangle by 2? Can they use the formula *base × height ÷ 2* to calculate the area?

ANSWERS

Question **1** a): Area of rectangle = 3 cm × 6 cm = 18 cm^2
Area of triangle = 18 cm^2 ÷ 2 = 9 cm^2

Question **1** b): Area of rectangle = 2 × 2 = 4 cm^2
Area of triangle = 4 ÷ 2 = 2 cm^2

Question **1** c): Area of rectangle = 4 × 11 = 44 cm^2
Area of triangle = 44 ÷ 2 = 22 cm^2

Question **2** a): 8 cm^2

Question **2** b): 5 cm^2

Question **2** c): 7 cm^2

Question **2** d): 22 cm^2

Question **3** a): Amelia is correct.

Question **3** b):

Base	Height
5 cm	4 cm
4 cm	5 cm
2 cm	10 cm
10 cm	2 cm
1 cm	20 cm
20 cm	1 cm

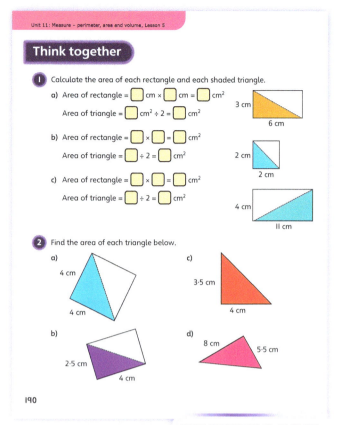

PUPIL TEXTBOOK 6B PAGE 190

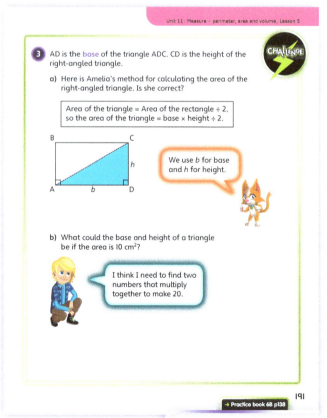

PUPIL TEXTBOOK 6B PAGE 191

Practice

WAYS OF WORKING Independent thinking

IN FOCUS Question ② requires children to think carefully when identifying the base and height of each triangle. Encourage them to form rectangles from the triangles to see this more clearly.

STRENGTHEN If children require support when calculating the area of a triangle, provide rectangles that, when folded diagonally, make the triangles shown in question ①. Ask them to identify the base and height of each triangle. Scaffold their thinking by asking: *What is the area of the rectangle? What is the area of each triangle?* In question ②, ask children to identify the base and the height of each triangle, highlighting these measurements in colour.

DEEPEN The problem presented in question ⑤ requires children to use their reasoning skills and implement their knowledge about the areas of triangles and rectangles to calculate a shaded area. Extend children's thinking by asking: *Is there a different way to solve this?* Present similar questions with triangles and rectangles where a shape has been cut out or removed from another shape.

ASSESSMENT CHECKPOINT Check whether children can work confidently when calculating the areas of triangles using the formula *base × height ÷ 2*. Can they problem solve when questions are presented in different ways?

ANSWERS Answers for the **Practice** part of the lesson can be found in the *Power Maths* online subscription.

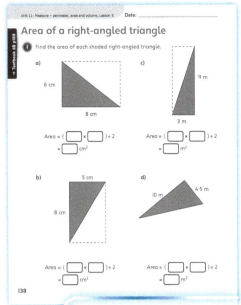

PUPIL PRACTICE BOOK 6B PAGE 138

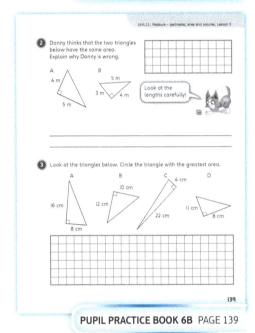

PUPIL PRACTICE BOOK 6B PAGE 139

Reflect

WAYS OF WORKING Independent thinking

IN FOCUS Use this question to check children's reasoning: can they explain how they use the area of a rectangle to find the area of a right-angled triangle? Encourage children to use the area of a rectangle to derive the formula *base × height ÷ 2*.

ASSESSMENT CHECKPOINT Assess whether children can describe the relationship between triangles and rectangles and use the formula for the area of a triangle with confidence.

ANSWERS Answers for the **Reflect** part of the lesson can be found in the *Power Maths* online subscription.

After the lesson ⏸

- Can children confidently find the area of a right-angled triangle by using the area of the rectangle?
- Can children identify the base and height of a right-angled triangle?
- Are children confident in using the formula for the area of a right-angled triangle?

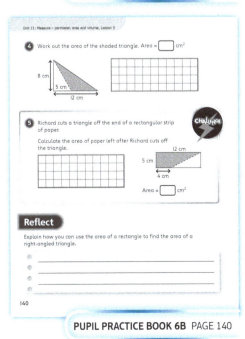

PUPIL PRACTICE BOOK 6B PAGE 140

Area of any triangle

Learning focus

In this lesson, children will apply their knowledge of area to calculate the area of any triangle.

Before you teach ⏸

- How will you help children to adapt the strategies they have learned so far to calculate the area of triangles?

NATIONAL CURRICULUM LINKS

Year 6 Measurement

Calculate the area of parallelograms and triangles.

ASSESSING MASTERY

Children can use the measurements of base and height and the formula *base × height ÷ 2* to calculate the area of a triangle.

COMMON MISCONCEPTIONS

Children may identify and multiply the wrong sides as the base and height of the triangle. Ask:

- *Have you been given enough information to find the answer or do you need more? Can you explain how to use the measurements you have been given to find the answer?*

STRENGTHENING UNDERSTANDING

Ask children to draw different triangles on squared paper or by using chalk outside on the playground, then ask them to measure the base and height to find the area.

GOING DEEPER

Challenge children to draw a triangle and calculate the area or ask them to draw triangles with a given area and then to find the missing sides. Ask children to draw triangles with a given area. How many triangles with the same area can they draw?

KEY LANGUAGE

In lesson: area, base, height, length, width, sides, square, rectangle, perpendicular, right-angled triangle

Other language to be used by the teacher: distance

STRUCTURES AND REPRESENTATIONS

Representations of triangles

RESOURCES

Mandatory: rulers, squared paper

Optional: paper straws (or similar), coloured pens, chalk, ruler

 In the eTextbook of this lesson, you will find interactive links to a selection of teaching tools.

Quick recap

Challenge children to draw a right-angled triangle that has an area of 10 cm^2.

Discover

WAYS OF WORKING Pair work

ASK

• Questions **1** a) and b): *Why is it important to know the area of triangular signs?*
• Questions **1** a) and b): *What strategies have you learned so far for finding the area of a triangle?*
• Questions **1** a) and b): *What measurements do you need to know?*

IN FOCUS For questions **1** a) and b), ask children to look at the triangles in the picture. Can they estimate the area of each triangle? Which of the triangles has the larger area?

PRACTICAL TIPS Provide children with isosceles and scalene triangles (already drawn and cut out). Extend reasoning skills by challenging children to cut each triangle in half along the line of symmetry (or, in the case of scalene triangles, from base to point) to form two right-angled triangles. Can they find the area of each right-angled triangle using the method they learnt in the last lesson and then add these areas together?

ANSWERS

Question **1** a): The area of the triangle on Lexi's sign is 42 cm^2.

Question **1** b): The area of Mo's sign is 600 cm^2.

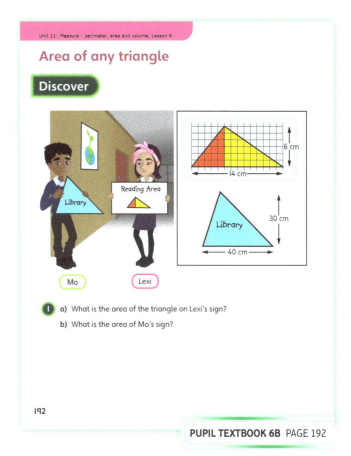

PUPIL TEXTBOOK 6B PAGE 192

Share

WAYS OF WORKING Whole class teacher led

ASK

• Question **1** a): *Look at the picture. How does it differ from the* **Discover** *picture? Why do you think it has been split like this?*
• Question **1** b): *Look at the picture. Why do you think the triangle is inside a rectangle? How can the area of the rectangle help Mo find the area of the triangle?*

IN FOCUS In questions **1** a) and b), it is important that children understand how they can use the given dimensions to derive the area of each triangle. Children should see how the area of the triangle and the area of the rectangle are linked, noting that the area of the rectangle is double the area of the triangle, even when it is not a right-angled triangle. Encourage children to highlight the base and height of each triangle and mark the right angle – this will help them to identify the rectangle. Ensure children are given the opportunity to practise making the links between the base and the height of a triangle and its area.

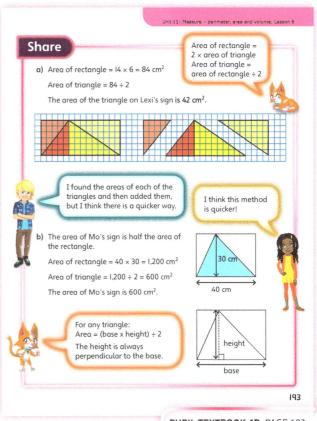

PUPIL TEXTBOOK 6B PAGE 193

Think together

WAYS OF WORKING Whole class teacher led (I do, We do, You do)

ASK

- Question **1**: *Can you explain the method used to find the area of each triangle? Why are you dividing by 2?*
- Question **2**: *What numbers could Max have multiplied? Why is that incorrect? What measurements do you need to know to find the area of a triangle? Which of the sides from the picture do you not need to calculate the area?*

IN FOCUS Question **2** gives children experience of finding the area of an obtuse triangle. Make children aware that, although the height falls outside the triangle, it is still perpendicular to the line that the base makes if it is extended. Explain that the base does not change in length when the line is made longer. Give children opportunities to discuss their reasoning in pairs before sharing with the class.

STRENGTHEN In questions **1** and **2**, it is important for children to recognise that they do not need to know the individual side lengths as long as they know the value of the base and height of the triangle. To strengthen understanding of this, provide triangles drawn on squared paper. Ask children to find the height and base by counting the squares inside each triangle, and then to use these measurements to find the area.

DEEPEN Question **3** challenges children to apply their reasoning skills. They should be able to use what they have learnt already to identify that both triangles have the same area because they have the same base and height. Remind children that they should be thinking of the formula for the area of a triangle. If children doubt that the height is the same, ask them to use a ruler to measure the height of each triangle. Revise parallel lines if needed.

ASSESSMENT CHECKPOINT At this point, children should display growing confidence when calculating the area of triangles. They should be able to explain which measurements they need to calculate the area of a triangle.

ANSWERS

Question **1** a): Area = (8 × 2) ÷ 2 = 8 cm^2

Question **1** b): Area = (6 × 3) ÷ 2 = 9 cm^2

Question **1** c): Area = (11 × 4) ÷ 2 = 22 cm^2

Question **2** a): Max used the slanting height to calculate the area. He should have used the vertical height.
Area = (6 × 5) ÷ 2 = 15 cm^2

Question **2** b): Base = 7 cm   Height = 4 cm
Area = (7 × 4) ÷ 2 = 14 cm^2

Question **3** a): Both triangles have the same area because they have the same base and the same vertical height.

Question **3** b): Children should draw a triangle with the same height as triangle A and B but a wider base.

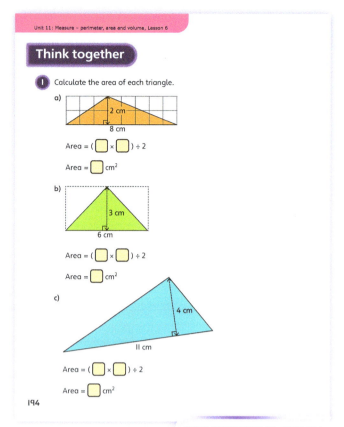

PUPIL TEXTBOOK 6B PAGE 194

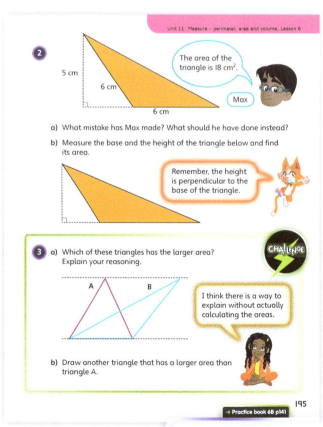

PUPIL TEXTBOOK 6B PAGE 195

Practice

WAYS OF WORKING Independent thinking

IN FOCUS Question ① requires children to find the base and height of each triangle and to use the formula for finding the area of a triangle. Sentence scaffolds are provided to support this.

In question ②, children consider triangles that have the same base and area. They should notice that the triangles also have the same height, but this does not mean all the triangles look identical.

STRENGTHEN In question ①, if children are unsure, present the triangles on squared paper so children can 'count' the base length and height. In question ②, allow children time to explore drawing triangles on extra pieces of squared paper.

DEEPEN The multi-step problem in question ⑤ requires children to calculate the area of a shaded area within a square. Children will have to calculate the area of the square then subtract the area of the other triangles to find the shaded area. The activity can be extended by asking children to find the height of the shaded triangle.

THINK DIFFERENTLY Question ③ addresses misconceptions children may have, such as using the base and a side length to find the area (instead of the base and height) or multiplying the base and height but not dividing by 2. Ensure children discuss the mistakes Ben and Alex have made and then find the area of each triangle. Note that some children may identify an alternative method – halving the base first and then multiplying by the height. Due to the commutative law, this method is perfectly acceptable.

ASSESSMENT CHECKPOINT Assess whether children are secure in their knowledge of the formula *base × height ÷ 2* to solve problems related to the areas or missing side lengths of different types of triangle. They should give clear, reasoned answers and their methods should show that they recognise how to use what they do know in order to derive what they do not in the context of area.

ANSWERS Answers for the **Practice** part of the lesson can be found in the *Power Maths* online subscription.

Reflect

WAYS OF WORKING Independent thinking

IN FOCUS Encourage children to be curious and to explore all the different methods they might use to answer this question. If children simply repeat the formula, ask them to explain why the formula works. Listen for children who link the area of a triangle to the area of a rectangle. To extend, ask: *Is it always, sometimes or never true that the area of a triangle is half the area of a rectangle?*

ASSESSMENT CHECKPOINT Can children explain different ways of calculating the area of a triangle? Can they draw diagrams and use the correct mathematical language when explaining their reasoning?

ANSWERS Answers for the **Reflect** part of the lesson can be found in the *Power Maths* online subscription.

After the lesson ⏸

- Which of the methods used in the last three lessons did children find most challenging?
- How well do you feel children have achieved the curriculum objective of being able to calculate the area of triangles?

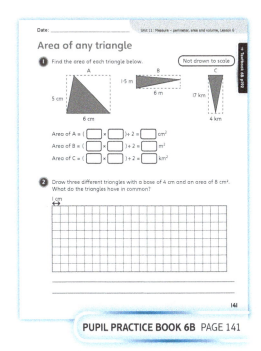

PUPIL PRACTICE BOOK 6B PAGE 141

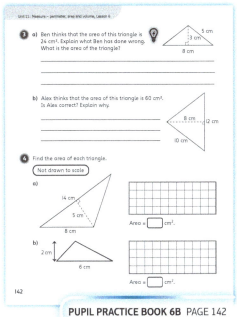

PUPIL PRACTICE BOOK 6B PAGE 142

PUPIL PRACTICE BOOK 6B PAGE 143

Area of a parallelogram

Learning focus

In this lesson, children will learn how a parallelogram can be rearranged into a rectangle to derive the formula for calculating the shape's area.

Before you teach

- Are there ways you can adapt this lesson to link it with other lessons or curriculum work?

NATIONAL CURRICULUM LINKS

Year 6 Measurement

Recognise when it is possible to use formulae for area and volume of shapes.

Calculate the area of parallelograms and triangles.

ASSESSING MASTERY

Children can use their knowledge of finding the area of a rectangle to calculate the area of a parallelogram. They can derive the formula for finding the area of a parallelogram and apply it correctly.

COMMON MISCONCEPTIONS

Children may multiply two sides of a parallelogram to find its area. Provide them with opportunities to calculate the areas of parallelograms and rectangles that have sides of the same length by drawing them on a square grid first. Children can count the squares inside each shape and establish that the areas differ. Ask:

- *How can you check that you are correct?*

STRENGTHENING UNDERSTANDING

Give children parallelograms drawn on squared paper for them to cut out and transform into rectangles by moving the triangles around. Have children measure the width and length of the parallelogram and the resulting rectangle with a ruler and see that the sides of the rectangle are different lengths to those of the parallelogram.

GOING DEEPER

Ask children to explore the difference between the areas of a parallelogram and a rectangle with sides of equal lengths. Ask: *Could they be the same? Can you predict what the area might be?*

KEY LANGUAGE

In lesson: area, square centimetres (cm^2), square metres (m^2), rectangle, width, length, height, base, parallelogram, formula

Other language to be used by the teacher: convert, dimensions, square

STRUCTURES AND REPRESENTATIONS

Rectangles and parallelograms drawn on squared paper

RESOURCES

Mandatory: rulers, squared paper

Optional: metre rulers, cardboard

 In the eTextbook of this lesson, you will find interactive links to a selection of teaching tools.

Quick recap

Ask children to draw a diagram that shows the difference between a kite, a trapezium and a parallelogram.

Discover

WAYS OF WORKING Pair work

ASK

• Question ❶ a): *What are the dimensions of each tile?*
• Question ❶ a): *When the parallelogram is transformed into a rectangle, which dimensions of the parallelogram match the length and width of the rectangle?*
• Question ❶ a): *How can you find the area of a rectangle?*

IN FOCUS In question ❶ a), children are asked to move part of a parallelogram to create a rectangle. They can make the connection between the length and height of a parallelogram and the length and width of a rectangle, thus relating to the formula for the area of a rectangle, *length × width*. To help children associate this with real-world situations, ask questions such as: *If you know the size of one tile, can you work out how many tiles are needed to cover a floor? What would happen if a builder made a mistake when calculating the area of each tile?*

PRACTICAL TIPS Give children a parallelogram to cut out. Ask them to use a ruler to draw a line perpendicular to the base, creating a triangle. Have them cut along this line and place the triangle on the other side, as shown in the picture. Children can then measure the height and length to find the area of the parallelogram.

ANSWERS

Question ❶ a): The area of the parallelogram is
30 cm × 20 cm = 600 cm².
So, the area of one tile is 600 cm².

Question ❶ b): Zac's method is 25 cm × 30 cm = 750 cm².
Zac is incorrect.
Emma's method is 30 cm × 20 cm = 600 cm².
Emma is correct.

Share

WAYS OF WORKING Whole class teacher led

ASK

• Question ❶ a): *How can you change a parallelogram to a rectangle? Is there another way to find the area?*
• Question ❶ b): *In the past, you have found area by counting squares. Is that how you should find the area here?*

IN FOCUS Questions ❶ a) and b) present a parallelogram and describe the process by which the formula to work out the area is derived. Children will see that the area does not change when the parallelogram is transformed into a rectangle. Ensure children understand that the base and height of the parallelogram are the length and width of the rectangle. Revise area with children, making sure they understand that area measures the space enclosed by a 2D shape. Question ❶ b) addresses a common mistake children make, of multiplying the lengths of adjacent sides of the parallelogram to find the area. Ensure they realise that the formula for the area of a parallelogram uses the base length and the height.

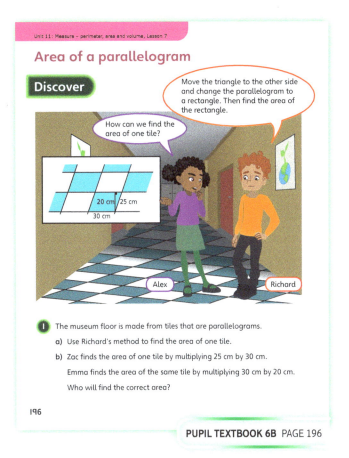

Area of a parallelogram

Discover

How can we find the area of one tile?

Move the triangle to the other side and change the parallelogram to a rectangle. Then find the area of the rectangle.

20 cm / 25 cm
30 cm

Alex   Richard

❶ The museum floor is made from tiles that are parallelograms.

a) Use Richard's method to find the area of one tile.

b) Zac finds the area of one tile by multiplying 25 cm by 30 cm.
Emma finds the area of the same tile by multiplying 30 cm by 20 cm.
Who will find the correct area?

196

PUPIL TEXTBOOK 6B PAGE 196

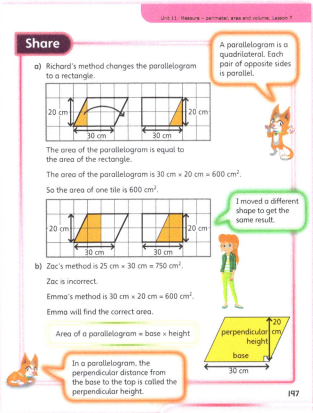

Share

a) Richard's method changes the parallelogram to a rectangle.

A parallelogram is a quadrilateral. Each pair of opposite sides is parallel.

20 cm   30 cm   20 cm
30 cm

The area of the parallelogram is equal to the area of the rectangle.

The area of the parallelogram is 30 cm × 20 cm = 600 cm².

So the area of one tile is 600 cm².

20 cm   30 cm   20 cm
30 cm

I moved a different shape to get the same result.

b) Zac's method is 25 cm × 30 cm = 750 cm².

Zac is incorrect.

Emma's method is 30 cm × 20 cm = 600 cm².

Emma will find the correct area.

Area of a parallelogram = base × height

In a parallelogram, the perpendicular distance from the base to the top is called the perpendicular height.

perpendicular height   20 cm
base
30 cm

197

PUPIL TEXTBOOK 6B PAGE 197

Think together

WAYS OF WORKING Whole class teacher led (I do, We do, You do)

ASK

• Question ❶: *Which method for finding the area do you prefer? Which is easier? Which is quicker?*
• Question ❷: *Which is the base of each parallelogram? Which is the height?*

IN FOCUS Question ❶ ensures children understand why the area of a parallelogram can be calculated using a similar formula to the area of a rectangle. The first two diagrams show how the parallelograms can be rearranged to form rectangles. Ask children to describe the steps required in their own words to assist understanding and retention.

STRENGTHEN Strengthen children's understanding of how each parallelogram is transformed into a rectangle by asking them to draw their own parallelograms on square paper and then calculate the area by transforming them into rectangles. Extend question ❶ by asking children to check the area of each parallelogram by using the formula. Continue this strategy in question ❷. Draw children's attention to parallelograms drawn in different rotations.

DEEPEN Question ❸ addresses the concept that a parellelogram can have two heights and two bases. Children should realise that as long as they pair the correct height and base, they will find the correct area. The area will be the same, whichever pair they use. For measurement b, children have to find the area using a given base and height, and then use this to find the missing height.

ASSESSMENT CHECKPOINT Can children describe the steps needed to calculate the area of a parallelogram by changing it to a rectangle? Can they identify the values of length and height and use these values correctly in the formula *area = base × height*?

ANSWERS

Question ❶ a): A: 5 × 6 = 30 cm²
   B: 2 × 4 = 8 cm²
   C: 2 × 3 = 6 cm²

Question ❶ b): A: 5 × 6 = 30 cm²
   B: 2 × 4 = 8 cm²
   C: 2 × 3 = 6 cm²

   Children should notice that the area is the same for both methods.

Question ❷ a): 20 cm²

Question ❷ b): 40 cm²

Question ❷ c): 42 mm²

Question ❷ d): 12.6 m²

Question ❸: *a* = 3 cm   *b* = 6 cm

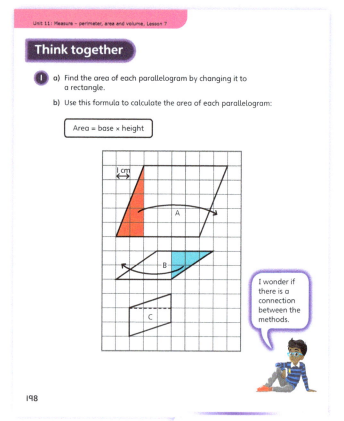

PUPIL TEXTBOOK 6B PAGE 198

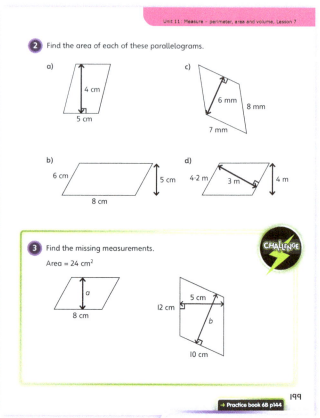

PUPIL TEXTBOOK 6B PAGE 199

Practice

WAYS OF WORKING Independent thinking

IN FOCUS In question **4**, children are asked to find missing lengths. They should identify which value is the *base* by using the fact that the *height* is perpendicular to the base. Children will need to use division to work backwards from the areas to find the missing measurements.

STRENGTHEN Support children in question **2** by encouraging them to shade the part of the parallelogram that moves, as in question **1**. Ask children to find the areas of the parallelograms in the 'rectangle way' and by using the formula. The better they understand why the formula works, the stronger their knowledge of area will be.

DEEPEN Question **6** challenges children to calculate the area of a compound shape made from two parallelograms. To extend, ask children to find the area of the grass on the school field as well. Children could then redesign the school field with a different path using parallelograms and calculate the area of the new path.

THINK DIFFERENTLY Encourage children in question **5** to consider the strategy they use to find the area of a parallelogram. Ask: *What is the same about all the parallelograms? What is different? Which sides of the parallelograms should be equal if the areas are equal?* To extend children's understanding, ask them to draw two other (different) parallelograms with the same area.

ASSESSMENT CHECKPOINT At this point, children should be secure in their knowledge of how to use the formula to find the area of a parallelogram. They should be able to present their answers using the correct unit of measurement.

ANSWERS Answers for the **Practice** part of the lesson can be found in the *Power Maths* online subscription.

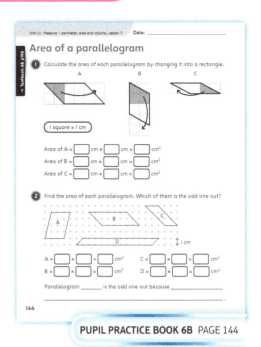

PUPIL PRACTICE BOOK 6B PAGE 144

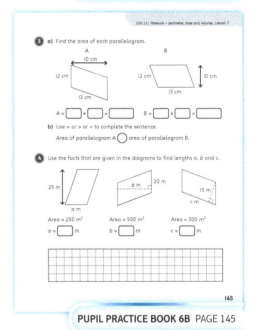

PUPIL PRACTICE BOOK 6B PAGE 145

Reflect

WAYS OF WORKING Independent thinking

IN FOCUS After children have looked at the diagram, ask them to state the formula for the area of a parallelogram. Ask them to explain how they can identify the base and the height.

ASSESSMENT CHECKPOINT Can children confidently explain how to find the area of a parallelogram?

ANSWERS Answers for the **Reflect** part of the lesson can be found in the *Power Maths* online subscription.

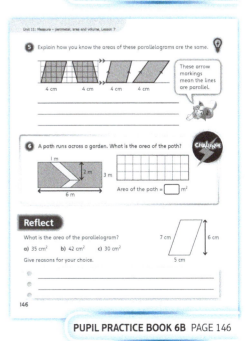

PUPIL PRACTICE BOOK 6B PAGE 146

After the lesson ⏸

- Do children understand how to calculate the area of a parallelogram using the formula?
- Are children aware of the links between the length and width of a rectangle and the base and height of a parallelogram?

Problem solving – area

Learning focus

In this lesson, children will apply their knowledge of area to solve problems, in particular when calculating the area of a composite shape or when finding missing measurements for a given area.

Before you teach ⏸

- How will you help children to use their knowledge of the areas of shapes to solve problems?

NATIONAL CURRICULUM LINKS

Year 6 Measurement

Calculate the area of parallelograms and triangles.

ASSESSING MASTERY

Children can use their knowledge of area and the properties of parallelograms and triangles to calculate their area.

COMMON MISCONCEPTIONS

Children may, when problem solving with area, multiply two given sides. They may multiply width and length without understanding the context of the question or what they are finding. They may not use the diagram given or may be unable to draw a diagram as described in the question. Ask:

- *What does the diagram show? Have you been given enough information or do you need more? Can you explain how to use the measurements you have been given to find the answer?*

STRENGTHENING UNDERSTANDING

To strengthen understanding, provide children with opportunities to model shapes concretely and move them around to compare their areas or make new shapes. Ask children to cut out shapes and then fold them to physically prove the equivalence of their areas.

GOING DEEPER

Challenge children to write down all the formulae for areas of shapes that they have learnt so far. Ask: *Can you draw the correct shape above each formula? Label the sides you need for calculating the area. What is the least information you need to find the area?*

KEY LANGUAGE

In lesson: area, length, square, rectangle, parallelogram, triangle

Other language to be used by the teacher: width, sides, distance

STRUCTURES AND REPRESENTATIONS

Representations of parallelograms and triangles

RESOURCES

Mandatory: rulers, squared paper

Optional: coloured pens, triangular tiles made from cardboard, chalk

 In the eTextbook of this lesson, you will find interactive links to a selection of teaching tools.

Quick recap

Challenge children to draw a rectangle, a triangle and a parallelogram that all have the same area.

Discover

WAYS OF WORKING Pair work

ASK

- Question **1** a): *What shapes can you see in the garden plan? Do you know the width and length of each path?*
- Question **1** a): *What shape is the overlapping part of the paths? What are the dimensions of the overlapping part?*

IN FOCUS Question **1** a) presents a practical situation in which knowledge of area is used. It is important to know the area of the path to make an informed estimate of the quantity of materials, such as gravel, concrete or bricks, needed to make the path. Children will need to identify the shapes involved and work out the order in which to complete the calculations. The centre of the path overlaps, so children will need to subtract the overlapping area to achieve the final answer to part a).

PRACTICAL TIPS Use chalk to mark out a similar shape to the garden plan on the ground outside. Ask two children to walk along the horizontal and vertical paths and describe the area of the path they walk. Challenge them to identify the dimensions of the 'overlapping part'.

ANSWERS

Question **1** a): $16 + 20 = 36$ m^2
$36 - 4 = 32$ m^2
The total area of the paths is 32 m^2.

Question **1** b): Area of the grass = $80 - 32 = 48$ m^2
The total area of the grass is 48 m^2.

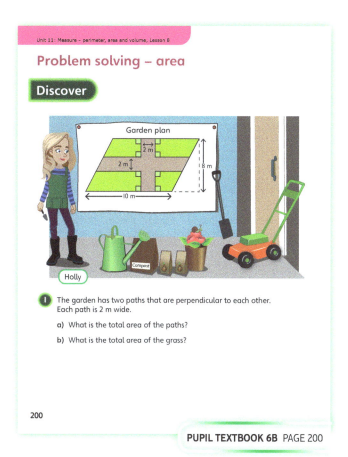

PUPIL TEXTBOOK 6B PAGE 200

Share

WAYS OF WORKING Whole class teacher led

ASK

- Question **1** a): *What shape is the vertical path? How can you calculate this area? What shape is the horizontal path? How can you calculate this area? Can you explain why you need to subtract the area of the overlapping part to find the total area of the paths?*
- Question **1** b): *How can you use the answer in part a) to find the total area of the grass?*

IN FOCUS At this point, it is important that children understand how they can use dimensions they are given to calculate the areas of shapes. This may be a good opportunity to revise the formula for the area of a parallelogram. Ask children to explain what height means and clarify any misconceptions. Ensure children are given adequate opportunity to practise finding the areas of different shapes.

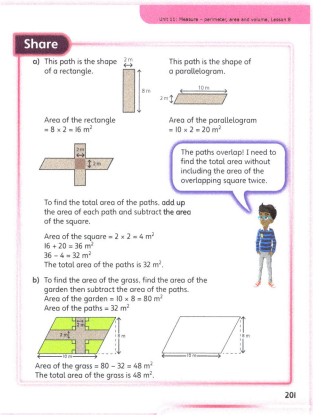

PUPIL TEXTBOOK 6B PAGE 201

237

Think together

WAYS OF WORKING Whole class teacher led (I do, We do, You do)

ASK

- Question ❶: *How can you calculate the total vegetable area? What information does Richard need to calculate the area of each flowerbed? How can you find the height of each triangle?*
- Question ❷: *How can you find the area of the bathroom floor? What shape is each tile? How can you calculate the area of each tile?*

IN FOCUS Question ❶ gives children experience with more complex compound shapes. Make sure they understand both methods used to find the area and can explain the steps needed for each method. Consider each unknown side in turn and ask: *How do you know what this measurement is?* Give children opportunities to discuss their reasoning in pairs before sharing with the class.

STRENGTHEN Question ❷ is an opportunity to ensure children understand clearly what the area represents. To strengthen their understanding, use chalk to draw a rectangle 120 cm by 60 cm outside on a flat surface. Make sixteen 30 cm × 30 cm triangular tiles using cardboard. Ask children to cover the whole area of the rectangle with tiles.

DEEPEN In question ❸, challenge children to work out the area of the path in as many ways as possible. One way is to calculate the area of the whole shape, then calculate the area of the grass and subtract the results. Some children may split the path into four rectangles, find the area of each part, then add the areas. Children will need to apply reasoning skills to know if all information is provided for each of their methods.

ASSESSMENT CHECKPOINT Check whether children display confidence when identifying how to calculate the areas of compound shapes in different ways. Can they explain how they know the value of a missing measurement or how to calculate a shape's area from the limited information given?

ANSWERS

Question ❶:

Isla:
Whole garden = 6 × 5 = 30 m²
2 larger vegetable triangles = (3 × 4) ÷ 2 = 6 m²
Medium vegetable triangle = (1 × 5) ÷ 2 = 2·5 m²
Small vegetable triangle = (1 × 1) ÷ 2 = 0·5 m²
Total = 6 + 6 + 2·5 + 0·5 = 15 m²
Flowers = 30 m² − 15 m² = 15 m²

Richard:
(4 × 6) ÷ 2 = 12 m²   (1 × 6) ÷ 2 = 3 m²
Total of flowers: 12 + 3 = 15 m²

Question ❷ a): Area of the floor = 60 × 120 = 7,200 cm²
or 72 m²

Question ❷ b): Area of each tile = (30 × 30) ÷ 2 = 450 cm²
or 4·5 m²

Question ❷ c): 72 ÷ 4·5 = 16
16 tiles are needed to cover the whole floor.

Question ❸ a): Area of the path = Area of the garden
– Area of the grass
Area of the path = 45·5 m² − 22·5 m² = 23 m²

Question ❸ b): Area of the grass = 22·5 m²
There is plenty of room for the tent.

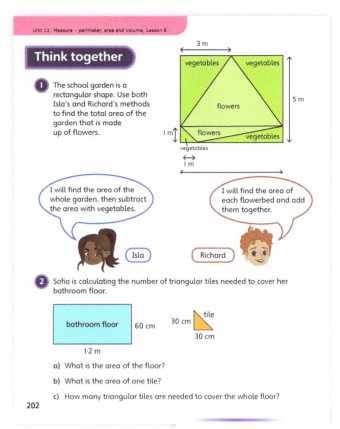

PUPIL TEXTBOOK 6B PAGE 202

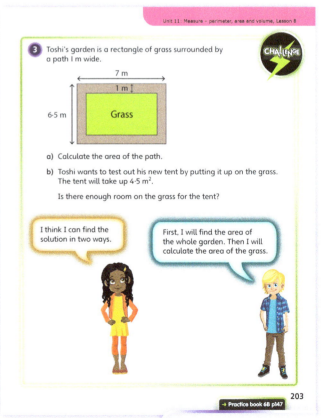

PUPIL TEXTBOOK 6B PAGE 203

Practice

WAYS OF WORKING Independent thinking

IN FOCUS In question **5**, ensure children discuss how the square is made. Ask: *How many rectangles are included in the square? What is the area of the whole square?* Remind children that the shape is a square, hence only one length is needed to find the area. Provide further examples if children require more practice before completing the question. Note that there is an alternative method that some children may identify – subtracting the area of the smaller square from the area of the larger square before dividing by 12.

STRENGTHEN In question **4**, if children are unsure how to find the area of each shape, encourage them to identify the height of the triangle. They can then find the area of the triangle and use this and the height to find the base length of the parallelogram.

DEEPEN Extend question **5** by asking children to find the dimensions of each rectangle (2 cm × 6 cm) and then determine if the rectangles can tessellate to fill the square with no gaps.

ASSESSMENT CHECKPOINT Assess whether children can apply their knowledge of compound shapes to solve problems related to area and/or missing side lengths. Can they give clear, reasoned answers and use methodology that shows they recognise how to use what they have learnt so far to derive what they do not know in the context of area?

ANSWERS Answers for the **Practice** part of the lesson can be found in the *Power Maths* online subscription.

Reflect

WAYS OF WORKING Independent thinking

IN FOCUS This asks children to reflect on what they have learnt about area in the last few lessons. Make clear to children that they should go back to the beginning of this unit.

ASSESSMENT CHECKPOINT Look for children who can give the formulae for calculating the area of a rectangle, a parallelogram and a triangle. Some children may also list what they know about the relationships between the areas of these shapes.

ANSWERS Answers for the **Reflect** part of the lesson can be found in the *Power Maths* online subscription.

After the lesson ⏸

- Are children able to use their knowledge of the properties of shapes and of area to solve problems?
- What opportunities can be provided for children to calculate the areas of shapes outside this unit?

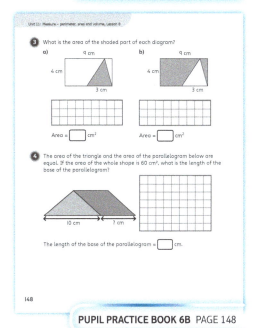

PUPIL PRACTICE BOOK 6B PAGE 147

PUPIL PRACTICE BOOK 6B PAGE 148

PUPIL PRACTICE BOOK 6B PAGE 149

Problem solving – perimeter

Learning focus

In this lesson, children will apply their knowledge of perimeter to solve problems, in particular when calculating unknown lengths and perimeters of composite rectilinear shapes.

Before you teach

- Are children confident with 'area' and 'perimeter'?
- How will you help children to adapt their strategies when solving a problem they have not come across before?

NATIONAL CURRICULUM LINKS

Year 6 Measurement

Recognise that shapes with the same areas can have different perimeters and vice versa.

ASSESSING MASTERY

Children can use their knowledge of perimeter and area to solve problems. They can find missing measurements in shapes that have equal perimeters.

COMMON MISCONCEPTIONS

Children may forget to include all the side lengths when finding the perimeter in more complicated, rectilinear shapes. Ask:
- *Have you added all the lengths of the sides in the shape to find the perimeter? Can you explain how to use the measurements you have been given to find the lengths of all the sides?*

STRENGTHENING UNDERSTANDING

Provide children with opportunities to model rectangles concretely, for example, ask children to use a ruler to measure the length of sides and prove their equivalence.

GOING DEEPER

Challenge children to set their own problems using rectilinear shapes. Say: *Write a question that involves calculating the areas of shapes with the same perimeter.* Ask: *What is the least information needed to draw the shape? How many steps are needed to solve the problem?* Encourage children to use their knowledge of area and perimeter of 2D shapes.

KEY LANGUAGE

In lesson: perimeter, area, hexagon, octagon, rectangle, square, enclosed, length, width, distance

Other language to be used by the teacher: rectilinear shape, total, triangle, sides, composite shape

STRUCTURES AND REPRESENTATIONS

Representations of 2D rectilinear shapes

RESOURCES

Mandatory: rulers, squared paper

Optional: paper straws (or similar), coloured pens

 In the eTextbook of this lesson, you will find interactive links to a selection of teaching tools.

Quick recap

Challenge children to draw three different shapes that all have a perimeter of 20 cm.

Discover

Pair work

ASK

- Question ❶ b): *What shape is the park? How will you find the perimeter of the park?*
- Question ❶ b): *What information can you use to find the total length of all of the sides of the field?*
- Question ❶ b): *If you were to put bunting all around the park, what information would you need to know?*

IN FOCUS Questions ❶ a) and b) explore the concept of perimeter of rectilinear shapes where some of the lengths are unknown. Children will need to look at known lengths to derive the information they need. Show children how the shorter, vertical lengths of the field will total the length stated on the parallel side of the field (150 m), and that the horizontal lengths on both sides of the field will have the same total.

PRACTICAL TIPS To help children visualise the vertical and horizontal lengths and totals, make the shape using two different coloured straws, one colour for the vertical lengths and the other colour for the horizontal lengths. When the straws are moved to be next to each other, children will see that the shorter lengths add up to the length of the side of the square.

ANSWERS

Question ❶ a): Danny ran 150 m + 150 m = 300 m.
Ambika ran 55 m + 71 m + 150 m = 276 m.
Danny ran 24 m more than Ambika.

Question ❶ b): The perimeter of the park = 150 × 4 = 600 m.
The perimeter of the field = 150 × 3 + 71 + 55 + 24 = 600 m.
The amount of bunting needed would be the same.

Share

Whole class teacher led

ASK

- Question ❶ a): *Can you explain why the three vertical parts of Ambika's route must add up to 150 m?*
- Question ❶ b): *How do you calculate the perimeter of a square? What information do you need to know?*

IN FOCUS For questions ❶ a) and b), it is important that children understand how they can use dimensions they are given to derive the side lengths that are not given. Ensure children are given adequate time and opportunity to notice the shorter vertical and horizontal lengths will add up to the given side length of the square. Ask children to draw the rectilinear shape of the field and use the information given to find all unknown lengths, before finding the perimeter.

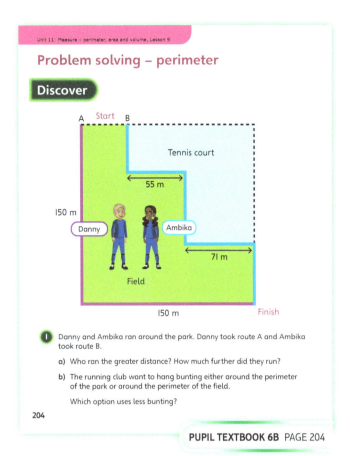

Problem solving – perimeter

Discover

❶ Danny and Ambika ran around the park. Danny took route A and Ambika took route B.

a) Who ran the greater distance? How much further did they run?

b) The running club want to hang bunting either around the perimeter of the park or around the perimeter of the field.

Which option uses less bunting?

204

PUPIL TEXTBOOK 6B PAGE 204

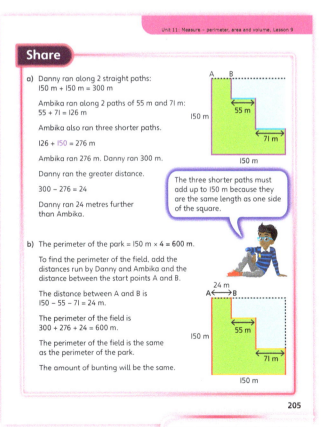

PUPIL TEXTBOOK 6B PAGE 205

Think together

Whole class teacher led (I do, We do, You do)

ASK

- Question ❶: *How can you work out the length of one side of the square? When the square is cut in half, which sides of the rectangles are the same as the sides of the original square and which are half the length?*
- Question ❷: *What does regular mean? How can you find the perimeter of a regular shape? How many sides does a hexagon have? How many sides does an octagon have?*

IN FOCUS Question ❷ gives children experience finding the perimeter of regular polygons. Make sure children understand that, although the shapes have a different number of sides, they have the same perimeter. Question ❸ asks children to use their knowledge of the area of squares to calculate the perimeter of the unshaded, rectilinear shape. Give children opportunities to discuss their reasoning in pairs before sharing with the class.

STRENGTHEN In question ❶, it is important for children to recognise that they should not generalise too early in the question. Rather than assuming or guessing what the answer should be, they need to prove their findings using calculations and diagrams, and by explaining their reasoning. If children say that the perimeter of the new rectangle is 20 cm, write the answer on the board and ask them to prove it. Working through mistakes in this way will strengthen and deepen children's understanding.

DEEPEN Question ❹ challenges children to apply reasoning skills. They should be able to use what they have learnt so far to identify possible widths and lengths of a rectangle when the perimeter is given. Ask: *What will the width and the length of the land be? Why does Dexter think the length and width must add up to 24?*

ASSESSMENT CHECKPOINT Check whether children can calculate the perimeters of rectilinear shapes with confidence. Can they solve problems that involve perimeter and area of 2D shapes? Can they explain how to find the value of a missing length and how to calculate a shape's perimeter when limited information is given?

ANSWERS

Question ❶: Perimeter of each rectangle is
10 + 10 + 5 + 5 = 30 cm.

Question ❷: Perimeter of the octagon = 9 × 8 = 72.
Length of one side of the hexagon =
72 ÷ 6 = 12.
The length of one side of the hexagon is 12 cm.

Question ❸: The perimeter of shape A is
9 + 9 + 5 + 5 = 28 cm.

Question ❹: The greatest possible area is a square
12 m × 12 m = 144 m^2.

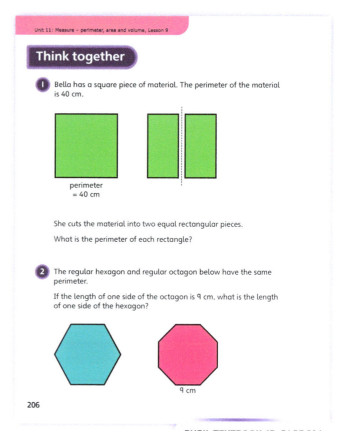

Unit 11: Measure – perimeter, area and volume, Lesson 9

Think together

❶ Bella has a square piece of material. The perimeter of the material is 40 cm.

perimeter
= 40 cm

She cuts the material into two equal rectangular pieces.

What is the perimeter of each rectangle?

❷ The regular hexagon and regular octagon below have the same perimeter.

If the length of one side of the octagon is 9 cm, what is the length of one side of the hexagon?

9 cm

206

PUPIL TEXTBOOK 6B PAGE 206

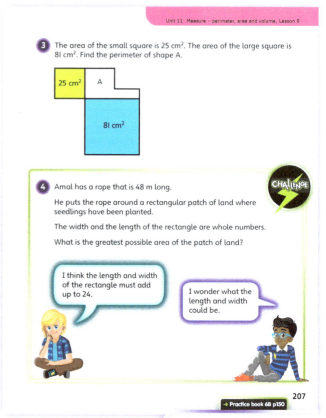

Unit 11: Measure – perimeter, area and volume, Lesson 9

❸ The area of the small square is 25 cm^2. The area of the large square is 81 cm^2. Find the perimeter of shape A.

25 cm^2 A

81 cm^2

❹ Amal has a rope that is 48 m long.

He puts the rope around a rectangular patch of land where seedlings have been planted.

The width and the length of the rectangle are whole numbers.

What is the greatest possible area of the patch of land?

CHALLENGE

I think the length and width of the rectangle must add up to 24.

I wonder what the length and width could be.

→ Practice book 6B p150

207

PUPIL TEXTBOOK 6B PAGE 207

Practice

WAYS OF WORKING Independent thinking

IN FOCUS In questions **2** and **3**, children work out missing lengths to find the perimeter of a shape when the area is given. Focus children's attention on the information given in the question. For example, in question **2**, children need to work out that each square has a length of 3 cm, not 1 cm. In question **3**, ask children to check their answers by putting the side lengths they calculate back into the question and checking that the area is correct.

STRENGTHEN In question **1**, if children are struggling to find the length of each race, have them highlight all the vertical lengths in one colour and the horizontal lengths in another to colour code the journey. Question **4** extends question **1** by asking children to look at two shapes that have different measurements and find the perimeter of each one. Children can again use coloured pencils, this time to match the equal sides.

DEEPEN The multi-step problem in question **5** requires children to investigate whether shapes with equal areas have equal perimeters. You can turn this activity into an investigation by asking children to find all the possible shapes made from the four triangles and to explore their perimeters. Ask: *Is it always, sometimes or never true that shapes made from the same number of tiles will have the same perimeter?*

ASSESSMENT CHECKPOINT Assess whether children are secure in applying their knowledge of perimeter to calculate missing side lengths or to find the perimeter of rectilinear shapes. They should give clear, reasoned answers and their methods should show that they recognise how to use what they do know to derive what they do not in the context of perimeter.

ANSWERS Answers for the **Practice** part of the lesson can be found in the *Power Maths* online subscription.

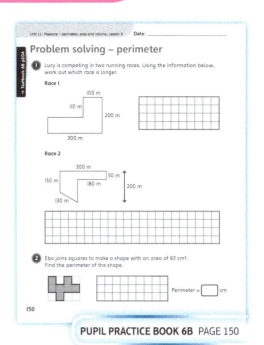

PUPIL PRACTICE BOOK 6B PAGE 150

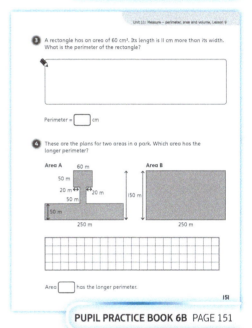

PUPIL PRACTICE BOOK 6B PAGE 151

Reflect

WAYS OF WORKING Pair work

IN FOCUS Children are asked to investigate what happens when a rectangle is cut into two equal parts. Ask children to work in pairs and think of different ways that the rectangle can be split. Ask: *Will the perimeter of the new shape always be smaller than the perimeter of the original shape?* Put the examples and answers that children provide on the board for everyone to see and encourage generalisations. Ask children to explain their findings clearly.

ASSESSMENT CHECKPOINT Look for children who explain their reasoning clearly and understand what perimeter means and how the perimeter is affected when the shape is split into equal parts.

ANSWERS Answers for the **Reflect** part of the lesson can be found in the *Power Maths* online subscription.

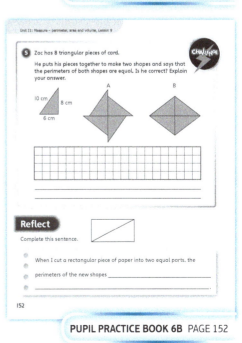

PUPIL PRACTICE BOOK 6B PAGE 152

After the lesson ⏸

- How well do you feel children have achieved the curriculum objective of being able to 'recognise that shapes with the same areas can have different perimeters and vice versa'?

Volume – count cubes

Learning focus

In this lesson, children will calculate the volume of cuboids and explore different shapes with the same volume.

Before you teach ⏸

- Do children have good knowledge of the times-tables?
- Do children remember what volume is?
- Can children estimate the volume of different solids?

NATIONAL CURRICULUM LINKS

Year 6 Measurement

Calculate, estimate and compare volume of cubes and cuboids using standard units, including cubic centimetres (cm^3) and cubic metres (m^3) and extending to other units (for example, mm^3 and km^3).

Recognise when it is possible to use formulae for area and volume of shapes.

ASSESSING MASTERY

Children can confidently calculate the volume of a shape by counting the number of cm^3 or m^3 that make the shape. They are able to find and compare volumes of cubes and cuboids and recognise that shapes with the same volume can have different dimensions.

COMMON MISCONCEPTIONS

Children may only count the cm^3 cubes they can see and may ignore the ones they cannot see. They may forget to add the hidden cm^3 to their existing volume calculation. Ask:

- *What does the volume measure? How can you check you are correct?*

STRENGTHENING UNDERSTANDING

Show children a cuboid made from multilink cubes or 1 cm^3 cubes, such as a 2 × 3 × 5 cuboid. Invite children to calculate the volume of the cuboid. Ask them to discuss the number of cubes in the cuboid, looking at the number in the bottom layer and determining how many layers there are. Place the cuboid in different positions. Ask: *Has the volume changed? How many cm^3 cubes can you not see?*

GOING DEEPER

Set investigative challenges for children to explore. Ask: *Can you make a cuboid with a volume of 20 cm^3?* Children should apply their knowledge of factors as they explore the width, length and height of each shape. Ask: *How can you organise your results so that you can see whether you have found all the possibilities?*

KEY LANGUAGE

In lesson: volume, length, **cubic centimetres (cm^3)**

Other language to be used by the teacher: measure, formula, estimate, width, cubic metres (m^3)

STRUCTURES AND REPRESENTATIONS

Cubes and cuboids drawn on squared and isometric paper

RESOURCES

Mandatory: isometric paper, 3D shapes made of cubes

Optional: multilink cubes

 In the eTextbook of this lesson, you will find interactive links to a selection of teaching tools.

Quick recap

Show children a small pot. As a class, discuss estimates for how many cm cubes will fill the pot up. Use real cm cubes to test these estimates.

Discover

WAYS OF WORKING Pair work

ASK

• Question ① a): *The volume of one multilink cube is 1 cm³. What does this mean?*
• Question ① a): *What is the length, width and height of each shape in the picture?*

IN FOCUS The picture presents two solids made with multilink cubes. For question ① a), draw children's attention to the number of cubes used to make each solid. It is important for children to realise there are cubes in each solid that cannot be seen. Encourage them to visualise the solid in layers. Ask: *How many cubes are in the bottom layer? How many layers are there?*

PRACTICAL TIPS Give children an opportunity to visualise the solids by using concrete representations. Provide each table with 16 cubes and ask children to first make Max's and Jamilla's solids and then explore cuboids made with all 16 cubes. Children will need directions and time to make the cuboids for question ① b).

ANSWERS

Question ① a): Jamilla and Max's solids each have a volume of 8 cm³. Jamilla is not correct.

Question ① b): The volume of the new cuboid is 16 cm³. Children could make the following cuboids: 2 × 2 × 4, 1 × 2 × 8 or 1 × 1 × 16.

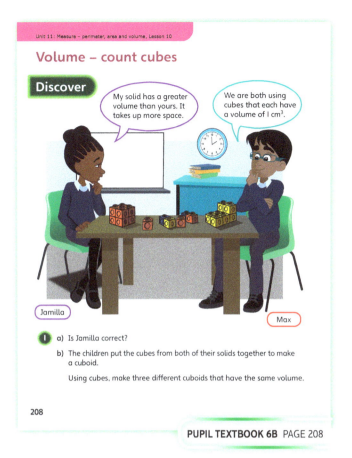

PUPIL TEXTBOOK 6B PAGE 208

Share

WAYS OF WORKING Whole class teacher led

ASK

• Question ① a): *How can you count the cubes you cannot see? How many cubes are there in the bottom layer of each solid? How many layers are there? How many cubes are there in total?*
• Question ① b): *What other solids could you make? How do you know that they are cuboids?*

IN FOCUS Ensure that children make conceptual connections between the solids split into cubes and the volume of each solid. Discuss how solids of different dimensions can have the same volume. Discuss the units used to measure volume. It is important for children to make the solids from question ① a) themselves so they can see what a volume of 8 cm³ looks like.

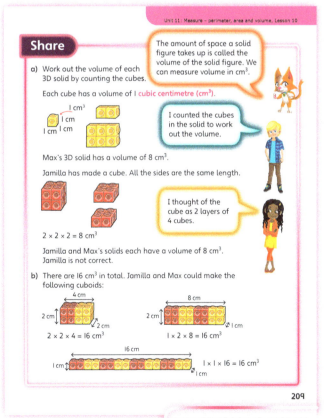

PUPIL TEXTBOOK 6B PAGE 209

Think together

WAYS OF WORKING Whole class teacher led (I do, We do, You do)

ASK

- Question ❶: *Can you describe the shapes using the words 'cm³ cubes' and 'layers'? How does knowing the number of cubes in each layer help you to find the volume?*
- Question ❷: *How is it possible to calculate the volume of a solid when not all the cubes are shown? Can you describe how you would use this method to work out the volume of each shape?*

IN FOCUS Questions ❶ and ❷ require children to find the volume of solids made with 1 cm³ cubes. Ask them to compare the questions, stating similarities and differences. Ensure children think about all the cubes in each solid, not just the ones they can see. Ask: *Can you imagine what the solid would look like if you held it in your hand? How would you describe it?*

STRENGTHEN Each time children encounter cuboids and cubes in these questions, strengthen their understanding by asking them to think about the number of cubes in the base. Provide multilink cubes or blocks for children to make the solids described in the questions. Ensure they recognise how their concrete representations reflect the pictorial representations on the page and the related multiplication facts.

DEEPEN To deepen children's understanding, use question ❸ to explore the connection between the volume of cubes and cuboids and the factor triplets that multiply to give the volume, such as $2 \times 2 \times 3 = 12$ and $3 \times 4 \times 1 = 12$ (so cuboids with these dimensions have a volume of 12 cubes). This will help children find all possible cuboids when presented with questions similar to **Discover** question ❶ b).

ASSESSMENT CHECKPOINT Check whether children display confidence when deriving the volume of a solid by counting the number of 1 cm³ cubes that are used to make the solid. Are they making progress towards finding the volume by multiplying the number of cubic centimetres in the base by the number of layers?

ANSWERS

Question ❶ a): 8 cm³

Question ❶ b): 11 cm³

Question ❶ c): 28 cm³

Question ❷ a): 20 cm³

Question ❷ b): 36 cm³

Question ❸ a): Max: $2 \times (3 \times 4) = 24$ cm³
Jamilla: $4 \times (3 \times 2) = 24$ cm³

Question ❸ b): A: 18 cm³   B: 24 cm³   C: 22 cm³
B has the greatest volume.
The total number of cubes is 64. This would make a $4 \times 4 \times 4$ cube.

Think together

❶ What is the volume of each of the following solids?

a)

⬜ cm³

b)

⬜ cm³

c)

⬜ cm³

❷ Work out the volumes of the cuboids.

a)

b)

210

PUPIL TEXTBOOK 6B PAGE 210

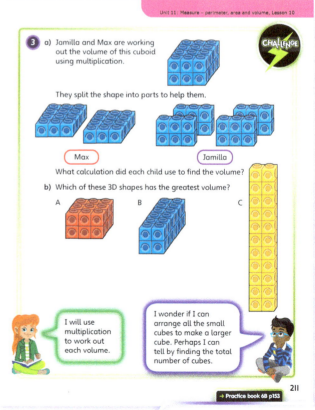

❸ a) Jamilla and Max are working out the volume of this cuboid using multiplication.

They split the shape into parts to help them.

Max   Jamilla

What calculation did each child use to find the volume?

b) Which of these 3D shapes has the greatest volume?

A   B   C

I will use multiplication to work out each volume.

I wonder if I can arrange all the small cubes to make a larger cube. Perhaps I can tell by finding the total number of cubes.

→ Practice book 6B p153

211

PUPIL TEXTBOOK 6B PAGE 211

Practice

WAYS OF WORKING Independent thinking

IN FOCUS The aim of questions ❸, ❹ and ❺ is to draw children away from a reliance on finding volumes by counting cubes. Revisit the common misconception of only counting the cubes that they can see. The more children make solids with a given number of cubes, the easier it will be for them to visualise the solid. Ask: *How many cubes are there in the base of your solid? Do all the layers have the same number of cubes? How many layers are there?*

STRENGTHEN If children find it difficult to understand that solids can have the same volume and different dimensions, spend time extending question ❷. Ask children to physically make one of the shapes shown using multilink cubes. Then have them rearrange the cubes to make other shapes.

DEEPEN Deepen children's understanding after they have completed question ❺ by asking: *Which of the following will reduce the volume of the cuboids by the greatest amount? 1. Removing a layer from the base. 2. Removing a layer from a side. 3. Removing a layer from the front.* When solving this activity, it is important that children have access to cubes to help them visualise and model the question.

THINK DIFFERENTLY On first inspection, children may answer 'Yes' to question ❻, assuming that a cube can be made with $9 \times 1 \text{ cm}^3$ cubes. Children will need to distinguish between their knowledge of square numbers and cube numbers. Give children nine multilink cubes so they can test their response. Extend their understanding by giving them many multilink cubes and asking them to compile a list of cube numbers through investigation.

ASSESSMENT CHECKPOINT Are children showing confidence in finding the volume of 3D shapes? Can they find the volume of a cuboid by multiplying the number of 1 cm^3 cubes in the base by the number of layers? Are children able to work out the correct volume when some cubes cannot be seen?

ANSWERS Answers for the **Practice** part of the lesson can be found in the *Power Maths* online subscription.

Reflect

WAYS OF WORKING Independent thinking

IN FOCUS In this question, children apply their knowledge of cubes and cuboids to explore if a cube can be made with $27 \times 1 \text{ cm}^3$ cubes. Ask children to make the solid and check that the volume they calculate matches the number of 1 cm^3 cubes they have. Some children may have calculated the value of cube numbers (such as $1 \times 1 \times 1 = 1$, $2 \times 2 \times 2 = 8$, and so on), or used their knowledge of cube numbers (1, 8, 27, and so on) to *know* the answer. Both of these methods illustrate children's ability to make the connection between cube numbers and volume. To extend, ask: *Can you make a different cuboid with the same number of 1 cm³ cubes? Will the volume change?*

ASSESSMENT CHECKPOINT Assess whether children recognise how to calculate the volume of a cube or cuboid and can explain their method clearly.

ANSWERS Answers for the **Reflect** part of the lesson can be found in the *Power Maths* online subscription.

After the lesson ⏸

- Have children mastered the concept of calculating volume?
- Are children ready to move on to using formulae to calculate the volume of shapes?

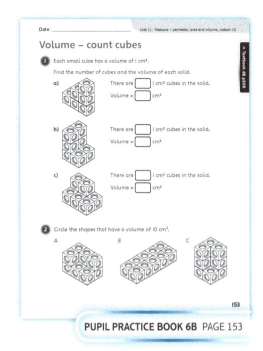

PUPIL PRACTICE BOOK 6B PAGE 153

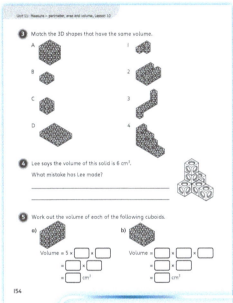

PUPIL PRACTICE BOOK 6B PAGE 154

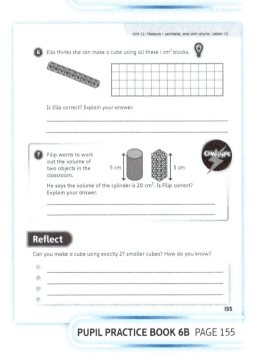

PUPIL PRACTICE BOOK 6B PAGE 155

Volume of a cuboid

Learning focus

In this lesson, children will calculate the volume of shapes, using the formula $V = l \times w \times h$, and find missing dimensions when the volume is given.

Before you teach ⏸

- In this lesson, children will use formulae to calculate volume. Would children benefit from a lesson starter to review calculation skills?
- Would children benefit from a quick recap of what they did in the last lesson?

NATIONAL CURRICULUM LINKS

Year 6 Measurement

Calculate, estimate and compare volume of cubes and cuboids using standard units, including cubic centimetres (cm^3) and cubic metres (m^3) and extending to other units (for example, mm^3 and km^3).

Recognise when it is possible to use formulae for area and volume of shapes.

ASSESSING MASTERY

Children can recognise the length, width and height of cubes and cuboids and use the formula for volume of a cuboid to find volumes in cm^3 or m^3.

COMMON MISCONCEPTIONS

Children may multiply the numbers given without paying attention to the units stated. For example, if a cuboid has dimensions 50 cm by 1 m by 2 m, children may calculate the volume as $50 \times 1 \times 2 = 100$. They may then be unsure what units to use for the answer. Ask:

- *Pretend the cuboid is in front of you. What does it look like? Which dimension is the smallest? Which is the largest? How can you check that the answer makes sense?*

STRENGTHENING UNDERSTANDING

Provide children with multilink cubes or cube blocks to model the cubes and cuboids in the questions. Encourage children to use a different colour (if available) for the bottom layer. Suggest turning the shape upside down to 'count' the area of the bottom layer.

GOING DEEPER

Set investigative challenges for children to explore, such as: *What is the effect on the volume when the height is doubled? When all dimensions are doubled, the volume is doubled – true or false?* Ask children to present diagrams or models to support their responses.

KEY LANGUAGE

In lesson: volume, length, width, cubic centimetres (cm^3), cubic metres (m^3), formula

Other language to be used by the teacher: measure, estimate

STRUCTURES AND REPRESENTATIONS

Cubes and cuboids drawn on squared paper

RESOURCES

Mandatory: multilink cubes, 3D shapes made of cubes

 In the eTextbook of this lesson, you will find interactive links to a selection of teaching tools.

Quick recap

Challenge children to each make a solid cuboid using exactly 12 cubes.

Discover

Pair work

ASK

- Question **1** a): *What is the length, width and height of each box?*
- Question **1** a): *How many cubes are required to cover the base of the box? How many layers of cubes are required to reach the top?*
- Question **1** b): *How can you calculate the volume of each box?*

IN FOCUS Questions **1** a) and b) require children to progress from counting cubes to thinking of volume as a stack of layers. Draw children's attention to what each of the dimensions represents in a solid. For example, length represents one side of the base, height represents the number of layers. Ask children to imagine the two boxes and discuss what they think the volume of each box will be. Provide each table with multilink cubes for them to make the cuboid and the cube. Were their predictions correct, too high or too low?

PRACTICAL TIPS Give children an opportunity to visualise the problem by using concrete representations. Provide a variety of small boxes for groups. Ask children to determine the volume of each box using multilink cubes or cube blocks. The groups should measure the width, length and height of each box using cubes. Ask: *What do these numbers represent? How many 1 cm^3 cubes can fit inside the box?*

ANSWERS

Question **1** a): 64 cubes fit in Aki's box.
60 cubes fit in Kate's box.

Question **1** b): *Volume = l × w × h*
$4 × 4 × 4 = 16 × 4 = 64$
The volume of Aki's box is 64 cm^3.
$5 × 4 × 3 = 20 × 3 = 60$
The volume of Kate's box is 60 cm^3.

Share

Whole class teacher led

ASK

- Question **1** a): *Explain Flo's first suggestion. How can you find the number of cubes in the bottom layer if you cannot count every cube? Discuss Flo's second method. Does it work for every cuboid?*
- Question **1** b): *Does it matter if the cuboid is in a different position and you are not sure which is the width and which is the length? When multiplying three numbers, does the order matter? Will the answer change?*

IN FOCUS For question **1** b), ensure children understand why *width × length × height* calculates the volume of the solid, and are not simply memorising the steps. If children are unsure, provide them with cm^3 cubes. Allow children to experiment, giving them the opportunity to calculate the volume of each shape themselves.

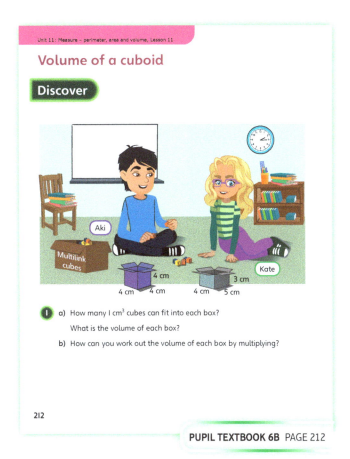

PUPIL TEXTBOOK 6B PAGE 212

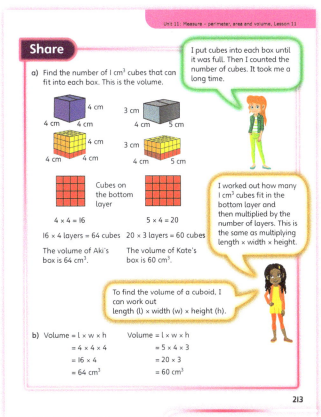

PUPIL TEXTBOOK 6B PAGE 213

Think together

Whole class teacher led (I do, We do, You do)

ASK

- Question ❶: *What information do you need to find the volume of a cuboid?*
- Question ❷: *What units will you use to measure the volume of each cuboid? Are the units for each cuboid the same?*
- Question ❸: *How can you use the formula V = l × w × h to find the missing dimensions? Why is there only the value of the length to find in part b)?*

IN FOCUS Questions ❶ and ❷ have been designed so children can practise finding the volume of cubes and cuboids when all three dimensions are given. Focus children's attention on the units used when calculating volume. Why is it important to say whether the volume is in cm³ or m³? Ask: *Can you imagine if you bought a box with a volume of 800 m³ rather than 800 cm³? Could a box with a volume of 800 m³ fit in your classroom?*

STRENGTHEN Each time children encounter cuboids and cubes in these questions, strengthen their understanding by asking them to pay attention to the numbers used. Ask children to investigate whether it matters if the height is bigger or smaller than the width or length. Help children to visualise what the shape would look like if the dimensions were swapped and discuss whether this would change the volume.

DEEPEN To deepen children's understanding, use question ❸ to explore the connection between the volume of a cuboid, its dimensions and the factors of a number. To extend, ask children to think of a cuboid that has three different prime numbers for the lengths of its sides. Ask: *What is the smallest volume the cuboid can have?*

ASSESSMENT CHECKPOINT Check whether children are displaying fluency when calculating the volume of a cuboid by multiplying its width, length and height. Children should be able to explain what each measurement represents.

ANSWERS

Question ❶ a): $4 × 3 × 3 = 36$ cm³

Question ❶ b): $5 × 5 × 2 = 50$ cm³

Question ❶ c): $10 × 3 × 4 = 120$ cm³

Question ❷: The volume of A is $4 × 5 × 6 = 120$ cm³.
The volume of B is $10 × 2 × 6 = 120$ cm³.
The volume of C is $4 × 1·5 × 20 = 120$ cm³.
Olivia is correct, they all have the same volume.

Question ❸ a): height = 2 cm

Question ❸ b): length = 10 cm

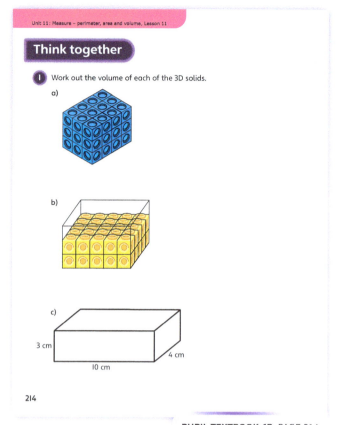

PUPIL TEXTBOOK 6B PAGE 214

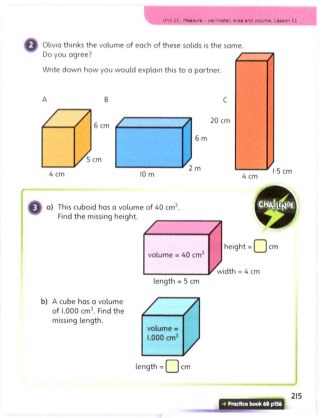

PUPIL TEXTBOOK 6B PAGE 215

Practice

Independent thinking

IN FOCUS The aim of question ④ is to find the missing length in a cuboid when the volume is given. Some children may multiply the two values given and then divide the volume by the answer. Others may divide the volume by one given dimension at a time. Another approach is to substitute all dimensions into the volume formula and work out the missing dimension, for example, V = ☐ × 8 × 5 = 480 cm³, therefore ☐ × 40 = 480 cm³, therefore ☐ = 12 cm. Discuss all approaches put forward by the class.

STRENGTHEN Question ③ moves away from the familiar to present a scenario where children calculate volume from the filling of a space with a material other than cubes. The method has not changed. Children will rely on multiplication to calculate the volume of the hole.

DEEPEN Question ⑦ provides a good opportunity to see how volume is used in real life. If children are not sure where to start, encourage them to draw a diagram on squared or isometric paper. Children can then model how many packets of tissues would fit on the base of the cardboard box and how many layers would fill the box. Encourage children to then make the link to the abstract: by dividing 12 cm by 3 cm, 2 cm or 4 cm will tell them the number of tissue packets that will fit along each side of the box. For example, the width of a tissue packet is 3 cm. 12 ÷ 3 = 4, so you can fit 4 packets along one side of the box if you align the widths to that side.

THINK DIFFERENTLY Question ⑥ presents an open-ended activity. After children have drawn the two diagrams required, extend by encouraging them to find all possibilities. Ask children to consider changes to the question, such as doubling the volume or changing 'greater than' to 'less than' in one or both places in the statement.

ASSESSMENT CHECKPOINT Assess whether children can calculate the volume of cubes and cuboids confidently. Children should be comfortable using a solid's volume to find its dimensions.

ANSWERS Answers for the **Practice** part of the lesson can be found in the *Power Maths* online subscription.

Reflect

Independent thinking

IN FOCUS The diagram states the height of the cuboid twice so children are presented with four values. It is important that children apply their knowledge of the formula to calculate the volume correctly. Ask: *What dimensions do you need to know to find the volume? Which numbers are multiplied to calculate the volume?*

ASSESSMENT CHECKPOINT Look for children who recognise how to calculate the volume of a cube or cuboid and clearly explain their method. Can children apply what they know to calculate the volume and work out missing lengths of real-world objects? Do they apply appropriate strategies to problem solving tasks that involve the volume of cubes and cuboids?

ANSWERS Answers for the **Reflect** part of the lesson can be found in the *Power Maths* online subscription.

After the lesson 📖

- Have children mastered the formula for the volume of cuboids?
- How well do you feel children have achieved the curriculum objective of being able to 'calculate, estimate and compare volume of cubes and cuboids'?

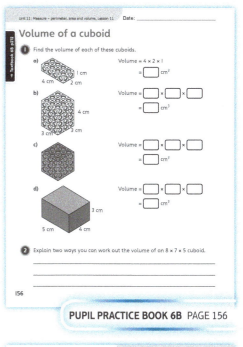

PUPIL PRACTICE BOOK 6B PAGE 156

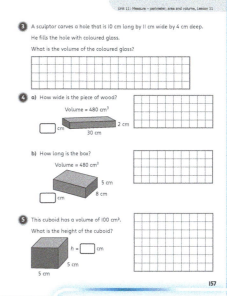

PUPIL PRACTICE BOOK 6B PAGE 157

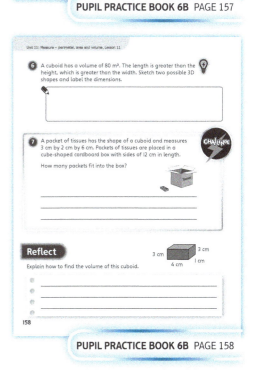

PUPIL PRACTICE BOOK 6B PAGE 158

End of unit check

> Don't forget the unit assessment grid in your *Power Maths* online subscription.

Group work adult led

IN FOCUS

- Question **1** assesses children's ability to use the correct formula to calculate the area of a parallelogram, then use the area to find a missing measurement in a triangle.
- Question **2** assesses children's knowledge of the correct formulae to calculate the areas of rectangles, parallelograms and triangles, and the volume of cuboids.
- Question **3** assesses children's ability to calculate the missing length in a cuboid, when the volume is given.
- Question **4** assesses children's ability to explore shapes with the same perimeter but different areas and vice versa.
- Question **5** is a SATs-style question where knowledge of how to calculate area is necessary to solve the problem.

ANSWERS AND COMMENTARY

Children who have mastered this unit will be able to accurately find the perimeter and area of triangles, parallelograms and rectilinear shapes by using the correct formulae. This includes examples where they are only given some of the shape's dimensions and need to derive those that are unknown. They will be able to apply their knowledge of volume to calculate the volume of different solids. They will be able to apply their knowledge of area and volume inversely to suggest the dimensions of a shape based on its area or volume. Children will be able to confidently explore the relationship between area and perimeter, using reasoning to explain their answers.

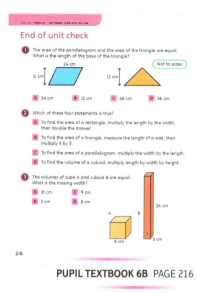

PUPIL TEXTBOOK 6B PAGE 216

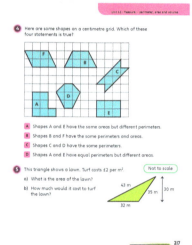

PUPIL TEXTBOOK 6B PAGE 217

Q	A	WRONG ANSWERS AND MISCONCEPTIONS	STRENGTHENING UNDERSTANDING
1	C	A suggests children believe the area of a triangle = base × height. B and D suggest children are unsure of what they are finding and simply add or multiply the values they see.	Provide different representations, both pictorial and concrete, to enable children to build conceptual connections. These may include the following:
2	D	A and B suggest children have confused the formula for the area of a 2D shape with its perimeter. C suggests children do not know the correct formula for finding the area of a parallelogram.	• Making 2D shapes out of cardboard. Children can measure the shapes and calculate their area and perimeter. • Exploring the area of 2D shapes with the same perimeter by bending a wire to make different 2D shapes.
3	B	A, C and D suggest children are not secure in calculating a missing length when the volume is given. Alternatively, children may have made an error while calculating.	• Exploring different solids that can be made using the same number of cubes.
4	B	A, C and D suggest children need more experience in exploring shapes with the same perimeter but different areas and vice versa.	When strengthening understanding, it is important that concrete and pictorial representations are not simply seen as the 'first steps'. Instead, encourage children to work backwards too – starting with abstract representations of area, perimeter and volume and then modelling these concretely and pictorially.
5	a) 480 m² b) £960	Calculating the area incorrectly suggests that children cannot identify the base and height of a triangle correctly.	

My journal

WAYS OF WORKING Independent thinking

ANSWERS AND COMMENTARY

Question ❶ a): I know that the area of the parallelogram is *108 cm²* because *the area is the base (which is 12 cm) multiplied by the height (which is 9 cm).*

Question ❶ b): I know that the area of this triangle is *24·75 cm²* because *the area of a triangle is found by multiplying the base by the height, then dividing by 2.*

If children are struggling to work out how to answer either question, ask:

• *How do you calculate the area of a parallelogram? How do you calculate the area of a triangle?*
• *What information do you need to know to calculate the area?*

Question ❷ : Any two rectangles labelled with the same area and with different correct dimensions would prove the statement to be false.

Question ❸ a): Shape A is the odd one out.

Question ❸ b): All the other shapes have an area of 12 cm².

Question ❸ c): Answers will vary; for example, shape B is the only shape with right angles.

Power check

WAYS OF WORKING Independent thinking

ASK

• *What did you know about area, perimeter and volume before you began this unit? What do you know now?*
• *How has what you have learnt made it easier to calculate the perimeter, area and volume of shapes?*

Power puzzle

WAYS OF WORKING Pair work

IN FOCUS The purpose of this puzzle is for children to explore the relationship between the volume of a shape and its dimensions. Question ❷ explores how the height of a cuboid with the same base changes when the volume increases. In order to solve the puzzle, children will need to apply their knowledge of volume – specifically how the length, width and height of a cuboid may change as the volume changes.

ANSWERS AND COMMENTARY

Question ❶ : The volume of the cuboid = 8 cm × 6 cm × 4 cm = 192 cm³. The volume of water is 192 ÷ 3 = 64 cm³. The volume of the cube = 64 cm³. There is enough water in the first tank to fill the second tank.

Question ❷ : The volume of the water in the tub containing the cube = 20 × 20 × 5 = 2,000 cm³. The volume of the water before the cube went in = 20 × 20 × 2·5 = 1,000 cm³. The volume of the cube is therefore 2,000 – 1,000 = 1,000. The dimensions of the cube are 10 cm³.

After the unit ⏸

• Can you think of opportunities to use the concepts of perimeter, area and volume in other curriculum areas?

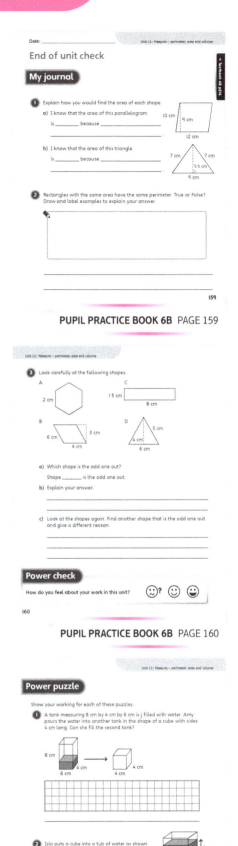

PUPIL PRACTICE BOOK 6B PAGE 159

PUPIL PRACTICE BOOK 6B PAGE 160

PUPIL PRACTICE BOOK 6B PAGE 161

Strengthen and **Deepen** activities for this unit can be found in the *Power Maths* online subscription.

Published by Pearson Education Limited, 80 Strand, London, WC2R 0RL.

www.pearsonschools.co.uk

Text © Pearson Education Limited 2018, 2023
Edited by Pearson and Florence Production Ltd
First edition edited by Pearson, Little Grey Cells Publishing Services and Haremi Ltd
Designed and typeset by Pearson and PDQ Digital Media Solutions Ltd
First edition designed and typeset by Kamae Design
Original illustrations © Pearson Education Limited 2018, 2023
Illustrated by John Batten, Diego Diaz, Adam Linley and Nadene Naude at Beehive Illustration;
Kamae Design; and Florence Production Ltd
Images: The Royal Mint, 1971, 1990: 46, 99
Cover design by Pearson Education Ltd
Back cover illustration Diego Diaz and Nadene Naude at Beehive Illustration

Series editor: Tony Staneff; Lead author: Josh Lury
Authors (first edition): Liu Jian, Josh Lury, David Board, Catherine Casey, Belle Cottingham,
Zhou Da, Zhang Dan, Zhu Dejiang, Wei Huinv, Hou Huiying, Neil Jarrett, Zhang Jing, Huang Lihua,
Yin Lili, Liu Qimeng, Timothy Weal, Paul Wrangles and Zhu Yuhong
Consultants (first edition): Professor Liu Jian and Professor Zhang Dan

The rights of Tony Staneff and Josh Lury to be identified as authors of this work have been
asserted by them in accordance with the Copyright, Designs and Patents Act 1988.

First published 2018
This edition first published 2023

27 26 25 24 23
10 9 8 7 6 5 4 3 2 1

British Library Cataloguing in Publication Data
A catalogue record for this book is available from the British Library

ISBN 978 1 292 45063 6

Printed in the UK by Ashford Press Ltd

For Power Maths online resources, go to:
www.activelearnprimary.co.uk

Note from the publisher
Pearson has robust editorial processes, including answer and fact checks, to ensure the
accuracy of the content in this publication, and every effort is made to ensure this publication
is free of errors. We are, however, only human, and occasionally errors do occur. Pearson is
not liable for any misunderstandings that arise as a result of errors in this publication, but it is
our priority to ensure that the content is accurate. If you spot an error, please do contact us at
resourcescorrections@pearson.com so we can make sure it is corrected.